Ralph W. Rader
English Department
University of California
Berkeley, CA 94720

D0820963

Ralph W. Rader
English Department
University of California
Berkeley, CA 94720

The Dilemma of Human Identity

The Dilemma of Human Identity

Heinz Lichtenstein, M.D.

Jason Aronson
New York

Lichtenstein, Heinz, 1904-
    The dilemma of human identity.

    Bibliography: 22 pp.
    Includes index.
    1. Identity (Psychology). 2. Psychoanalysis.
3. Existential Psychology.   I. Title.
BF 697. L52   155.2   77-87146
ISBN 0-87668-230-1

Classical Psychonalysis and Its Applications:

A Series of Books
Edited by Robert Langs, M.D.

Langs, Robert
THE TECHNIQUE OF
PSYCHOANALYTIC
PSYCHOTHERAPY, VOLS. I AND II

THE THERAPEUTIC INTERACTION,
TWO-VOLUME SET

THE BIPERSONAL FIELD

THE THERAPEUTIC INTERACTION:
A SYNTHESIS

Kestenberg, Judith
CHILDREN AND PARENTS:
PSYCHOANALYTIC STUDIES IN
DEVELOPMENT

Sperling, Melitta
THE MAJOR NEUROSES AND
BEHAVIOR DISORDERS IN
CHILDREN

Giovacchini, Peter L.
PSYCHOANALYSIS OF CHARACTER
DISORDERS

PSYCHOTHERAPY OF PRIMITIVE
MENTAL STATES

Kernberg, Otto
BORDERLINE CONDITIONS AND
PATHOLOGICAL NARCISSISM

OBJECT-RELATIONS THEORY AND
CLINICAL PSYCHOANALYSIS

Console, William A.
Simons, Richard D.
Rubenstein, Mark
THE FIRST ENCOUNTER

Nagera, Humberto
FEMALE SEXUALITY AND THE
OEDIPUS COMPLEX

OBSESSIONAL NEUROSES:
DEVELOPMENTAL
PSYCHOPATHOLOGY

Hoffer, Willi
THE EARLY DEVELOPMENT AND
EDUCATION OF THE CHILD

Meissner, William
THE PARANOID PROCESS

Horowitz, Mardi
STRESS RESPONSE SYNDROMES

HYSTERICAL PERSONALITY

Rosen, Victor
STYLE, CHARACTER AND LANGUAGE

Sarnoff, Charles
LATENCY

Heinz Lichenstein
DILEMMA OF HUMAN IDENTITY

Simon Grolnick,
Leonard Barkin, Editors
in collaboration with
Werner Muensterberger,
BETWEEN FANTASY AND REALITY:
TRANSITIONAL OBJECTS AND
PHENOMENA

ARONSON

SERIES INTRODUCTION

Heinz Lichtenstein has brought to psychoanalysis a most remarkable historical and philosophical erudition, a distinctive medical training in Germany, and a wide clinical psychiatric experience there, in Switzerland, and in the United States, where it was combined with a distinguished teaching career. His psychoanalytic work and broad concern for the human condition has inspired him over the past forty years of social and individual turmoil and change to repeated investigations of human identity, its development and maintenance. Interested in relatively unexplored therapeutic issues and endeavoring to offer psychoanalytic insights to basic and universal questions, Lichtenstein's clinical and theoretical work has given rise to a series of comprehensive papers on identity and sexuality; the philosophically thorny problem of conceptualizing human identity; the development of the self, including the vicissitudes of narcissism and superego functioning; and, finally, the influence of cultural change on human identity. Unmatched in any body of literature, his work shows a special sensitivity for integrating specific clinical problems with broader social issues and the nuances of man's essential identity—in all its potential stability and openness to crisis. This is a volume addressing itself to some of mankind's most pressing current concerns, one that, while offering no easy solutions, suggests many unique and important conceptualizations. Lichtenstein's work ranks with the finest psychosocial and clinical psychoanalytic researches, and represents classical psychoanalysis at its best, in its endeavors to comprehend its subject—mankind and the individual—from his deepest intrapsychic secrets and structure to the broadest sociocultural questions.

Robert Langs, M.D.

ACKNOWLEDGMENTS

What I owe to whom in the development of my approach to the issues debated in this volume will, I hope, be conveyed to the reader by the text with sufficient clarity.

There are, however, individuals who have personally taken part in the efforts of which this book is the result. They trusted me enough to give me the confidence to continue my exploration into problem areas often dark enough to deter the search. Among those without whose faith I would not have continued, and to whom I owe a very personal debt of gratitude, I will place first three psychoanalysts who were at one time my teachers, and later accepted me as a colleague. They are the late Ernst Kris, Dr. Phyllis Greenacre, and Dr. Edith Jacobson. They opened for me the way into the theory and practice of psychoanalysis. Neither can I forget, for their open-mindedness toward and acceptance of my first psychoanalytic papers in English, Drs. John Frosch and Nathaniel Ross. They have never withdrawn their initial support.

During my life in Buffalo, N.Y., starting in late 1939, I was fortunate enough to renew a relationship that went back to my first semester in Freiburg, Germany: I met again Professor Marvin Farber, Distinguished Professor of Philosophy at the University of Buffalo, whose friendship and encouragement was never in question, and who represented an important link between my European and my American existence. From Buffalo I also established ties to the psychoanalytic group in Rochester, N.Y., first and foremost in the person of the late Dr. Sandor S. Feldman, who became the founder and inspiration of what is now the Western New York Psychoanalytic Society. When Dr. S. Mouchly Small became Professor and Chairman of the Department of Psychiatry at the School of Medicine of the State University of New York at Buffalo, I could always count on his complete support of my clinical and theoretical interests, thus enabling me to devote a considerable part of my time to thought and reflection on the issues presented in my articles.

A great change occurred with the arrival of Professors Norman N. Holland and Murray M. Schwartz at the Department of English at the State University of New York at Buffalo in the late sixties. It was their initiative that led to the founding of the Group for Applied Psychoanalysis at the University, followed by the establishment of the Center for the Psychological Study of the Arts. To my contacts with this group I owe a most important stimulation and exposure to new dimensions of knowledge that have influenced my thinking in many ways. This collection would never have occurred without the encouragement and practical help which I received from Professors Holland and Schwartz. I hope the book, the result of their initiative, will be worth their persistent efforts.

After the collection of papers was accepted for publication by Dr. Jason Aronson, it was Dr. Robert J. Langs who guided me patiently to take the necessary steps that must precede publication. Without his help, and the perceptive advice and sensitive understanding of Mrs. Jan Blakeslee, who transformed a mere collection of articles and manuscripts into a coherent text, I would have failed in my efforts. I will always feel indebted to the tireless efforts of Mrs. Jean Connelly, who never hesitated to do the typing and retyping of the often nearly illegible drafts of the chapters of this book.

Whatever I have been striving for is, however, the result of the cooperation of two people over many years of a shared life. Without my wife's capacity to create a world in which I could live with a sense of authenticity, all my efforts would have been futile.

Chapter 1 first appeared under the title "Zur Phanomemologie des Wiederholungszwanges und des Todestriebes" in *Imago* 21 (1935): 446–480. It was reprinted in translation, with permission of

Sigmund Freud Copyrights, Ltd., London, in *The Annual of Psychoanalysis,* 1975.

Chapter 2 first appeared in the *Journal of the American Psychoanalytic Association* 9 (1961):179–260. Reprinted by permission.

Chapter 3 appears here for the first time.

Chapters 4–6 first appeared in the *Journal of the American Psychoanalytic Association* 11(1963):173–223. Reprinted here by permission.

Chapter 7 is a greatly revised version of material that first appeared with chapters 4-6 in the *Journal of the American Psychoanalytic Association 11(1963):173–223.*

Chapter 8 first appeared in the *International Journal of Psycho-Analysis* 45:49–56. Reprinted by permission.

Chapter 9 first appeared in the *International Journal of Psycho-Analysis* 46:117–128. Reprinted by permission.

Chapter 10 was presented as a lecture at the invitation of the Department of Psychiatry of Georgetown University, Washington, D.C., in February 1965.

Chapter 11 first appeared in the *Journal of the Americal Psychoanalytic Association* 18(1970):300–318. Reprinted by permission.

Chapter 12 was first presented at a panel discussion, Current Status of the Theory of the Superego, reported by Stanley Goodman, M.D., in the *Journal of the American Psychoanalytic Association* 13(1965):172–180. Presented here in revised form.

Chapter 13 first appeared as Chapter 8 in *The Unconscious Today: Essays in Honor of Max Schur,* ed. Mark Kanzer, pp. 147–176, New York: International Universities Press, 1971. Reprinted here by permission.

Chapter 14 first appeared in *The Annual of Psychoanalysis* 2(1974): 349–367. Reprinted by permission of the publisher, International Universities Press, Inc.

Chapter 15 first appeared in the *International Journal of Psychoanalytic Psychotherapy* 2(1973):149-173. Reprinted by permission of the publisher, Jason Aronson, Inc.

CONTENTS

I can scarcely express what I but dimly perceive—and yet I think I perceive it—that you may judge the more clearly I will put it in the most homely form possible—I will call the *world* a School instituted for the purpose of teaching little children to read—I will call the *human heart* the *horn Book* used in that School—and I will call the *Child able to read, the Soul* made from that *school* and its *hornbook*. Do you not see how necessary a World of Pains and troubles is to school an Intelligence and make it a soul? A Place where the heart must feel and suffer in a thousand diverse ways! Not merely is the Heart a Hornbook, It is the Minds Bible, it is the Minds experience, it is the teat from which the Mind or intelligence sucks its identity.

—John Keats

The Dilemma of Human Identity

INTRODUCTION

In the early thirties, while I was still practicing "neuropsychiatry" in Germany, my search for a new, more integrated vision of man than either existentialist philosophy or scientific medicine had to offer led me to the work of Freud. I sensed that there was, in Freud's approach to the great contradictions of human existence, an attempt to reach out beyond Cartesian dualism. As the philosopher Hans Jonas (1966) has so poignantly stated, "so constitutive for life is the possibility of not-being that its very being is essentially a hovering over this abyss, a skirting of its brink: thus being itself has become a constant possibility rather than a given state, ever anew to be laid hold of in opposition to its ever-present contrary, not-being, which will inevitably engulf it in the end" (p. 41). As I became more intimately familiar with the writings of Freud, I was as fascinated by their monumental grandeur as I was impressed with their fragmentary nature. Freud's theory of drives, for instance, culminated, after several revisions, in a cosmic vision of a life instinct—represented for Freud by Eros, conceptualized as a drive toward life—opposed by an even more powerful death instinct, to which all life must eventually succumb. There were many psychoanalysts who objected, for quite valid theoretical reasons, to the antithesis of Eros and death instinct. Obviously, it was impossible to demonstrate for the death instinct any psychological basis such as had been made evident for the libidinal drives. Hartmann, Kris, and Loewenstein (1947), for instance, felt that Freud's concept of the death instinct was a biological hypothesis, outside the realm of psychoanalytic observation. What to most psychoanalysts appeared demonstrable psychologically were aggressive impulses. Thus, the concept of a libidinal drive opposed by an aggressive instinct became part of the structural theory, and was offered as a more acceptable conceptualization of Freud's theory of instinctual dualism.

As a matter of fact, however, this construct belongs to a very different dimension of theoretical thought. An aggressive drive refers to impulses of single individuals, either human or animal. Freud's death instinct was impersonal, not even something that could be derived from psychological observation, except by hypothesizing a turning-outward of this instinct, which would thus manifest itself as aggression. There is no doubt that Freud originally conceived the death instinct as a cosmic principle, to which everything living would finally succumb, but the drive theory he envisaged remained a majestic fragment, a building block, as it were, for a vision even more encompassing than the new psychology psychoanalysis was creating. Was it perhaps also an effort "toward a philosophical biology" in the sense in which Jonas has used the term?

In the foreword to his *The Phenomenon of Life* (1966), Jonas writes

The . . . investigations seek to break through the anthropocentric confines of idealist and existentialist philosophy as well as through the materialist confines of natural science. In the mystery of the living body both poles are in fact integrated. The great contradictions which man discovers in himself—freedom and necessity, autonomy and dependence, self and world, relation and isolation, creativity and morality—have their rudimentary traces in even the most primitive forms of life, each precariously balanced between their being and not-being, and each already endowed with an internal horizon of "transcendence." We shall pursue this underlying theme of all life in its development through the ascending order of organic powers and functions: metabolism, moving and desiring, sensing and perceiving, imagination, art and mind—a progressive scale of freedom and peril, culminating in man, who may understand his uniqueness anew when he no longer sees himself in metaphysical isolation.

Only very recently have I become acquainted with the important philosophical essays of Hans Jonas, who obtained his doctorate in philosophy in the late twenties in Marburg, Germany, where I at the time was a medical student and where I too had been exposed to the philosophies of Edmund Husserl and Martin Heidegger. Now, in Buffalo, in November 1974, I was reading Jonas's *The Phenomenon of Life*, in which he expressed concerns which had begun to preoccupy me many years ago. I believe that most psychoanalysts reading these quotations from Jonas will concede that the phenomena described by him constitute a perception of life not at all alien to that of psychoanalytic theories, particularly as Freud had presented them in *Beyond the Pleasure Principle*. Jonas's language is, however, in his own words, that "of critical analysis and phenomenological description," and thus it is foreign to the terminology of psychoanalytic theory. In my early attempts to understand the significance of Freud's ideas for a new approach to a study of the existential structure of human reality, I felt that Freud's *Beyond the Pleasure Principle* contributed fundamental insights, but my doubts that his insights could be conceptualized in terms of a drive dualism led me to write "Phenomenology of the Repetition Compulsion and the Death Instinct" (chapter 1), where I attempted to preserve the essence of Freud's existential awareness while suggesting a revision of the drive dualism that Freud used in his paper. I proposed that what Freud calls the death instinct is the very antithesis of a drive concept—that it is the principle of entropy, to which indeed all life finally succumbs. I also suggested that the nature of drive was not what Freud believed it to be—a move toward restoration of an earlier state—but rather a reaching out for a state of being which transcends the actual conditions of mortal existence. I believed that it was possible to detect in drives a moving in the direction of timelessness and permanence. This seemed to me especially true with regard to the sexual drive, which, at least in its human manifestations, reached out for a state of ecstasy that carried it beyond both the biological function of procreation and its role in reducing drive tension. I concluded that if the existing fragments of psychoanalytic theory were ever to become a consistent approach to the problems of the "existential structure of human reality" they must move away from the Cartesian dichotomy of human reality and must also avoid, in Jonas's words, the "anthropocentric confines of existentialism."

I did not for many years envisage that I would, within the context of psychoanalytic exploration of the "human reality," come even slightly closer to the issues raised in my first paper. This does not mean that the problems were not lingering on as unsettled issues. My concern regarding the "existential structure of human reality" and its close relationship to the problems of psychiatry and to the work of Freud led me, in a 1948 review of Jean-Paul Sartre's *Age of Reason*, to state that "modern psychiatry does not take for granted that man's existence is synonymous to thinking, reasoning existence. [The psychiatrist] has learned that man can lose his *facultas cogitandi* without losing the faculty to be—and he calls this insanity. . . . Whatever technical names he uses, he is describing an existential structure of human reality. This existential structure was, for psychiatry, rediscovered by Sigmund Freud."[1]

It was still a long time before this very general idea turned into a specific problem that demanded a specific answer. It centered upon the issue touched on in the quotation above: at what moment of development does the child partake of the state of being human? Raising this question leads us to another area of Freud's work that he left unfinished, even though, late in life, he became aware of its significance for a more comprehensive view of the process of "becoming human." In his renewed efforts to clarify the stages of female sexuality, he confronted the preoedipal phase of development, and he felt as if he were discovering a lost civilization:

Our insight into this early, pre-Oedipal phase in girls comes to us as a surprise, like the discovery, in another field, of the Minoan-Mycenean civilization behind the civilization of Greece. Everything in the sphere of this first attachment to the mother seemed to me so difficult to grasp in analysis—so grey with age and shadowy and almost impossible to revivify—that it was as if it had succumbed to an especially inexorable repression. [1931, p. 226]

Today, we know that the preoedipal phase has a crucial significance in the emergence of any human being, girl or boy, from a symbiotic stage to the slow growth of human individuality. It is fair to say that the most pioneering work in psychoanalysis after Freud has been in the area of early childhood development. From this research have come new insights affecting every aspect of psychoanalytic theory and clinical work. The names of Melanie Klein, Anna Freud, D. W. Winnicott, J. Bowlby, R. A. Spitz, Margaret Mahler, and E. James Anthony are just a few milestones on the long road of discovery that is still far from its final destination.

But even more disquieting than the answers that these researchers have been able to offer are the questions they have raised regarding the "existential structure of human reality." To illustrate the nature of these questions, I shall quote from the recent work of Mahler and her coworkers: "For the more or less normal adult, the experience of himself as both fully 'in' and fully separated from 'the world out there' is taken for *granted as a given of life.* Consciousness of self and absorption without awareness of self are two polarities between which he moves with varying degrees of alternation and simultaneity. But this, too, is the result of a slowly unfolding process" (1975, p. 3; my italics). This process, however, turns out to be not a certainty at all. As the authors describe it:

In the study of infantile psychosis, both in the predominantly autistic ... and in the predominantly symbiotic syndromes ... children were observed who seemed either unable to enter or ever to leave the delusional twilight state of a mother-infant symbiotic common orbit. ... In consequence of one or the other of these solutions, adaptation to the outside world ... and individuation leading to the child's unique personality do not unfold evenly from an early stage onward. Thus, essential human characteristics get blunted and distorted in their rudimentary stage, or fall apart later on. [1975, p. 6]

Thus we are forced to conclude that the most important aspect of the "existential structure of *human* reality" is its high degree of uncertainty. There is never more to be said than that human existence remains a mere possibility *if* all the complex prerequisites for human individuation are met by the right human environment at the right time for each stage of human development.

It is my contention that our growing awareness of this high degree of uncertainty about the chance of an infant developing into a human individual carries us beyond Freud's implicit view of human development. Freud was fully aware of the precarious balance of the existential structure of human reality. His understanding of the reasons for this precariousness has made possible the new questions that studies such as Mahler's have raised. Freud took, however, more for granted about the earliest stages of childhood than Mahler's research permits us. Freud would have expected any human being to be struggling with conflicts—between Id and Ego, Ego and Superego, between Id and Superego—and he clearly saw that there were, indeed, conflicts so severe as to destroy the possibility of any balance that would permit even a limited stability. What Freud did not envisage was that it it always questionable whether a human infant will reach the stage where structures and consequently conflicts in the sense of the structural theory can develop. In the words of Ricoeur (1970, p. 439), it was Freud's "prior positing of the *sum* at the heart of the *cogito*" that already implied a view of human existence going beyond Cartesian principles. Now we must take into account the radical fact, emerging from studies of early child development, that even the *sum*—the "I am"—cannot be taken for granted. Thus, Mahler and her coworkers state: "We use the term identity to refer to the earliest awareness of being, of entity—a feeling that includes in part, we believe, a cathexis of the body with libidinal energy. It is not a sense of *who* I am but *that* I am; as such, this is the earliest step in the process of the unfolding individuality" (1975, p. 8). This implies that in the very strictest sense the experience of existing has, in human beings, to be evoked, "teased out" by some specifically human interaction, at first between mother and child and later between family and child.

I have been quoting Mahler's work so extensively because it appears to me to lend support to some of the propositions developed in my "Identity and Sexuality" (see chapter 2) and derived from my experience with adult patients undergoing psychoanalysis. Over the years I had gained the impression that many of my more severely disturbed patients were profoundly torn between an overwhelming yearning to return to a symbiotic state of existence and an equally compelling urge to assert their separateness as individuals. Their unresolvable conflicts seemed due to the fact that both symbiosis and separateness were equally threatening to the existential structure of their human reality. Symbiosis implied to them a ceasing-to-be, a dissolution of their reality as persons. Individual separateness, on the other hand, doomed them to total isolation, as if they were suspended in the void. Anna Freud (1952) has described this in terms of an alternation between negativism and emotional surrender (*Hoerigkeit*). The clinical diagnosis could vary: severe depressive states, perversions, borderline type of personality, character neurosis, might all be applicable. While it seemed possible to interpret the specific symptoms that troubled these patients in the dynamic terms of the structural theory, it did not seem that this was really feasible with regard to their basic predicament: the dilemma of symbiosis versus separateness. To refer again to Ricoeur's formulation, their *sum* at the heart of the *cogito* seemed to have failed them. Or, in Mahler's terms, they did not lack a sense of *who* they were, but *that* they were. While they had an intellectual awareness of their existence, they were lacking, in Eissler's terminology (1958a), an "emotional conviction" of their being. I gradually came to believe that this conviction cannot be taken for granted as a self-evident aspect of the human reality, but that it has to be acquired. To offer a plausible hypothesis of this acquisition, based on clinical observation, appeared therefore to be in the interest of the evolving body of psychoanalytic theories as well as of its potential implications with regard to the reality of human existence.

I shall not repeat here the theses developed in "Identity and Sexuality." I wish rather to direct attention to an entirely intuitive characterization of the existential structure of human reality coming from an unexpected, but authoritative source. I am referring to John Keats's justifiably famous concept of "negative capability" as a prerequisite for the creative imagination—especially relevant since Keats also saw a connection between creativity and the problems of human identity.[2] Keats introduced the term *negative capability* in a letter to a friend and commented on it with the terse statement: "That is when man is capable of being in uncertainties, Mysteries, doubts, without any irritable reaching after fact and reason." Leavy amplifies the concept as follows: " 'Negative capability' then would be the capacity to give free rein to the imagination. The disparate, absurd, inchoate, illogical, impossible would not present stop-signs. . . . All that prevents that from happening is the restraint ordinarily imposed in the face of 'uncertainties, Mysteries, doubts' and a need for the security of 'fact and reason'; it is these that block the flight of fancy." Keats linked these "negative capabilities" with the poet's "lack of identity": "A Poet is the most unpoetical of anything in existence; because he has no identity—Not one word I ever utter can be taken for granted as an opinion growing out of my identical nature—the identity of everyone begins to press upon me."[3]

Keats dealt here with the difference between the poet and the nonpoet, whom he saw as a logical, reasoning individual and characterized as "consequitive" man. Leavy points out that Keats overemphasized the contrast between reason and imagination by limiting the concept of reason to "antipoetical," strictly factual thinking. In this antithesis it is to imagination that Keats attributed all the qualities that were for him essential characteristics of being human, while he believed that reaching "after fact and reason" has a dehumanizing, "heartless" quality about it. I believe that it is not doing any violence to Keats to claim that what he was trying to capture in his concepts of negative capability and lack of identity was the existential structure of human reality. Our present knowledge of the mental processes we consider basically human permits us to reformulate Keats's insights. We have to dare to expand negative capability and lack of identity to characterize what sets "being human" apart from any nonhuman way of existing. Negative capability and lack of identity do not define per se the poet versus other forms through which human existence may manifest itself—such as reasoning and judgment—but they separate the totality of "being human" from every nonhuman mode of existence.[4] Animals have indeed "positive capability" and "identity"—but not "imagination" in Keats's sense. Their "positive capability" consists of their unreflective preadaptedness to their environment, and their "identity" is the total unambiguity of their state of being. Animals may be frightened, in pain, suffering, but "being in uncertainties, mysteries, doubts" we do not attribute to them. It is, however, this ambiguity of the state of being which defines the existential structure of human inner reality. Keats's statement "that which is creative must create itself" describes the very process of the psychological birth of the human infant, and beyond that, implies that this process of self-creation is a permanent "rebirth." To claim that the potential to create a poem distinguishes human beings from animals might sound like romantic indulgence. It is, however, quite compatible with Jonas's suggestion that what determines man's "specific difference" in the animal kingdom is man's capacity for image-making:

"The crudest and most childish drawing would be just as conclusive as the frescoes of Michelangelo. Conclusive for what? For the more-than-animal nature of its creator; and for his being potentially a speaking, thinking, inventing, in short 'symbolic' being" (1966, p. 158).

If we accept that it is negative capability and lack of identity that define the existential structure of human reality, we come closer to the predicament of those patients who could never accept their own yearning for a symbiotic union nor endure a separate individuality. They seemed to be prevented from "creating themselves." The questions arise how this dilemma came about and whether it can be resolved. Perhaps Keats's assertion that the poet has no identity because "the identity of everyone else begins to press upon me" implies a uniquely human way to create "identity" out of symbiotic fusion. I do assume that in the prestructural stage of development human beings must create themselves in accordance to an image "pressed upon them"—I compare it to "imprinting"—by their mothers. This is the only path to an identity that humans have, since they are not endowed with the positive capabilities that enable animals to exist unambiguously, never questioning that they are or who they are.

The "imaginative" or "symbolic" identity that is part of the existential structure of human reality remains a variation of the symbiotic state and not its total abandonment. It may be described as an identity made possible by one's response to another's perception of one's existence. I described this process as a kind of "mirroring" in my paper on narcissism (chapter 8). Such identity can never be taken for granted. It has to be recreated throughout life. In this sense, man is the most endangered species: there is never any certainty that, once born, he is going to become human. And if he does, it is still always at issue whether he will remain human.[5] This is due to the fact that the identity human beings are able to create for themselves is maintained only through a specific kind of interaction with another one from whom an affirmation of the reality of existence can be obtained. Implied in this affirmation is, however, not only the certainty that I am, but an ever growing awareness of another one that I am *not*. This polarity—to borrow a term from Jonas—in one's experience of the other one excludes the possibility that human identity is a solipsistic state, an existence in and by oneself without an essential awareness of an otherness. This condition pervades human identity regardless of the stage of development, though it originates in the infant's preverbal relationship with the mother. It is she who provides affirmation for the infant that it is there, existing, but it also conveys to the child its mother's otherness and, therefore, its own.

Thus the existential structure of human identity comes into being in a social matrix, from which the development of the specific societal structure of *human* social organization must be derived. But the mother-infant social matrix has unique characteristics that can be considered as fateful for many of the structures of human ways of relating to other humans. It is, above all, a relationship pervaded by the extreme inequality of mother and infant. It is not a relationship between two persons, but a form of coexistence between one overpowering being and another one which long remains in a position of unconditional surrender to the power of the other. In fact, even as the infant separates slowly from the original symbiotic state, mother and child respond to each other as if they were extensions of one another, both physically and psychically. In this most intimate interaction, the child is affirmed as being there as the mother's extension, on the basis of the nonverbal responses of mother and child to one another. In turn, the child perceives its mother as the most important part of its physical and emotional being. This type of relatedness, whose primary aim is not nourishment but a heightened sense "that one exists," constituting a mutually affirmative response to each other's being, defines also an essential aspect of human sexuality. It seems, in fact, throughout adult life the strongest motive for sexual intimacy—independent of the procreative functions of sexuality as a biological need.

Insofar as this prototypical emotional eroticism between mother and child builds the child's sense "that he is," human nonprocreative sexuality appears instrumental in the creation of an identity man does not possess as a "given" state of being. According to the mother's specific expectations of the child, all nonverbally communicated, the child will "create itself" as he understands those expectations. Simultaneously, the child makes demands about the ways in which it wants its mother to affirm its being. All of these "mysteries" can lead to infinite variations, both in the way individuals expect to be affirmed, and in the conditions of relatedness that find their primary expression in the language of sexuality. The close link between sexuality and identity maintenance and reaffirmation is one of the reasons that human sexuality is inseparable from human imagination. It also throws light on the compulsive and irrational quality of human sexuality. I dealt with some of the extreme hazards growing out of these conditions in "The Malignant No" (chapter 13). Human identity, because it is based on negative capability, depends so much on another person's response that this other person may ultimately become a threat, just as the mother's power to affirm the child's existence may make her the one person the child must in the end radically separate from.

Gedo and Goldberg (1973), among others, reject the use of the concept of identity in the context of separation-individuation. They agree with Kohut that "its use is an attempt to straddle the gap between two disciplines, social and individual psychology, without really belonging to either" (p. 64). I think that this position oversimplifies the issue, overlooking the fact that human *existence* straddles the gap between individual and social ways of being from the beginning to the end. The infant begins with a symbiotic stage not strictly definable as either individual or social. As the child slowly separates from the mother, it becomes another one in relation to her. Thus, its beginning individuality is experienced in terms of a changed relationship with someone else. Its individuality emerges from a state of *primary oneness*, then into a primitive way of relatedness—at first confined to an I-you relatedness—which is the primary *social unit*. One aspect of the dilemma of human identity is the fact that outside a relatedness to another one it collapses. Only by contrasting themselves one to another can human beings become separate, can they acquire or create an identity. The integral role of the other in the creation of an identity constitutes a grave danger, a profound threat to one's identity through loss, abandonment, or enforced separation. The dangers are real, and they make the alternative—regression to the symbiotic stage, with loss of identity—an always threatening possibility.

This special "existential" imbalance is at the root of the precariousness of human existence. It is also the motive behind the need for a "support system" for human beings, who must maintain their capacity for separateness, but cannot exist without being embedded in patterns of relatedness. The societal order in which human beings live may constitute this kind of support system: its function then is to protect the

growing child—by methods of child-rearing, family structure, etc.—
from symbiotic arrest, and at the same time from the dangers of inner
isolation. I believe the facts support an assumption that there is a
causal relationship between the specific forms of "being human" that
develop within a particular societal structure, and the conditions for
survival that prevail within the environment with which a group has to
cope. Thus, under certain conditions some ways of "being human"
become preferred to others. This preference for a particular choice
among the many options of "how to be human" finally crystallizes in
those patterns of being human that are referred to as "social identities,"
for instance, that of a tribe of hunters or of fishermen.

While it might be in the interest of group survival to produce such
"preferred ways to be human," this achievement does in fact intensify
the "dilemma of human identity" by creating new and very hazardous
possibilities. The more effective a societal organization becomes in
promoting the development of certain favored ways of being human,
the more pervasive becomes its conviction that its preferred way is *the*
way to exist. In other words, societies tend to foster the belief that
human beings are born with "positive capabilities," namely, those that
in any particular society have been promoted by unconscious processes
of selective molding. The result is an increasingly powerful antagonism
toward any alternative ways of being human. These may be disdained
as "not truly human" or may be perceived as serious threats to the
stability and viability of the society collectively. For the individual
whose sense of existence depends on affirmation by the group,
tendencies toward such alternate ways of being human may create
profound anxieties of isolation and may undermine the conviction of
existing. Thus, the efforts of social groups to protect themselves
against the dangerous dilemmas of human identity by supporting
collective safeguards against them, does, paradoxically, create a new
danger: varying degrees of antagonism against those whose difference
is perceived as a threat. I am inclined to believe that wars, the ostracism
of certain groups as "untouchables," etc. are not the result of aggressive
drives. Rather, aggression is one of the defensive manifestations of the
inner contradictions of the dilemma of human identity. The well-
known emotional conflicts of the adolescent or young adult who has to
find for himself or herself an acceptable "social role" indicate the
precarious balance brought about by the necessity to repress or deny

important aspects of his or her own way of being human. Keats himself is an example of the existential hazards that endanger an exceptional way of being human, even in an individual endowed with the genius to create himself symbolically through the medium of poetry. May we not wonder whether his premature death was the price he paid for an effort to bridge the chasm opening up in the depths of this particular human identity? Problems concerning "social identities" are derivatives of efforts to find a way out of the *inherent* dilemma of human identity, which is an inseparable aspect of being human from the day of a child's birth.

It would be hopeful to look at these disturbing predicaments of human existence with the optimistic expectation that a general increase in human tolerance for different ways of "being human" would offer a solution. There are, however, limits to what one may expect of tolerance. It is certainly true that in the modern Western world differences between alternative ways of being human are tolerated that would not have been in the Middle Ages—nor would they be today in certain cultural settings. This is due mostly, however, to worldwide changes in the perception of reality, which also delimits one's interpretation of one's own place in the universe. For the majority of people in the United States, for instance, the Darwinian theory of evolution is no longer the same profound threat to their perception of reality that it was a hundred years ago; their interpretation of themselves as existing within the framework of that reality is not seriously endangered by Darwin's theories. It is, however, well known that there are still groups of people who consider evolutionary theory quite incompatible with their perception of the world and, consequently, of their own existence. This fact might indicate that tolerance for differences is not primarily a "moral issue," though it is usually treated as such. It rather seems to reflect the structure of a person's or a group's reality perception, and therefore measures the relative vulnerability of an individual or a group to changing realities which inevitably affect his or its own sense of existence.

Many of the members of the young generation today aim at an almost unrestricted tolerance for a wide range of patterns of being human. In a world that is almost totally lacking in a consensus about what is to be regarded as "real" and what as "human," such unlimited tolerance is an understandable ideal. The difficulty for such young people is that they are compelled to consider justifiable every pattern of being human—and it may not be possible to maintain a sense of human existence without affirming it by sharing it with others. Not infrequently, these young people develop a profound uncertainty about whether they are "real," since it is most difficult for them to obtain a convincing affirmation of their reality from others, whose experience of being human excludes them. It often leads to a regression toward a symbiotic state of being, which may express itself through impersonal sexuality, drug use, and submersion in such collective experiences as rock concerts. I have tried to deal with some of these problems in my papers dealing with the "generation gap" and the problem of reality perception. It seems, in fact, unwarranted to assume that there is any way to deal with the dilemma of human identity that eliminates all risks and hazards.

This view will not be acceptable to those who expect from a restructuring of society a resolution of what I call here the dilemma of human identity. I have already stressed that the particular structure of a society has an important influence on the manifestations of the phenomena I have discussed. It seems also likely that particular societies—for instance, a society based on slave labor, with the consequent promotion of an inherently symbiotic pattern—are bound to jeopardize possibilities for a balanced equilibrium between separateness and symbiosis. The technological society, on the other hand, has fostered extremes of functional group interactions, potentially deleterious for the development and maintenance of a conviction of one's own existence as a person. Technological society seems particularly apt to interfere with the conditions necessary for the psychological birth of the infant and its progress toward separation and individuation. I nevertheless believe, as stated before, that a typically human society develops as a way to reduce the dangers inherent in the existential structure of human reality—the dilemma of human identity being the most hazardous and pervasive of these dangers, in all stages of human life. Thus, I cannot conceive that this problem, which begins with the birth of the human infant, could be secondary to any other of the multifarious dangers threatening human existence.

Freud did not hesitate to confront uncomfortable findings about the reality of being human, even if these findings contradicted our most cherished expectations of what human reality ought to be. I have, in some respects, expanded on Freud's ideas, not trying to diminish his contribution to our understanding of the existential structure of human reality, but rather as an homage to his lifework, which he, knowing he had to leave much unfinished, expected other generations to carry on. I believe that Freud would have been in agreement with the way Jonas characterizes his own philosophy of the phenomenon of life: "The reader will . . . find nothing here of the evolutionary optimism . . . with life's sure and majestic march toward a sublime consummation. He will find life viewed as an experiment with mounting stakes and risks which in the fateful freedom of man may end in disaster as well as in success" (1966). I cannot see in this philosophy anything incompatible with Freud's expressed views of man's fate, though I suspect that Freud might not have shared Jonas's profound scepticism toward the evolutionary process itself. Since Freud's time psychoanalysis has moved in a direction which has tended to transform into mere possibilities many assumptions once taken for granted or considered simple givens. One can no longer assume that a child will develop object relationships on the basis of a predictable pattern of psychosexual development. Rather, we now see such a development as contingent on the child's successful emergence from the separation-individuation stage. Another example of an assumption that we may no longer take for granted is the inner awareness "that I am." It is not an expectable certainty of ego development. Only a child that experiences an affirmation of its own being by the mother will achieve a conviction of the reality of its existence.

These shifts from near certainty to mere possibility are more than modifications of psychoanalytic theory. They are, rather, a reevaluation of the existential structure of human reality. They have a profound influence on our judgment of social issues, moral problems, and therapeutic priorities in preventive psychiatry. They present the structure of human reality as depending on a harmonious confluence of all the necessary conditions; without this the possibility of human existence remains questionable and may in fact not offer itself again. This does not only hold true for the psychological birth of the individual human child. The potential failure of the "psychological reproduction" of homo sapiens must also be taken seriously. I do not view this, however, as a proclamation of therapeutic nihilism. On the contrary, I believe that what we have learned as psychoanalysts about the precariousness of the existential structure of human reality makes it a therapeutic responsibility to envisage the extreme consequences that might arise from the failure to see what is at stake if we insist on taking human existence for granted.

There is no one who would not rather accept as "self-evident truths" the assuring faith of the signers of the Declaration of Independence "that all men are created equal; that they are endowed by their Creator with certain inalienable rights: that among those are life, liberty and the pursuit of happiness." It is, however, no longer our inalienable right to take our hopes for mankind as givens. Human existence finds itself in a twilight of uncertain possibilities. We must face the challenge of new questions and not hesitate to suggest new answers to old problems. What recent explorations about the existential structure of human reality seem to reveal is not essentially different from what a more universally informed thinker said almost thirty years ago: "Man is essentially an unbalanced animal who, nevertheless, exists; this means that he is not precisely and solely an animal, for to an animal, existing is always equilibrium, or if not, it is ceasing to exist, succumbing. To this paradoxical lack of balance man owes all his grace and all his disgrace, all his misery and all his splendor" (Ortega y Gasset 1973, p. 246).

NOTES

1. In rereading that review of Sartre, I found that I had touched upon a number of issues taken up in greater detail in the essays in this volume. It may perhaps be relevant to quote at length the passage in which this sentence occurred:

Is morbidity a general structure of human existence? The psychiatrist does not hesitate to answer the question in the affirmative. To be able to become "morbid"—to be psychoneurotic, addicted, perverted; and indeed, insane is not just an "accident" that happens to some human freaks or "degenerates." It is a basic potentiality of human existence itself. Everybody is aware of the fact that human existence is lived in the face of death. The psychiatrist knows of another death than the physical one. He knows that human existence—any human existence—can be destroyed by disintegration. Modern psychiatry does not take it for granted that man's existence is synonymous to thinking, reasoning existence. He has learned that man can lose his *facultas cogitandi* without losing the faculty to be—and he calls this insanity. He has discovered the intimate connection between an individual's hold on reality and his freedom to choose. He has observed that disintegration deprives a person not only of the experience of reality (to use Heidegger's term: his being-in-the-world), but makes him subject to the compelling power of impulses that take control of his action against the decisions of his reasoning mind. The stages of disintegration are the stages of being compelled to do what one has not chosen to do. According to the aspect of an individual's life that has come under the domination of compulsion—instead of freedom to choose—the psychiatrist classifies the phenomena of disintegration of human existence. Some forms are nearly universal, he calls them psychoneuroses. Others represent the complete "loss of reality," he labels them psychoses. Whatever technical names he uses, he is describing an existential structure of human reality. This existential structure was, for psychiatry, rediscovered by Sigmund Freud. In one of his early writings Freud (Totem and Taboo, *Standard Edition* 13:92-93) pays tribute to the understanding of life that the ancient people betrayed in recognizing the ever-present demonic powers that threaten human existence. Freud gave these "demonic powers" a modern name; he spoke of the forces of the "Id" in man, and claimed they were unconscious. He felt that clinical "normality" was a particular state of equilibrium between the reasoning powers of man and the hidden forces of the *Id*. This equilibrium, according to Freud, could be disturbed under certain conditions. This would mean that man can fall under the domination of "demonic powers." In Freud's own words, this would mean the loss of the "ability to choose," to become driven by powers that man is unable to control.

2. I owe a debt to Stanley A. Leavy, whose excellent paper "John Keats's Psychology of Imagination," (*Psychoanalytic Quarterly*, 39(1970):173-197) made me aware of Keats's importance for psychoanalytic theory. I am grateful also to Professor Robert Rogers of the Department of English at the State University of New York at Buffalo for his furthering of my awareness of Keats's significance for psychoanalysis.

3. Leavy feels that Keats's concept of identity "has particular appeal at present, because so much has been said lately about identity and the absence of it, or its negative forms, and its comes as a little shock that Keats looked on identity as a barrier to creative work."

4. That concepts like "negative capability" and "lack of identity" were perceived and formulated by a poet, and not by a philosopher or scientist, is, of course, anything but accidental: they appear to emerge from a vision that is closer to "primary-process" insights than one would expect in a "rational thinker."

5. "While the tiger cannot cease being a tiger, cannot be detigered, man lives in the perpetual risk of being dehumanized. With him, not only is it problematic and contingent, whether this or that will happen to him, as it is with the other animals, but at times what happens to man is nothing less than *ceasing to be man.* And this is true not only abstractly and generically but it holds for our own individuality" (Ortega y Gasset 1939).

Part I

Identity and Sexuality

Chapter 1

REPETITION COMPULSION AND
THE DEATH INSTINCT:
A PHENOMENOLOGICAL APPROACH

When an author experiences the reappearance in print of a piece of his own writing of forty years ago, he cannot help but be seized with the uncanny feeling of encountering his double. He knows that the person he is hearing is himself, though the revenant is speaking a now foreign tongue, a language belonging to an altogether different time, place, and intellectual climate, linked to a period he may have vainly aimed to forget. He also cannot help wondering how those who have known him in his later years as a fellow member of the American Psychoanalytic Association will respond to the strange voice that they hear speaking in the pages of this first paper.

It is because of the enormous gap in thought and method of reasoning between the early paper and much later ones that I feel an obligation to write these introductory remarks to this paper, which I have translated into English and edited for the present-day reader.

It is obvious that the paper was not written by a psychoanalyst. It clearly reflects the powerful influence of Edmund Husserl and Martin Heidegger, who shaped my philosophical thinking as a student. But, in my own judgment, the paper shows the even greater impact of Freud's ideas on my thinking about certain basic questions of existence. These questions deal first with the issue of permanence within change (temporality), which appears in the early paper but is equally central for the identity concept developed later in "Identity and Sexuality." Second, there is the continuity of the quest for a specific psychological function of sexuality in man outside of procreativity. It is assumed that this function goes beyond the aim of reduction of sexual tension. Both the early paper and the later ones see sexuality as effecting a heightened sense of being for the individual, though there are differences in the psychological understanding of such a state between the early and the later papers. Third, the question is raised whether aggression, even destruction, is not linked to man's unconscious striving to transcend his transitoriness by means of aggrandizing his sense of self by control and domination of other persons and nature. This "will to existential affirmation," and not a death instinct, may account for human aggression. Finally, Freud's insights into a principle beyond the pleasure principle form a central theme in the first paper. The thesis that Freud had perceived in the repetition compulsion a key to the concept of identity maintenance—continuity of personal identity within temporality—is taken up twenty years later in "Identity and Sexuality."

I may add that these apparent continuities came as a surprise to me, since I had not read my early paper for many years—perhaps in an effort to extinguish the memory of a period when questions of life and death, of meaning and absurdity, confronted everybody most personally and directly. Olinick (1957), in an inspired paper on "Questioning and Pain, Truth and Negation," says: "Etymologically, historically, and psychologically, linkages are demonstrable between questioning, the search for knowledge and truth, the pain of torture and ordeal, guilt and anxiety, and sense of justice." If he is right, I am willing to believe that the radical questioning concerning "Being" and "Nothingness" that pervades my early paper is a necessary corollary to the circumstances under which it was written: Through unconscious perseverance of this questioning, the transition from "then" to "now" became possible without a break in the sense of inner continuity.

Since Freud's introduction of the concept of the death instinct in *Beyond the Pleasure Principle* (1920), no generally accepted viewpoint regarding the nature of this type of drive has been able to assert itself within the psychoanalytic school of thought. There are still theorists who feel they must reject this conceptualization of Freud's. In contrast, Freud, in his latest writings, put increasing emphasis on the fundamental significance of this concept in the context of his "dualistic theory of drives." Any effort undertaken with the aim of clarifying the points at issue will always have to take as its starting point the theoretical steps leading to the introduction of the concept of a death instinct. According to Freud's own affirmation, the theoretical bases on which the postulate for the existence of a death instinct rests are twofold: first, the theoretical considerations developed in his 1920 paper; second, the "sadistic contributions which have attached themselves to Eros" (1923, p. 46). The theoretical deduction of the death instinct from the empirical fact of the repetition compulsion in *Beyond the Pleasure Principle* shall now be briefly restated, in view of the decisive significance that these ideas of Freud's assume in the thesis to be presented here.

Having demonstrated the existence of a compulsion to repeat with several (clinical) examples and having assigned to it the rank of one of the most basic reaction patterns of mental life, Freud raised the fundamental issue of how the phenomenon of drive in general is linked to the compulsion to repeat. In his answer, Freud asserted the following: Repetition is essentially a restoration of an earlier existing condition. This very tendency toward restoration of an earlier state of being illuminates to us the nature of the interrelatedness between drive in general and repetition. The most general drive characteristic is constituted by a tendency to restore something existing earlier, aiming, accordingly, toward repetition of a previous state. Freud demonstrates this "conservative nature of drives" by references to a variety of biological phenomena, and then draws this conclusion: The aim of all drives cannot consist of anything other than the ultimate repetition of the inorganic state of nature which, for unknown external causes, had been transcended at one evolutionary stage. Considering the inorganic matter as the matrix from which the living substance originated, Freud put the final aim of all drives as a striving for the restoration of death, death being the condition that was earlier than life. Freud thus arrived at the concept of the death instinct by a process of deductive reasoning, directly derived from the empirical fact of the repetition compulsion.[1]

REPETITION, RETROGRESSION (PROGRESSION)

Freud's interpretation of the concept of repetition indubitably represents the key to an understanding of his deduction of the idea of the death instinct from the repetition compulsion. He defined repetition as "restoration of a previously existing state." One can indeed say that Freud used these two terms synonymously. The question must be raised, however, whether it is phenomenologically justifiable to use the concepts "repetition" and "restoration" as if they were equivalent terms. One has only to keep before one's mind's eye a model of any repetitive occurrence—the labors of Sisyphus, for instance, who was condemned to eternal repetition—to notice the difference. Though we immediately become aware that the first phase of the phenomenon of repetition represents a return to a state which has already been traversed before, all that can be asserted regarding that first phase is that repetition *begins* with a restoration of a previously existing state. Once this stage of restoration has been reached, however, it is not held on to, but is immediately abandoned again. There is an instant redirection of the process. The movement of repetition does not lead in the direction of an ever-earlier phase of a developmental process. Rather, by reversing its direction, the movement returns to the position already held at the beginning of the repetition. What specifically characterizes the phenomenon of repetition is this immutably linked alternation between an initial phase of backward movement followed by a subsequent forward movement. Sisyphus' labor is constituted as eternal repetition only because he must roll the rock anew to the top of the mountain from which it had just plummeted. We are, however, not obligated to make the descent into Hades in order to study repetition phenomena: if we stay in the natural world, we are offered sufficiently impressive experiences of repetition in the regular sequence of the alternating seasons, or the recurrent rhythm of the change from day to night. In these phenomena we can recognize clearly the biphasic movement by which a phenomenon establishes itself as repetition: an initial phase that moves toward restoration of a previous condition, followed by a return to the beginning—one could think of the phases of repetition as countervailing movements, each of which annuls the effect of the other. If one were to represent repetition by a simple graphic delineation, the circle would be a suitable image of its movement. And, indeed, both the seasons and the sequence of day and night are the immediate consequences of the circular movement of the earth.

The phenomenology of retrogression is radically different. In contrast to the phenomenon of repetition, retrogression is uniphasic, continuous in the direction of its movement toward an unequivocal end stage. Accordingly, retrogression lacks the necessary reversal of direction, i.e., a progressive phase, which characterizes repetition. Rather, retrogression remains constant in its backward movement. Its graphic image is not a circle, but a straight line moving toward a zero point.[2]

In contrasting the phenomenological description of "repetition" on the one hand, with "retrogression" on the other, it becomes apparent that these phenomena not only do not overlap, but are also mutually exclusive of one another: Where there is repetition, retrogression cannot take place, and vice versa. Again Greek mythology can help us to clarify the point: Penelope used repetition in what she did to her famous garment. There was an initial phase of retrogressive movement when she unraveled the woven threads of her garment at night. This retrogressive movement was reversed during the day by reweaving the gown. Had Penelope let herself be overcome by the momentum of her retrogression, the garment would have been unraveled into threads. Her whole effort would not have made any sense, and no suitor would have fallen victim to the deception. The story serves us beyond its function as a paradigm. We become aware that the effect of repetition may consist in the fixation of a particular phase within a retrogressive[3] movement in time. With this, we are focusing on a central aspect of the phenomenon of repetition: It is the intimate link between repetition and the experience of time in man.

REPETITION AND TIME EXPERIENCE

While we do not intend to enter the complex psychological and philosophical problems presented by the concept of time, we must nevertheless direct our attention to the relation between repetition and the phenomenon of time. The fact that the time dimension of occurrences is the reason for the impossibility of repetition, in the strict sense of the term, is one of the oldest philosophical perceptions. This is indeed what the famous dictum of Heraclitus affirms by its assertion that nobody is capable of diving into the same river twice. It is, however, equally evident that the time quality of experience is what establishes the condition for the possibility of repetition. The concept of an "again" can make sense only within a sequence that extends from a past to a present into a future. These two assertions are not mutually exclusive. Rather, only their coexistence throws the appropriate light upon the phenomenon of repetition. The idea of a repetition, which implies a recapture (in German, literally, *Wieder-holen*) of what is past, presupposes the reality of time experience. If time were a continuum, extending uniformly toward the past and the future, something imposed from without upon the current of events, like a yardstick for measuring—under such circumstances, repetition, in the literal sense of recovering the past, would be a possibility. This conceptualization of time is, however, an abstraction, which makes sense only as a form of measuring inanimate physical processes. Its use is legitimate as the "physical" time concept, i.e., the time concept applicable to physics. In contrast, "experienced" time (see Bergson 1888, and Heidegger 1927), is inherent in the state of being alive. This time is experienced as flowing only in one direction: namely, from the future through the present into the past. The experienced time (*le temps vécu* of Bergson) is "irreversible": Everything living has "it's" time, and as this time "runs out," it implies a simultaneous and continuous change of the essence of what it is to be alive—*nos et mutamur in illis.*[4] Within the experienced time it is, therefore, not possible to repeat (in the sense of recapturing, recovering) the past: Heraclitus' stress on time's irreversibility correctly describes the subjective mode of time experience in the sense of one's lifetime.[5] These reflections make it apparent that repetition stands in a special relationship to the subjective experience of time: whenever there is the aim to actualize repetition within the course of a (human) life, repetition stands in opposition to time. That is to say: *Repetition is an attempt or a tendency to transcend the irreversibility of the flow of time*, to recapture, as it were, the time which has disappeared, to compel time to stand still. This is the meaning of the fixating effect of repetition, a fact to which reference was made before in contrasting the respective phenomenologies of repetition, retrogression, and progression. Amid the immutable changes to which everything is exposed that exists in time and is determined by time, repetition effects a kind of duration, albeit often a mere appearance of duration. Indeed, the only mode of duration accessible to anything living is, strictly speaking, duration by means of repetition. If we wish to bestow duration to customs otherwise soon to be forgotten, we can accomplish this only by means of repetition. Such repetitions, frequently of a symbolic kind, are our traditional customs, such as our holidays and various celebrations: they endeavor to recapture an event from the past, to endow such an event with duration within time, or, as we are wont to say, to keep whatever happened "alive" within ourselves regardless of the passage of centuries.[6] In the end it is in this way that repeatability becomes a direct scale of value by which we measure the sense impressions that crowd our very lives. An experience has for us a "permanent" value only if it is capable of an intrapsychic, if not a real, repetition. In contrast, experiences take on the character of being "fleeting" ("transitory"), if they are not capable of such repetition. The factual singularity and irretrievability of all occurrences causes mental anguish, which is all the more painful to endure, the more intensively we feel in ourselves a yearning for the recapture of a unique experience. Still, in the face of his actual knowledge, as if in spite of it, man seizes upon repetition in order to make time yield to him duration, indeed, eternity. Repetition, duration, eternity are thus established as phases in a continuum based on the inner negation of the passing of time. Repetition effects "permanence in time"; the eternal repetition becomes the conceptual form which enables human thought to adumbrate an image of eternity.

Friedrich Rueckert[7] (1822) succeeds, in his moving poem "Chidher," in conveying through imagery eternity as compared to human transitoriness, by juxtaposing an eternal and immutable repetitive occurrence to the mutability of everything merely temporal. The refrain (my translation) after each stanza of the poem—

> And as centuries come and wane
> I shall travel these roads again

—holds out the promise of a repetition ad infinitum, and this image constitutes the poetic representation of eternity. But it is not only the poet who represents eternity to us through the image of a repetition ad infinitum. That individual life is capable of infinite repetition, thus contradicting the time-bound, fleeting momentariness of life—this is affirmed by every mythology of the beyond, be it formulated in terms of metempsychosis, or resurrection, or any other manner of life after death. Neither have the philosophers, from antiquity to modern times, succeeded in finding a more adequate symbol for the idea of eternity than that of an endlessly repetitive movement. Aristotle saw the circular motion of the celestial bodies of the first heaven as the eternal moving principle from which everything that exists derives its movement. Friedrich Nietzsche, the most radical and uncompromising thinker of the last century, believed that he had found an eternity that actualizes itself through eternal repetition, as formulated in his doctrine of the eternal recurrence.

In retrospect, the reasoning as developed here permits us to state that the concepts of repetition and of retrogression, phenomenologically viewed, lead us to the conclusion that these two phenomena are not identical. On the contrary, they constitute fundamental opposites. Repetition effects the suspension of any retrogressive or progressive movement. Psychologically, repetition offers the only possibility of creating the experience of duration compatible with the inner reality of time. Finally, as an idea of repetition ad infinitum, repetition symbolizes the concept of eternity, insofar as eternity is perceived as time-determined, in contrast to a perception that would place it "beyond time."

THE RELEVANCE OF THE PHENOMENOLOGY OF REPETITION FOR THE PSYCHOLOGICAL INTERPRETATION OF THE REPETITION COMPULSION

What does the application of the phenomenological analysis of repetition yield to our understanding of the repetition compulsion as an empirical psychological phenomenon? We take as our point of departure Freud's acknowledgment that the existence of a repetition compulsion had to be recognized not only as a basic characteristic of mental life, but as an inherent characteristic of the phenomenon of life itself. We must therefore conclude that the primary, most elemental drive quality of the living substance aims at repetition, constituting thus an antithesis to retrogression, an antithesis to change through the passage of time, an antithesis to time itself. The tendency inherent in the repetition compulsion is directed toward fixation within the flow of time, toward duration—indeed, we must dare say it: toward eternity. The meaning of the "conservative nature of everything living" reveals itself to us, in exact conformity with the literal sense of the word, as a tendency to "conserve" the living substance, i.e., to protect it from the change brought about by the "progress of time."[8] This interpretation of the repetition compulsion seems, at first glance, to place us in opposition to Freud's opinion. It appears, however, as if Freud (1920) saw the relation between drive and temporality, at least to some degree, in an antithetic way similar to the view presented here: ". . . unconscious mental processes are in themselves 'timeless.' This means in the first place that they are not ordered temporally, that time does not change them in any way and that the idea of time cannot be applied to them" (p. 28).

This characterization of unconscious mental processes in their relation to time does not seem at all incompatible with the view presented here: that the most elemental, primary tendency of what constitutes the drive quality is its opposition to, its negation of the fact of temporality. The unconscious mental processes follow a pattern that seems to imply that there is no time, that time is incapable of bringing about changes in them. And this, while the individual is subjected to continuous change through time. We would expect, therefore, that even the forces prevailing in the unconscious would adapt themselves to the changes in the individual's life conditioned by the passage of time. Yet such an adaptation, as Freud could demonstrate incontrovertibly with regard to the unconscious, does not ever occur.

This imperviousness of the unconscious to time is demonstrated by the manifestations of the repetition compulsion in the course of psychoanalytic therapy, which Freud discusses at length in *Beyond the Pleasure Principle* (1920, pp. 18ff). "The patient behaves in a purely infantile fashion," according to Freud (p. 36), which in the context implies: the repetition compulsion leads to a behavior that does not take into account the changes that time has brought about in his personality (i.e., he is now an adult, not a child), nor does he act consistently with what defines his personality in reality. Rather, he conducts himself during therapy as if nothing had changed for him since the first days of his life. The repetition demonstrates in this situation its fixating character. It takes on the quality of a defiance against the acceptance of the changes imposed by time; it becomes a rebellion against having undergone the process of becoming older with the passage of time. By its exclusive effort to remain fixated at a particular phase of life, it becomes an obstacle for any further growth. It is, however, possible to interpret the characteristic manifestation of the transference through repetition in another way that further supports the thesis presented here concerning the aim of the repetition compulsion. It can be claimed that transference, insofar as it is a repetition phenomenon—for example, a repetition of a libidinal attachment to the father—demonstrates clearly the conserving, "time-suspending" effect of repetition. In the suggested example, the image of the father is preserved from destruction through the passage of time by means of repetition as transference. This preservation of the living father is effected through repetition in the transference. The father, who at one time had become a libidinal object, also becomes subjected to the power of the repetition compulsion. In this way, he remains forever "alive" (in the unconscious), even if, in reality, he has passed away a long time ago. Thus, the time-suspending quality of the drives can bestow eternal life to the father. This result is in accordance with the proposition that the elemental tendency of the drives aims by means of repetition to achieve permanence and eternity in time. It is equally compatible with Freud's derivation of the concept of the deity from the father image.

The examples discussed so far have dealt with the work of the repetition compulsion within a stage of development characterized by drive patterns of already considerable complexity. What is subject to repetition in these and similarly structured situations are definite reaction patterns of the individual living through stages of typical psychosexual development. It is, however, possible to apply the concept of repetition compulsion in a much more primitive sense when speaking of drives in general, which would, so far as the development of the individual is concerned, have to be described as "prehistoric." What I am thinking of is the innate compulsion of every drive to repeat the steady alternation between tension and gratification. It seems to me that the most elemental phenomenon that can be observed with regard to the drives is just this: every drive, having reached the acme of gratification, descends to a low point of need depletion, at which point renewed tension leads to renewed striving for gratification. This steady alternation between gratification and need depletion appears to me to merit the name of a repetition compulsion. One may dare to say that this repetitive phenomenon characterizes the essence of what constitutes a drive among all other psychic activities . Except for the drives, there is no other tendency within the whole of mental life for which the compulsion to repeat is a *sine qua non*. If this is indeed the case, the most pertinent question arising from the thesis presented previously is this: Does the interpretation of the phenomenon of repetition as a pattern of motion tending to effect the actualization of permanence within temporal change make sense if applied to the elemental repetitiveness of drive gratification per se? If we examine one of the self-preservative drives, for instance, hunger, with this question in mind, one is forced to admit that the natural effect of the gratification of this drive seems indeed to result in obtaining the longest possible life-span for the individual. Obviously, living matter would reach the end of its viability much more quickly if it were not organized so as to be capable of reconstructing itself by means of the steady repetition of food intake. As we apply the same question to the sexual drives, if we limit ourselves to the procreative function of sexuality,[9] we merely ask whether procreation uses repetition for the actualization of permanence within temporal change. This question can patently be answered in the affirmative. The "biological immortality" of the living substance is evidently the result of procreation.

But this "immortality" is accomplished by nothing other than an immense repetitive production of living mortal individuals. By means of this repetition of the individual through procreation, and by nothing else, has the living substance succeeded up to now in defying the destroyer Time. It seems, therefore, justified to maintain—in view of the elemental repetitive propensity of the organic living substance—that repetition within the realm of biological existence can be interpreted as a striving toward permanence, and possibly toward eternity, within time.

RETROGRESSIVE PHENOMENA
IN THE PHYSICAL SCIENCES:
THE CONCEPT OF A "PRIMAL DUALISM"

In the preceding pages, Freud's interpretation of the repetition compulsion as a manifestation of the retrogressive tendency inherent in living substance has been challenged. A detailed presentation of a thesis justifying the challenge was offered. Does this imply that I aim to refute altogether the existence of a retrogressive tendency as an intrinsic quality of the living substance? Not at all. It is merely considered untenable to interpret the *repetition compulsion* as a manifestation of the retrogressive tendency. Freud's delineation of retrogression as indicative, within the context of a living organism, of the inertia of matter has, however, in my opinion, made us aware of a phenomenon which is not only an undeniable fact, but which deserves a central position in every biological approach to mental functioning. What force, then, does retrogression represent? Where can it be demonstrated in biological and mental life, if it is *not* conceptually compatible with repetitive phenomena (repetition compulsion)? It is merely a restatement of a proposition suggested by numerous analysts (Alexander 1921, Bernfeld and Feitelberg 1931, Westerman-Holstijn 1930) to claim that the most universal retrogressive phenomenon dominating the totality of both inanimate as well as animate natural processes appears to be none other than the entropy principle established in physics. The pattern of energy changes subsumed under the concept of entropy unquestioningly deserves the designation of a retrogressive process. The process is unequivocally directed toward a decrease (in this case, of motion), its course is continuous, and it shows no reversal of direction. Given unlimited time, it would, in theory, come to an end only after having reached a minimum state of motion, an absolute inertia. If one measures this ultimate state against the condition of life represented in *any* living substance, one may choose to follow the example of Boltzman (1844-1906) by speaking of this ultimate state of thermodynamical equilibrium as the "heat death of the universe."[10] That this retrogressive tendency of the inorganic matter is, as long as a life lasts, delayed by counteracting processes, follows from the fact of life, though this fact in itself is not explainable in terms of known physical laws. On the other hand, the unavoidability of death for all living units left to themselves leads to the conclusion that those unknown forces capable of halting temporarily the retrogression of matter to the state of maximum entropy, in the end, do falter. Life must yield to the general retrogressive tendency of the laws of physics, to which the very building blocks of the living substance must submit. For this reason it seems consistent to view all those phenomena which herald the death of the organism as the direct manifestations of the retrogressive physical processes.[11] Examples may be general physical decline, aging, and possibly certain types of degenerative diseases. In contrast, the drives appear to represent the biological manifestations of those unknown forces that are counteracting the laws of physical retrogression. Our affirmation of the phenomenon of retrogression in nature is in agreement with Freud's view. It is also supported by numerous other authors who see these phenomena as representing the entropy principle of physics.

Does it, then, not follow that one must accept the concept of a death instinct too? The opposition among psychoanalytic theorists to the introduction of the concept of a death instinct was obviously directed not against the acknowledgment of the phenomena described by Freud, but against conceptualizing them as a *drive*. Such opposition, I believe, is justified, for repetition is an inherent characteristic of the drive. In it, according to the thesis presented here, a basic tendency to approximate permanence becomes manifest. Thus, retrogression and drive are indeed incompatible, both phenomenologically and conceptually. The retrogressive principle defined as entropy in physics represents absolute nonrepetition, irreversibility per se. In terms of its relation to the drive concept, it is its antithesis, the fundamental nondrive quality, if such a coinage may be permissible.[12] To view the drives as the psychic representation of those forces which seem capable of overcoming the law of entropy nevertheless leaves unanswered the question of the nature of such forces. We are here confronting the mystery of the nature of the living substance. One may engage in a variety of speculative thoughts, but that is not the same as formulating a comprehensible theory. In its absence, all we can see is the clash between the laws of physics as expressed in the entropy principle, which, if operating exclusively, must be destructive of all life, and those unknown, life-sustaining processes. The latter, demonstrable psychologically as drives, can be said to aim at duration in time, if not at eternal existence. In biological terms this battle constitutes the "primal dualism." It is a credible assumption that it is ultimately this "primal dualism" which forms the basis for Freud's dichotomy of drives, even though he uses a conceptual approach differing from the one presented here.

Both biological and psychological theories must start out from this fact: we do not know a state prior to the beginning of this struggle between the great powers of life and death; nor do we know anything about its future outcome. Are we in any way capable of conceptualizing any direction toward an ultimate aim? One might be inclined to answer all too hastily: obviously, the preservation of life. A host of objections to such an answer come to mind. If the drives represent what opposes in nature the law of entropy, for the sake of mere "preservation of life," how could this be reconciled with the reality of destructive drives? We cannot doubt the reality of drives aiming at the destruction of life. Freud's other chief argument for the introduction of a "death instinct" was, aside from the phenomenon of the repetition compulsion, the fact of the demonstrability of destructive drives. To find an answer to this dilemma, we must make the decision to take another step, even at the risk of entering unknown territory.

THE ARCHETYPICAL IDEAS
OF "NOTHINGNESS" AND OF "BEING"

Since Freud essentially equated the aim of the life instinct (Eros) with the preservation of life as we know it, he could not help but arrive at the conclusion that drives that are patently indifferent to the preservation of life must belong to a totally different category of biological phenomena, aiming toward the opposite of life—in other words, death instincts. At this point certain doubts deserve to be raised. In Freud's conceptualization of Eros and death instincts, the aims toward which these two drives are supposed to move belong each to a radically different conceptual "scale." The final state that the retrogressive tendency of physical processes approaches is conceptualized as that ultimate inertia (thermodynamical equilibrium) which Boltzmann characterizes as the "heat death of the universe." As the final state toward which Freud's Eros is aiming, we envision a general concept of "life." The latter is a condition existing in reality. The "heat death of the universe" does not exist in reality, but is the ultimate hypothetical state of equilibrium postulated for an infinite retrogressive motion of which we, in reality, always only see the beginning. The concept of a "heat death of the universe" expresses in words the final implication of Boltzmann's mathematical equation concerning the fundamental law of physics that bears his name. In reality, all physical processes merely approximate this ultimate state without, however, fully attaining it. "Life," on the other hand, is an actual state, of which we cannot claim with certainty that its known factuality constitutes the theoretical limit of its organizing principle (i.e., Freud's life instinct).

Thus, there is a danger that our image of the struggle between retrogressive forces on the one hand and life forces on the other is a distorted one: this is so, because we are operating on the one side with a mathematically definable ultimate state (maximum entropy), contrasting it on the other side, one might say, with a chance configuration represented by "life." In order, therefore, to arrive at a figurative representation of the opposing primal forces that would approach the true situation more exactly, I deem it necessary to set against the ultimate state of physical equilibrium, expressed in the entropy principle, a corresponding ultimate state that would define the "limit" toward which the opposing "death-delaying," i.e., life-building forces could be thought to be carried by their impetus. For the sake of a sharp distinction, I shall refer to the state of thermodynamical equilibrium, as defined through the entropy principle, as the archetypical idea of "Nothingness," and the corresponding opposing state, implying the "ultimate state" toward which "life" can be said to move, as the archetypical idea of "Being." "Life," meaning the condition that is known to us, would have to be conceptualized as being somewhere "in between" the ideas of "Nothingness" and "Being." The concept of a "heat death" can be exactly defined only through a mathematical equation; it defies translation into any ordinary verbal conceptualization. The same ought to apply to the definition of the archetypical idea of "Being": ideally, it should be expressed with the same mathematical precision as its counterpart. In its absence, it may suffice, within the context of this paper, to sketch a quasi "formula" to serve as a definition of its "locus." The concept of the thermodynamical equilibrium ("heat death of the universe") could be won by projecting the motion of physical processes into infinity. Correspondingly, in order to approximate the archetypical idea of "Being," one must project into infinity the surge of forces thought of as being capable of stemming the increase of entropy. According to the thesis presented here, the drives are seen as representing such a power, balancing the retrogression toward maximum entropy.

The question must then be asked: Toward what state of being is life propelled by the drives? Assuming there would be no obstacles for the realization of the ultimate aims of the drives, whereto would their thrust propel the movement of life? Up to now, we have mostly spoken of drives in general, without placing any weight on their differences. So long as the central interest was directed toward the study of certain universal characteristics of drives (i.e., repetition), this neglect of their differences was justifiable. But when we raise the question concerning the ultimate reach of the drives, it becomes necessary to stress the difference between self-preservative and sexual drives. Reflecting on the ultimate aims of the self-preservative instincts, one is able to say that their aim is nothing more than to preserve permanently a biological equilibrium which reduces to a minimum one's awareness of the retrogressive forces within the living substance. We come close to the basic idea by stating that the self-preservative instincts aim to maintain forever the organism's full possession of its given powers. They tend to approach an ideal that we find fully developed in the Greek gods on Mount Olympus: they are pictured as eternally youthful, as always in perfect health, implying an assurance that these conditions won't change, inasmuch as gods are immortal. These deities are, however, merely idealized human beings; therefore, even the ultimate attainment of the aim of the instincts of self-preservation still remain within the known sphere of the basic limitations of living individuals.

What answer can we give to the question of the ultimate aim of the sexual drives? The immediate aim of the sexual drives is the instantaneous attainment of orgastic pleasure; it is this specific aim through which they are differentiated from any other drives[13]. The question of what constitutes their ultimate aim would consequently have to be answered consistently: a state of permanent sexual pleasure. But what is the psychological nature of sexual pleasure (lust), an experience that is usually discussed in a manner implying that it is an end in itself, something that would not admit of any further psychological elaboration?[14] If one wants to chance an attempt to comprehend conceptually the "content" of the feeling of sexual gratification, one can, as a general description, speak of a profound sense of a heightened experience of one's being. One could thus tentatively define pleasure or happiness as the experience of a heightened sense of one's being, while unpleasure would correlate to a diminished sense of one's being. This leaves the question of how a heightened sense of being, such as happiness or ecstasy, can be differentiated from our "average" way of experiencing our existence. Here we return to our interpretation of the repetitive character of drives as constituting a tendency to delay the passing of time, to force time to grant permanence, to grant eternity. If these are truly the most elemental tendencies of drives, it would be a legitimate expectation that, at the height of sexual satisfaction, this aim attains a degree of actualization: in other words, the transcending of temporality has been, to some extent, accomplished.

If this interpretation of the experiential quality of orgastic pleasure is valid, one should be able to demonstrate that experiences of happiness and ecstasy do coincide with a reduction of our consciousness of the experience of time, which ordinarily constitutes an ever-present awareness of our consciousness. I believe that psychological observation confirms this thesis. Every lover knows that at the height of happiness time seems "to stand still," that past and present appear to be powerless to assert themselves against a state in which seemingly the present is permanence in actuality, completely at rest in itself. Every great love reaches out for permanence. The fact that all lovers vow "forever," is not just an empty phrase, but the appropriate expression of the essence of the experience of profound happiness. For this very reason, the most bitter disappointment for all human beings is the experience of the transitoriness of even this ecstatic bliss.

The older a person grows, the less he is able to experience a pure, unalloyed happiness, for the sense of temporality has become too deeply rooted in consciousness. The kind of happiness of which the awareness of temporality is an integral part is described as "wistfulness." Wistfulness implies that the knowledge that it is impossible for a heightened state of being to be permanent has become part of one consciousness.

In a passage in Nietzsche's (1883) *Thus Spoke Zarathustra*, the essential relationship between the sense of bliss and the experience of having transcended temporality is stated with utmost clarity: A state of supreme happiness is described in the following quotation from the chapter entitled "At Noon."

> What happened to me? Listen! Did time perhaps fly away? Do I
> not fall?
> Did I not fall — listen! — into the well of eternity?
> What is happening to me? Still! I have been stung, alas — in   the
> heart?
> In the heart!
> Oh break, break heart, after such happiness, after such a sting!
> Did not the world become perfect just now?[15]

Such an elevated sense of one's being, as Nietzsche describes it, deserves to be characterized as an ecstatic experience. One can derive another insight into the psychology of ecstatic bliss, aside from the essential connection between supreme happiness and the sense of "timelessness," in Nietzsche's prose poem: the incapacity to experience and bear such ecstatic states for more than a very brief moment of lightning illumination, as it were. "Oh break, break heart," read the Nietzschean lines, touching upon the imminence of death in a state of supreme happiness. It does appear very understandable that this should be the case. For the "suspension" of temporality is equivalent to the dissolution of the bond between life and the living substance, of which temporality is an inherent aspect. Such break of life with the living substance is, however, equivalent to death.

It seems that this nexus can throw some light on the link between love and death. For love to actualize its aim toward eternal being, it would be necessary for it to break its ties with the organic conditions of life. Perhaps an awareness of this closeness of death to the experience of ecstasy is reflected in the Latin *"Omne animal est triste post coitum."* If our reflections concerning the nature of the experience of happiness must lead us to conclude that orgastic pleasure, too, has its source in a momentary suspension of the experience of time, there does not appear any reason to disavow such consequences. They are supported by descriptions of the orgastic experience which stress a sense of absolute fulfillment in the actuality of being, a flowing of all psychic power into the fulfilled Now of the lived moment. Thus, one might describe orgasm as the biological form of the ecstatic experience: the well-known close relation in antiquity between states of orgiastic mania on the one hand and true ecstatic inspiration on the other becomes at once meaningful.

We are now able to define the sexual drive as aiming to achieve an ecstatic climax of the sense of being. This permits its distinction from the self-preservative drives. The ideal aim of the latter remains always within the range of the biological conditions of living. The sexual drive, however, represents a move in the direction of a state of being whose true realization implies a going-beyond the limits of the biologically defined individual. This transcendent impetus of the sexual drive is manifested, within the biological range, in the fact of procreation, by means of which the individual can be said to explode the limits of his biological singularity. Of equal importance, however, is the boundary transgression which expresses itself in the psychological aim of the experience of orgasm, through which a state of being is approached that lies beyond all possibilities of a biologically defined existence. The Latin word for "going beyond limits" is *"transcendere,"* and what inherently aims at "going beyond" is a transcendent phenomenon. It is, therefore, permissible to offer the formulation that the impetus underlying the sexual drive is a biologically conditioned tendency to go beyond the limits of one's own state of being, i.e., a tendency toward transcendence. The realization of such a tendency *within* temporality, is, of course, only possible in the one way in which any aim to attain permanence can approximate reality within a temporal world: by repetition. This train of thought contains the answer to the question raised in the preceding pages, which had, at that stage, to be left open. It is the question of whether the compulsion to repeat the satisfaction of the sexual drive, too, constitutes the only obtainable temporal mode of a primary quest for permanence of being. Based on the preceding exposition, the question must be answered unequivocally in the affirmative.

We have reached the point now where a further question can be raised: Is it possible to deduce from this direction of the drives toward transcendent gratification an archetypical idea of "Being," i.e., in a manner similar to the way science could derive an archetypical idea of "Nothingness" from the direction of physical motion in nature toward a limit defined by the entropy principle ("heat death of the universe"). We are in the position to state that, by means of the sexual drives, actually existing man moves toward a heightened sense of being, which includes absolute permanence and, therefore, timelessness as its attributes. These two defining concepts, "timelessness" and "permanence," appear to represent to us the "formula" for the archetypical idea of "Being." By means of the drives, the actual state of being continuously adumbrates this ideal but, being temporal, it is never able to attain it. The archetypical idea of "Being," defined by timelessness and permanence, is totally incapable of any concrete conceptualization. In its abstractness it is comparable to the entropy principle. It does not do more than describe a direction of motion that we can observe psychologically in the aims of the actual drives.[16]

CONCLUSIONS

The reflections of the preceding section were considered necessary in order to counter a possible objection against the proposed interpretation of the drives as representing processes working against the effects of the Second Law of Thermodynamics (entropy principle). This objection is founded on the demonstration of the role of sadism in instinctual life. We have now, however, come to see that the aim of the drives, expressed in terms of an archetypical idea of Being, is by no means tantamount to the concept of "preservation of life as it exists," but represents rather an antithesis to such aim. Consequently, there is no longer any need for the conceptual construct of a death instinct in order to find an explanation for the destructive tendencies of the drives. The drive propulsion toward a heightened sense of being—in the direction of an archetypical idea of Being—displays an indifference to life as it exists in reality. This indifference can turn into absolute ruthlessness under the impact of a certain type of psychological development. We know that the stage of orality is closely related to the development of sadism. The concept of oral sadism permits one to postulate a situation that is characterized by the exclusive use of the devouring of other living entities as a means of attaining a heightened sense of the existence of one's *own* person. Those threatened with being devoured would naturally conceive such behavior as destructive aggression. This is precisely the dilemma of a belligerent nation. The aggressivity of such a national unit, intent on incorporating neighboring populations, impresses those threatened with attack as a manifestation of destructive design. The attackers themselves, however, are animated not by a death instinct, but a most decisive urge toward a heightened sense of their own being, an urge that has become so dominant that it brings about an indifference toward the mere "preservation of life," i.e., individual lives. This brief remark may suffice to sketch the outline of a schema that would allow us to reconcile the existence of destructive drives with the proposed role of the drives as carriers of a trend culminating in a heightened sense of being.

Finally, there are a few more conclusions worth mentioning briefly, which also derive from the proposed thesis of a "primal dualism." A more complete conceptual analysis showing the derivation of sadism, and some other psychic phenomena, from the theoretical premises developed here would require separate treatment. These phenomena are all related to the biological and psychological impossibility of achieving the heightened sense of "being as permanence" by means of sexual orgasm. Through continuous repetition no more can be realized than a fleeting moment of ecstasy, limited by the simultaneously occurring exhaustion of the vital energies. A new understanding of other important psychological phenomena follows directly from this unresolvable dilemma, phenomena that can be subsumed under the concept of "sublimation." It is understandable that human beings have been reaching out, since time immemorial, for a more perfect, more lasting way to the experience of bliss than is obtainable through the intense, but fleeting sensation of sexual orgasm, an only imperfect attainment of the ecstatic height of the sense of being. The various practices of mystical cults aim directly at the creation of a state of permanent ecstasy. Within the tradition of classical Occidental thought, at least, the more usual way to overcome the awareness of temporal transitoriness has been the striving to partake in the sense of permanence by means of the spiritual surrender of the individual to the archetypical forms of being which were conceived as the actuality of a timeless and permanent state. What has been considered an "Ideal" was nothing but a conviction that a specific "aspect of being" was in fact timeless and permanent. This conviction finds its synthesis in the triad of the archetypes of the Good, the Beautiful, and the True. There is no doubt that the psychological rationale for the profound satisfaction that people have derived, and still derive, from the devotion to these "ideals" is rooted in the notion that through such participation—what Plato called methexis—the temporal, fleeting moment of human existence itself approaches the timeless duration of these archetypes of Being. Through this form of sublimation, the actualization of the innermost trend of drive activity—i.e., the transcendence of temporality by means of a heightened state of being approaching timeless permanence—would be more closely approximated than the pure biological, "predetermined" orgastic ecstasy could ever be.

With this, our reflections concerning the phenomenology of the repetition compulsion and the death instinct have come to their end within the limits to be observed. It may seem that the thesis presented here contradicts the original Freudian doctrine concerning the antagonism of life and death instincts. It is, however, my belief that, ultimately, I have been able to confirm the basic justification for the conception of a cosmic dualism. It is this conception—called here "primal dualism"—which I have attempted to demonstrate as the essence of Freud's theory of drives. An effort has been made, on the other hand, to show to what degree the critique of Freud's formulations as expressed by psychoanalytic theorists is a legitimate one. Such critique must, however, not lead to a blindness regarding the psychological and biological realities contained in Freud's hypothesis of Eros and the death instinct. That the analysis presented here might have contributed to the clarification of the difficult conceptual problems involved, is my hope. I must confess my fear, however, that my chosen approach to the treatment of the subject matter might have aroused some consternation in many readers devoted to psychoanalytic research. Against the objections of such readers I feel justified in defending myself with Freud's (1920, p. 37) own words in *Beyond the Pleasure Principle*: "The outcome may give an impression of mysticism or of sham profundity; but we can feel quite innocent of having had any such purpose in view. We seek only for the sober results of research or of reflection based on it; and we have no wish to find in those results any quality other than certainty."

NOTES

1. According to Freud's proposition, repetition of what existed earlier is a basic characteristic of all drives, including, consequently, the life (sexual) instincts as well. Freud emphasized, however, that such a tendency to restore an earlier existing condition cannot as yet be considered validated by

empirical evidence concerning the sexual drives. For the time being, only certain hypothetical assumptions offer support for the thesis, as developed in *Beyond the Pleasure Principle*. For this reason, only the empirical derivation of the death instinct from the repetition compulsion, as outlined above, will be considered as the basis for the theoretical discussion presented here.

2. There is no simple graphic representation for the movement of retrogression, comparable to that of repetition. Retrogression cannot be conceptualized without introducing a quantitative notion in a very general meaning of the term. In whatever form one might attempt to think of retrogression concretely—e.g., as a steadily decreasing energy potential, as a sound diminishing evenly in intensity, or as a process of biological dedifferentiation—there is always the implication of some "plus" that undergoes a change that in some specific respect impresses as a leveling off to a "minus" condition.

3. The same applies to a progressive motion: In both cases there are monophasic "linear" processes, not different from one another compared to the contrasting "cyclic" movement pattern characteristic of repetition phenomena. For this reason a description of the phenomenology of the movement of progression has not been undertaken here.

4. *"Tempera mutantur, nos et mutamur in illis"* (The times are changed, and we are changed with them).

5. It is not possible, within the limits of this paper, to do justice to Kierkegaard's treatment of the phenomenon of repetition (1843).

6. This type of repetition may miscarry in terms of its psychological aim: the more mechanical the repetition is, the more it brings to consciousness the factual impossibility of repeating the past, instead of the intended aim of experiencing duration through repetition.

7. Addendum 1973: Friedrich Rueckert (1788-1866) was a professor of oriental languages and a well-known romantic poet. Many of his poems still live in the German literary and musical tradition, having been set to music by composers from Schumann to Mahler. Rueckert used many oriental themes in his poetry. "Chidher" is based on Mohammedan legends pertaining to Alexander the Great. Chidher, who accompanied the king on his conquests, is said to have been the only follower of Alexander who discovered the spring of eternal life, which the king failed to find. Thus Rueckert refers to Chidher as "the eternal young one." The poem contrasts Chidher's eternal life-view with the transitoriness of everything human. "Eternal cities," "eternal oceans," etc., have disappeared when Chidher returns to the same regions after intervals that seem beyond the grasp of ordinary mortals, but seem like yesterday to Chidher on his voyage through eternity.

8. In contrast, Freud obviously understands the term "conservative" as synonymous with "moving backward" or "being retrogressive."

9. We may, however, look at the sexual drive as aiming toward the experience of pleasure. Then we must ask another question: Does the drive to repeat sexual pleasure in ever-new actualizations represent the manifestation of a striving toward the ultimate aim of permanent bliss? And is, perhaps, the repetition of sexual pleasure a "substitute" for that never-realizable, perfect state of permanent blissfulness, since this kind of permanence is incapable of actualization within the limits of temporality? At this point in our argument we are not yet ready to answer this question satisfactorily, but we shall return to it later.

10. Addendum 1973: for a discussion of Boltzman, see Schroedinger 1944.

11. Westerman-Holstijn (1930) expresses himself along similar lines: "Insofar as the inanimate matter exerts a more or less powerful influence on the living substance, the tendencies characterizing the inanimate matter impose their influence on the behavioral vicissitudes of the living unit to a greater or lesser degree.... We recognize them in the fact of dying, aging, sleep, inertia, fatigue, as well as in certain symptoms of toxic psychoses and drug reactions."

12. This antithesis appears to be the reason for Freud's repeated emphasis on the fact that the death instinct cannot be directly observed as one among other drives. Thus, he postulates that the death instinct must be assumed to do its work silently. If, however, the "death instinct" represents the retrogressive law of inorganic, inanimate substance, it is clear that it cannot be demonstrated among the drives because the inorganic (retrogressive) motion *cannot* be represented by a drive, i.e., an inherently repetitive phenomenon. If there is any psychic representation for retrogression, one might perhaps search for it in the phenomenon of temporality, which is experienced as irreversible.

13. It is psychologically incorrect to characterize the sexual drives as procreative drives. Procreation is a biological effect, which is brought about by the satisfaction of the sexual drive. Psychologically considered, procreation cannot be viewed as the immediate aim of the instinctual sexual desire.

14. The performance of sexually exciting acts is not equivalent to the experiential psychological "content" of orgasm. It is general knowledge that the acts that are performed with the aim of experiencing sexual pleasure are extraordinarily varied; they are, in fact, of opposite nature in different individuals. Every sexual act is always merely a means, the particular method, by which the individual attains "his" or "her" sexual pleasure. It is a probable assumption that the sexual gratification thus produced, in spite of the differences in the ways of its attainment, is in its emotional quality a very similar personal experience for all individuals.

15. The same thought is even more precisely expressed in "The Drunken Song": "Joy wants the eternity of all things, wants deep, wants deep eternity." A comparison may be offered with the verses in the second part of Goethe's "Faust" (1832), in which Faust states his reason for having just experienced the "highest moment" of his life:

Then could I bid the passing moment:
"Linger awhile, thou art so fair!"
The traces of my earthly days can never
Sink in the aeons unaware.
And I, who feel ahead such delights of bliss,
At last enjoy my highest moment — this.

In these lines one may trace all the essential aspects which were claimed to structure the experience of supreme happiness: the sense that the transitory moment has been transformed into everlastingness. This gives rise to an instantaneous affective conviction that one's being has been removed from the destructive power of temporality and is partaking in the experience of eternity.

16. I believe I am correct when I see similarities between the result of my attempts to arrive by psychological means at an archetypical idea of Being and the old ontological derivation of the idea of an *"ens perfectissimum"* (Ferm 1950).

Chapter 2

IDENTITY AND SEXUALITY

Antes muerto que mudado: "Rather dead than changed"
— Inscription on a portrait of John Donne

GENERAL BIOLOGICAL CONSIDERATIONS CONCERNING THE ROLE OF NONPROCREATIVE SEXUALITY IN MAN

In his *Outline of Psychoanalysis* Freud (1940) summarizes the main results of psychoanalytic research concerning the sexual function as follows:

a. The sexual function does not start with puberty, but begins soon after birth with clear manifestations.
b. It is necessary to make a sharp distinction between the concepts sexual and genital. The first concept is wider and includes many activities which have nothing to do with the genitals.
c. Sexuality is defined as the function of gaining pleasurable gratification from specific bodily zones. This function is placed in the service of procreation only secondarily. Often both functions do not completely fuse. [tr. by author]

Since Freud first postulated these three fundamental theses regarding sexuality (1905), his observations have been confirmed, enlarged, and are today almost universally accepted. It must be said, however, that while Freud's great discoveries concerning the sexual function threw new light on many obscure areas of human psychology, they also introduced many new problems that did not exist before Freud's formulations. One of these problems is contained in the third of Freud's statements concerning the sexual function: according to Freud, the sexual function does not appear to be identical with the function of procreation. In the case of human sexuality this seems to be an undeniable fact. Whether such a sharp distinction between sexuality and procreation exists in the same degree in the animal world is a more controversial matter. If there is, as most authorities seem to assume, a significant difference of degree between the role played by nonprocreative sexuality in man and in the animals, the question arises: what is, biologically and psychologically, the function of nonprocreative human sexuality?

We all know, of course, that according to Freud the function of sexuality is the obtainment of sexual gratification. This statement does not answer the question, but merely shifts its emphasis. What, then, is the biological and psychological function of sexual gratification? Psychoanalysis had a hard enough fight to prove even the observational fact that sexuality and procreation were not, from the start, linked together. Consequently most of the psychoanalytic contributions marshal their data and their arguments just to prove that this is so. There are comparatively few psychoanalytic contributions to the problem of what psychological and biological function sexuality has per se, i.e., independent from the function of procreation.

The two great classical contributions to this problem are Ferenczi's *Thalassa: A Theory of Genitality* (1924), and Wilhelm Reich's *The Function of Orgasm* (1927). Both of these attempts to interpret the meaning of the sexual function are based on broad, cosmological theories concerning the life processes themselves. The function of sexuality in the individual is understood as a manifestation of these cosmological principles. One can therefore do justice to these two works only by a critical evaluation of the basic cosmological ideas proposed in them—a task outside the scope of this paper. (For a discussion of Ferenczi's essay see Bernfeld 1937, and, more recently,

Fluegel 1953.) Among recent authors, Masserman (1952) has suggested that sexuality is what he calls one of the basic *Urdefenses* of man as well as animals. According to Masserman, it is

> only in the stages preliminary to coitus that one adult human being can feel that his desires begin to dovetail with those of another, yet perhaps it is only at the acme of the orgasm that for a precious little while at least, human suspicion and enmities are completely submerged in an oceanic feeling of mutual ecstasy and forgetfulness. Is it any wonder then, that man, as all other organisms seem to do, should cherish this most exceptional of experiences, that in his case particularly, preoccupations with sexuality in relation to its concomitant interpersonal and social phantasies should subtly pervade nearly every human thought and act from childhood to death?

According to Masserman, sexuality is one of three *Urdefenses*—the others being the denial of mortality and the fantasy of omnipotence—which man needs as "comforting delusions . . . if he is to live in a world in which every material phenomenon is a possible danger and every human relationship a potential threat." This explanation of the function of nonprocreative sexuality as an *Urdefense* against man's all-pervading fear for his survival does not seem convincing to this writer. Far from providing for man an ever available "biological opiate" against the pains of life, the compulsive character of man's sexuality is, as analysts know, rather bound to increase the occasions and the possibilities for anxiety. Kubie (1941) has impressively demonstrated the biological reasons for this clinical observation. Kubie has shown that the greater the time lag between biological need and gratification of the need, the greater will be the role of psychological elaboration of this need. Thus, there arises greater possibility for distortion and anxiety. Since of all the biological needs the time lag between the biological basis for sexual desire and its gratification is by far the longest, Kubie shows that human sexuality, with its relative independence from vital biological needs, introduces more possibilities for phobic compulsive patterns and anxieties than any other biological need. It would, therefore, seem that Masserman's explanation of the function of sexuality as an *Urdefense* against the fears to which every living being is exposed oversimplifies the problem.

Perhaps the problem of the function of nonprocreative sexuality has been relatively rarely investigated, because its answer is taken for granted: it is considered implied in the definition of the psychoanalytic drive concept. This drive concept is based on a general biological principle, described by Freud as the constancy principle, today often equated with the principle of homeostasis (Cannon 1932). According to this principle, the maintenance of an equilibrium within the biological milieu is one of the most fundamental biological regulatory principles. Among the many biological functions that serve this principle, sexuality is just one. According to this view, sexuality would have the function, by means of a specific form of energy discharge, of guaranteeing the homeostatic equilibrium of the organism. This view was, for instance, expressed by Hendrick (1939), when he broadly equated Cannon's principle of homeostasis with Freud's pleasure principle. Whether these two concepts can properly be equated was questioned by Orr in 1942. More recently Kubie (1948, 1956) has devoted a series of papers to a searching analysis of the concept of instinct in psychoanalysis and its relationship to the principle of homeostasis.

On the basis of an exhaustive study of the literature of all those fields of science which have investigated the phenomena referred to as instinctual patterns, including experimental psychology, animal psychology, physiology, and biology, Kubie attempts a conceptual integration of the knowledge gained in all these various fields of research with the experiences of psychoanalytic observation. Some of his conclusions are pertinent to the theme of this paper. Basing his concept of instinct on Freud's definition that an instinct represents a demand which the body makes on the mental apparatus, Kubie investigates the specific way in which such a demand of the body is translated into the experience of a biological need. Kubie discusses the bodily demands for oxygen, for water, for maintenance of tissue substance as examples of relatively well-known homeostatic body processes, becoming manifest through the instinctive needs of respiration, thirst, and hunger. In these instances the demand which the body makes on the mental apparatus, while complex, can, according to Kubie, be related directly to homeostatic body processes. This, however, is not the case with regard to the sexual drives. Kubie

(1948) states, however, that there is a significant inverse relationship between sexuality and hormonal influences on the evolutionary scale:

> The basic neural pattern for sexual behavior appears to be inherited in a relatively undifferentiated form throughout the vertebrate series; . . . on this inherited pattern hormones exercise a decreasing influence as one ascends the evolutionary scale; while in the same evolution the patterns of sexual behavior become increasingly modifiable by intricate and subtle psychological influences.

In Kubie's view (1956), it is characteristic for the human species "that the gratification of the individual can be totally dissociated from survival needs for the species through masturbation, fellatio, anal intercourse, homosexuality, and the use of contraceptives." In this broad generality, the human specificity of this dissociation is denied by most students of animal behavior. Ford and Beach (1951), for instance, summarize these findings as follows:

> Those animal species whose evolutionary status most closely approximates our own ... are known to indulge in sexual intercourse under conditions in which such relations cannot possibly result in fertilization. ... One sees, then, evidence for an evolutionary change from strict periodicity of sexual behavior in the female to relative absence of such behavior rhythms. This change cannot be an abrupt one. Instead it is progressive with lower mammals representing one extreme, human beings the other.

The authors thus agree with Kubie's claim that, ascending the evolutionary scale, sexuality becomes less and less identical with the procreative function. They furthermore stress the important point that this increase in the nonprocreative function of sexuality parallels the increase of the cerebral cortex in the higher animals. This parallelism between increase in cortical substance and function and independence of the sexual from the productive function raises important and interesting problems. Since it is obvious that the increase in the size and complexity of the cortical brain is an expression of an increase in its significance and role in the functioning of the higher organisms, the question arises whether we are entitled to assume that there is analogously an increasing biological significance attached to the nonprocreative sexual function as such in the higher animal; and whether this is particularly the case in the human species, where it would manifest itself in the fact that sexuality becomes largely independent from the procreative cycles and begins to pervade all human behavior to a much more complete degree than seems to be the case in the animals, particularly in the lower animals. Briefly, is the relative independence of sexuality from procreation an indication of a specific human way of functioning?

The following hypothesis is proposed as an explanation of these correlations: Just as the increase in the development of the cortex is the biological expression of the ego functions as a means of adaptation, winning in man ascendancy over instincts, i.e., "preformed structural automatisms" (Brun 1951), in the same way human nonprocreative sexuality must take over an important function which in the animal (particularly in the lower animal) is fulfilled by preformed automatisms. What function could this be? It is a widely held view that the preformed structural automatisms equip the lower animal, in the words of Brun, "not only with a general disposition to behave in view of a certain goal and in a certain direction, but also with the *realization* of the behavior as a so-called instinctive action." Brun continues:

> according to Freud we would say that with these low animals not only the *drive* as such has been fixed in the hereditary memory but also the *object representation of the drive*: this causes the rigidity of most instincts of insects, their firmly established reaction structure. ... Von Uexküll [1921] has described this object representation specific to the species ... by the pertinent expression 'schema,' which means: inborn schedule.

It is now suggested that this schema, this preformed structural automatism, provides the lower animal, in contrast to man, with what we would like to call a fixed identity, an identity within relatively narrow limits of typical behavior. Identity, as a fixed behavioral pattern, can exist only where preformed automatism exists. With the gradual loss of truly instinctive preformed automatism, there is a parallel loss of a fixed behavioral identity both for the individual and the species. This comparative lack of behavioral identity removes from man much of the instinctual rigidity of the animal. Man can assume, compared to most animals, an almost infinite variety of behavioral identities. He is near-protean in his behavioral character, a fact which enables him to adapt himself to almost any environmental change. For his adaptability, however, he is forever threatened with loss or breakdown of his identity, a danger unknown to the animal under natural conditions. Man has forever to struggle with the need to define himself, to create an identity not basically inherent in him by dint of inborn automatisms. The attempt shall be made in this chapter to demonstrate, on the basis of psychoanalytic observation, that human identity is established by a specific use of the nonprocreative sexual function. Throughout life, human identity has to be maintained by processes which are unique both for the human species as v ell as for each individual. It should be emphasized that these processes are manifold, comprising many forms of nonsexual behavior which are not treated in this chapter. This chapter is confined to the task of collecting evidence that nonprocreative human sexuality is instrumental in establishing the earliest and most basic outlines for the development of behavioral or existential identity. This identity is a prerequisite of the conscious awareness of a sense of identity, but the former can and does exist independently from the latter.

PART I: IDENTITY, IDENTIFICATION
AND THE SENSE OF IDENTITY

"The study of identity," says Erik H. Erikson (1950a), "becomes as strategic in our time as the study of sexuality was in Freud's time." Unfortunately, in trying to define the concept of identity we face a bewildering complexity of phenomena. Erikson (1956) gives this account of the difficulties inherent in a definition of the concept of identity:

At one time . . . it will appear to refer to a conscious *sense of individual identity*; at another to an unconscious striving for a *continuity of personal character*; at a third, as a criterion for the silent doings of *ego synthesis*; and, finally, as a maintenance of an inner *solidarity* with a group's ideals and identity. In some respects the term will appear to be colloquial and naive; in another, vaguely related to existing concepts in psychoanalysis and sociology.

There is, furthermore, a lack of clear differentiation between the concepts of identity and the so-called sense of identity, as well as the concept of the self. As Erikson (1959) points out: "the term identity covers much of what has been called the self by a variety of workers, be it in the form of a self-concept (George H. Mead 1954), a self-system (Harry S. Sullivan 1953), or in that of fluctuating self-experiences described by Schilder (1935), Federn (1952), and others." (See also Moustakas 1956.) Under these circumstances we must concentrate on two groups of questions: (1) Where and in what form does the psychoanalyst in his clinical work encounter phenomena that touch upon the complex problems of identity? (2) Can these clinical manifestations of problems of identity be described in terms of psychoanalytic theory of the personality, i.e., in dynamic, genetic, and structural concepts? This paper will deal with the first group of questions in Part I and Part II, while Part III will be devoted to an attempt to outline problems of the second group.

The Clinical Approach to the Problem of Identity
At the panel on Problems of Identity (Annual Meeting of the American Psychoanalytic Association, Chicago, May, 1957; abstracted in the *Journal of the American Psychoanalytic Association* 6:131-142), the concept of identity was discussed by Eissler, Greenacre and Mahler. Because of its particular helpfulness, I shall begin this part with the definition of the concept of identity offered by Greenacre (1958a):

> The term *identity* has two significant faces—an inner and an outer one. It means, on the one hand, an individual person or object, whose component parts are sufficiently well integrated in the organization of the whole that the effect is of genuine oneness, a unit. On the other hand, in some situations identity also refers to the unique characteristics of an individual person or object whereby it can be distinguished from other somewhat similar

persons or objects. In the one instance, the emphasis is on likeness, and in the other on specific differences.

Most adults seem to accept their own identities unquestioningly, or at least without much contemplation except under rather unusual circumstances, such as when coming out of an anesthetic, being alone in a foreign country, or that even rarer instance of having some experience which is or seems almost completely new. Otherwise only young children, philosophers, artists, and certain sick individuals concern themselves constantly with questions of their own identities. Yet many problems subsidiary to the over-all one of identity have been the basis of a considerable section of our psychoanalytic study.

Identity in its general range is a term of flexible and functional rather than absolute meaning. *Identity* is closely related to identification, whether as an inner process of psychic development or an act of recognition by a human being toward an outer object, animate or inanimate. If we think of the identity of a house, what we will emphasize will depend in good measure on our purpose in singling out that house. We may tend to think first of the appearance of the house, its structure, and then of its location in the community. It will be identified or recognized not only by the material of which it is built, its form and arrangement of its rooms, but by its similarity to or dissimilarity from other structures, its accessibility and any distinctive thing in its immediate surroundings. Thus it is "the house with seven gables," or "the brick house at the end of the block," or "the Victorian monstrosity beyond the A & P," or occasionally simply "No. 9 Smith Square." Only those who have lived in it or done some work there will think of it much in terms of its inner functioning, and then mostly if they can compare and contrast it with other houses in which they have lived or worked. Here the simile must be dropped.

My point is simply that inner structure or organization is likely to be taken for granted unless there is trouble or need for repair—i.e., house or body pain and danger, or unless there is some other organization whose functioning is held up for comparison. The *sense* of identity, or awareness of identity involves comparison and contrast—with some emphasis on basic likeness, but with special attention called to obvious unlikenesses. In the case of the ailing house or person, the contrast is with the well or undamaged state. But in general a sense of identity involves some relation to others and has a socially determined component—with a degree of observation both by the person himself and/or through another person. Even for the individual, his inner sense of himself is not enough to produce a sense of identity. His self-image, based as it is on a fusion of implicit, but generally not clearly focused awareness of his own form and functioning with his wishes as to how he would like to appear and function (forerunners and derivatives of identifications and ideals) forms the core on which his sense of his own identity is built. But this core, in so far as the fusion is relatively firm, is comparatively muted and stable. The sense of the self-image is maintained and perhaps vitalized by the continual redefinement which accompanies comparison and contrast with others.

Greenacre's approach to the concept of identity, while referring to normal and pathologic experiences of identity, is essentially a descriptive-phenomenological one, reminding us thus that the concept of identity, even as applying to human identity, is only one aspect of a much wider problem. The range of this problem become visible when Greenacre emphasizes the two faces of the term identity, one stressing the likeness and the other the specific differences of persons or objects. This double orientation of the term identity appears to be a special aspect of the fact that the concept of identity can be perceived only as relative to its opposite, the idea of change. We are thus reminded of time and change as universal phenomena that have often been interpreted by philosophers as the essence of being itself.[1] Against the all-pervading change, the phenomenon of identity appears, as it were, as a contradiction. Referring to the changes in inanimate nature, we may even say that identity is change arrested, and that this relative "arrest" of physical and chemical change is what distinguishes the animate from the inanimate in nature (for the view of Schroedinger, see Part III of this chapter). Life, as a biological as well as mental phenomenon, can be defined as identity in change. This was what Cannon (1932) had in mind when he said: "Organisms, composed of material which is characterized by the utmost inconstancy and unsteadiness, have somehow learned the methods of maintaining constancy and keeping steady in the presence of conditions which might reasonably be expected to prove profoundly disturbing." And further on: "The coordinated physiological processes which maintain most of the steady states in the organism are so complex and so peculiar to living beings that I have suggested a special designation for these states, homeostasis." The Greek word *homoios* does indeed mean "identical."

We can arrive in this way at a general definition of instincts, insofar as they serve the maintenance of life, as guarantors of biological identity. Thus we can see that when we postulate a close link between the phenomenon of instinct and the problem of identity, we have done nothing but to make explicit a correlation inherent in the concept of instinct itself. The maintenance of identity being thus tantamount to the maintenance of life itself, we would expect that man, whose instinctual drives are no more "than innate dispositions to act in a certain manner" (Brun 1951), but no longer structural automatisms of great rigidity, must find means to "acquire" an identity, and having acquired it, must develop a means to maintain it. It is our thesis that (1) nonprocreative sexuality in man is used to acquire a primary identity *(Uridentitat)*. (2) Psychoanalytic evidence makes it also probable that the maintenance of identity in man has priority over any other principle determining human behavior, not only the reality principle but also the pleasure principle. (3) Once sexuality has acted as a pace setter, the maintenance of human identity is accomplished by complex means, many of them of a nonsexual nature. We turn first to psychoanalytic clinical findings concerning a relationship between sexuality and phenomena pertaining to identity.

Psychoanalytic Evidence for a Correlation
Between Sexuality and the Emergence of Identity

Since the recent contributions of Greenacre (1957, 1958a), Mahler (1958), and Eissler (1958) have in numerous respects been the point of departure for this presentation, their findings shall be reviewed first. The three authors deal thoroughly with the interrelationship between psychosexual development and the emergence of the sense of identity. Greenacre focuses her discussion on the development of the early body image. On the basis of her observation she reaches the conclusion that "the body areas which are ... most significant in comparing and contrasting and establishing individual recognition of the body self, and that of others, are the *face* and the *genitals*. ... They are obviously of basic importance in the sense of identity." Greenacre finds that these decisive steps toward the establishment of a sense of individual identity take place "before there is a very full sense of individuation of the own body and when the simplest body image is still in process of being assembled." More precisely, Greenacre traces these developments to a period "after six months of age and extending into the second half of the second year. During the latter part of this time, however, and especially during the third year, the gradual increase in genital feelings—clitoral and phallic—gives endogenous sensations and pressures from within a kind of sensory peg which combines locally with the body imagery produced by visual and tactile appreciation of the own genitals and those of the other." Greenacre claims "that some degree of fusion [of the images of the own organs and those of an individual of the opposite sex] is practically universal." The fusion of this incorporated image with the image obtained from the own body under specially unstable conditions is, as Greenacre had shown in earlier studies (1953, 1955), important in connection with fetishism, where "problems of the sense of identity are always present." Greenacre's observations show clearly that even where there is a stable core concerning the sense of identity, it changes during life following the stages of body maturation and psychological growth. Greenacre (1958a) feels that

> no sense of adult functional identity can be completed until after adolescence. ... But even then there are further changes occurring later in life, e.g., in sickness, in the involuntary period and in senescence. Under most circumstances the sense of the own identity follows with the organizational structural identity but it always remains receptive to the influence of changes in the individual's relationship to his environment.

Mahler (1958), on the basis of clinical observation of children, reaches many conclusions similar to those of Greenacre:

> We conceive of the sense of self-identity as arising from alternation of two kinds of experience, namely pleasurable bodily

contact with the nursing mother and also pleasurable reunion with her during sleep, alternating with interpolated periods of wakefulness. During the gradually prolonged periods of wakefulness occur probably libidinization of the body surface and all those transitory phenomena which form the perceptual ideational borderland between the self and the object world.

Stressing her conviction that the decisive events leading to either normal or disturbed feelings of identity must be assumed to go back "not only to a preverbal stage, but all the way to a stage before images were formed," Mahler specifies two crucial periods of identity formation. The first is during the first year of life, possibly with decisive events occurring between one and a half to three years. According to Mahler, during this second eighteen-month period of life, self-differentiation in terms of separation (individuation) from the object occurs. "The second crucial period of personality development during which integration of the feelings of self-identity as separate from the object world takes place extends from three years up to latency." To Mahler it seems that

the most consequential maturational happening occurs with the phallic phase. The massive concentration of libido in the sexual parts of the body image occurs independently from environmental influences. It causes per se important shifts of cathexis in terms of body-image representations emerging via pregenital libidinal phases, and bisexual identifications to firm establishment of sexual identity.

This second phase of integration of the body image and feeling of identity depends, in Mahler's experience, on a number of important conditions, all of which stress the fundamental significance of successful integration of pregenital and genital development in the formation of the sense of identity.

Eissler (1958), in contrast to Greenacre and Mahler, emphasizes much less the interrelationship between body image and sense of identity. He defines the sense of identity as the experience that "I AM I," and calls this the experience of self-cognizance. Self-cognizance is, for Eissler, a specific, often powerfully conscious awareness of one's own uniqueness and inner continuity in all the changes of the personality during his life. Eissler does postulate a relationship between this sense of personal identity and sexuality, in that the final form of the sense of identity as self-cognizance is established fully only "at puberty, with incipient or established genital maturity." This final achievement of a personal sense of identity is, for Eissler, indicative of the emergence, at puberty, of a fourth structural system, which is differentiated in function from id, ego, and superego, integrating all three: this fourth structural system is serving the function of a self and the sense of personal identity. Eissler thus makes explicit a problem which Greenacre and Mahler pose only implicitly through their strong emphasis on the interrelationship between sexuality, body image, and sense of identity: the relationship of the problem of identity to the theoretical framework of psychoanalysis, in terms of the structural concepts of the id, the ego, and the superego.

Eissler's definition of the sense of identity as self-cognizance is akin to Spitz's approach to the problem of self and identity. Spitz (1957) differentiates between "I," the "ego," and the "self" as follows:

We consider the "I," like later on the self, to be a product of the awareness of the ego. We have described . . . the precursor of the "I," namely the infant's awareness of a "non-I." This emerges at the three-months level. The infant works out in the subsequent three to six months an awareness of the "I" in virtue of actions performed in his relations with the "non-I." The "I," therefore, is to be conceived as a cognitive precipitate of experience. In contrast to this, the ego as a system is a construct of psychoanalytic theory.

[Spitz goes on to describe the development of the "I" into the self.] The self is also a cognitive precipitate of experience, on a higher level of integration than the "I." . . . Genetically, the self can be traced to the "I," . . . The self . . . is the product of intrapsychic processes which take place as a result of the vicissitudes of object relations. In the precursor stage of object relations, the object was a constituent part of the "non-I," out of which it is segregated step by step, beginning as part object. It achieves the dignity of love object as a result of emotional interchanges which develop progressively into true object relations.... The ever-increasing cathectic investment finally compels the ego to become aware of the "I's" function in the unfolding object relations. *Through this awareness of the ego the "I" now achieves identity as the self.*

Spitz (Spitz et al. 1949), like Eissler (1958), equates the sense of identity and the sense of self, and both are for him "products of the awareness of the ego." In contrast to Eissler, Spitz traces the beginning of awareness of the self to around fifteen months of life, a much earlier phase than Eissler would postulate for his concept of self-cognizance, which Eissler assumes to reach its full development only around puberty. This would seem to imply that "awareness" as used by Spitz does not imply the same type of fully conscious inner experience that Eissler has in mind. Of special importance appears Spitz's emphasis on the emergence of the awareness of the "I" and self in the unfolding relations to love objects. Here we can see a link to the positions of Greenacre (1957, 1958a) and Mahler (1958), where the early contact with the nursing mother is perceived as instrumental in the development of the emerging sense of identity. While not referring specifically to the role of primitive sexual experiences in the development of a sense of identity, Spitz stresses the fact that the self is "on the one hand closely connected to the body and its functions, on the other to the exchanges in the course of object relations." In fact, Spitz sees in the emotional object relation "a defense against a growing awareness of separateness. When the child is gradually and progressively deprived of bodily closeness and skin contact, he replaces them by forming emotional ties." Spitz's propositions would thus tend to confirm the assumption of very close correlations between primitive body contacts, experienced by the child in its relation to the love object, and the emergence of the sense of self. It should be noted here that Spitz (Spitz et al. 1949), Eissler (1958), as well as Jacobson (1964) and Mahler (1958), when referring to "identity," imply an "awareness of," or a "sense of" identity—hence the equating of "sense of identity" and "sense of self." In contrast, I differentiate between the concept of identity and the "sense of identity": the former characterizes the capacity to remain the same in the midst of change, the latter a consciousness of such continuity of sameness. In differentiating between "identity" and "sense of identity" I follow Greenacre (1958a).

To summarize: psychoanalytic findings support a close correlation between emergence of identity and development of object relations. The development of object relations in man is, however, traditionally conceptualized in terms of various stages of identification (Freud 1921, Fenichel 1953, Hendrick 1951, Jacobson 1954, 1964, Spitz 1957, Grinker 1957). Thus, "identifications . . . determine characteristics of the component parts of the personality and, in compound, delineate the self" (Grinker 1957). A clarification of the relationship between identification and identity is, therefore, necessary. This is all the more the case because, in my opinion, the concepts implied in the term *identification* tend to keep out of view many phenomena essential to an understanding of the problems of identity.

Individuation Through Identification
in Present-day Psychoanalytic Theory
The concept of individuation has varied historical and philosophical connotations. It is used here, in conformity with psychoanalytic terminology, to characterize the emergence of the "separate individual" from its earliest symbiotic fusion with the mother passing through certain typical phases of growth. The literature dealing with the early stages of infantile development is vast (for a review of the field, see Kris 1950b), but it confronts the student of psychoanalytic theory with some of the most controversial issues (Riviere 1936, Waelder 1937, Glover 1945, 1956, Hartmann and Kris 1945, Hartmann et al. 1947, Bibring 1947, Federn 1952, Winnicot 1953, Balint, A. 1949, Balint, M. 1949, 1952b, 1955, Fairbairn 1952, Zetzel 1955). I shall attempt to trace the relation of some of these controversies to the problem of identity, even though only a very sketchy outline of the conceptual issues is possible in this chapter.

The issues appear to arise from the difficulty in defining the nature of the early mother-infant relationship. The authors agree on its singular character. Ferenczi and his followers gave much emphasis to it and described its special character variously as *Dual-Einheit* (Hermann 1936), *Zwei-Einigkeit* (Hoffmann 1935)—both terms rendered in English as "dual unity." Alice Balint (1949), Mahler (1952), and Benedek (1949) have used the term "symbiotic relationship." Spitz

(1945, 1946) applied Freud's (1905) term "anaclitic" to characterize the uniqueness of the early mother-child relation. All these terms express the fact that the relation between mother and infant does, from the infant's viewpoint, and also in terms of the mother's (unconscious) experience, represent an inner state of oneness, in which there is no differentiation between the infant's I and the mother. The controversy relates to the question whether this lack of differentiation between infant and mother means that the infant must be described as "objectless" in his early stages, or whether from the beginning there is object relation albeit in a unique form. Michael Balint (1949) formulated the conceptual issue very clearly:

> It will be very likely argued against the assumption of primary object love that the infant does not know of any external world; accordingly it is nonsensical to think that it can build up any relation to such objects not yet existing in his mind. . . . [This objection] only shows the overwhelming power of the hypothesis that the whole mind, and with it the Id, could only be thought of as originally narcissistic. It is true, a mind that maintains no relationship to the external world is logically the simplest proposition, but does it follow that the logically simplest form must be in reality the most primitive one? This is a fallacy of which we psycho-analysts are not the only victims.

Since love and hate, hostile and destructive impulses require a differentiation between a "subject" that loves, hates, wants to destroy, etc., an "object," it is obvious that this conceptual issue of an "objectless" or "object-related" infantile mind plays a decisive part in the controversies concerning the theories of Melanie Klein and her school (Klein 1948, Riviere 1936, Waelder 1937, Glover 1945a, 1956, Bibring 1947).

While Ferenczi (1949) and many of his followers insist on what is variously called passive, archaic, or primary object love (Balint, A. 1949, Balint, M. 1949, 1952b, 1955), *Anklammerungstrieb* [drive to cling to] (Hermann 1936) as the earliest "object-directed" manifestation of the infant, other authors have strenuously objected to this concept. Waelder (1937), Hartmann (1939), Spitz (1957), Jacobson (1964), and others have considered the assumption of primary object love as incompatible with both the libido theory and the structural concepts of psychoanalysis. These authors reason that to an infant a primary love object would imply that the infant, like the lower animal, possesses an innate "object representation of a drive" (Brun 1951). Such an assumption, by blurring the differentiation of human drives from animal instincts, is considered by the opponents of the concept of primary object love as incompatible with the very core of psychoanalytic theory. They furthermore point out that the evidence from clinical material as well as from direct child observations clearly indicates the *gradual* emergence of the differentiation between the I and the not-I (object). Some of these authors do, however, share Balint's doubts whether Freud's (1914, 1920, 1923a, 1924b, 1926, 1940) concept of primary narcissism is the most appropriate one to define the early undifferentiated stage. Jacobson (1964), for instance, rejects the notion of primary object love, but is fully aware of the theoretical difficulties implied in the concept of primary narcissism, as formulated originally by Freud.

> In view of the fact that the infant, though gaining gratification from an "object"—the mother's breast—is as yet unaware of anything but pleasurable or unpleasurable sensations, we are entitled from the psychological point of view to call his drive manifestations, in general, "narcissistic." But it is of relevance to realize that they do not represent drive discharge only toward the inside, "on the self"; that from birth on the infant has at his disposal biologically predetermined, though limited, channels for discharge to the outside, which is the precursor of object-related discharge.

Jacobson thus finally arrives at the conclusion that one may be compelled "to dispose of the concept of primary narcissism." (See also Loewenstein 1957.) The conceptual issue is, therefore, not as Balint seems to assume, centering upon the problem of primary narcissism.

Is it then merely a question of terminology, a choice between the term "primary object love" and the concept of a "precursor of object-related discharge" in Jacobson's formulations? I do not think so. There is a fundamental problem hidden behind this controversy of "primary love object" versus early "objectless" infantile condition. But the problem is, I believe, not basically a psychoanalytic problem, but one of Western philosophy in its relation to the foundation of modern science. I refer to the impact of the Cartesian Revolution (Frondizi 1953, Meyer, R. W. 1948) on the conceptual approach to man and reality in science. Descartes's distinction (1931a, b) between the "subject" *(res cogitans)* and the "object" *(res extensa)* made modern science possible, but left unsolved the question: how does the "subject" manage to "perceive" the object, or, how does the "outside" reality enter the "inside" of the subject? Ever since Descartes these problems have moved Western philosophical thought, with Leibnitz's philosophy (1949) being one of the greatest efforts to bridge the gap between the *res cogitans* and the *res extensa*.

This basic issue has, of course, been recognized by numerous authors. Its importance for psychological theory has been particularly great, and it is probably not an exaggeration to say that all scientific systems of psychology constitute either a conscious or an implied attempt to come to terms with the Cartesian heritage. While academic psychology has, on the whole, accepted the Cartesian method of reasoning as synonymous with scientific reasoning per se, there have been notable exceptions, such as the work of William Stern (1919, 1921, 1938), which is based on the philosophy of Leibnitz. It is impossible to deal with the psychology of Stern in this context, but it must be said that it is exactly the Cartesian split of mind and body—subject and object—which motivated Stern's psychology of personalism.

Psychonalysts have been aware of this fundamental issue as well, though the importance of the Cartesian tradition in science for the formulation of psychoanalytic theory has not received a systematic study. There have, however, been references to the problems involved. To name just one example, Milner (1957) states the issue as follows:

Of course this idea of two fundamental differences [i.e., incorporated environment and external environment] was not something I had only just begun to think about. I had once even succeeded in answering examination questions on the history of philosophy. I had to start with Descartes and learn how he made the distinction between mind and matter, and how this became the foundation of modern scientific achievement. But now I had not only found, after years of uncomfortable experience, that it was an urgent task to bring these two together again; I had also found that the making of the distinction was not only an intellectual achievement, it was also an emotional one, having a long history of accepted disillusion behind it.

In psychoanalytic theory, the Cartesian subject-object juxtaposition is quite obvious in the concept of a subject confronting an "external reality." The task "to bring these two together again" had been assigned to the concept of identification, and it forms the basis for the theory of individuation through identification. Identification is a concept designed to make it understandable how the "inside" (subject) becomes capable of "relating" to what is "outside" (object). How the process of identification is accomplishing the task in the present-day view of representative psychoanalytic theorists must now be discussed in some detail.[2]

The Process of Identification
as Described by Jacobson and Grinker

Discussing the advance from preoedipal identifications to ego identifications, Jacobson (1964) distinguishes several steps. "The earliest infantile stage is represented by the mother-child unit, a situation which of course cannot be described as yet in terms of identification which is a process." According to Jacobson, the next step, depending on sufficient maturation of the perceptive function, leads, via the constructive influence of frustration, to a beginning discovery of the self and the love object.

> Induced by such ... experiences of frustration, deprivation and separation from the love object fantasies of (total) incorporation of the gratifying object begin to arise, expressive of wishes to re-establish the lost unit.... Thus the earliest wishful fantasies of merging and being one with the mother (breast) are the foundation on which all future types of identifications are built. [On this foundation develops now] a more active type of identification from the child's increasing efforts to imitate the love objects....Since these originate in the close, empathetic ties between the mother and the child, they start out from what we may call primitive affective identifications. The fact that the

mother is able directly to induce affects in the baby by way of her own affective expression ... is well known, but difficult to explain. Observations on infants leave little doubt that the child begins very early to perceive, to respond to and to imitate the gestures, the inflection of voice and other visible and audible affective manifestations of the mother. We may surmise that the mere imitation of such parental emotional expression can influence the child's own discharge patterns in a sufficient degree to induce identical affective phenomena. ... But his playful imitations of what the parents do are first only forerunners of true ego identifications. ... This presupposes a transition from desires for a complete union with the mother to strivings to become only "like" her. Such strivings ... indicate the progress from wishes for a total to fantasies of only partial oral (anal, visual, respiratory) incorporation of the love object.

[Concerning this transitional stage of identification, Jacobson has this to say:] At this stage the child is still apt to believe that imitating the mother, "playing mother," means being or becoming mother. Such magic, illusory fantasies indicate how much the child wants to maintain the mother as part of himself and to adhere to the primitive aims of identification: the merging of maternal and self-images without distinction of and regard for the external and his own, inner reality. The main progress manifests itself in the child's growing desire to achieve this goal no longer only by way of oral gratification from the love object, but also by activity of his own.

[Finally the child reaches the stage of true ego identifications.] The processes leading to ego identifications set in with the transition from the stage of infantile dependency to ego independence. They mark the introduction into the psychic organization of a new time category, of the concept of the future. Moreover, they presuppose the ability to perceive and distinguish single physical and mental features of the love objects. Thus the early infantile wish to achieve oneness with the love object yields to desires to become like the object by the mechanisms of "partial introjection" only. This realistic aim can be reached by way of deep-seated modifications of the ego which now really assumes certain characteristics of the object.

Grinker (1957), in discussing identification, emphasizes the unsolved questions implied in the concept:

> How are the patterned processes of the external human environment internalized to form identifications? The answer to this is usually according to the oral pattern and its transactional experiences. But I have stated before, "the more we have learned about the structure and the function of the mouth in the human organism, the more dissatisfaction there is with our current psychoanalytic formulations. . . ." There are many systems of relationship between the neonate and the external environment that are not included when we talk about the oral pattern. . . . How do we reconcile these manifold transactions [i.e., visual, auditory, tactile, and deep sensibilities] between the neonate and its mother with the oral pattern of incorporation which seems to lead to the process of psychological introjection which forms identifications? This is an extremely difficult question to answer. . . . What is introjected? We may say that this is always a patterned relationship between the subject and the object. . . . The patterned relationships, however, develop not only from instinctual need plus gratification, but also include nuances of frustration leading to suffering and pain, influencing the introjected pattern identified as within the self to be as painful or as pleasurable as the child's early experiences. Thus, the frustrating mother is, as it were, what the subject experiences within himself, and the self becomes like the bad mother.

In quoting Jacobson and Grinker I have been striving to illustrate the proposition that identification is a concept designed to make understandable how the "inside subject" gradually becomes capable of relating to what is "outside." Both Jacobson and Grinker operate with this subject-object juxtaposition. But it may well be that these categories are not appropriate to the phenomena they are expected to explain, just as the classical cause-effect categories of physics have shown themselves to be inappropriate for the conceptual problems of atom physics (Bohr 1948, Lenzen 1954).

Seen in this way, theoretical controversies in psychoanalysis appear as manifestations of the inappropriateness of the traditional concepts used to describe the phenomena rather than as real disagreement concerning the latter. The controversy concerning "primary object love" versus "objectless" primary infantile experience is an example for this type of theoretical controversy. In this instance, both groups use terms that are the outgrowth of the Cartesian distinction of *res cogitans* and *res extensa* while intending to describe phenomena to which the distinction of subject and object, of inside and outside, are inapplicable. Even when describing animal behavior these categories fail to do justice to the phenomena. When Brun (1951) describes the lower animals as having not only the drive toward the object fixed in what he calls their hereditary memory, but also the "object representation of the drive," he implies a primary, not acquired relationship between inner and outer world which is incompatible with the Cartesian distinctions. Thus Brun feels compelled to adopt von Uexküll's (1921, 1934) concept of the "schema" as a term designating the innate object representation characteristic for a particular species. The concepts of subject-object, inside-outside are not only not helpful in describing such phenomena, they are, in fact, making them inaccessible for observation. I feel the same to be true concerning the concept of identification in it relation to the problem of identity.

There is, of course, a phenomenon *properly* described as identification. Grinker (1957) defines it as an "unconscious state of having become part or total the same, in that a person thinks, feels and acts after the fashion ... of the one taken as a model." But it must be questioned whether this process is the *general* method by which individuation takes place. Von Uexküll's concept of the "schema" may indeed be a more appropriate concept to approach these phenomena, although it is not directly applicable to man. The animal's innate "schema" refers to the innate object representation of a drive; we have in this schema the guarantee for each animal's identity—not a *sense* of identity, or any form of awareness, but a guarantee of "living sameness" within change, of continuity as an individual of a particular species. The animal's *Umwelt* is defined not as an "external environment," but it rather represents a range of experience within which certain identities become recognizable, such as the identity of the animal's prey, its equals, its foes. Thus the animal's *Umwelt* delineates its identity.[3] We therefore must find a concept permitting a delineation of identity which is appropriate to the human condition.

Some Phenomenological Aspects
of Identity in the Human Infant

The concept of identification, implying the Cartesian subject-object juxtaposition, obscures rather than elucidates the phenomenon of identity. This becomes particularly impressive when the concept of identification—as in the study of individuation—is used to examine the gradual emergence of identity in man. Jacobson (1954, 1964), for instance, says "that the earliest infantile stage is represented by the mother-child unit, a situation which of course cannot be described as yet in terms of identification which is a process." It is after the breaking up of this unit, induced, among other factors, by experiences of frustration, deprivation, and separation from the love object, that, according to Jacobson, the re-establishment of the lost unit is pursued by processes of identification with the mother. The implication of this theoretical approach to individuation is that the human being must, in order to become himself, strive to be like somebody else—the mother.

In contrast, I am inclined to see in the early mother-child unit, and not in its breaking up, the primary condition for identity in man. While man does not have the innate identity of the animal which rests upon an innate "schema" or an innate object representation, the very extremeness of the symbiotic relation of the human child to his mother—usually described as the long dependency of the human infant on the mother—becomes the very source of the emergence of *human* identity. The human infant is not equipped with an innate *object* representation, but it may be equipped with an innate *Umwelt,* even though there is not yet the mature differentiation between an I and a not-I. One may describe this as a kind of polarization within the mother-child unit: in this unit the mother-*Umwelt* would correspond to the surrounding total organism, and the infant to an organ within this totality. Just as an organ within an organism is both "separate" and "symbiotic," the infant is one with the mother, but simultaneously there is a primary relatedness of a part to a whole. This symbiotic universe cannot be described in Cartesian terms of subject and object, but it can be described as organized: the organ of an organism has an identity in terms of its function within the organism; thus, the maternal

Umwelt (which includes the unconscious of the mother) ordains an organ-function to the child, and it is this primary function in which I see the nucleus of the emerging human identity. Even as an adult, I believe, man cannot ever experience his identity except in terms of an organic instrumentality[4] within the variations of a symbiotically structured *Umwelt*. Man, insofar as he consciously expresses his sense of identity, must do it in terms of what he is for someone else: his king's subject, his parents' child, the mother of her children, etc. This is usually referred to as a person's social role, and is used as an evidence that human identity can be defined only within a cultural pattern. To me, however, it appears that man's identity is not a *consequence* of an existing social or cultural pattern. Rather, the emergence of social and cultural patterns is possible only because man, in contrast to the animal, must define his identity, and this definition of himself reflects his fundamentally symbiotic way of existing: man defines himself as an instrument, an "organ" serving a function. Eissler (1958) touches upon the problems involved here. After defining identity as the ego's experience of being identical with itself, which Eissler calls the experience of "self-cognizance," he adds the following most important remark:

> It should, by the way, not lightly be assumed that the capacity for self-cognizance has existed in all historical eras: this is still a question for historical research. An ancient Pharaoh, for example, would perhaps have rejected such a proposition as "I am I" and have said rather "I am all my subjects—and much more," or "I am Egypt," or, probably, "I am the world." And a subject of that Pharaoh might easily have said: "I am not I; I am an insignificant extension of the Pharaoh." The proposition "I am I," the sense of being identical with oneself, is probably only a relatively recent development in the history of man.

It is striking that Eissler, in spite of his awareness that the sense of identity, as a conscious inner experience, is a relatively late historical acquisition, insists on defining identity as the "I-am-I" experience. In contrast, I believe that identity in man is an experience of a potential instrumentality for another one: one who can be loved by mother, by father, then later on by his community, etc. "I am I," as a definition of existence. It has, therefore, often been this expression "I am I" by which the Deity is defining Itself in contrast to man.

A Hypothesis Concerning Human Individuation

If we must search for a terminology which does not use concepts implying the subject-object juxtaposition, we might look for attempts made already along these lines. Some of the terms introduced by the ethologists (Von Uexküll, 1921, 1934, Lorenz, 1935, Tinbergen 1951) appear to have been motivated by similar considerations: the study of animals and their *Umwelt* seems to me to be a non-Cartesian approach, attempting to bring together the "isolated" animal and its "external environment." For this reason, I have in the preceding pages made use of the *Umwelt* concept. The task of describing the processes of individuation without recourse to the concept of identification is the next step in any attempt to overcome the subject-object dilemma, and, by doing this, to gain a more complete access to the problems of human identity than has been possible up to now.[5]

As an effort in this direction I suggest the use of the well-known concept of "imprinting" for the description of certain aspects of early infant-mother interaction.[6] Imprinting, in the definition of Lorenz (1935), "is the name we have given the process by which the releaser of an innate reaction to a fellow member of the species is acquired." It is characterized by three observable facts. It is influenced by conspecific living material, it is restricted to critical phases of ontogenesis, and it is irreversible (Lorenz 1937). The Innate Releaser Mechanism (IRM) is defined as "the innately determined readiness of an animal to respond with a certain action to a certain stimulus combination. It is an innate neurosensory correlate to a specific stimulus combination" (Lorenz and Tinbergen 1938).

Obviously, imprinting and innate releaser mechanisms, if applied to human development, are used as an analogy. What makes this analogy possible are two striking similarities in early phases of individuation. First, that certain responses on the part of the infant to the mother seem to be restricted to "critical phases of ontogenesis"; secondly, that the effect appears to be irreversible. But aside from these characteristics of timing and of irreversibility, what other analogy is there in the human situation to the "imprinting" stimulus combination, and what analogy could be found to an innate releaser mechanism in an infant? I

believe that there are such analogies, that, in fact, they have been
described by psychoanalytic observers of early infant-mother relation
(Boyer 1956). The imprinting stimulus combination would be the
individual and unique unconscious wishes, the unconscious needs of
the mother with regard to her child. This idea, indeed, was suggested by
Spitz (Spitz and Wolf 1949) when he expressed the belief that infants
respond directly to the mother's unconscious wishes. Even Spitz's
concept of "reciprocal identification" (1957) appears to me to imply a
form of unconscious, symbiotic communication between mother and
infant. Bak's (1939) and Hermann's (1929) use of the concept of a
"flowing-over" mechanism seems to refer to a direct communication
from the mother's to the infant's unconscious. In her paper on
"Problems of Identity" Mahler (1958) describes the emergence of
identity as follows:

> In order to understand normal as well as disturbed feelings of
> identity, we have to go back not only to the preverbal stage, but all
> the way to a stage before images were formed. . . . We need to go
> back to primitive modalities of perception if we are to attempt any
> systematic study of the development of the sense of identity. There
> exist ... primitive somatic identification of flowing-over
> mechanisms or, should we say, assimilatory kinds of mechanisms
> which involve cathecting the apparatus of touch, smell, taste, and
> temperature, and also . . . the kinesthetic sense and that of a deep
> sensibility.

It is undeniable that Mahler aims at finding a concept appropriate to
the phenomena she is describing. It must appear that the concept of
identification is not quite satisfactory for Mahler. For this reason she
uses Bak's and Hermann's flowing-over concept, and introduces the
concept of assimilatory mechanisms.

Disregarding the fact that Mahler does not distinguish between the
concept of identity and the concept of a sense of identity, we
concentrate on Mahler's contribution to the phenomenology of the
symbiotic *Umwelt*. We could then say that the primitive flowing-over
stimulations described by her so succinctly may well constitute the
analogy to the "specific stimulus combination" of the ethologists. But
here is an important difference between the imprinting of the birds and

the "imprinting" of the infant: the specific stimulus combination, conveyed to the infant by the mother, is "specific" in a more individual sense than the term implies when used by the ethologists. It is a stimulus combination which is specific for the *individual* mother, and once the infant has been stimulated that way, the infant "recognizes" *his* mother by the specific individual combination of stimulations as well as frustrations long before there is a true perceptive recognition. This, at least, is a propostion which does not seem improbable to me. In the animal, the specificity is apparently less individual and structured generally in a simpler way. But this differentiation in the meaning of "specific stimulus combination" (Lorenz and Tinbergen 1938) does not invalidate the analogic use of the concept of imprinting.

Another important point which is not explicitly made by Mahler, but does not appear to contradict her findings, is that the primitive stimuli which cathect the apparatus of touch, smell, taste, etc., must be seen as "messages" conveying to the infant a great deal about the mother's unconscious wishes concerning the child. The way the mother is touching, holding, warming the child, the way in which some senses are stimulated, while others are not, forms a kind of "stimulus cast" of the mother's unconscious, just as a blind and deaf person may, by the sense of touch, "cast" the form and the personality of another person in his mind. Here we are on more familiar territory: numerous psychoanalytic authors (Lacan 1953, Greenacre 1957 1958a, Mahler 1958, Eissler 1958, Ellis 1959) have talked about the "mirroring experience" and have shown conclusively that such mirroring experiences are intimately linked with the emergence of both body image and "sense of identity." I feel that the term *mirroring* overemphasizes the visual element of the experience. It would seem that the primitive modalities of "somatic recognition" between mother and infant described by Mahler in the quoted passage constitute a kind of mirroring experience, but the "image" of oneself that the mirror conveys is at this early age—a stage "before images formed" (Mahler 1958)—outlined in terms of sensory responsiveness, not as visual perception. This would appear to be an important point, because these sensory responses are simultaneously "outlining" a first "*Umwelt-*otherness" and a first *Umwelt*-defined identity. Moreover, these responses as well as the primitive stimuli that elicit them form a continuous interchange of need creation and need satisfaction between the two partners of the symbiotic world. While the mother satisfies the infant's needs, in fact creates certain specific needs, which she delights in satisfying, the infant is transformed into an organ or an instrument for the satisfaction of the mother's unconscious needs.

It is at this point that I see a link between sexuality and the emergence of identity in man. An interaction between two partners where each partner experiences himself as uniquely and specifically capable of serving as the instrument of the other's sensory gratification—such a partnership can be called a partnership of sensual involvement. I believe that this type of relationship is, in the adult, established in the sexual involvement of two individuals. In the primitive sensory interchanges taking place between mother and infant one could see the precursor of adult sexuality. This proposition does not yet, however, permit us to see the link between this mother-infant interaction and the problem of identity in man.

I have delayed raising the question whether there is, in the human infant, an analogy to the innate releaser mechanism of the animals, corresponding to the "imprinting," for which we did see analogies in the specificity of the mother's "stimulus combination." This latter question can be answered in the affirmative only if we make certain assumptions which have formed the basic propositions of this paper, namely, that man does not have "an" identity, that his identity is an artifact, a creative act, and that for this reason loss of identity is a specifically human danger, and maintenance of identity a specifically human necessity. If, by contrast, human individuation is understood as a process of identifications, this phenomenon cannot come into view. The concept of identification, implying a subject-object juxtaposition, must always come to an understanding of man as becoming gradually aware of himself as "subject" confronting other "subjects" and the world of "objects." This traditional approach fails to come to grips with the problems of human identity. The consequence of this is that the Cartesian split between *res cogitans* and *res extensa* is carried into our approach to man in nature and man in history. It creates pseudo-problems, such as "biological" versus "cultural" schools of thought.

I believe the proposition that man is distinct from the animals in not having an innate identity can avoid many pseudocontroversies, and widen the scope of psychoanalytic understanding. But if the proposition that man has no innate identity is taken seriously, we must demonstrate how the human infant acquires an identity. I see the answer to this question in the "imprinting" of an identity on the human child by the mother. The mother does not convey a *sense* of identity to the infant but an *identity:* The child is the organ, the instrument for the fulfillment of the mother's unconscious needs. *Out of the infinite potentialities within the human infant, the specific stimulus combination emanating from the individual mother "releases" one, and only one, concrete way of being this organ, this instrument.* This "released" identity will be irreversible, and thus it will compel the child to find ways and means to realize this specific identity which the mother has imprinted upon it.

The Innate Releaser Mechanism has, then, an analogy in the human infant in so far as there is an innately determined readiness in the human infant to react to the maternal stimulations with a "somatic obedience" experience. This "obedience" represents, however, fulfillment of the child's own needs: in being the instrument, the organ for the satisfaction of the maternal Otherness, the full symbiotic interaction of the two partners is realized for both of them. It would, however, be a mistake to see this "organ" or "instrumental" identity as too narrowly defined. The mother imprints upon the infant not *an* identity, but an *"identity theme."* This *theme* is irreversible, but it is capable of variations, variations that spell the difference between human creativity and "a destiny neurosis." What in the adult is referred to as his social identity (Erikson's ego identity)—being a worker, a farmer, a hunter, etc.—is, at its best, a successful variation of the identity theme imprinted upon the infant. At its worst, it is an artificially imposed part, the playing of which is experienced as alienation by the individual, because it is incompatible with his identity theme. But we do not yet deal here with the possible variations of the identity theme. It is the origin of identity in man that we have been trying to correlate to the imprinting upon the infant of an identity theme, and this identity theme, in turn, appears at first in the form of an "organ instrumentality."

Man thus makes use of nonprocreative sexuality in a unique way: he becomes an instrument for the fulfillment of another one's needs, needs which are conveyed and perceived as primitive modalities of sensory interaction within a symbiotically structural *Umwelt.* This link between sexuality and imprinted identity is supported by the observation of many psychoanalysts of a correlation between body image, sexuality, and identity problems (such as in fetishists: Greenacre 1953, 1955). It seems necessary, however, to test the theoretical propositions suggested here through their application to a more fully presented clinical example.

PART II: SEXUALITY AND THE EMERGENCE OF THE
"IDENTITY THEME" IN A CASE OF SEVERE SEXUAL PATHOLOGY

Anna S: A Case History

A twenty-three-year-old girl entered treatment in order to extricate herself from a life situation that was rapidly destroying her spiritually as well as physically. The main issues were: prostitution, conflicts arising from homosexual relations, periodic drinking, suicidal impulses. More exactly, she came for help because she could no longer endure the anxieties, depressions, and the overwhelming sense of despair and loneliness that had, in her opinion, gradually driven her to the type of life that she had been leading approximately since her sixteenth year. There were many more manifestations of serious pathology than those mentioned: there were phobic anxieties, like fears of rats and cats; compulsive spending of money, often on quite useless things, which kept her in a state of chronic indebtedness; alternating periods of compulsive eating, and inability to eat; periods of incapacity to do any kind of work, not only sustained work on a job, but cleaning up her room, etc., which were followed by a kind of frenzied overactivity, where she would, for instance, clean house for several consecutive days, continuing even at night. There were, in short, few facts of her life that could be described as normal. It was, therefore, all the more striking that in the face of so much pathology one could not but acknowledge that her fundamental sense of reality appeared intact. While she acted abnormally in so many areas, and was prey to so many morbid emotional states, she herself could clearly distinguish those actions and those feelings as abnormal, and could describe quite clearly how a healthy person would act and feel.

To speak of an intact sense of reality in this patient oversimplifies matters, however. In the sense that she had no gross distortions, such as delusional interpretations of reality, and did very little rationalizing concerning her actions, in this sense her contact with reality was intact and her judgment intelligent. A psychological test, taken at a late stage of the treatment, confirmed this intitial impression: she was, indeed, of "superior intelligence." There was, however, a most peculiar discrepancy between her clear awareness of her actions, their implications for her chances of finding any kind of fulfillment of her wishes for happiness in her life, on the one hand, and her feeling about herself as a person, about her self. The fact that she had been a prostitute, working both as a "call girl" and in houses of prostitution, had nothing whatsoever to do with the way she felt about herself as a person.

The person she considered to be, in her own words, her "real self," was someone who had been, by the circumstances of her upbringing, deprived of any chance of education, which pained her greatly. She was proud to have educated herself by her reading, which was of a high standard and included many books dealing with ethical and religious problems as well as books on psychology—it was in this way that she arrived at the conclusion that she needed psychoanalytic help. She considered herself seriously interested in the arts: she loved music, went to concerts, attended ballet performances. She had an appreciation for painting, and she enjoyed poetry. Her self-education had remained spotty and haphazard, but she seemed to possess a good sense of value in both literary and artistic matters. This person sincerely striving to "improve herself" was her "real self." The girl who lived and was known to others as a prostitute was not "really herself," although she never denied "the facts" of her life. She looked upon herself somewhat like a person who, for some reason outside of himself, has to play a social role totally disconnected with his original position in life: while he may acknowledge that he is a forced laborer in a prison camp, he knows that he "really" is a scientist, a musician, or a one-time political leader.

The patient came for treatment because she was to some degree aware of this inner contradiction: she hoped that treatment would help her to become what she felt she "really was." Due to this complete divorce of her "real self" from the role she lived, her attitude about moral issues involved in prostitution was equally contradictory: one side of her insisted that "real good people" had probably no sex life at all—though she knew that this was not so—while for herself she considered prostitution as morally rather irrelevant: it was a mysterious fact of her life that she felt unable to explain, but it was not comparable to "real" crimes like stealing or killing. She most definitely believed in moral principles: one might say that she firmly believed in the validity of the Ten Commandments. She was, in fact, something of a do-gooder. She often went out of her way to do something helpful for other people; she would, for instance, offer her time to orphanages, or invite some lonely old women for Christmas dinner. Moreover, her guilt feelings were very intense when she felt that she had done something wrong, such as lying. Her confusion about her sex life was certainly most remarkable; in spite of her many years of indiscriminate promiscuity she was rather prudish in many respects: she would never use profane or obscene words, nor was she indifferent when other people used them. While she was very matter of fact about her experiences, she was never cynical. Thus, if we describe her sense of reality as intact insofar as the functions of reality testing are concerned, the sense of her own, inner reality, her sense of identity, was eminently disturbed.

Anna S. was the illegitimate child of a woman who at the time of Anna's birth had been only sixteen years old. Anna's mother was born in the United States from first-generation European immigrants. The family seems to have just managed to eke out a marginal economic existence, but culturally, at least on the grandfather's side, there was a tradition of achievement in the fields of music and the theater. Several brothers of the grandfather had been successful as good musicians in the United States, but the grandfather himself, according to the patient, gave up his career as a musician on the urging of his wife in order to open a small and never really successful business. The grandmother was a very religious woman who could never accept the illegitimate grandchild, and prayed quite openly for its early death in order to remove the disgrace from the family. In contrast, the grandfather was warm and affectionate to Anna, and she remembered him as the only member of the family who had given her unconditional love during her early years of life.

These early years had been most confusing. Anna was born in a home for out-of-wedlock children, and had probably stayed there during the first year of her life. She insisted that she had some memory of this early period of her life and that it was a pleasant memory. She believed that she had received very loving care from a nurse who liked her as a baby. Afterwards she lived for awhile with the grandparents, until finally, when she was three years old, her mother married a man whom Anna considered for many years as her father, although there must have been some confusion about this, too. She knew members of her real father's family, whom she called uncle and aunt, respectively. She never met her real father since he had moved to a different part of the country before she was born. But his picture had often been shown to her, and it was never quite clear how much she knew or perceived of her illegitimate birth even before her stepfather, in a fit of rage, divulged it to her when she was nine years old. What she did know was that her parents were not happy with each other, that her stepfather was very often mad at her. He frequently beat her, but she also remembered him beating her mother. The picture of the stepfather was certainly a very disturbing and frightening one to the child. He seemed to have been a very unbalanced individual, at times friendly, but prone to unpredictable rages. Anna claimed that once, when her mother was away in a hospital, he had made sexual advances to her. Anna was very sure that later he had been committed to a mental hospital. He certainly was not an adequate provider. Whenever the family had some money it seemed to have been earned by her mother, who had become a successful singer in vaudeville. It was there that Anna's mother met her husband, who also made his living in show business. Anna grew up in the vaudeville and show business world, and claimed to have performed as a child dancer from an early age on, being part of an act presented by her parents. The theater world, for all its attractions, was as unsteady as everything else in Anna's life: not only because it meant travel and constant change, but also because the parents were often out of work. Thus periods of excitement and gaiety alternated with periods of drabness, poverty, and gloom, and often actual hunger.

More than anything else, however, it was the relationship to her mother that had a profoundly unsettling effect on Anna. While her stepfather was rather consistently a threatening figure in Anna's life, her relationship to her mother was intensely ambivalent, being at once both passionate and deeply resentful, reflecting the mother's ambivalence toward the child. For Anna, her mother was the most beautiful woman whose love she constantly was seeking. She had seen her on stage, admired by the audience as well as by her colleagues in the theater. Everybody seemed to like her, people were captivated by her good looks, charm, and her beautiful voice. Anna knew that she was an attractive and vivacious child, but would never be as beautiful as her mother. She had a natural gift for dancing, but no singing voice whatsoever. But worst of all, she never knew where she stood with her mother. True, her mother had never left her, and in some way had always taken care of her. When Anna was little, her mother often placed her in foster homes, while the mother was traveling with a vaudeville group. Anna remembered vividly the many times that she had to say "good-bye" to her mother, never knowing for sure whether she would return. She always did, and while this might have indicated that she did indeed care for the child, Anna deeply felt that for some reason her mother did not really love her, yes, seemed to be ashamed of her. Her mother would be proud of Anna's early stage successes, and of the fact that everybody seemed to consider her a cute little girl. At the same time, however, she would criticize her looks, her freckles, the color of her hair, the shape of her teeth—nothing seemed to be exactly right about her. To increase Anna's confusion, the mother often wanted Anna to give her (Anna's) age as much younger, or, when this was unbelievable, to make her appear as a younger sister and not as her child. The mother also seemed to imply that Anna was the reason for all kinds of physical troubles that the mother had—allegedly caused by Anna's birth. Anna was fully aware that her mother often told lies about her. For most of her childhood she did not understand the reason. In spite of all this, she had no doubt that her mother did not love the man whom Anna called father. There was a secret alliance between Anna and her mother against this man. Mother seemed nicer to Anna when they were all alone, without the stepfather, and when there was nobody to whom Anna's age and her relationship to her mother had to be explained. The mother did not do anything to further Anna's abilities, for instance, in dancing, and Anna hardly received any regular schooling because the parents changed domicile so often.

The result of all this was a passionate wooing of her mother: Anna's one aim was to be what her mother wanted her to be. She became her mother's most ardent lover, and tormented her with her rages of jealousy. She plotted throughout her childhood against her stepfather, at first surreptitiously, later when she knew she was not his child, quite openly: she and her mother should leave the stepfather and live for each other only. When her mother did not do what Anna wanted,

Anna's passion would turn into rage. She would say and do things in order to hurt and humiliate her mother. She described herself as a "she devil," when it came to fighting her mother, but she had never any doubt that she was fighting, even as an adult, for one thing only: that her mother would give up any other tie and live for her only.

When Anna was fourteen years old, she almost accomplished her aim. After years of fighting between the parents, and years of warfare against the stepfather on the part of Anna, the mother decided to leave her husband. Anna, though still a minor, immediately set herself the task of providing for her mother. She knew her mother well: unless she could appear on the stage, she was unable to take care of herself, not to speak of herself and an adolescent girl. Anna knew that her mother was more childlike than herself, that she expected to be taken care of by admiring people, and she could apparently charm people into doing just that. After leaving the stepfather, Anna knew that she would have to work to keep herself and her mother alive. She falsified her age, took jobs in factories, sold Fuller brushes, etc., in order to have her mother all for herself. She claimed that she worked in those years like a robot. But she lost out: shortly after having left the stepfather, her mother became romantically involved with another man, who wanted to marry her. As it turned out, the man was married already, and her mother was heartbroken when the truth came out.

For Anna, her mother's love affair had an even deeper effect: it was evidence of her total failure to win her mother. She had done her utmost "to take care of Mother," and her mother had turned to a man—a man Anna never ceased to hate. She felt betrayed and decided to run away. She was only fifteen years old then, but she knew the break was final. With her show business experience and some lying about her age, she found a job as a dancer in a night club. This was a club popular with both male and female homosexuals. Anna knew this, but it rather appealed to her. She liked homosexual men because they were, in her experience, more artistic and less brutal than other men, and she felt attracted to Lesbian women. Her first great love had been a schoolteacher whom she had adored passionately. Later, she had fallen in love with a girl in a factory who was a Lesbian.

The club in which she began to work was by no means exclusively frequented by homosexuals. One day a man offered Anna a large sum of money if she could prove to him that she was still a virgin. Anna felt intrigued by this monetary approach to sex, and acceded to the man's request to have intercourse with her. She found the experience painful and very unpleasant. She also had some physical contacts with girls and had decided that the caresses of girls were much more emotionally satisfying. Her introduction to sexual experience seemed to set free forces in her that she could not control. In later life, she always blamed her mother's "betrayal" of her for the course of events. Shortly after her first intercourse with the customer of the club, she found herself in debt and in urgent need of money. Some girls who worked in the club suggested that she work as a call girl in a hotel—as they had done. In this way she would get the money in a short time. Anna without hesitation accepted this suggestion. At first she worked for three weeks as a call girl. Just as with the first man, she did not like the experience. She remembered that she often was afraid, suffered from nausea and vomiting—but she kept on "working."

From then on, her life followed a pattern: there was homosexuality with often deep emotional involvement, and there were experiences as a prostitute. Sometimes she would be a call girl, sometimes she would enter houses of prostitution. Finally, she began drinking periodically. In general, there was a rather typical sequence of events. First, she would fall passionately in love with a girl. As long as she was sure of this girl's love, she would neither drink nor engage in prostitution. At times she would live with a girl, in her own words, as wife and husband, she feeling as the wife. During such times she would take on a regular job and have no particular interest in men. But these relationships tended to disintegrate sooner or later. Anna was as intensely possessive of her female lover as she had been of her mother. Soon, with or without reason, she began to torment her friend with jealousy. She found herself unable to maintain any stable relationship of this kind for any length of time. She would become depressed, and drinking would develop. As her despair and her sense of inner isolation and loneliness would mount, she would engage in prostitute activities, often ending with a kind of "flight" into a brothel. It was there, she claimed, that she gradually regained a degree of inner composure, and then she would leave—and the vicious circle would start all over again: a Lesbian love relationship would lead to fear of desertion, fear of desertion would create panic and depression (there had been one serious suicide attempt) and depression would lead to excessive drinking and prostitution.

The foregoing summary presents only an outline of the complex history and symptomatology of this patient. Those aspects that have been reported appear indispensable to the main thesis of this paper: the correlation between (nonprocreative) sexuality and the emergence and maintenance of identity in man. The problem of identity was thematic in this patient not only by way of inference from her symptoms, it was a conscious preoccupation of Anna. Again and again she would ask: "*Am I* a prostitute? They say: a whore is whore, once a whore, always a whore. I do not want to believe it, *I know it is not what I really am.*"

This preoccupation with the problem of their identity has impressed other observers as an important characteristic of the personality of prostitutes (Deutsch, H. 1929, 1942). Agoston (1929, 1946) considers it the basic feature, common to all patients of this type he had opportunity to observe. He describes it as the "I-am-not-I defense," which characterizes the individuals as pseudo personalities, a term introduced by Agoston to indicate that these patients deny their real selves by a mask of toughness and cynicism, in order to hide an infantile, shy, deeply anxiety-ridden personality. According to Agoston, the I-am-not-I defense uses the denial of one's identity in order to escape feelings of guilt, a guilt not based on the antisocial actions of these patients, but on the unconscious incestuous fantasies acted out by these individuals. Helene Deutsch (1944) goes so far as to state that many prostitutes actually lead double lives, which would establish them as closely related to people with multiple personalities. There can be little doubt then that a gross disturbance of the sense of identity is often associated with, if not a prerequisite of, prostitution.

Anna's many verbalizations of uncertainty concerning her "real self" did not impress the observer as a denial type of defense in the sense of Agoston. Rather the confusion and uncertainty indicated a painful awareness of disconnected identities. She could not arrive at an integrated sense of identity, because the identity experience based on her actions did in no way correspond to the inner experience of her "real" self. If prostitution served Anna as defense, the danger against which this defense was directed was the threat of being loved as a woman by a man, particularly the fulfillment of such love by sexual union. More exactly, prostitution was for Anna a defense against the experience of shame that overwhelmed her when a man tried to flirt with her, court her, or wanted to make love to her because he liked her. To escape this deeply disturbing sense of shame she went to extreme lengths to make the relationships with men as businesslike and matter of fact as possible. She had a set of rules that a man who wanted to have intercourse with her should follow. He should not use with her any names of endearment. She liked it best if the man came out quite straightforwardly with his desire to have sexual intercourse with her. He should neither pretend to be affectionate, nor should he be vulgar or brutal. If a man offered her a specified amount of money in exchange for her services, this made her much more confortable. To have sex relations for money was, in fact, a condition that enabled her to enter into a sex relationship, because it made it very obvious to the man and to her that, in her own words, "she was not *really* in it, that she *really* did not participate in it." Thus, prostitution was for Anna a defense against the danger of involvement with men that would have "really" affected her "real" self.[7] Aside from the business approach to sex she used other means to exclude herself from "real" participation in the experience: she would try hard to think of something that had nothing to do with the present sexual experience, perhaps concentrating on what she would buy next time when shopping. As soon as the experience was over, she would rush into some other activity that would take her mind away from the sexual experience.

Agoston explains this frequently observed behavior by attributing to prostitutes a special kind of castration fear, which he called existential castration fear. By this he means a fear of actual total destruction of one's existence. This would be a concept corresponding to Jones' concept of "aphanisis" (1927). Prostitutes, Agoston believes, are children of parents who consciously or unconsciously aimed at destroying the child. According to this line of thought, the prostitute would fight her fear of being destroyed by exposing herself to the danger under conditions that would give her the reassurance: I have experienced sex inumerable times with inumerable men, and they could not do anything to me. This would imply that the basic danger is sexual experience, while in the case of Anna the danger which she perceived is the emotional involvement. This raises the question under what conditions can *love* become an unbearable threat to an individual? I believe that this problem can be solved in the context of an inquiry into the emergence of identity in man, especially in the discussion of the relationship of identity to the concept of metamorphosis.

Anna was aware that she felt threatened in her relationship to such men who could be potential husbands. If the man was much older, possibly a grandfather type of man, she could permit herself much deeper emotional responses than with younger, marriageable males. She had had several close relationships with older men which did not always include sexual relationships. For a long time Anna persisted that her only "real" trouble was that she could not endure loneliness.(Schmideberg 1953, Greeson 1953, Sullivan 1953). For her, loneliness was a reason for all the contradictory aspects of her behavior. She would, in her opinion, be quite content if a girl she loved would remain forever faithful to her: then she would not have to feel lonely and she would not need any men at all. She described again and again that loneliness was an experience of intolerable intensity, undistinguishable from profound anguish, as if, in her words, she would go out of her mind.

Exploring the inner experience of what she called loneliness, which seemed also to include a degree of depersonalization and derealization, she one day divulged that there were certain fantasies accompanying the state of loneliness. In fact, she had oftentimes tried to write down these fantasies, giving them a kind of poetic form. This had happened before she entered treatment, and she was hesitant to show what she had written. She finally brought them to the treatment session. Their essence consists of what shall be called the Mad Lover fantasy. Anna talks about an imaginary lover, who is a "madman." He comes to make love to her, but while doing so, he destroys both her body and her mind; this she imagines to be an ecstatic experience of happiness. The title of the following example is "Return." It shall be quoted verbatim:

Ah, he quiets Sanity, for I hear the sounds of my lover's footsteps.—Is that you beloved, is that you returning to Drown in my madness, to baptize me with the Sweetness of our foolishness? Oh, bring back the strange but happy love.—Bless you, and drink with me my blood to quench our starved thirstiness.—*Farewell, loneliness* of Sanity, for madness has come to save my Soul. Hold my hand, lead me through the gates of Hell where we may rejoice to the Sins of humble men. Embrace me oh madness, let my nakedness and nudity quench thy thirst for madness with love of a longing heart.

The following lines were untitled:

Don't leave me, for with you I am not alone. Keep me safe in your oblivion, safe from the haunting night with its thousands eyes upon my naked soul—for the love I have for you, I need you, for when you leave I find my Self in a reality upon this God's hell on earth, to breathe only the contemptuousness of man's Sanity. Come back, come back, my Sweet love, don't turn me out, let me bathe my Soul in your torment, bleed my body of its blood for a Smooth Vintage of men's liqueur. Let me drink to our holy madness, to our love of Solitude, Oh madness, I love you, come back to keep me free from Sanity.

Anna S.: Tentative Interpretation of an Identity Theme

I am of course aware of the fact that there is no difficulty in interpreting the dynamics of a case like Anna's in terms of modern psychoanalytic thought. In the interpretation offered here I deliberately confine myself to the attempt to demonstrate the irreversibility of the "identity theme" as an "independent variable," which, by its seeming disregard for the individual's most important needs (including self-preservation), impresses us easily as evidence of the death instinct, as masochism (Bergler 1949, Loewenstein 1957) or as aggression turned against the self (Freud 1915a, 1924b, Jacobson 1953, 1964).

Returning to the Mad Lover fantasy of the patient, I shall concentrate on an exploration of what it may reveal concerning this patient's identity theme. It is obviously a fantasy representing a desire for symbiotic fusion with the lover, expressed in archaic oral concepts of being devoured by the Madman. This experience of being devoured (drunk) is anticipated as ecstatic union with the lover, and this union is to imply a joyful "liberation from sanity." Since we are to reconstruct an imprinted identity theme from these fantasies, we must interpret them as a response to the unconscious "imprinting" message from the mother to the child. What, then, did a mother convey to an infant that imprinted upon the child the identity to be someone's "drink of blood"?

Since it is impossible to transcribe in concepts taken from the space-time world of the adult the archaic language of the unconscious, we can give only an approximation of its meaning: the mother wants the child to satisfy her needs by becoming and remaining a part of her—her "lifeblood" (see Boyer [1956], quotation by Wangh, p. 250). She thus excludes from the child any identity theme that is compatible with separateness as an individual. We should nevertheless point to the fact that even this type of identity theme has a range of variations. They may be transcribed by the concept of being another one's "essence"— "essence" connoting, according to Webster's Dictionary, both what is permanent and unchangeable as well as a distilled extract. This "identity theme" touches upon Eissler's (1958) transcription of an ancient Egyptian's identity as "being an extension of Pharoah." We find striking verbalizations of similar "identity themes" in the works of some religious mystics, for example, Angelus Silesius (1623-77). In his almost untranslatable German verses we find the following: "Ich bin nicht ausser Gott, und Gott nicht ausser mir. Ich bin sein Glanz und Licht, und er ist meine Zier [I am not separate from God, nor is He separate from me. I am His luster and light, and He is my adornment]." Even more striking in the context of the paper are the following verses with their oral imagery: "Nimm, trink, so viel du willst and kannst, es steht dir frei: Die ganze Gottheit selbst ist deine Gasterei [Take, drink as much as you wish and can, it is all for you to choose: God Himself in His wholeness is your feast]" (Silesius 1657). In Anna, the emphasis is on her being the feast of another one, but the oral language serves in both cases the thought of being both inseparable and being the "essence" of the other one.

It is this incompatibility of Anna's identity theme with a high degree of separateness[8] which gives rise to a multitude of dillemmas. One of these dilemmas becomes articulate (in the Mad Lover fantasy) in the equation of sanity with loneliness, of ecstasy with "freedom from sanity." It does indeed make sense in view of psychoanalytic insight into early stages of mental development to equate the emergence of the "sane" mind with the process of individuation: sanity does imply the capacity to differentiate between the I and the not-I. Symbiotic experiences, blurring the person's boundary between himself and the "objects" of the "real world," are, if they dominate the individual's perception of himself and the world, an important characteristic of insanity. Thus, Anna is expressing quite clearly the nature of her dilemma: in order to be sane, she would have to accomplish a high degree of separateness as an individual. But in order to be "herself" according to her symbiotically perceived identity theme, separateness means loss of her identity. As long as she remains separate and sane, she suffers from an unbearable sense of loneliness, close to a feeling of depersonalization, because she is, indeed, in danger of loss of her identity. "Imprinted" with a symbiotic identity theme, the patient finds herself between the Scylla of loss of sanity and separateness—the madness of her Mad Lover fantasy—and the Charybdis of loss of identity (loneliness)—depersonalization.

Our clinical terminology is still quite unsatisfactory for the distinction between pathology based on disturbances in the processes of differentiation of the separate individual from the symbiotic mother-infant unit on the one hand, and deviations occurring in the development of the sense of identity of the individual. What are rather crudely, if conveniently, labeled borderline states, pseudoneurotic schizophrenias, etc., probably contain processes whose dynamics are basically different. This becomes apparent when we see that phenomena like fugues, amnesias with "loss of identity" (Geleerd et al. 1945), "as if" personalities (Deutsch 1942), patients with narcissistic object choice (A. Reich 1953), and many other conditions are all defined in terms of what one may call "near psychoses." Perhaps the development of the concept of ego distortion (Waelder et al. 1958) is an acknowledgment of the need for more specific dynamic differentiation of such "near-psychotic" states. The case of Anna S. can be used to demonstrate how psychosislike conflicts arising from the irreversible character of an individual's identity theme may appear, but also how dynamically and prognostically different they are from schizophrenic processes.

The maintenance of a person's identity theme having priority over all other needs, in Anna's case, "symbiotic existence" (identity theme) has priority over "sanity and separateness" (self-preservation). The application of this proposition permits an interpretation which is also different from the customary ones with regard to those aspects of Anna's pathology that appear to be manifestations of self-destructive drives. We suggest that the sadomasochistic ruminations of the Mad Lover fantasy can be understood as attempted realizations of the identity theme. The attempt to live such a symbiotic existence cannot but lead to conflicts with the necessities of mental development through the accomplishment of genuine individual separateness.

The conflicts between the compelling force of the identity theme on the one hand and Anna's needs can also be seen in certain phases of her sexual pathology. Anna's sex life is characterized by her fluctuation between homosexual experiences with intense emotional involvement, and unemotional, "businesslike" heterosexual experiences. The less the male represented a lover or husband, the more she could permit herself genuine feelings for him; the more he was considered by her as a love object, the more extreme became her incapacity to respond emotionally to him. This fluctuation would go on for awhile and consist of "faithful" homosexual relationships interrupted by promiscuous heterosexual experiences. At a certain point in the cycle, however, she became overwhelmed with the "despair of loneliness" and it was at this moment that promiscuity gave way to the radically impersonal pattern of prostitution.

The suggested interpretation of prostitution in terms of an imprinted "symbiotic" type of identity theme makes it understandable why homosexuality plays an important part in the psychology of prostitutes. This has been known to observers long before there were psychoanalytic studies of this problem. To name just one example, we may refer to Zola's *Nana*. Among psychoanalysts, Agoston (1946), Barag (1937), Helene Deutsch (1929, 1942), Glover (1945b), and Schmideberg (1946), have confirmed the older observations by their study of the dynamics of such cases. Studies of prostitutes such as those by Greenwalt (1958) and Murtagh and Harris (1957) tend to give the impression of wide similarities in the personalities of these patients, making one suspect that a "symbiotic" type of identity theme may be an important factor in the general problem of prostitution. We will therefore try, on the basis of the clinical material provided by the case of Anna S., to understand the inner connection between a "symbiotic" identity theme and prostitute behavior.

Once we have transcribed Anna's identity theme as "being another's essence," it becomes understandable why the child "imprinted" with such "identity theme" would encounter special problems both in her early relationship to the mother as well as in the later one to the father. The difficulty consists essentially in the fact that the relationship to the mother must remain totally frustrating, while the relationship to the father, in so far as it may promise fulfillment of the identity theme, is overwhelmingly threatening. To be the "essence" of another person's life implies one's irreplaceability for another one. In the case of Anna, this "being the irreplaceable essence" has the particular "symbiotic" connotation we have been stressing throughout. But the fulfillment of this identity theme cannot succeed with Anna's type of mother: the symbiotic "essence," the "life-giving food," is for a woman like Anna's mother quite definitely a man rather than her child, particularly not a daughter. Due to the special circumstances of Anna's mother's unhappy marriage, Anna felt encouraged to make at least a valiant attempt to replace the stepfather as the "essence" of her mother's life.

We have here an opportunity to see how the identity theme undergoes variations corresponding to the stages of psychosexual development. While the character of Anna's identity theme emphasizes a realization in the archaic forms of orality, as in the Mad Lover fantasy, Anna seems to have been able to develop a variation of her identity theme, permitting her to offer herself to her mother as a "phallic child." The material emerging during the treatment gave ample evidence of her attempt to become a phallus: she was, during her early years, anxious to have "large feet," and prayed that she would not develop any breasts. Even as an adult, she was often confused about her body image: for instance, whether she was petite, or large and strong. At some phase of her life she was consciously uncertain whether she was a boy or girl. From early childhood her greatest wish had been to become a dancer. While one cannot exclude the influence of the theatrical environment on her thinking, the role of phallic identification in dancers has been stressed by psychoanalysts (Erikson 1947). I assume that this phallic variation of Anna's identity theme constituted an important defense against the much more threatening implications of the oral-devouring fantasies expressed in her Mad Lover fantasy. If her identity had to be implemented in a symbiotic relation as another one's "organ," it would indeed be safer to offer herself as a phallus to another woman. In this way, she would have fulfilled her identity theme, while at the same time not exposing herself to total annihilation. As a woman's symbolic phallus, she would be a symbiotic, but essential organ or extension of another one. Thus, her efforts to implement her identity theme through a homosexual "symbiosis" become understandable. But this effort was bound to fail:

first, she could not compete with her mother's heterosexual love objects; second, her mother wanted her to be an "organ," a "part" of her, but as a form of a decorative appendix without individuality, not as her "essential" part.

In her later homosexual relationships with Lesbian women, Anna never felt that she was as symbiotically "essential" to her friends as her identity theme demanded: she could never satisfy herself that any of these friends ever regarded her as the "life-giving" part of themselves. Since the Lesbian woman denies her femininity, unconsciously claiming male characteristics, the meaning of her homosexuality runs counter to the underlying fantasy of Anna's homosexuality. Anna's phallic identification implies: I can add to you what you need—while the Lesbian girl claims: I have everything. Consequently the fulfillment of her symbiotic identity theme was possible only in a relationship to a man, because only a man could convey to her the experience of being his very "essence." The inner obstacle for the implementation of her identity theme in a relation to a man is the archaic character of symbiosis: its fulfillment is experienced by her as a threat to her very existence, since it implies being devoured as life-giving essence and thus being destroyed by the man.

How then could she realize her identity of oral symbiotic fusion with the man, and still retain a safe minimum of separateness to guard her sanity? Anna tried to solve this fatal dilemma by a desperate method: she permitted a "devouring" sexual use of her body, only safeguarding her sanity by separating her "real self" from this "consummated body." In short, she became a prostitute. While submitting sexually to a man, the prostitute permits the man to treat her as an extension of himself, negating completely her individual separateness, and thus her "real self" in Anna's terminology. She endeavors to share this symbiotic fantasy of the man by setting "inner limits" as to the meaning of the sexual act (Milner 1957). By the "business ritual" between her and the male partner she emphasizes that she is no longer a "person," but a thing or an "organ" of the man. This strict isolation protects her against the danger of "emotional symbiosis" which would unavoidably threaten her with complete dissolution or absorption in the other one.

The inner connection between a symbiotic identity theme and prostitution has not escaped the perception of great writer-psychologists. Thus Thomas Mann in the *Confessions of Felix Krull*

(1955) describes the encounter of his hero with a prostitute in the following poignant passage:

> Only after the nocturnal vehicle had again set itself into jogging motion did our conversation begin. . . . It was without introduction, this conversation, it was without polite conventions of any sort; from the very beginning it had the free, exalted irresponsibility that is usually a characteristic only of dreams, where our "I" associates with shadows that have no independent life, with creations of its own, in a way that is after all impossible in waking life where one flesh-and-blood being exists in actual separation from another. Here it happened, and I happily admit that I was moved to the depth of my soul by the intoxicating strangeness of the experience. We were not alone and even less were we as two: for duality ordinarily creates an inhibiting social situation—and there could be no talk of that here. My darling had a way of putting her leg over mine as though she were simply crossing her own; everything she said and did was marvelously unconstrained, bold and free as lonely thoughts are, and I was joyously ready to follow her lead. . . . her speech was broken and ungrammatical; indeed, she really did not know German at all, so that her words and expressions were often completely absurd and verged strangely upon the irrational—a fact that increased the dreamlike quality of her company. It must be especially and specifically noted, however, that her behavior was devoid of any frivolity or lightmindedness; instead she maintained in all circumstances— and how strange the circumstances sometimes were!—a severe, almost fierce seriousness, both then and during the whole time of our association.

Symbiotic identity themes might be a typical stage in the normal development of girls, as may be concluded from A. Katan's observation (1951) that temporary prostitution fantasies appear with great regularity at certain stages of adolescence. See also Deutsch (1929), Cohn (1928), Wittels (1935).

The possbility that an individual assumes the identity not only of being another person's bodily part and extension, but the identity of a "bought" object or acquired property of someone else raises issues of great complexity. One of the issues is the well-known one of "alienation." Fromm (1955), in *The Sane Society*, devotes a chapter to the phenomenon and concept of alienation, which he defines as "the fact that man does not experience himself as the active bearer of his own powers and richness, but as an impoverished 'thing,' dependent on powers outside of himself, unto whom he has projected his living substance." The central role of the concept of alienation in Marx's philosophy (Meyer 1934, Venable 1945) can only be mentioned here.

For me, alienation is, however, but one aspect of an even more central human problem: this problem derives from man's lack of an innate "identity," thus compelling him to define himself in terms of his instrumentality for someone or something else. This implies that man is the protean animal, capable of "infinite" identities. For this phenomenon I suggest the term *metamorphosis* (see Chapter 6, p. 184). I consider metamorphosis a unique human problem, implying both unique human potentialities as well as unique human dangers. Among the former, the potentialities usually referred to as creativity have to be mentioned, among the latter man's unique capacity of being "false," i.e., of being an imposter (Deutsch 1955, Moustakas 1956, Greenacre 1958c, d), can serve as an example. True and false, in man, are not merely logical but existential categories. It is in the context of these problems that the phenomenon of alienation must be considered. Prostitution can be understood as one specific form of alienation, but not the only one. Erikson's (1956) concept of "negative identity" and related phenomena described by Greenson (1954), A. Reich (1953), Waelder et al. (1958), and others would appear to explore similar territory. The phenomenon of metamorphosis seems also related to the observations described by Klein and her school (1948, 1955) under the headings "ego splitting" and "projective identification" (see also chapter 3).

There are clinical observations bearing on the theme of a person experiencing himself as an object or thing. They are important both clinically and theoretically. Such observations have been contributed by Mahler (1958) in cases of child psychosis. Such a child may not be able to decide whether inanimate objects in his environment are "himself" or not. Mahler speaks of "dissociation of identity," which is characterized by "the loss of the innate human faculty of discrimination between animate and inanimate, the living and the dead." This "primal discrimination" is, in Mahler's view, part of the primitive "flowing-over mechanism" (Bak 1939) and "seems to depend on and consist of impressions of warmth, resiliency, turgor, deep tactile sensations between two living higher organisms at contact with one another." Mahler's characterization would thus attribute the possibility of a human being acquiring a "human" or a "thing" identity to those very processes which in this paper have been described as the infant's being imprinted, during its earliest contacts with the mother, with an individual identity theme.

The Case of Anna S.: Conclusions and Problems

The interpretation of prostitution as a pathological form of maintenance of an identity theme appears to be supported by the psychological development that took place in Anna while under treatment. The therpeutic problem in Anna's case can be defined in terms of the range of variations of her identity theme. Was she capable of a less pathological form of implementation of this theme—an implementation that would not compel her to become fused with the other person as an alienated "organ-" or "thing-form" of herself? Could one expect, for instance, a gradual transformation of Anna's identity theme to that specific symbiotic feminine surrender to a man that writers and poets insist on ascribing to prostitutes? Has this cliché of the prostitute transformed into a woman capable of a unique type of love a psychological basis in the propensity of women with a certain type of identity theme for both prostitution and a special capacity of "blending" with a symbiotically loved man? The following letter, written by Anna sometime after the treatment had come to an end, may perhaps contribute to the exploration of this question. Beyond that (and more important) is, however, the evidence it offers concerning the irreversibility of an individual's identity theme. While it shows that Anna fell in love with a man, she loves symbiotically to such a degree that one cannot help wonder what would happen to her if this love would end in tragedy. I doubt that Anna would be able to deal with a loss of the love of her friend, Ray, without relapsing into some form of pathology consistent with her symbiotic identity theme. The letter is quoted verbatim except for the elimination of some minor irrelevant passages:

Never before have I felt peace of mind with anyone, warmth and feeling of wanting to do. I feel so much part of him that when he tells me something that was unpleasant to him, no matter what . . . I hate the thing or person for it. I feel it displeased him and that makes it terrible. If he is very tired, fatigue takes hold of me, and I seem to share his feeling, and usually end up relieving him of it. Does real loving make one feel a part of another? When he makes love to me I really feel that I'm way down deep inside of him, that his arms are my arms, etc. When he laughs, and he does not often, but he really does, I am filled with sheer glee. When he is sad I long to whitewash all that has caused him his miseries and I feel compassion so deep that I usually have indigestion. . . . I seem not only to suffer these days with my own grieves but his too if only it could lessen his, it would be worth it, but it does not. . . . Guess I never did get to mention [during treatment] all the thoughts that were plaguing me, but I do feel better just the same. Women should not have to work at a public job for money, they should not be career women as this makes them men. They should have a man to take care of that part, but they should be good and do all they can to make him happy. How can I like work when all it ever did was make me feel like a boy . . . when I worked at 13 to 15 for my mother and then what did she do? She left me for that terrible [n]. I worked while she went to the mountains and had a grand time. It was then that I met Lola [her first homosexual love] and I became lost until [I met] Ray. I sold Fuller brushes, cleaned house, cooked for a family and played house to support her. . . . She is having good feelings now that Ben [mother's second husband] has awakened her to the duties that were long ago hers. Now the story is "we *both* love you," not her alone. Think she is afraid of me alone. Once I threw her into a swimming pool and she was almost drowning. I wonder if being an orphan for real could have hurt as much.

A clinical example has been presented to support the proposition that an irreversible identity theme emerges in the early relationship between mother and infant. The process by which this identity theme is established has been compared to the "imprinting" of certain animals described by ethologists. The maintenance of the identity theme is claimed to have priority over all other needs—those emanating from drives as well as those representing powerful ego interests. The identity theme appears thus as an independent variable the vicissitudes of which can be traced in the symptomatology of the patient. The proposition of a theme of identity as an independent variable influences directly the role which we attribute to the drives in a given life situation. For instance, destructive, devouring orality may be seen as a form of implementation of an identity theme of "being somebody's part." The case history also illustrates the correlation of nonprocreative sexuality to the establishment of a theme of identity. In a case of an individual with an archaic identity theme the reinforcement of this theme may manifest itself as severe sexual pathology. We cannot, however, introduce propositions of this kind without raising the question of their compatibility with the dynamic and structural concepts of psychoanalysis. The third part of this chapter will be devoted to a clarification of these issues.

PART III: IDENTITY AND THE STRUCTURAL
CONCEPTS OF PSYCHOANALYSIS

The nature of the structural concepts of psychoanalysis and their relationship to the earlier formulated drive concepts form the central issues of modern psychoanalytic theory. In view of the fact that the contributions to these topics are numerous, complex, and often controversial (their scope and dimension are well indicated in Bellak, 1959—papers presented at a conference on Conceptual Problems in Psychoanalysis), it is necessary to restrict the discussion in this part to the more limited question of the relationship of the structural concepts to the concept of identity. This discussion must take up the earlier stated approach which views psychoanalysis as one attempt to deal with the fundamental issues left by the Cartesian revolution in Western scientific thought.

It has already been emphasized that psychoanalysis is not the only effort in the field of psychology to overcome the Cartesian split between *res cogitans* and *res extensa,* between "mind" and "body," between man as a historical and man as a natural being. One may claim, however, that psychoanalysis is the most radical attempt to overcome the split between man (mind) and nature (body) by the application of the evolutionary principle, established so firmly in biology and sociology during the nineteenth century, to the study of the emergence of the human mind (Toomey 1959). It is certainly not without justification to look upon Freud's work as a psychological version of the *Descent of Man*. There can be no doubt that Freud was aware of the necessity to free psychology from the implications of the *res cogitans*. Hartmann (1956a) attributes to this awareness Freud's hesitation to introduce the ego concept into psychoanalytic theory. According to Hartmann, "Freud disliked what the philosophers had said about the ego and was suspicious of its metaphysical implications." Freud's suspicions were certainly justified when we consider how the metaphysical substantialism, which, according to Frondizi (1953), had permeated Descartes's own understanding of the *ego cogitans* as a "thinking *substance*," has crept into psychoanalytic theory by means of the equation of problems of identity with problems of self-awareness or a "sense of identity." Since this point has been stressed previously, it will suffice to add here one example referring not to general theoretical issues, but to clinical observation. The example is chosen because it demonstrates that the equation of problems of identity with those of a sense of identity, and thus with ego function, actually obscures important phenomena rather than illuminates our psychoanalytic understanding of them. In a paper on "Amnesia and Allied Conditions," Geleerd, Hacker, and Rapaport (1945) describe the feeling of personal identity as one aspect of the integrative functions of the ego. They note, therefore, with some surprise that in cases of amnesia and "loss of identity" important ego functions such as "a high degree of reality testing seem to be retained."[9] This example illustrates that, in order to avoid implied substantialist meanings of the Cartesian *ego cogitans*, we must insist on postulating that in man identity is neither innate nor inherent in the concept of the ego. Only then it becomes possible to see that man, in contrast to the animals, is compelled to "create" his identity. It is this step that Freud did not take when he attempted to free the ego concept from the philosophical and metaphysical implications referred to by Hartmann. How much these implications have affected the development of psychoanalytic theory will be traced in the following pages. I believe that this outline, brief and incomplete as it is, will place the intent of this paper into the proper perspective within the questions and issues of modern psychoanalytic theory.

Beyond the Pleasure Principle and the Problem of Identity

The influence of the Cartesian tradition on conceptual problems of psychoanalytic theory can be illustrated by a brief recapitulation of the two theoretical positions taken in the "Two Principles of Mental Functioning" (1911) as against those set forth in *Beyond the Pleasure Principle* (1920). In brief, the theoretical position of the "Two Principles" is an attempt to apply the principle of evolution to the emergence of a human mind, and to describe the specific method by which a characteristically human mind could be thought to evolve on the basis of the known biological laws operating in the higher animals. Freud accomplishes this by taking as his biological basis the operation of a principle akin to that of homeostasis—"law of constancy of excitation" for Freud—applying it to the study of the human mind in the form of the pleasure-unpleasure principle.

This "principle" does not only imply that the restoration of a hypothetical equilibrium of "excitation" is experienced as pleasure, and a disturbance of this equilibrium as unpleasure. It rather implies that in man there is *no other* "innate" or "preformed" biological steering mechanims at work to safeguard the adaptation of the human species—no other, that is, in comparison with the preformed structural automatisms or instincts (Brun 1951) of the animals, which "fit them" into their appropriate *Umwelt*. Because there is *no other* biological safeguard for man's survival but the pleasure principle—serving through evoking unpleasure, as a signal for approaching biological danger—man, and man alone, must evolve a system for testing the *Umwelt* conditions in order to delay the immediate restoration of equilibrium long enough in order, as Freud puts it in the words of G. B. Shaw, "to be able to choose the line of greatest advantage instead of yielding in the direction of least resistance" (1911). For the animal, the "choice" has been made by its "preformed structural automatisms," its "instincts." Man, having no instincts in this sense, must learn to "choose."[10]

In man, there is an *evolutionary necessity* that he develop a "reality principle" whose primary function it is to delay the operation of the pleasure principle. The substitution of the reality principle for the pleasure principle, in Freud's own words, denotes no dethronement of the pleasure principle but only the safeguarding of it. "A momentary pleasure, uncertain in its results, is given up, but only to gain in a new way a sure pleasure, coming later" (1911). If we remain aware that the term *pleasure* means in this context adaptive equilibrium between man as a biological entity and its *Umwelt*, we can see why Freud could, in the "Two Principles," indeed believe that he had found in a simple biological principle of adaptation the method by which the evolution of the human mind became understandable: in order to survive, man had to test his *Umwelt*; to do this, he had to develop his sense organs in a special way, which had in turn led by evolutionary steps to the development of memory, of judgment, of action based on judgment of reality, and finally to the emergence of the thought processes as a form of "trial action" (Rapaport 1951b). Thought processes made the development of language possible, and with this development human consciousness made its appearance.

In the "Two Principles," then, Freud perceives the pleasure principle as the most important adaptive principle in man, though, at times, it has to be "safeguarded" by the capacity of delayed action, i.e., the reality principle. To prove the validity of this evolutionary hypothesis it was necessary to show that *every* manifestation of the human mind, normal as well as pathological, could be interpreted as a derivative of the operation of the pleasure principle and of the "safeguarding" reality principle. Freud, in his clinical work, became more and more convinced, however, that this was, in fact, not possible: there were manifestations of the human mind that were pointing to a something "beyond the pleasure principle." This mysterious force Freud described as the "repetition compulsion" (1920). After weighing the possibility that the repetition compulsion could be a disguised form of the operation of the pleasure principle, Freud rejects this idea: "Enough remains which justifies the proposition of a repetition compulsion, and it appears to be more basic, more drive-like than the pleasure principle which it has suspended." Freud introduced the concept of the repetition compulsion to explain certain phenomena in human behavior that seem to indicate that many individuals, far from following a course of survival by adaptation to reality, did everything in their power to repeat painful and even self-destructive types of experience. There were also other observations, like the play of children, where repetition appears to be a more compelling urge than pleasure, because children would insist on repeating certain experiences even if they would suffer while undergoing these experiences.

Before retracing the new theoretical position to which Freud arrived in *Beyond the Pleasure Principle*, I want to make clear my own position with regard to the phenomenon of the repetition compulsion, because otherwise the following theoretical considerations would lack clarity. It is my contention that the repetition compulsion is a manifestation of the necessity for maintenance of the "theme of identity." Identity, in man, requires a "repetitive doing" in order to safeguard the "sameness within change" which I believe to be a fundamental aspect of identity in man. We may refer here to Greenacre (1958a), who stresses the need for "maintenance" of identity in the following words: "the sense of self-image is *maintained* and perhaps vitalized by the *continual redefinement* which accompanies comparison and contrast with others." As proposed in the previous sections, the maintenance of the identity theme does indeed appear to have priority over any other principle, including the pleasure principle. I believe, moreover, that Freud, in *Beyond the Pleasure Principle,* was aware that he was dealing with problems of identity. To substantiate this contention, only one statement shall be quoted: "It is evident that the repetition, *the rediscover of identity,* is in itself a source of gratification" (my italics).

In treating the problem of identity, however, Freud followed the Cartesian tradition by assuming that where there was an ego, there was continuity of identity. On the basis of this assumption, it becomes necessary to look for some other compelling reason which would explain the many repetitive phenomena in man, which so often make man appear to be engaged in the pursuit of unhappiness. As we know, Freud came to postulate a death instinct in order to account for the compulsive, drivelike power of the repetition compulsion. The introduction of the death instinct meant a radical deviation from his position in the "Two Principles." In spite of Freud's effort, in *Beyond the Pleasure Principle,* to save the evolutionary approach concerning the emergence of the human mind, it has become more and more apparent that the failure to link the repetition compulsion to the problem of human identity has greatly weakened the evolutionary character of psychoanalytic theory. At least one can say that what is still left of the evolutionary genetic elements of psychoanalytic theory is hard to reconcile with the Cartesian implications of many of the structural conceptualizations.

The Effect of the Theoretical Propositions
of Beyond the Pleasure Principle *on Psychoanalytic Theory,*
Especially the Structural Concepts

The far-reaching effects on the inner consistency of psychoanalytic theory caused by Freud's introduction of the death instinct have so often been described that only a few points will be made here that are relevant in the context of this paper. That there is a close link between Freud's formulations regarding the psychic apparatus and its structure and his assumptions of two primary drives—libido and death instinct—has been stressed by Hartmann, Kris, and Loewenstein (1949). These authors do not accept the concept of a death instinct, but postulate instead an aggressive drive which is distinct from the libidinous drives. Since from their viewpoint the decisive conceptual advance represented by Freud's structural formulations is beyond doubt, they seem to me to underestimate the grave difficulties inherent in postulating two primary drives on the one hand, and the emergence of psychic structure on the other.

The change from the position taken in the "Two Principles" to the one postulated in *Beyond the Pleasure Principle* consists of the fact that in the earlier paper Freud saw the human mind evolving as a result of a basic biological principle of *adaptation*—the pleasure principle. Given the special human conditions (lack of innate instinctual adaptive mechanism), the adaptive propensities of the life process had to give rise to the evolution of a human mind. In *Beyond the Pleasure Principle,* however, the question is reversed: not only is the life process not adaptive, but it aims at its own cessation. It becomes, in fact, a mystery how under these conditions life could ever have evolved a functioning human mind. Bibring (1941) has set forth a similar view concerning the consequences of the formulations in *Beyond the Pleasure Principle:* "But as soon as the fundamental view of life was changed and it was no longer regarded as moving in an orbit but along a linear course, its basic trend had also to be differently regarded. The principle of constancy was accordingly replaced by the nirvana principle, the trend of which was to effect a complete leveling down of all difference of potential—to reach zero potential."

The introduction of the theory of the primal instincts (life and death instincts) fundamentally changed the model of the human mind as set down in the "Two Principles." According to Bibring, "the theory of the primal instincts—was founded upon an essentially changed concept of instincts." According to this new concept,

> instinct was not a tension of energy which infringed upon the mental sphere, v hich arose from an organic source and which aimed at removing a state of excitation in the organ from which it originated. . . . It was no longer possible to maintain a strict contrast between a mental apparatus regulated by principles and instincts pressing in upon it from outside, since the instincts themselves now stood revealed as fundamental principles of life.

In this later view of Freud's, the "Two Principles" have been replaced in the following manner: "The Nirvana principle expresses the trend of the death instincts, the pleasure principle represents the claim of the libido (life instincts), while a modification of the latter, the reality principle, represents the influence of the external world" (Freud 1924b, 1926, 1940).

If, according to the position taken in *Beyond the Pleasure Principle,* there is no adaptive principle recognizable in the propensity of the human organism toward a biologically defined equilibrium, it is logical to look for it elsewhere. Modern psychoanalytic theory has done just that, and the result has been the equation of the ego system with adaptive regulation. While for Freud in the "Two Principles" the inherent adaptive propensity of the pleasure principle was supposed to lead to the emergence of the ego from the id, modern psychoanalytic thinking has all but abandoned this hypothesis in favor of an entirely different ego concept. The most radical steps in this redefinition of the principles of mental functioning have been taken by Hartmann. Developing over the years the ideas laid down in his *Ego Psychology and the Problem of Adaptation* (1939), Hartmann (1950, 1951, 1952, 1956a, b), in cooperation with Kris and Loewenstein (1945, 1947, 1949), has introduced into psychoanalytic theory new and radical concepts such as that of the autonomous sphere of the ego, of an undifferentiated phase, of neutralization (in contrast to sublimation). He has established in psychoanalytic theory the formulations regarding the two primary drives—aggression and libido—as a cornerstone of present-day psychoanalytic thinking. It is indeed impossible to overestimate the impact of these writers on modern psychoanalytic theory. Through their work, the conceptual crisis in psychoanalysis, initiated by the new formulations of *Beyond the Pleasure Principle* and their theoretical consequences, appears to have been staved off.

One may characterize the resultant changes as an approach toward a psychoanalytic operationism, although from the viewpoint of operationism (Frenkel-Brunswik 1954, Ellis, A. 1959) the reformulations initiated by Hartmann do not go far enough. It is, however, recognized by representatives of modern operationism that under Hartmann's guidance "psychoanalysis has undergone, during the last few decades, some modification in the direction of including just those problems which it previously neglected" (Frenkel-Brunswik 1954). These are specifically mentioned as the study of processes of perception, learning, and thinking. In this way modern psychoanalytic theory has become more closely integrated with academic psychology and sociology, particularly with learning theory and studies along developmental lines, such as the work of Piaget (1954). From the viewpoint of the clinical psychoanalyst, modern ego psychology has made it possible to deal with many phenomena that could not have been dealt with on the theoretical basis of the "Two Principles," and for which some of the new concepts introduced in *Beyond the Pleasure Principle* might have proven disastrously at odds with the observable facts.

To see the full scope of the conceptual difficulties arising from the formulations in *Beyond the Pleasure Principle*, and the operational usefulness of Hartmann's reformulations, it may be well to quote from the important work of Jacobson (1954, 1964). Jacobson has formulated the difficulties inherent in the assumption of a primary destructive drive with particular clarity. There can be no doubt, according to Jacobson, that the concept of a destructive drive is useful in our understanding of many clinical observations such as psychosomatic diseases or psychotic disorders. But, Jacobson reasons, destructive drives cannot be considered primary qualities of the biological system in the sense of Freud's primary masochism:

There are significant differences between the psychic economy in such pathological, regressive states and the original (infantile) economic and discharge conditions of which they are remindful.

These disorders show convincing evidence of self-destructive, not only psychological but also physiological, processes of which we feel nothing in the normal sleeping and in the healthy, early infantile childhood state. Quite on the contrary, the sleeping state is recuperative and the embryonal state serves the psychophysiological building up of the organism. . . . We face the question whether our psychoeconomical considerations make it advisable at all to adhere to the concepts, not only of primary narcissism, but also of a primary masochism, i.e., of a death instinct. The assumption that those unobservable, inner physiological discharge processes in the infant many also provide for a harmless diffused discharge of small amounts of aggressive energy is certainly untenable. [Jacobson then refers specifically to Freud's position in *Beyond the Pleasure Principle*:] Freud tried to resolve this problem by assuming that in the primary narcissistic-masochistic state the presence of life instinct prevents self-destruction. But how should this occur? We understand that fusions between libido and aggression render the destructive drives harmless. This process, however, develops at a much later infantile period, connected with and probably increasing the neutralization of the drive.

Jacobson thus shows clearly the tremendous complications to which the introduction of destructive drives leads in devising a consistent theoretical model of the human mind. Jacobson finds Hartmann's distinction between the system ego and the self most useful in solving the problem. The concept of the self mirrors, in the words of Jacobson, "the state and the characteristics, the potentialities and abilites, the assets and the limits of our bodily and mental ego: on the one hand, of our appearance, our anatomy and physiology; on the other hand of our conscious and preconscious feelings and thoughts, wishes, impulses and attitudes of our physical and mental activities." Following Hartmann, Jacobson sees in the self, fully equipped with all the defensive potentialities of the ego, the battlefield of libidinous and aggressive drives.

In view of these indubitable merits of the reformulation of psychoanalytic theory stimulated by Hartmann's work, it is not surprising that a number of unresolved problems, stemming ultimately from the issues raised by Freud in *Beyond the Pleasure Principle*, have not received all the attention I feel they deserve. There is without a doubt a rather widespread sense of discontent with the hypothetical model of the human mind as modern psychoanalytic theory has developed it. Hence, attempts at bringing the model up-to-date, such as Colby's (1955) and Rapaport's (1951, 1952), can be regarded as indications that the new, ego-psychological model does not completely fulfill the theoretical needs for which it was designed. Grinker (1957) has perhaps most decisively expressed the difference between the Freudian model and the model of modern psychoanalytic theory when he says that

> it is more concerned with opposition of instinctual drives and reality, resulting in defenses and symptoms, than with cohesive, integrating, organizing, or homeostatic principles. Like the biologists who are attempting to supplement the stability or homeostatic principle with concepts which include growth, learning and evolution, psychoanalysts are now separating a conflict-free sphere of the ego concerned with development and learning using so-called "neutralized energy."

I believe that there is an alternative solution to the difficulties stemming from Freud's new departure in *Beyond the Pleasure Principle*. The reason for suggesting such an alternative solution is my conviction that the reformulations of psychoanalytic theory introduced by Hartmann are such that in spite of their seemingly operational advantages they lead ultimately to the reintroduction of an ego concept that is much closer to the Cartesian *res cogitans* than the Freudian ego concept of the "Two Principles." Hartmann's introduction of the concept of autonomous ego functions, which have to be recognized as independent variables, has been a theoretical step the magnitude and radical nature of which has not yet been completely appreciated. It implies, as Hartmann has always stressed, that very important—indeed, possibly the most important—ego functions cannot be derived from the conflicting forces within the personality, but rather must be viewed as prerequisites for the development of conflict. This position does not regard the pleasure principle as it functions in man (i.e., without "safeguarding" innate adaptive automatisms) as a principle of evolution from which the emergence of a specifically human mind can be derived. On the contrary, Hartmann (1948, 1956) has always consistently emphasized that he does not see how the Freudian notion of a reality principle, evolving out of the conditions under which the pleasure principle is functioning in man, can be maintained. For Hartmann, only a system capable of *anticipating* future gratification could give the pleasure principle any adaptive propensities. Such a system anticipating future gratification can only be, Hartmann stresses, an ego system. Thus, only an independent ego function, existing as a Anlage in the human mind, can introduce an adaptive safeguard into a biological system working under the special dangers characteristic for man.

Since Hartmann and those who share his theoretical views assume that libidinous and aggressive drives, both under the sway of a non-adaptive pleasure principle, are to be considered primary drives, the destructive potentialities of such a system are indeed enormous. They are another danger added to that of loss of instincts (preformed adaptive automatisms) in man (Brun 1951). Even the vastly more autonomous ego of Hartmann is not capable of counteracting the destructive potentialities of the drives, unless one assumes that the dangerous drive energy is transformed into a nondestructive neutralized energy. Thus, the binding of aggressive energy emerges as an important function of the ego. In contrast to the view presented in the "Two Principles," the "weak link" in the hypothetical model of a human mind is no longer the power of the sexual drives, which have escaped the adaptive influence of the reality principle, but the inability of the undeveloped ego system to cope with the aggressive drives.

The infant that is exposed to repeated experiences of disappoint-ment will be in danger of being overwhelmed by the aggressive drives which his weak ego cannot neutralize. The child may be prevented from endowing object and self-representations with lasting libidinous cathexis and from establishing firm boundaries between them. They may remain partially fused and unduly cathected with aggressive forces. This will profoundly affect not only the libidinous development, but also the ego, and, as we shall see, superego formation. If supported by constitutional factors, it may predispose the child for psychotic development. [Jacobson 1964]

As this quotation shows, the libidinous drives are often synergistic with the ego in the task of keeping the aggressive drives in check—a point made by Hartmann (1952) as well: "It is not always advisable to conceive of the relationships between ego and id as if they were just two opposing camps. The object of research is the great variety of the developing ego functions, in their antagonistic but often also synergistic interdependence with the id, and their differential consideration." In contrast, Greenacre (1957) has recently raised the question whether "aggressive" manifestations must always imply destructive or hostile aims. Greenacre makes the important point that "hostile aggression implies a sufficient degree of individuation for there to be a sense of self and the others against whom activity is directed." The significance of the question raised by Greenacre lies in the fact that it points clearly to a correlation between aggression (as destruction) and the process of individuation, i.e., with the problem of identity. This correlation is indeed decisive.

To summarize: the steps that psychoanalytic theory has taken begin with the "evolutionary model" of the "Two Principles." The discovery of phenomena that seemed to indicate a "principle beyond the pleasure principle" led to the introduction of the repetition compulsion. With the repetition compulsion Freud encountered, I believe, the problem of "maintenance of the identity theme." Due to the influences stemming from the Cartesian tradition on Freud (equation of ego and identity), Freud did not see the repetition compulsion as the manifestation of the necessity for man to maintain his identity. Rather, he looked for another drivelike principle beyond the pleasure principle. We know that he saw this new principle in the death instinct. The introduction of the death instinct undermined the inner cohesion of the psychoanalytic theory, as Bibring and others have pointed out. On the other hand, the death instinct or its modification as a primary aggressive drive did seem a necessary assumption in order to apply psychoanalytic principles to numerous clinical phenomena. Thus, while Freud's new formulations in *Beyond the Pleasure Pinciple* opened new avenues for clinical research in psychoanalysis, they left psychoanalysis in the throes of unsolved theoretical dilemmas. On the clinical level, the work of Jacobson illuminates these theoretical difficulties (apparent in her criticism of such concepts as primary narcissism and primary masochism). Hartmann's concept of the autonomous sphere of the ego with all its radical new formulations offered an alternative. But this theoretical alternative was accomplished by abandoning the evolutionary basis of psychoanalysis in favor of what appeared to be a more operational approach. The operational purity of this new approach becomes questionable when it simultaneously reinforces the elements of substantialism inherent already in the Cartesian tradition of psychoanalysis. These theoretical issues have their very tangible counterparts in the concrete problems to which psychoanalytic theory is applied.

Unity of Theory and Practice in Psychoanalysis

The fact that psychoanalytic theory is directly and immediately relevant for its practical application has been stated by Freud as well as by many other psychoanalysts. Practical application refers not only to questions of psychoanalytic technique, but also to the kind of problems psychoanalysis is applied to. Thus, one may say that the introduction of the concept of an aggressive drive has a direct bearing on the development of psychosomatic medicine, and the formulation of the structural concepts has had considerable influence on the study of thought processes (Rapaport 1951, Jacobson 1953), psychosis (Jacobson 1954), early phases of mental development (Jacobson 1953; 1954, Spitz 1945, 1957, Spitz and Wolf 1949) as well as the creative processes (Kris 1952). What, then, we must ask ourselves, are the practical consequences of the theoretical formulations that Hartmann introduced into psychoanalytic theory with the intent to reintroduce an adaptive principle—or, in Hartmann's terminology, a "reality principle in a wider sense,"—in contrast to the reality principle of the "Two Principles," which merely safeguards the function of the pleasure principle?

Since for Hartmann (1939, 1956) this adaptive principle is the ego, it becomes for him a "necessary assumption that the child is born with a certain degree of preadaptiveness. . . . the very system to which we attribute these [perception, memory, mobility, etc.], the ego, is also our organ of learning." I believe that the consequences of these new theories are twofold: they have made it possible, as emphasized already, to include in the realm of psychoanalytic investigation vast new areas of ego-psychological studies, and have made possible also an integration of psychoanalytic psychology into the mainstream of academic psychology.

However, these achievements became possible only by sacrificing an important aspect of psychoanalytic theory as envisaged in the "Two Principles,": its applicability to the dual existence of man as a biological and as a historical being. Freud viewed man as an organism whose unique biological characteristics, namely, the loss of instinctual adaptedness to its *Umwelt,* made survival dependent on its evolution into a being with consciousness, i.e., a being capable of historic existence. This formulation is an understatement: man *must* exist as a historical being, or not exist at all. Historical existence, in the terminology of this paper, is an existence with a self-defined, self-created identity, an existence without "preformed" adaptive identity. Animals, while they undergo evolution, do not, in the human sense, have a historical existence. In other words, Freud's concept of man as the biological entity that must evolve into historical existence, if it is to survive, was a profoundly evolutionary one, making possible a dialectic approach to the evolution of a human mind and of history as a manifestation of this evolution.[11] It opened a way to avoid not only a purely mechanistic understanding of the biological nature of man, but also the dangers of a metaphysical (substantialist) interpretation of man's historical existence. When in *Beyond the Pleasure Principle* Freud made his basic changes of the model of a human mind as conceived in the "Two Principles," the applicability of the new model to man's dual existence as a biological and historical being became clouded, if not lost.

Hartmann's new theories do not restore the evolutionary (dialectical) character of the model of the "Two Principles." In fact, the model as seen by Hartmann introduces an ambiguity into psychoanalytic theory which has never been clearly resolved. The ambiguity consists in the fact that Hartmann's model is open to a mechanistic interpretation (for instance, a drive concept as an energy which must be "neutralized" in order not to destroy the "balance of power" in the intricate system of adaptive and not adaptive principles[12]), as well as to a metaphysical (substantialist) interpretation when it emphasizes the concept of the autonomous ego which is hardly distinguishable from the *ego cogitans* of Descartes.

It is probably this hybrid character of Hartmann's views that has made them useful as "working hypotheses": they reflect a still largely mechanistic thinking applying to physiological and biological phenomena in the natural sciences and a Cartesian approach to ego psychology. This ambiguity has prevented Hartmann's (1950) often emphasized distinction between the concept of the ego as a psychic system and the self as referring to the total personality from breaking the conceptual impasse of modern psychoanalytic theory. The impasse prevents a successful approach to such issues as sublimation, alienation, and a psychoanalytic theory of the self. This is due, I believe, to the impossibility of dealing with these phenomena meaningfully without correlating them to man's need to define or "create" his own identity.

Modern ego theory and the structural concepts permit us to study a life situation as it developed genetically, to analyze the conflicting forces, weigh the impact of autonomous ego elements, etc., contributing to the finally resulting balance or imbalance within the total system of a personality. in short, they offer a form of vector analysis of the personality. We do not attain, however, an understanding of the forces within an individual as manifestation of a process of general evolution—an evolution carrying the inanimate matter through various forms of living entities to man and his dual existence in the world of nature and of history. Having abandoned Freud's basic idea that the conflicts observable within the individual are a psychological representation of a cosmic process of evolution, modern ego theory has limited the role of conflict to that of an intrasystemic source of adaptive imbalance. This limitation of modern ego theory is probably felt by Grinker (1957) when he says: "We need a term to apply to a supra-ordinate process which functions in integrating the sub-systems, including the many identifications that constitute the ego, ego-ideal, and superego, and in organizing behavior into available social roles."

I doubt that what is needed is merely a new term. We have to go back to the dialectic-evolutionary position implied in Freud's concept of the human mind as presented in the "Two Principles." The new principle that Grinker seeks is in fact a very old principle: it is the principle beyond the pleasure principle which Freud set out to define in terms of the repetition compulsion.

The Concept of an Identity Principle

Can one, then, define a "principle" which re-establishes the function assigned by Freud (1911) to the pleasure principle—namely that of a basic biological adaptive principle from which it is possible to derive the evolutionary emergence of a human mind—but which, unlike the pleasure principle, encompasses those phenomena which led Freud (1920) to postulate a repetition compulsion? I propose to describe such a principle as the "identity principle": it is meant to refer to a fundamental biological phenomenon, "more basic, more drive-like than the pleasure principle" (Freud 1920). Such a principle—if I understand his intentions correctly—probably comes close to what Hartmann implied when he spoke of a "reality principle in a wider sense which would be the prerequisite for the functioning of a pleasure principle."

I shall confine myself to listing some basic characteristics of the phenomena of identity establishment and maintenance as they have appeared in the course of the preceding discussion. Identity maintenance as such is not confined to the human personality. It was repeatedly emphasized that the capacity to maintain or hold on to an identity is a fundamental characteristic of all living organisms, one to which we refer when we think of "self-preservation" and "self-reproduction." I spoke of "change arrested" to describe this character of living organisms. Thus, identity establishment and maintenance must be considered basic biological principles—principles defining the concept of living matter itself. As soon as a living organism ceases to maintain its identity we speak of its decay—which describes its return to the laws of physical and chemical interactions. The fundamental differences between the natural laws prevailing within the biological realm and those which affect inanimate processes are decisively defined by Schroedinger (1945) from the viewpoint of modern physics.

The orderliness in the unfolding of life springs from a different source [than . . . the order of exact physical law coming forth from atomic and molecular disorder]. It appears that there are two different "mechanisms" by which orderly events can be produced: the "statistical mechanism" which produces "order from disorder" and the new one, producing "order from order". . . . We cannot expect that the "laws of physics" derived from [the order-from-

disorder principle] suffice . . . to explain the behavior of living
matter, whose most striking features are visibly based . . . on the
"order-from-order." principle. . . . We must be prepared to find a
new type of physical law prevailing in it.

This new physical principle is for Schroedinger "nothing else but the
principle of quantum physics," through which, according to Schroedinger, "living matter evades the decay to [thermodynamical]
equilibrium."[13] While I cannot follow Schroedinger into the intricacies
of quantum theory and its application to biological processes, his
emphasis on a different physical principle prevailing in the realm of
living organisms, setting them apart from the order of inanimate events
in nature, appears to justify the introduction of the concept of the
"identity principle." Insofar as this principle attempts to apprehend
both the biological as well as the psychological phenomenon of
identity in change, it goes beyond the facts of physics and biology, but
it does not seem to contradict modern thought in these fields.

  Before the application of quantum theory to biology, the concept of
homeostasis emphasized the same idea that Schroedinger stresses,
namely that in the living organism the natural laws of physics and
chemistry function in a unique way, enabling the living organism to
"evade decay" (Schroedinger) and thus making possible a living
continuity or an identity in change. Homeostasis, while describing one
aspect of the maintenance of biological identity, does not, however,
describe the full range of the "identity principle." This insight has been
a contribution of psychoanalytic observation. While Freud's law of
constancy, on which his concept of the pleasure principle was based,
seemed at first to imply that a homeostatic principle was the only
adaptive principle effective in man as a living organism, the
observations presented in *Beyond the Pleasure Principle* proved this
assumption untenable.

  Recent contributions have made the subordination of homeostasis
under the necessity of maintenance of identity even more evident.
Greenacre (1958a) has emphasized that identity is "dependent on the
intrinsic body-organizational structure." From certain observations
one may arrive at the conclusion that the homeostatic equilibrium will
prevail only as long as it is compatible with the intrinsic body-
organizational structure defining biological identity. The studies of

Spitz (1945) of infants suffering from hospitalism would suggest such interpretation. Since these children did not suffer from any observable lack of physical care, it is hard to understand why their homeostatic equilibrium was so very precarious as Spitz's observation of their high death rate would suggest. Spitz attributes the retardation as well as the early death of many of these children to the emotional climate, the lack of mothering from which these children suffered. In the light of the importance of the mother-infant relation in terms of establishing and maintaining the infant's identity theme, the idea that infants may die when this reinforcement (Greenacre 1958a) of their identity theme is lacking seems consistent with the propositions presented previously.

The identity principle sets the conditions for the kinds of homeostatic processes realized within the organisms: the latter must vary greatly throughout animate nature, and those that prevail in a given organism prevail only as long as they are compatible with the organism's identity. This compatibility is secured in the animals largely by those preformed, innate automatisms which we call instincts. The instincts are the safeguards of the animal's identity, but they protect the individual animal's survival to a lesser degree. When the maintenance of the animal's identity becomes incompabible with the satisfaction of his needs, even the animal is often more likely to die than to "give up" its identity. Animals in captivity seem often rather to die from starvation than to adapt to a change in the pattern of their identity.

In man, the establishment and maintenance of identity is different from the animal's insofar as man's identity is not guaranteed by instinctual, innate automatisms. It is, however, not different in commanding absolute priority over any other need. Thus, while not a drive, the identity principle does act more like one than the pleasure principle which it is quite capable of suspending: it is absolutely compelling, while the drives—even hunger—are only relatively compelling. But it would not seem appropriate to call this fundamental biological principle a drive. Identity, indeed, is the prerequisite for the possibility of any drive, because the concept of a drive presupposes a living organized continuity (Freud 1915a). Drives as well as ego functions appear to be functions (in the mathematical-logical sense) of the identity principle.

Whether a drive will appear as aggressive or libidinous might reflect the means through which the individual is dealing with his task of identity maintenance, which in turn depends on his attained phase of individuation. The more the personality has retained a symbiotic, fusion-type individuation, the more likely are the drive manifestations to show aggressive-destructive features: the indifference toward boundaries of organismic separateness—so characteristic for the aggressive-destructive drives—is also an inherent quality of all archaic-symbiotic stages of individuation. Thus, the postulation of "an" aggressive drive, or a death instinct, may not be necessary in order to explain aggressive-destructive phenomena such as are prevalent in sadomasochism.

Aside from the theoretical difficulties inherent in the task of deriving sadism and masochism from some primary biological principle (Bonaparte 1952), the suggested approach is also in accordance with modern scientific thought: thus Nils Bohr (1948) has suggested that the concept of "complementarity" may be useful not only in modern physics, but in biology, sociology, and psychology as well. According to Bohr, "the conditions for analysis and synthesis [in psychology] exhibit a striking analogy with the situation in atomic physics, in that seemingly incompatible concepts pertain to mutually exclusive situations characterized by a different drawing of the line between subject and object." Whether "libidinous" and "aggressive" drives could, in this way, be functions of the state of differentiation between subject and object remains at least a conceptual possibility.

If the identity principle is not a drive, it is nevertheless not an ego function, but a biological organizational principle, the true nature of which we do not yet completely understand. In order to understand it, we would have to know what it is that makes possible the relative "arrest in change" which is tantamount to living. We would have to know the reason that arrangements of molecules, at some point, behave like living substance, instead of chemical materials (Schroedinger 1945). The identity principle, representing a general biological principle, includes perhaps even the concept of preadaptedness that Hartmann (1939, 1956) stresses so often as a necessary assumption concerning the living substance. But a question must be raised at this point: if the drives are described as functions of the identity principle, how can identity in man be correlated to the sexual drive? This has been claimed in the previous parts of this paper; but how can this proposition be reconciled with the emphasis on the priority of the identity principle over the pleasure principle, and the subordination of both drives and ego under the identity principle?

The answer, I believe, lies in the fact that while we cannot, strictly speaking, refer to a drive before there is a functioning, continuous, organizational identity, there is an innate body responsiveness, a capacity, probably more developed in the human infant than in animals, to respond to contact with another person with a specific kind of somatic excitation which is not a drive, because it has no direction, but which is the innate prerequisite for the later development of a drive. This responsiveness to body contact—so convincingly described by Mahler and her coworkers (1952, 1958, 1953, 1955)—is probably heightened by the other person's emotional interest in provoking this particular somatic excitation, i.e., by what we may call another person's seductive intent. We might hesitate to use the word seduction in order not to conjure up old ghosts of sexual seduction theory, but if we take the concept of seduction in a broader sense, it implies the kindling of desires by one person in another one, desires which, without this kindling effort, would perhaps never, or at least not in this form, have arisen in the object of stimulation. Thus, in this sense, one may say that infants—like those victims of hospitalism described by Spitz (1945)—can die, or not develop, because nobody has taken the interest to seduce them to live. This responsiveness we may call sexual because it forms the matrix of later sexual development. In man it is used to imprint an identity upon the human infant, which, according to the thesis of this paper, has no innate preformed identity comparable to that of the animals. Again we must define with greater clarity what is meant by these propositions.

There is, of course, an innate, intrinsic body-organizational structure in man without which he never could acquire an identity (Greenacre 1958a). But while the animals have an innate actual identity—this is completely true probably only for the lower animals— man has only an innate potential identity, in fact, an almost infinite range of potential identities. This range, while freeing man from the rigidity and relatively poor adaptability of the animal, has its peculiar dangers which are specific to man. When Greenacre says that "only young children, philosophers, artists, and certain sick individuals concern themselves constantly with questions of their own identity," she puts her finger on a selected group of humanity that has always been most perceptive to the fundamentals of the "condition of man." In the course of this paper some of the dangers arising from man's range of potential identities have been described. We will here only repeat that these dangers are intimately related to the fact that the actualization of the one identity—the identity theme—among the infinite potentialities occurs under the irreversible impact of the mother's use of the somatic responsiveness of the human infant. Once the identity theme becomes actualized, we recognize in it an irreversible principle of evolution taking hold in the life of the individual, a principle representing the phenomenon of life itself, and thus linking man with his evolutionary past. But this principle beyond the pleasure principle is at the same time transforming the individual life into an individual existence, because, through interactions between the identity theme and the now emerging drives and the ego interests, the variations of the theme of identity become manifest as creative activities leading to social roles—and thus the biological infant gives birth to historical man. Thus, the concept of an identity principle would permit us to integrate the subsystems of id and ego, and may very well lead us to a new understanding of ego ideal and superego. By reintroducing an evolutionary principle into psychoanalytic thought, the identity principle can make us understand the process by which, from inherent necessity, the biological equipment of man forces him to become the creator of a manmade world within the natural world. It is, however, ultimately not a new principle or even a new term. It is the repetition compulsion, the "beyond the pleasure principle," seen in a different perspective.

There may accrue other theoretical gains from this reapproachment to the problems raised by Freud in *Beyond the Pleasure Principle*, aside from bridging the artificial gap between the so-called biological versus the so-called cultural approach in psychoanalysis. We may, for instance, be able to distinguish the concept of the self from that of the total personality. It may recommend itself to define the self as the total potential range of all possible variations of the individual's identity which are compatible with his identity theme. (Similar ideas concerning the self are implied in Eissler's paper [1953].) Around the criteria of compatible and incompatible variations may develop an approach to a psychoanalytic theory of the meaning of morality. It does not serve any purpose, however, merely to list further problems to which the propositions developed in this paper may be applied without elaborating them.

There is, however, one characteristically human phenomenon which appears as a manifestation of the identity principle in man. I believe that this is the phenomenon of work, as implied in the concept of man as *homo faber*. Work in man is different from what has been called work in animals, because it is experienced as a compelling need, the absence of which we consider pathological (Greenson 1953), a need without any direct relatedness to the problem of physical survival. Work, in the sense in which we use it here, refers not to useful work as contrasted to leisure. Human work is an inner need for meaningful activity, which may consist of "useless" painting as much as "useful" inventing of a new machine. Just as nonprocreative sexuality in man assumes a special significance that it does not have in the animal, serving the establishment of the primary identity theme in man, work, in man, serves the maintenance of the individual's identity theme: through it most of the possible variations of the identity theme find their expression. Work in the animals seems closely related to self-preservation, as sexuality in the animals is related to procreation. The maintenance of man's identity theme through the phenomenon of work *not* directly related to survival leads to the creation of the "work world" in man: thus, we arrive at the conclusion that "culture" is a manifestation of the identity principle. A biological system like that of man, devoid of instinctual adaptedness and therefore devoid of innate identity, can only exist by safeguarding its identity in the creative historical existence which becomes visible in the "work" of culture. It has become customary to emphasize that outside a cultural and social context, an individual cannot acquire and maintain an identity. This should not be denied, but the relationship is a reciprocal one: there cannot be culture unless there is this particular living being whose fundamental biological imbalance can only be stabilized through a never-ending process of work guaranteeing identity reinforcement, identity maintenance, and identity recreation.

Erikson (1950a) has quoted Freud as saying that the capacity to love and to work constituted the essence of what is specifically human in man. This paper was intended as a variation on this Freudian theme.

NOTES

1. The interrelatedness of identity and change is also expressed through the concept of causality as "uniformity of sequence of phenomena" (Lenzen 1954). Meyerson (1908) has in fact defined causality as "Identity which is expressed by the equality of cause and effect." The metaphysical dimensions of this problem have been stated by Heidegger (1957).

2. I am indebted to two relatively recent contributions to the history of Western philosophic-scientific tradition by Frondizi (1953) and R. W. Meyer (1948). A nonspecialist, but concise treatment of these problems and their impact on modern scientific ideas is given by Drucker (1957). A paper by Toomey (1959), which deals with the philosophical implications of psychoanalytic conceptualizations, came to my attention after the termination of this paper.

3. The German word *Umwelt* conveys an idea of confluence of subject (inside) and object (outside). Loewald's (1951) differentiation between "paternal" and "maternal" reality experience might correspond to the distinction between "external" reality and *Umwelt*.

4. Angyal's ideas on man's tendency "to become an organic part of something that he conceives to be greater than himself" (1956) emphasize, to some extent, the same phenomena described here, although his conceptual outlook differs in many other respects.

5. The difficulties in defining the concept of identity, which Erikson (1956) enumerates, can be attributed to the as yet unsolved task of describing the process of individuation in non-Cartesian concepts.

6. The use of this term for certain phenomena of human growth and development has been suggested not only by Grinker (1957) but by Konrad Lorenz (1935) himself when he says about the "imprinting" observed in birds: "It has no equal in the psychology of any other animal, least of all a mammal. However, I would like to point out certain analogies in human psychology, which appear in the form of pathological fixation on the object of an instinct." After I wrote this paper, I became aware of Murphy's (1958) reference to the concept of imprinting in the context of human psychological development. I also regret that the important contribution of Bowlby (1958) could not be considered since it became available only after this paper had been written. This also applies to the novel and significant use of ethological concepts in Schur's revision of a theory of anxiety (1958).

7. Cf. Marion Milner's (1957) concept of creating a "frame" for anxiety-producing activities: "the frame marks off an area within which what is perceived has to be taken symbolically, while what is outside the frame is taken literally. Symbolic of what? We certainly assume that it is symbolic of

the feelings and ideas of whoever determined the pattern or form within the frame. We assume that it makes sense, for instance we assume that people on the stage are not just there by accident." See also Bergler (1951).

8. The concept of symbiosis has a certain vagueness as it is used in psychoanalytic writing. It may refer to a totally undifferentiated state of real fusion between infant and mother, or it may describe a perception of oneself in terms of being "inseparable" from another one from whom one is differentiated.. Since I have taken the position that human identity can be defined only in symbiotic terms, symbiosis has both a "normal" as well as a "pathological" phenomenology. A study of phases of symbiotic development might be an important supplement to the ontogenetic phases of psychosexual development. Concerning the conflict between "separateness" and "fusion," see also Kramer (1955).

9. More recently, however, Rapaport (1951b), commenting on a paper by Claparede on the experience of me-ness, no longer seems to equate the me-ness experience with ego functions.

10. Cf. Goethe's remark: "Die Tiere werden durch ihre Organe belehrt, Der Mensch belehrt die Organe [Animals are instructed by their organs, Man instructs his organs]" (1830).

11. An evolutionary dialectic, in the precise formulation of J. A. Schumpeter (1954) perceives of "reality, as we know it from experience . . . as an evolutionary *process* evolving from inherent necessity, instead of being a set of phenomena that seek a definite state or level, so that an extraneous factor—or at least a distinct factor—is necessary in order to move them to another state or level as the analogy to Newtonian mechanics suggests."

12. Greenacre's (1957) objections to the term and concept of neutralization seem to be based on the mechanistic connotations of this metaphor. Concerning neutralization and sublimation, see Kris (1955).

13. Szasz (1952) has based his objections to the concept of a "death instinct" very much on its incompatibility with modern physics and biology. This argument is probably scientifically valid, but I doubt that it comes to grips with the phenomena underlying Freud's introduction of the "death instinct": i.e., the unique character of identity maintenance in man. Schroedinger's contribution (1958) to the problems considered here appeared after this paper was completed.

Part II

Views of Human Identity

INTRODUCTION

While human identity involves the capacity to remain the same in the midst of change, it is not immediately self-evident what changes and what remains the same. To paraphrase John Locke, we do not hesitate to believe that an individual whom we know as an adult, or in old age, is the same who at one time was a newborn child. What does this assumption of sameness refer to? On the other hand, if this person, in old age, suffers from senile dementia, when we know him to have been a knowledgeable and brilliant individual during his adult life, we might state that he or she is no longer the "same person." It is, therefore, not surprising that different observers of the human condition arrive at diametrically opposed viewpoints concerning the essence both of change and of sameness of individuals. In the following essays I deal with different approaches to the phenomenon of sameness in the midst of change. In selecting authors who have contributed important studies aimed at developing a consistent theory of sameness and change in the context of human lives, it seems impossible to avoid confronting three central manifestations of sameness-within-change: These I have referred to as self-transformation, self objectivation, and metamorphosis.

Self-transformation is a process in time: individuals are changing, for instance, while undergoing an educational experience. Self-transformation refers to fundamental changes not only in behavior, but in perception of reality. It thus describes an aspect of the historical process. The concept of development in history, for instance, from an agrarian civilization to a scientific-technological one, can be described as self-transformation. Self-objectivation refers to the acquisition of a definable role, such as that of farmer, soldier, or priest, and to the ascription to such social roles of the function of assuring the individual's sameness in a changing world. Metamorphosis describes the extreme possibility of a person's being transformed into somebody or something that is incompatible with the idea of sameness: in its most extreme form, it envisages the possibility of a human being changing into an animal as in Franz Kafka's story of that title, or into an inanimate thing. The term is, however, also used in a less radical way: Doctor Faustus, for instance, changes from an aging, unworldly scholar into a youthful and reckless seducer under the power of Mephistopheles.

The thesis presented in the following essays claims that only a concept of human identity—of sameness in the midst of change— which makes it possible to account for the phenomena of self-transformation, self-objectivation and metamorphosis as potentialities coexisting in every individual can reflect the inner, the social and the historical realities of being human. Such a concept does not only function as the keystone on which a psychoanalytic psychology would have to rest. It would seem equally essential for other sciences dealing with any aspects of the human condition, such as social science and history. The following essays can, therefore, be described as dealing with the interface of psychoanalysis and those sciences that cannot escape confronting the dilemma of human identity.

Chapter 3

JOHN LOCKE
ON PERSONAL IDENTITY

Having devoted a great deal of thought to problems pertaining to the nature of human identity, of self and related issues, I was surprised to discover just recently that one of the most searching investigations of these themes had been published in 1694 in the second edition of Locke's *Essay Concerning Human Understanding.* Locke added to the second edition of his work a chapter (chapter 27), entitled "Of Identity and Diversity," whose appearance constituted an event in the history of European philosophy. It led to an intellectual controversy beginning in Locke's lifetime, continuing, however, long after his death in 1704, and offering even today a challenge to philosophical debate. Among those who participated in this philosophical and also theological confrontation were the highest intellects of the era, men such as Berkeley, Hume, Leibniz, and Bishop Joseph Butler (1692-1752), whose *Dissertation of Personal Identity* is still quoted as the most decisive criticism of Locke's views. But in spite of all the questioning that Locke's approach to the problem of personal identity has provoked, A. Flew, whose critical essay appeared in 1951, praises him for his achievement in uncovering the appalling difficulties in the task he had set himself and adds: "His insights are the more remarkable since he had to struggle for them through a rank growth of baffling terms—'immaterial substances,' 'Selves,' 'thinking substances,' 'rational souls'."

What are the "appalling difficulties" concerning personal identity which Flew credits Locke with uncovering? Essentially, the problem is, how can the concept of sameness—which is, after all, what "identical" means—be applied to a person who is, obviously, constantly changing from birth to old age, physically, mentally, and behaviorally? In spite of this obvious fact we apply, with little doubt, the characterization of sameness to people we have seen growing up from infancy to adulthood. We are, in addition, even more convinced that we, ourselves, are the same person in spite of all the changes we have lived through since the beginning of our lives. How this sameness in the midst of change is possible, objectively as well as subjectively, is the central problem that Locke attempts to solve in his *Essay*, and he surprises us with his psychological, indeed, psychiatric, observations.

This problem is, in my view, still central for any theory of the personality such as psychoanalysis offers. It is also still unresolved, even though psychoanalytic literature, rather grudgingly, has added "identity problems" to its vocabulary. Some psychoanalysts, indeed, still hesitate to consider the term "identity" as a bona fide psychoanalytic concept. The introduction of this concept is largely due to Erikson's pioneering work, and since, in Erikson's usage, identity predominantly, though not exclusively, refers to a person's perception of himself through the eyes of others within a social context, it may appear to be defining an individual's social role, and therefore not to be germane to psychoanalytic theory. The remarkable fact that the problem of personal identity was not a theme in Freud's work creates in the minds of many psychoanalysts an added suspicion that the concept may be used to introduce surreptitiously "culturalist" or "existentialist" ideology into the legacy of Freud. It is true that, as it is used today, the concept of identity has an intangible quality about it, especially since it has invaded the popular language, where it refers to the manifold manifestations of the malaise of our times, retaining a vagueness that obscures rather than clarifies the nature of the problems it is supposed to describe. For all these reasons I feel that an examination of Locke's presentation of the problem of personal identity may clarify the basic questions that must be dealt with, whenever we are confronting, as psychoanalysts do, the mystery concerning "the nature of the bond which unites a person"—to use Flew's paraphrase of Hume (see Flew 1951, p. 63).

Locke opens his inquiry into identity and diversity as follows:

Another occasion the mind often takes of comparing, is the very being of things, when considering *anything existing at any determined time and place*, we compare it with *itself existing at another time*, and thereon form the ideas[1] of *identity* and *diversity*. When we see anything to be in any place in any instant of time, we are sure (be it what it will) that it is that very thing, and not another which at the same time exists in another place, how like or indistinguishable soever it may be in all other respects: and in this consists *identity*, when the ideas it is attributed to vary not at all from what they were that moment wherein we consider their former existence, and to which we compare the present. . . . When therefore we demand whether anything be the *same* or no, it refers always to something that existed such a time in such a place, which it was certain, at that instant, was the same with itself, and no other. . . . That, therefore, that had one beginning, is the same thing; and that which had a different beginning in time and place from that, is not the same, but divers. That which has made the difficulty about this relation has been the little time and attention used in having precise notions of the things to which it is attributed.[2]

For Locke, identity and diversity mean different things according to which category of being they are applied to, i.e., their definition always implies ontological problems. The highest category of being is for Locke the being of God: "*God* is without beginning, eternal, unalterable, and everywhere, and therefore concerning his identity there can be no doubt." Locke does not use terms like "categories of being," but speaks of "substances," though it is clear in the context that he uses "substance" in an ontological sense. He can, therefore, designate God as a substance, and contrast his category of being with "Finite Intelligences" and "Bodies," the latter being synonymous with "[inanimate] matter." The problematic category of being or "substance" is the one Locke defines as "Finite Intelligences" or "Finite Spirits." Locke describes them as "having had each its determinate time and place of beginning to exist, the relation to that time and place will always determine to each of them its identity, as long as it exists."

This broad definition of "Finite Spirits" includes all "living creatures," plants, animals, men and persons.

It is Locke's thesis that identity and diversity mean something different, according to the "substance" or category of being to which they are applied. While the differentiation of plants and animals is customary, Locke's distinction of "man" from "person" requires comment. For Locke, the terms "man" or "men" refer exclusively to the biological or animal characteristics of human beings, while "person" applies to the conscious, thinking and moral aspects of being human. Locke's distinction of three "substances"—God, living creatures and inanimate matter—and his attempt to deal with each of them as separate categories of being bring into focus the fact that the problem of personal identity could only become a philosophical and psychological issue when it was no longer considered self-evident that what constituted a person was divine origin—man's endowment with an immortal soul from which derived his unalterable identity. Personal identity without the postulation of a soul—or a *res cogitans* or a monad—became a specific problem of empirical philosophy and scientific psychology, and Locke was only too keenly aware how immense a problem it turned out to be.

The issue concerning the identity of living creatures as contrasted with "particles of matter" is presented by Locke as follows:

In the state of living creatures, their identity depends not on a mass of the same particles, but on something else. For in them the variation of great parcels of matter alters not their identity: an oak growing from a plant into a great tree, and then lopped, is still the same oak; and a colt grown up to a horse, sometimes fat, sometimes lean, is all the while the same horse: though, in both these cases there may be manifest change of the parts; so that truly they are not either of them the same masses of matter, though they be truly one of them the same oak, and the other the same horse. The reason whereof is, that, in these two cases—a *mass of matter* and a *living body*—identity is not applied to the same thing.

A living body, be it a plant, an animal or, in Locke's terminology, "man," is characterized by having "an organization of parts in one coherent body, partaking of one common life. . . . For this organization, being at any one instant in any one collection of matter, is in that particular concrete distinguished from all other, and *is* that individual life. . . . it has that identity which makes the same plant (p. 443) [Locke applied the same argument to animal and "man"] . . . during all the time that they exist united in that continued organization." These statements, were, however, a challenge to an older and hallowed tradition which Locke has in mind in what follows:

> He that shall place the identity of man in anything else, but, like that of other animals, in one fitly organized body, taken in any one instant, and from thence continued, under one organization of life, in several successively fleeting particles of matter united to it, will find it hard to make an embryo, one of years, mad and sober, the *same* man. . . . If the identity of *soul alone* makes the same *man*; and there be nothing in the nature of matter why the same individual spirit may not be united to different bodies, it will be possible that . . . men, living in distant ages, and of different tempers, may have been the same man: which way of speaking must be from a very strange use of the word man, applied to an idea out of which body and shape are excluded.

For Locke "it is not the idea of a thinking and rational being alone that makes the idea of a man in most people's sense: but of a body, so and so shaped, joined to it: and if that be the idea of a man, the same successive body not shifted all at once, must, as well as the same immaterial spirit, go to the making of the same man."

Having thus defined the meaning of identity with regard to inanimate matter, living organisms such as plants and animals, and man in terms of "one fitly organized body," Locke is now ready to approach the problem of personal identity. It is with regard to this problem that, in the words of Locke's editor, Fraser, "the perplexities arise which Locke meets in this chapter." He starts with a definition of the problem:

> To find wherein personal identity consists, we must consider what person stands for; which, I think, is a thinking intelligent being, that has reason and reflection, and can consider itself as itself, the same thinking thing, in different times and places; which it does

only by that consciousness which is inseparable from thinking, and, so it seems to me, essential to it: it being impossible for anyone to perceive without *perceiving* that he does perceive. When we see, hear, smell, taste, feel, meditate, or will anything, we know that we do so. Thus it is always as to our present sensations and perceptions: and by this everyone is to himself that which he calls *self*:—it not being considered in this case, whether the same self be continued in the same or divers substances. For, since consciousness always accompanies thinking, and it is that which makes everybody to be what he calls self, and thereby distinguishes himself from all other thinking things, in this alone consists personal identity, i.e., the sameness of a rational being: and as far as this consciousness can be extended backwards to any past action or thought, so far reaches the identity of that person; it is the same self now it was then; and it is by the same self with this present one that now reflects on it, that that action was done.

This definition of personal identity as consciousness of one's present and past perceptions and thought processes contradicts, however, many facts of psychological observation. Locke is very much aware of this, as is evident from the following continuation of the above quotation:

But it is further inquired, whether it be the same identical substance. This few would think they had reason to doubt of, if these perceptions, with their consciousness, always remained present in the mind, whereby the same thinking thing would be always consciously present, and, as would be thought, evidently the same to itself. But that which seems to make the difficulty is this, that this consciousness being interrupted always by forgetfulness, there being no moment of our lives wherein we have the whole train of all our past actions before our eyes in one view, but even the best memories losing sight of one part whilst they are viewing another; and we sometimes, and that the greatest part of our lives, not reflecting on our past selves, being intent on our present thought, and in sound sleep having no thoughts at all, or at least none with that consciousness which remarks our waking thoughts,—I say, in all these cases, our consciousness being interrupted, and we losing the sight of our past selves, doubts are raised whether we are the same thinking thing, i.e., the same *substance* or no. Which, however reasonable or unreasonable, concerns not *personal* identity at all. The question being what makes the same person: and not whether it be the same identical substance, which always thinks in the same person, which, in this case, matters not at all: different substances, by the same consciousness (where they do partake in it) being united into one person, as well as different bodies by the same life are united into one animal, whose identity is preserved in that change of substances by the unity of one continued life. For, it being the same consciousness that makes a man be himself to himself, personal identity depends on that only, whether it be annexed solely to one individual substance, or can be continued in a succession of several substances. For as far as any intelligent being *can* repeat the idea of any past action with the same consciousness it had of it at first, and with the same consciousness it has of any present action; so far it is the same personal self. For it is by the consciousness it has of its present thoughts and actions, that it is *self to itself* now, and so will be the same self, as far as the same consciousness can extend to actions past or to come.[3]

It does not seem to me too far-fetched, when reading a formulation like "different substances, by the same consciousness . . . being united into one person" to be reminded of Freud's description of "the mental apparatus as a compound instrument, to the components of which we will give the name of 'agencies'; or (for the sake of greater clarity) 'systems.'" That these various systems ("substances" for Locke) were to be understood as "being united into one person" was taken for granted by Freud, just as it is taken for granted by modern ego psychology that the "tripartite model" of the personality presupposes the unity of the person. In view of this seeming similarity between Locke's ideas and the concept of psychoanalytic theory, it is all the more noteworthy that these shared assumptions did not lead to similar types of questions: questions concerning "the nature of the bond which unites a person." Though one may argue that Freud implicitly touches in some of his statements on the problem of personal identity—such as in the later to be quoted remarks concerning "multiple personalities"—

it was never a central issue for him, nor did it become a subject of investigation until rather late in the development of psychoanalysis. Why this is so, would seem to be a question meriting serious reflection, especially in view of the history of the problem of identity. It seems to be due to a position, never precisely formulated, which accepts the "unity of the person" as a self-evident phenomenon. This appears to be so, in spite of the perception of human development as a process of transformations from birth to adulthood, implying shifting body images, thought patterns and forms of relatedness to others.

How an individual, undergoing these transformations, can still remain the same would indeed appear to be a more fundamental issue to psychoanalytic theory than it was in Locke's era. It was Bishop Joseph Butler in his *Dissertation of Personal Identity* who made the point against Locke's theory that represents most tellingly the theological objection of his era: "One should think it self-evident that consciousness *presupposes*, and cannot *constitute* personal identity." To this classical critique Fraser makes the comment that Locke "views [personal] identity as manifested in consciousness, and not in the mystery of its ultimate constitution, the *conscious manifestation* concealing rather than *revealing* the substance on which they depend" (p. 468).

Locke's thinking was certainly far less removed from theology than modern psychoanalysis is. Why is it then that Locke searched for an answer to what may *constitute* personal identity, while psychoanalytic thinking seems almost to "presuppose its existence"? Locke's theory that personal identity is constituted by consciousness and memory did, indeed, lead to "strange perplexities," in Butler's words. Could it be that the discoveries of psychoanalysis were already unsettling enough in their implications concerning human existence to justify the postponement of yet another blow to man's narcissism? Locke himself admits that his assumptions lead to many "strange suppositions," however pardonable "in the dark concerning these matters." Among them are the questions whether one individual can have two or more identities, and whether several persons, who may have lived "at different times, may have been the same person." Strange as such possibilities may sound, they clearly refer to phenomena not unfamiliar to the psychiatrist, as is obvious in the following question raised by Locke:

Suppose I wholly lose the memory of some parts of my life, beyond a possibility of retrieving them, so that perhaps I shall never be conscious of them again; yet am I not the same person that did those actions, had those thoughts that I once was conscious of, though I have now forgot them? To which I answer, that we must take notice what the word *I* is applied to; which, in this case, is the *man* only. And the same man being presumed to be the same person, I is easily here to stand also for the same person. But if it be possible for the same man to have distinct incommunicable consciousness at different times, it is past doubt the same man would at different times make different persons; which, we see, is the sense of mankind in the solemnest declaration of their opinions, human laws not punishing the mad man for the sober man's actions, nor the sober man for what the mad man did—thereby making them two persons: which is somewhat explained by our way of speaking in English when we say such an one is "not himself" or is "beside himself" in which phrases it is insinuated, as if those who now, or at least first used them, thought that self was changed; the self-same person was no longer in that man.

What Locke implies here is nothing less than the possibility that personal identity—the capacity to remain the same in the midst of constant change—has its limits. It may, in fact, not exist at all in the strictest sense. Rather, the individual may harbor in himself the potential for more than one person. Freud came very close to a similar view, though he only hinted at such phenomena. I am referring to Freud's remarks in *The Ego and the Id*, made in the context of his discussion of the ego's object-identifications:

If they obtain the upper hand and become too numerous, unduly powerful and incompatible with one another . . . . it may come to a disruption of the ego in consequence of the different identifications becoming cut off from one another by resistances; perhaps the secret of the cases of what is described as "multiple personalities" is that different identifications seize hold of consciousness in turn. Even when things don't go so far as this,

there remains the question of conflicts between various identifications into which the ego comes apart, conflicts which cannot after
all be described as entirely pathological.

Perhaps this is the closest that Freud came to raising the problem of
personal identity—in the sense of raising the question of "the nature of
the bond which unites a person." It is obvious that phenomena like
"multiple personalities" raise this issue like few others.[4]
   For Freud, it was the concept of object-identifications that offered
the clue to individual development. It finally led to one of Freud's most
sweeping, but also most controversial hypotheses concerning the
specifically human quality of human ontogenesis. In attemtping to
answer the question of how to account for the "higher side of man,"
manifesting itself by the acquisition of religion, morality and a social
sense, Freud postulated the phylogenetic acquisition of guilt and love
as a derivative of the conflicts surrounding the patricide of the brothers
within the primal horde. Unconscious memories of these conflicts are
acquired by the id, and preserved for all later generations by heredity.
"Thus, in the id . . . are harbored residues of the existence of countless
egos: and, when the ego forms its superego out of the id, it may perhaps
only be reviving shapes of former egos and be bringing them to
resurrection" (*The Ego and the Id*). Through this highly imaginative
hypothesis, based on a Lamarckian view of heredity of acquired
characteristics, Freud was able to see the core of the individual—his or
her personal identity—as being constituted of unconscious memories
of his "own personal prehistory" blended with inherited unconscious
memories of preceding generations.
   The introduction of the controversial phylogenetic thesis would
establish the individual's capacity to remain the same in the midst of
change. It would also permit an understanding of such phenomena as
"multiple personalities," based on "residues of countless egos," leading
to the occasional "resurrection of former egos." It thus appears that
Freud's reliance on unconscious memories, personal as well as
inherited ones, is not so far removed from Locke's bold effort to
constitute personal identity on the basis of memory. Locke, too,
envisages the possibility that consciousness may unite existences and
actions very remote in time into the same person:

I once met with one, who was persuaded his had been the *soul* of Socrates (how reasonable I will not dispute; this I know, that in the post he filled, which was no inconsiderable one, he passed for a very rational man. . . .)—would anyone say, that he, being not conscious of any of Socrates actions or thought, could be the same *person* with Socrates? . . . But though the same immaterial substance or soul does not alone, whereever it be, and in whatsoever state, make the same *man*; yet it is plain, consciousness, as far as ever it can be extended—should it be to ages past—unites existences and actions very remote in time into the same *person*, as well as it does the existences and actions of the immediately preceding moment: so that whatever has the consciousness of present and past actions, is the same person to whom they both belong. . . . For as to this point of being the same self, it matters not whether this present self be made up of the same or other substances—I being as much concerned, and as justly accountable for any action that was done a thousand years since, appropriated now by this self-consciousness, as I am for what I did the last moment.

That both Locke and Freud derive a sense of accountability for an individual's action from deeds committed prior to their biological existence seems a remarkable confluence of their thoughts, even though Locke bases his argument upon the possibility of extension of consciousness beyond the lifespan of an individual, while Freud postulates a hereditary sense of guilt originating with prehistoric man. Locke specifically raises the question whether it could happen that "one intellectual substance . . . . have represented to it, as done by itself, what it never did, and was perhaps done by another agent." He concludes that "such a representation may not possibly be without reality of matter of fact, as well as several representations in dreams are, which yet whilst dreaming we take for true." Having stated this possibility, he recoils from the thought by invoking the "goodness of God; who as far as the happiness or misery of any of his sensible creatures is concerned will not, by a fatal error of theirs, transfer from one to another that consciousness which draws reward or punishment with it." (This retraction on the part of Locke has been criticized by Flew, who calls it Locke's "capitulation as a philosopher.")

It might appear far-fetched for a psychoanalyst to explore the inquiry of a seventeenth-century philosopher, like Locke, into the problems of personal identity. I believe, however, that Locke's contribution is relevant for the discussion about the identity concept in modern psychoanalysis. There is, as I remarked, a tendency among psychoanalysts to be suspicious of raising this issue. What we can learn from Locke is that identity and diversity are among the fundamental categories in the process of cognition, as fundamental as, and perhaps related to, such concepts as space and time. Just as space and time have other meanings applied to physical phenomena than they have when applied to intrapsychic experience, so it is with the concept of identity, when we refer to the identity of a person.

All the criteria that may be valid when we describe identical objects in space fail us when we deal with living things, like plants or animals. When we attempt to define the meaning of the identity of a person, the difficulties become staggering indeed. Locke was not deterred by these complexities. He pursued the questions that have to be asked when we speak of personal identity, often carelessly, as if it was a natural given. His answers might perplex us, as they did his contemporaries, and some might indeed not be supportable. But Locke can convince those who try to understand him that he is at all times directing his and our attention to real phenomena that are genuine aspects of the problem of the meaning of *sameness* when applied to persons. That we meet in this process strange phenomena—the puzzle-cases, in the words of Flew—compels us to acknowledge the existence of poorly understood regions of human experience.

If the relevance of Locke's inquiry would not be apparent enough by the rigor of his critical questioning, the response to his theses on identity by the great minds of the age would be added demonstration that what he compelled his readers to think about was indeed of vital concern to human understanding—whether one agreed with his answers or not. Even contemporary philosophers, while often critical of his answers, do not deny the validity of his questions. Last, but not least, I consider it of great significance that Freud, separated from Locke by several centuries, finds himself confronted by problems described by Locke in a manner that is, in spite of the different language of much earlier intellectual tradition, sufficiently similar to be recognizable as dealing with the same observable facts.

Perhaps it is not superfluous to point out some similarities in the personal development of Locke and Freud. Locke was no professional philosopher, just as Freud was no professional psychologist. Locke was at one time a practicing physician, at other times an experimental scientist. He was about forty years old when he embarked on the work that made him famous, *An Essay Concerning Human Understanding*, about the same age as Freud when he turned from neurophysiologic research to the exporation of the mental apparatus. Both men had the boldness to develop theories that became the objects of intense controversy. I am inclined to believe that if two thinkers of this type, even though separated by time and intellectual tradition, converge with regard to what they *observe*, we have good reason to trust their judgement concerning the reality of the problems. Both Locke and Freud faltered, however, in their attempted solutions of the problem of personal identity: Locke could not really, without introducing some "strange suppositions," prove that consciousness or memory *alone* constitute personal identity. Freud, in what is perhaps his closest approach to the problem of personal identity (I refer to his theory of object-identifications) introduced his phylogenetic theory of human development, which anchors personal identity and the inheritance of all *human* characteristics—religion, morality and social sense—in the unconscious memory of parricide, and the ensuing conflicts about it.

It would not be quite wrong to say that Freud, with this phylogenetic theory of inherited guilt, ingenious as it is, capitulated as a psychoanalyst, to paraphrase Flew's critique of Locke. It is my belief that Freud might have preferred to capitulate rather than leave a theory of the personality without an answer to the problem of personal identity, without any theory of "the nature of the bond that unites the person." It does, however, not entitle psychoanalysts today to pretend that this answer exists. Unless one is willing to accept Freud's phylogenetic theory of human development—and there are few psychoanalysts who are willing to do so—Freud's theoretical efforts will remain incomplete without an attempt to face the question of personal identity, in the spirit of Locke's inquiry, but with the background concerning the vicissitudes of mental development that we owe to Freud. I hope that the following chapters dealing with varying aspects of the problem of identity are a contribution to this task.

NOTES

1. "The phenomena presented by external and internal realities, whether received, retained, or elaborated, are called 'ideas' by Locke" (Fraser, in his edition of Locke's essay, p. lviii).

2. The difficulty is acknowledged by modern philosophers as well. Thus, B. O. Williams (1964) states: "In the case of material objects, we can draw a distinction between identity and similarity. This notion of identity is given to us primarily though not completely, by the notion of spatiotemporal similarity. In the case of character, however, this distinction cannot be drawn; ... Nor can this distinction be drawn in the case of memories."

3. Fraser (p. 451) comments in connection with this passage that a strict interpretation of Locke's text implies that Locke thought of personal identity as "making itself the same by its memory of itself, and thus in memory creating, and not merely discovering itself." In another comment to the above passage, Fraser points out that Locke suggests elsewhere "that a substance of a man is perhaps 'material'—as it may 'have pleased God to make consciousness one of the qualities or powers of organized matter'."

4. R. J. Stoller (1973) has recently dealt with these problems.

Chapter 4

THE LONELY CROWD:
HISTORY AND SELF-TRANSFORMATION

There are perhaps no endeavors that illuminate more poignantly certain aspects of the dilemma of human identity than the seemingly kaleidoscopic rearrangement of human identities in the historical process. For this reason David Riesman's *The Lonely Crowd* (1950), a work that set itself the task of studying changes in the American character during the preceding four or five decades, offers a particularly apposite subject of study. To give an adequate presentation of Riesman's hypotheses and to discuss them intelligently within the scope of this paper offers many difficulties. Some of these are due to the fact that I am not a social scientist, and am therefore inadequately informed about many subjects that Riesman deals with in his work. There are, however, difficulties which must be attributed to the character of Riesman's ideas: they lend themselves to interpretations in several contradictory and mutually exclusive ways. This conceptual ambiguity becomes apparent in the contributions to a work (Lipset and Lowenthal 1961) intended to review and reappraise Riesman's thesis and its impact on the social sciences. Not only do the interpretations of Riesman's theories by various experts in the social sciences and related fields profoundly contradict one another, but Riesman himself revises, in a final chapter of this book, many important positions which he originally took in *The Lonely Crowd*.

In their contribution to the volume, Messinger and Clark (1961) state the difficulty quite succinctly:

To accept Riesman's *explicit* theoretical and strategic leads is to run the risk of losing grasp of the analytic posture and substantive insights that we feel make this work important. To disregard these leads, however, is to be left without a stated framework within which to proceed, as well as to discount much that Riesman obviously takes quite seriously." [p. 73]

The two authors propose to resolve this dilemma "by showing that Riesman himself furnishes an *implicit* theory of man's social conduct and follows a latent strategy of inquiry and analysis" (p. 73). I believe that this distinction of an explicit from and implicit theory can also be applied to a study of Riesman's *implicit psychology* and what it has to contribute to the dilemma of human identity in historical change.

Riesman's *explicit* psychological theory leans strongly on Erich Fromm's ideas, especially the latter's concept of social character. With the help of this explicit psychology Riesman aims to make understandable the changes in the American character structure during the last half century. These changes, the existence of which is questioned by other social scientists (Lipset 1961), are manifested in "broad shifts in behavioral and affective styles, and in the tone and organization of life" (Messinger and Clark 1961, p. 73). Riesman attempts to explain these changes on the basis of a general theory of the correlation between historical process and social character formation.

Since the social function of character is to insure or permit conformity, it appears that the various types of social character can be defined most appropriately in terms of the modes of conformity that are developed in them. Finally, any prevailing mode of conformity may itself be used as an index to characterize a whole society. [Riesman et al. 1950]

Riesman sees this link between character and society as forged by three mechanisms, each characterized by a *source of direction*—tradition-direction, inner-direction, and other-direction. While no society ever wholly consists of only one type, any particular individual or society can be characterized by the one mechanism on which *principal* reliance is placed. Riesman sees a historical sequence of development from tradition- to inner- to other-direction.

The historical process as Riesman interprets it, can be described as follows:

> In the tradition-directed society . . . goals and their implementation through specific acts are prescribed to a much greater degree than in the subsequent stages of societal development. . . . The focus[is] on "securing external *behavioral* conformity." With inner-direction these . . . ties begin to break down. . . . Increased personal mobility . . . and rapid technological innovation, among other factors, necessitated greater freedom in the implementation of goals, an emancipation of goal-fulfillment from the specifications of a tradition that no longer proved adequate. But, although the goals changed, they remained inescapably destined—by the exigencies of an expanding society and economy. . . . And such goals were implanted by parents and other adult authorities in the young, who—knowing their destination—had to arrive at it as best they could. With the development of a highly industrialized society and its mature economy . . . what had previously been areas of daring innovation in an inner-directed society become institutionalized, "built into" society. The attainment of these goals by the society greatly diminishes them as a source of direction for the individual. . . . In this last stage, society becomes characterized by other-direction wherein the individual looks to his peers—and those formidable peer-surrogates, the mass media—for his source of guidance. Here the goals are no longer set but ever shifting, and only the mechanism of direction itself remains. [Parsons and White 1961]

I have quoted from Parsons and White's paper because it is admirably succinct in stating in the briefest possible way the basic tenets of Riesman's characterological approach to history.

Riesman (1950) attributes to tradition-directed, inner-directed, and other-directed individuals distinctly different emotional responses to social pressures: "One way to see the structural differences between the three types is to see the differences . . . in the emotional sanction, control, or 'tuning' in each type" (p. 25). For the tradition-directed person "the sanction for behavior tends to be the fear of being *shamed*." In the inner-directed person "getting off course may lead to the feeling of *guilt* . . . one prime psychological lever of the other-directed person is a diffuse *anxiety*" (p. 25f.) While comparing control mechanism of the inner-directed person to a gyroscope, and that of the other-directed person to a radar set, Riesman does not want us to take his typology and the imagery concerning the control equipment too literally. He warns against thinking in terms "of a separate body, 'society' making certain demands on people and testing out various processes." Riesman believes that "any number of ways of insuring characterological conformity may exist in a given society. Those which have been successful in preserving a coherent society are transmitted as unconsciously as they arose . . . by their historical success, they preserve themselves for study and investigation" (p. 30). History is viewed as a *struggle* between character types. "The struggle of classes and societies may . . . be viewed, to some extent, as a struggle among different characterological adaptations to the situation created by the dominance of the given mode of insuring conformity" (p. 31).

Within *any* given society Riesman distinguishes three "universal types" of personalities. There are, first, the *adjusted* personalities who are "the people who respond in the character structure to the demands of their society"; secondly, there are those "who do not conform to the characterological pattern" (p. 287). These latter ones Riesman calls *anomics,* "who [are] frequently neurotic, but . . . outwardly conform most of the time while paying so high a price for this behavioral conformity as to develop psychosomatic symptoms" (p. 288). In all societies there are a number of individuals whom Riesman calls *autonomous* individuals. The latter "are *capable* of conforming to the behavioral norms of their society . . . but . . . are free to choose whether to conform or not" (p. 287). The autonomous person is capable of breaking the conformity pattern so that "people can envisage adapting themselves not only within the narrow confines of the animal kingdom but within the wide range of alternative possibilities illustrated . . . by human experience to date" (p. 292). Riesman adds: "We obviously know much less about those whom I call autonomous. Many will even deny that there are such people, people capable of transcending their culture at any time or in any respect" (p. 290). However, he sees in the autonomous person the very hope of mankind, the "saving remnant" who, "by converting present helplessness into a condition of advance, . . . lay the groundwork for a new society" (1949).

The outline of Riesman's theory of man's historical transformation in terms of characterological typology represents correctly, I believe, his present position. In *The Lonely Crowd*, as it was written in 1950, considerable emphasis is placed on two other aspects concerning historical change. One of these aspects deals with the importance of the population curve as a quasi-biological pace-setter of historical change. The other emphasizes a transformation in human conduct, presenting the thesis that once the drudgery of labor has been eased by the emergence of modern industrial society, not work, but play will emerge as the royal road to autonomy. Both these theses have been abandoned or at least modified by Riesman. In *The Lonely Crowd* he assumes "that changes in population and technology everywhere are the chief correlates for changes in the social character" (p. v). Riesman proposes "some possible relationship between the population growth of a society and the historical sequence of character types" (p. 7). He sees the three character types (tradition-, inner-, and other-directed) correlated to three specific phases of the population curve in such a way that societies in the phase of "high growth potential" develop tradition-directed types, societies during "transitional population growth" develop inner-directed personalities, and societies of "incipient population decline" develop other-directed character types (p. 9ff.). Even though today Riesman no longer adheres to the population theory, its importance lies in the fact that it expressed his attempt to develop his typology of social character into a deterministic theory of history, "a quasi-evolutionary notion of the sequence of character types" (Riesman and Glazer 1961).

The other aspect of Riesman's earlier formulations in *The Lonely Crowd* refers to his theory of play. Play is for Riesman "a kind of extreme or limiting case of the leisure and consumption [i.e., in contrast to production] sphere" (p. 308), which permits him to place any activity not directly related to industrial production into the category of play, such as Charles Ives' composing symphonies when not selling insurance (p. 325). According to this interpretation, "play may prove to be the sphere in which there is still some room left for the would-be autonomous man to reclaim his individual character from the pervasive demands of his social character" (p. 326). In contrast to play, work is viewed as conforming to the economic demands and prejudices of industrial society (p. 308). Leisure and play are thus presented as freeing the modern, overconforming men from "their loneliness in a crowd of peers" (p. 373). In *The Lonely Crowd* Riesman sees in the development of leisure activities the hope for a Utopian society where men can devote themselves to the development of "the enormous potentialities for diversity in nature's bounty and men's capacity to differentiate their experience . . . so that [the individual] will not be tempted and coerced into adjustment or, failing adjustment, into anomie" (p. 373).

These earlier views of Riesman concerning work, leisure, and play are important for an understanding of his implicit psychology, even though today Riesman believes that "leisure itself cannot rescue work, but fails with it, and can only be meaningful for most men if work is meaningful" (Reisman and Glazer 1961).

In the work by Lipset and Lowenthal (1961), we find some careful psychological studies concerning Riesman's character types. Most important is Elaine Graham Sofer's paper, "Inner-direction, Other-direction, and Autonomy: A Study of College Students." Sofer, using attitude questionnaires, arrives at the conclusion that her investigation "can afford no direct confirmation of Riesman's theory, either in terms of showing a particular relationship between the form of a society and the character structures to which it gives rise, or even in the more limited sense of showing that in our society individuals can indeed be shown to be increasingly other-directed in their character mechanisms" (p. 345). Actually there are no clearly defined psychological categories which correspond to Riesman's distinction between inner- and other-directed personalities. Sofer feels that perhaps terms such as "self-orientation" versus "field-orientation" would permit a clearer psychological understanding of the differences which Riesman has in mind (p. 337). Having applied these criteria to her investigation, Sofer concludes that

a finer analysis of the cases uncovers a range of possible personality configurations that evidently can underlie inner-direction, other-direction, or autonomy. Despite the clear personality weakness of the other-directed subjects revealed by the projective tests, we have seen that there is no significant difference in the over-all Rorschach "adjustment" ratings for this group versus the "self"-directed subjects. Scores of the personality inventory suggest, moreover, that a pattern of worried self-concern . . . is more characteristic of inner-direction and autonomy than of other-direction. [p. 340]

Sofer is also unable to confirm Riesman's assumption that within the three types of social character, individuals may be either adjusted, anomic, or autonomous. On the basis of her test results Sofer concludes that "those who have succumbed to the more exaggerated forms of other-direction in our society do not appear to have the ego resources to deal adequately with either the internal or the external world, the cognitive or the emotional aspects of their motivations and their perceptions" (p. 340). On the other hand, Sofer points out that "the personality configurations of those who reject other-direction range from the near-schizophrenic individual to those with strong egos who are evidently able to integrate the 'inner,' the 'outer,' and the 'other' in creative and truly autonomous ways" (p. 342). This result indicates that while "inner-directed" personalities may be, in Riesman's terminology, adjusted, autonomous, or anomic, the same is not true with regard to "other-directed" personalities.

The discrepancy between psychological findings on the one hand and the formulations of Riesman on the other points to a basic incompatibility between Riesman's typology and any of the currently available psychological models. This becomes apparent in the totally different interpretation of inner-direction and other-direction on the part of different psychologists. Thus Brodbeck (1961, p. 55) interprets other-direction as an index of a change in values. In contrast to Sofer, Brodbeck arrives at the conclusion

that the "inner-directed" have a narrower frame of attention, since they emphasize "the development of" character rather than "the expression of" personality. The expanding frame of reference that comprises "other-direction" leads them *to respect the person* beneath the role or duty occupied, to look deeper than how duties or role relationships are carried off, so as to discover ways in which roles can be redefined more creatively in terms of individual potentialities for fuller expression. The "inner-directed" appear, on the other hand, more respectful of roles and role-behavior than of persons.

It appears then that, in order to arrive at any psychologically meaningful conceptualization of *inner-directed* and *other-directed,* these terms must be taken out of the context of Riesman's explicit psychological theory, and reformulated in terms of the personality theory of the individual psychological investigator. Then, by a process of analogic reasoning, the various investigators may arrive at some definition of inner-direction and other-direction which is meaningful within their own personality theories.

This confusion is due, I believe, to the fact that the psychologists who have attempted to apply Riesman's concepts of character types to personality study have taken his *explicit* psychological terminology at its face value. "Character" is a concept in good standing in most schools of psychology. "Direction" may be understood as referring to "goal-directedness" or motivation; inner-direction or other-direction may sound, to a psychoanalyst, vaguely familiar: he may be reminded of Jung's "introvert" and "extrovert," or even think of a somewhat vague analogy with the Freudian distinction of ego libido and object libido. I believe, however, that these psychological-sounding concepts have no relationship to the psychological contexts from which they seem to be borrowed.

Interestingly, this is more clearly recognized by the sociologist Dahrendorf (1961, pp. 179ff.) in his essay in *Culture and Social Character* than by the psychologists Sofer and Brodbeck. He says:

The word "character" (and its alternative, "mask," which, signigicantly enough, Mr. Riesman employs occasionally) seems to stem from the same context as another well-known category of sociological analysis: that of "role." Both invoke somewhere in their etymological history the image of a stage on which actors appear in given masks, characters, roles, parts. Originally, all these words indicated clusters of tasks, attitudes, and behaviors that were given to an actor from outside, that were, in other words, neither of his own making nor even of his own choosing. "Society" or, to be more precise, certain social reference groups, define roles, characters, parts for individuals who occupy given positions. By learning his parts the individual becomes a member of society; the parts are ... the imprint left by society on the presumed *tabula rasa* of the individual at birth.

It seems to me that the *tabula rasa* concept of the human personality is indeed the key to Riesman's implicit psychology. Inner-direction and other-direction are not psychological orientations indicative of the prevalence of certain particular needs of the individuals, but imposed directives, by which societal agencies "direct" the production of a certain type of individual. For Riesman, the social character is the "more or less confining strait jacket which is imposed upon [the individual]" (p. 5) by society so that the individual's drives can be "harnessed to perform the culturally defined tasks" (p. 4).

According to Allport (1957, pp. 6-7), the *tabula rasa* concept of the human mind is part of the tradition of Anglo-Saxon philosophy:

There is a basic difference in philosophical assumptions regarding the nature of mental life, the Lockean tradition being dominant in England and America; the Leibnitzian and Kantian on the Continent.... The Lockean tradition, in brief, holds that man's mind by nature is *tabula rasa* (environmentalistic leaning): mind does what it is made to do (a leaning toward reactivity and behavioristics).... By contrast, the Leibnitzian and Kantian positions have been dominant and, in my opinion, are still dominant on the Continent. To Leibnitz, as to Kant, the intellect was perpetually self-active (not merely reactive).... to [Leibnitz], the inner and spontaneous workings of the mind were at least as important as its contents or productions. His concept of the self-active monad easily became the "person" who, with his entelechtive strivings, pursued a unique destiny.... It was easy for such a unit to become differentiated into strata, the higher levels of which are bent on autonomy and self-actualization.

The *tabula rasa* concept assumes in Riesman certain extreme, mechanistic features expressed in a peculiar technological as well as technocratic imagery.

The conformity of the individual [in tradition-directed society] tends to be *dictated* to a very large degree by power-relations among the various age and sex groups. . . . The culture *controls* behavior minutely and, . . . careful and rigid etiquette *governs* the fundamentally influential sphere of kin relationships . . . [p. 11]. As the situational controls of the primary group are loosened— the group that both *socializes* the young and *controls* the adult in the earlier era—a new psychological *mechanism* appropriate to the more open society is *"invented": it is a psychological gyroscope.* This *instrument, once it is set by* the parents and other authorities, keeps the inner-directed person . . . *"on course"* even when tradition . . . no longer *dictates* his moves." [p. 16; my italics]

The other-directed character is provided with a *"control equipment"* which Riesman compares to a *radar device* which is highly sensitive to any kind of messages received from the environment (p. 26).

Riesman's choice of technological analogies cannot be considered coincidental. This is borne out by the fact that his concept of the human personality is completely static, as I shall presently show, so that human development has to explained by a *vis a tergo,* which pushes it along in this or that direction; it is also shown in Riesman's attempt to interpret historical transformation of human identity as "character struggle," when, in his own words, "character" is so unchangeably molded that only under the most powerful of outside pressures does it yield to change. Such outside forces are "variations in the basic conditions of reproduction, livelihood and survival chances, that is, in the supply of and demand for human beings" (p. 9). In order to explain the fact that the "strait jacket" of the social character permits any change at all, Riesman needed the population-curve theory: under the crushing pressure of these external forces, character did not really *change* from within: it had to be readjusted to the new circumstances, by replacing certain of its mechanical features, such as a gyroscope, with a radar set. Thus it should not take us by surprise when Riesman, after giving a detailed description of such historical struggle of characters (p. 291), arrives at the conclusion that "this epic has the quality not of human history but of animal life." Given Riesman's characterological viewpoint, he can hardly be expected to arrive at any other conclusion. The reason for this is the fact that the concept of character, psychologically, is in man the phenomenon closest akin to the instinctual behavior pattern of the animal.

Fromm, whose psychology Riesman adopts as his explicit psychological theory, states this very precisely:

> Character can be defined as the *(relatively permanent) form in which human energy is canalized in the process of assimilation and socialization* [i.e., in his relationships to the natural and the human environment]. . . . This canalization of psychic energy has a very significant biological function. . . . The character system can be considered the *human substitute for the instinctive apparatus of the animal.* [1947, p. 59; my italics]

"Social character," as Fromm defines the term, refers to "the nucleus of the character structure which is shared by most members of the same culture in contradistinction to the *individual character* in which people belonging to the same culture differ from each other" (1949). Such a concept of "social character" can, according to Fromm, be abstracted only by taking as "relatively fixed at any given historical period" the social structures within which individuals operate in a given society (1949). Thus, character is an essentially static aspect of the personality, and social character a decidedly unhistorical abstraction. Erikson (1959, p. 147, n.) has made this very clear:

> I prefer to speak of a "sense of identity" rather than of a "character structure" or "basic character." In nations, too, my concepts would lead me to concentrate on the conditions and experiences which heighten or endanger a national sense of identity rather than on a static national character. . . . Here it is important to remember that each identity cultivates its own sense of freedom.

In striking contrast Riesman feels that the conception "that 'Man is born free; and everywhere he is in chains' [should be interpreted] to mean that man is born a slave—a slave to his biological and cultural inheritance—but that he can become, through experience and experiment, increasingly free" [p. 300].

This unhappy slavery which Riesman sees everywhere is rooted, in my opinion, not in man's biological and cultural inheritance, but in the conceptual dehumanization of man's social relations and in the automatization of his biological propensities. This mechanization is one aspect of Riesman's implicit psychology, a psychology dominated by the image of La Mettrie's *L'Homme Machine*. Freud, whose psychology Riesman sees as founded on a narrow biological basis which he rejects in favor of a typology that he considers to be "already a socially-patterned one" (Riesman and Glazer 1961, p. 427), did not view man as a slave of his biological inheritance, but rather saw in the latter the guarantee of human freedom: ". . . a desire for freedom . . . may . . . spring from the remains of their original personality, which is still untamed by civilization. . . . It does not seem as though any influence could induce a man to change his nature into a termite's. No doubt he will always defend his claim to individual liberty against the will of the group" (1930, p. 96). Riesman does not believe in the possibility that human freedom may emanate from an original layer of the personality: in his view, man can become free increasingly through experience and experiment. I wonder how this can come about if man is born a slave, i.e., if he is so constituted that from birth he is completely dominated by forces far more powerful than himself. It would, indeed, be completely inexplicable in terms of Riesman's implicit psychology, based on a *tabula rasa* concept of the human mind—a mind which is thought to be the product of social engineering.

Fortunately, Riesman does not aim at mere formal consistency. Rather, he permits the conceptual system to bend under the weight of psychological evidence. This evidence shows that man does not always conform to social patterns, just as he is not completely bound by his biological equipment. Riesman admits that there are individuals who are capable of either conforming or not conforming: the autonomous personalities. He does not explain how this ability to make choices comes about, as Freud (1911) attempted to do in terms of a theory of mental evolution. Riesman simply postulates the existence of autonomy. Having first adopted the *tabula rasa* theory of the human mind, he shifts, when it comes to autonomy, to the position of continental psychology based on Descartes, Leibniz, and Kant. While for these philosophers, human autonomy was a manifestation of a divine *ego cogitans*, Riesman simply ascribes to man autonomy as a near-mystical quality, a spiritual variant of spontaneous generation. He does not seem to assume that all men are capable of autonomy, but that there is a sufficient number of them to constitute the "saving remnant" which will guard the humanity of man against the forces of society and biology. Among the manifestations of autonomy are creativity and self-realization. In *The Lonely Crowd*, Riesman thought them to be impeded by work, and developed by play. Play would expand the area of autonomy and human freedom.

In my opinion, the concept of autonomy leads to a self-contradiction in Riesman's theoretical constructs. I must agree with Brodbeck (1961), who refers to it as a *deus ex machina*. The self-contradictory character of Riesman's implicit psychology—*tabula rasa* plus entelechtive autonomy—becomes even clearer when one describes *The Lonely Crowd* as dealing with the human possibility of alienation as well as autonomy. Seeman (1959), dealing with the concept of "alienation as self-estrangement," quotes Fromm's definition of alienation as "a mode of experience in which the person experiences himself as an alien. He has become, one might say, estranged from himself" (1955, p. 120). Seeman comments:

> To speak of "alienation of the self" is after all simply a metaphor, in the way that "alienation from popular culture," for example, need not be. The latter can be reasonably specified. . . . but what is intended when Fromm . . . and the others speak of self-estrangement? Apparently, what is being postulated here is some ideal human condition from which the individual is estranged . . .
> To be self-alienated, in the final analysis, means to be something less than one might ideally be if the circumstances in society were otherwise—to be insecure, given to appearances, conformist. [1959, p. 789ff.]

The "ideal condition" of which Seeman speaks, is, it seems to me, nothing else than Riesman's autonomy. This seems to be borne out by the title of the last chapter of *The Lonely Crowd*: "Autonomy and Utopia." For Riesman, if we are to take seriously his statement that man is born a slave, but can become increasingly free, man is born alienated, but may approximate the ideal human condition of autonomy by means of experience and experiment. This order of the sequence of autonomy and alienation appears to me quite incompatible with any developmental psychology. Alienation, in whatever variation of meaning it is used, does not indicate an innate, but an acquired psychological state, caused by definable psychological conditions. Riesman does not specifically say that man is born alienated; but to refer to man as being born a slave can hardly refer to anything else than an alienated state. Riesman's conceptualizations seem here to depart entirely from the psychological basis that his terminology—his *explicit* psychology theory—appears to suggest. What is implied here is, in my opinion, a hidden theological approach: it is a modern, secular disguise for a theology with a neo-Manichaean outlook.

According to Runciman (1955, p. 173), "there is one characteristic quality in any dualistic [neo-Manichaean] church. Man, to escape from the vileness of his body, must seek to make himself spirit as far as may be. This is done by a gnosis, an experience that is usually won by an initiation ceremony. Thus a class of initiates arises, a spiritual aristocracy." In neo-Manichaeanism, man is also born a slave, and only by a special experience can he become more spiritual, as for Riesman man can by experience become more autonomous. But the similarity goes further.

> Most sects divided mankind into three categories, according to the amount of divine sparks that existed in each man ... these [three categories] were: the Spirituals ... who were full of divinity ... next the Psychics ..., who had a little spark in their souls but were not assured of salvation ... finally there were the Materials ... men without spark who return inevitably to the dust from which they came. [Runciman 1955, p. 7ff.]

Are Riesman's autonomous, adjusteds, and anomics not merely the twentieth-century sophisticated successors of those more simple, but more straightforwardly theological typologies? The self-contradictory nature of Riesman's views in *The Lonely Crowd* can thus be described as being due to a combination of a mechanistic, static concept of the personality with the spirituality of neo-Manichaean theology.

We ask ourselves how this strange theoretical hybrid could have been offered by one of the most perceptive, most erudite, and most genuinely humanistic social scientists. Perhaps we should wonder even more why this theoretical system continues to exert a powerful impact on modern social science, social psychology, and last but not least, on certain members of the younger generation of psychoanalysts. I am persuaded that no work of scientific character can have the impact that Riesman's book has had unless it contains a psychological truth, unless it depicts a psychological reality that modern man confronts. I believe that the psychological truth of Riesman's *The Lonely Crowd* is its reflection of the dilemma of human identity in transformation. Its inner contradictions are in fact the expressions of this existential dilemma. Human identity is an experience of inner continuity in change. If we concentrate on the change, we cannot get hold of the continuity and sameness. What we can observe in the history, both of nations and of individuals, is that they are in constant flux. In our own time, these changes are occurring at a rate which leads to an all-pervasive sense of self-estrangement or alienation. Riesman has narrowed down this aspect of the dilemma of identity in historical transformation to a change in "social character." The problem of human identity in the process of self-transformation is thereby externalized—indeed, mechanized. It remains, I believe, still a task for psychologists appropriately to conceptualize these inner experiences of self-transformation (Strauss 1959). Such attempts will always have to deal with the equally difficult task of accounting for the sense of inner continuity in self-transformation. Here Riesman has turned to the concept of autonomy, which, as I have indicated, is only a thinly disguised version of the age-old idea of man's immortal soul. Thus Riesman's conceptual ambiguities illuminate the paradoxical nature of the dilemma of human identity: paraphrasing Riesman, we may state that man, when he looks around him at the world into which he is born, may well consider himself a slave to the accidents of his natural and social conditions. But as he looks into himself, he cannot but discover a sense of inner continuity, of autonomy and freedom, which Freud did not hesitate to attribute to the original layer of the human personality. Riesman, in *The Lonely Crowd*, has attempted to "resolve" the dilemma of identity in transformation through a characterological typology. This attempt, I believe, did not succeed. But Riesman has spotlighted a basic issue that remains a challenge for all students of the human condition.

Chapter 5

THE CONTRIBUTION OF
ERIK ERIKSON

In contrast to Riesman, Erik Erikson's basic perception of human self-transformation is that of an ordered and structured process. This applies both to the individual life cycle and to historical developments. For Erikson, transformation implies essentially a process that I shall call self-objectivation. Through self-objectivation man attains both a social and a historical identity. History is for Erikson the continuum of individual life cycles. While each life cycle fulfills itself in the emergence of a socially definable identity, the specific "style" of such self-objectivation imparts on the historical process a definable, "epochal" character, and is at the same time imbued by the character of the epoch. Rapaport, (1959, p. 16) in his introduction to *Identity and the Life Cycle*, a reissue of three papers characterizing three decisive levels of Erikson's conceptualizations of problems of identity, states that "Erikson's theory (like much of Freud's) ranges over phenomenological, specifically clinical psychoanalytic and general psychoanalytic-psychological propositions, without systematically differentiating among them." The comparison to Freud's "theory making" is justified in that Erikson does not hesitate to formulate his thoughts in terms not free from a certain ambiguity—an ambiguity that is seen as an integral aspect of the phenomenon of identity itself. In Erikson's writings the dimensions of this ambiguity unfold until in his *magnum opus, Young Man Luther* (1958), he confronts the reader with the full range of problems which I have called here the dilemma of human

In his early paper "Ego Development and Historical Change" (1959), Erikson states, "The conscious feeling of having a *personal identity* is based on two simultaneous observations: the immediate perception of one's self-sameness and continuity in time; and the simultaneous perceptions of the fact that others recognize one's sameness and continuity" (p. 23). This statement contains the essence of the aspect of the dilemma of human identity which centers upon self-objectivation versus the subjective experience of the "actuality of being." Because I believe that these two ways of experiencing one's identity are mutually exclusive, i.e., man loses the one when he is experiencing the other, I am speaking of a dilemma of human identity. Erikson seems in the quoted passage to assume that these two "observations" can and do occur simultaneously in man. But in his work as a whole I discover an awareness that these "simultaneous" observations are actually mutually incompatible as psychological experience, i.e., that they really cannot be simultaneously conscious in the same individual. This becomes evident in Erikson's work on Luther. There he states that in "the language of the uncorrupted core of all spiritual tradition . . . the identity of knowing transcendence" (pp. 178ff) can only be discovered by man when the possibility *for any social definition of identity is shattered beyond any restoration.* Thus, the original formulation that identity is based on two *simultaneous* observations is now revised. Between these two stages of conceptualization Erikson is willing to accept the *ambiguity* of the phenomenon of identity: "I can attempt to make the subject matter of identity more explicit only by approaching it from a variety of angles—biographic, pathographic, and theoretical; and by letting the term identity speak for itself in a number of connotations" (1959, p. 102).

Erikson begins with the study of what *can be* described and conceptualized. Thus the emphasis appears concentrated on the fact that *others* recognize one's sameness and continuity and indirectly bestow a sense of identity on the one who is thus "recognized." This led to the development of the concept of ego identity. "What I propose to call ego identity concerns more than the mere fact of existence, as conveyed by personal identity; it is the ego quality of this existence." This ego quality is defined by Erikson as "a conviction that the ego is . . . developing into a defined ego within a social reality. . . . Ego identity, . . . in its subjective aspect, is the awareness of the fact that there is selfsameness and continuity to the ego's synthesizing methods and that these methods are effective in safeguarding the sameness and continuity of one's meaning for others" (1959, p. 23).

This safeguarding of one's sense of sameness and continuity for others Erikson describes in the same paper as "a vitalizing sense of reality [derived] from the awareness that [the growing child's] individual way of mastering experience (his ego synthesis) is a successful variant of a group identity and is in accord with its space-time and life plan" (p. 22). This, then, is the definition of identity as a process of self-objectivation. Through this process of self-objectivation the individual is, within the social context, capable of talking about the "who" that he is, in "objective" terms: these objective terms are defined as the social role of the individual. The question must be raised whether the vitalizing effect of self-objectivation on the individual's sense of identity is not contingent on the perception of the objectivated self in *human* terms, such as to be somebody's child, father, husband, etc. Self-objectivation may, however, introduce elements of dehumanization in that the individual may experience himself as a mere "cog in the machine rather than someone who runs it" (Bettelheim 1960, p. 57). Identity as self-objectivation may thus come into conflict with the individual's existential identity, a concept introduced in Erikson's *Luther* as identity which is "defined by the relationship of each soul to its mere existence" (p. 177).

This concept of "existential identity" makes its appearance only in Erikson's later writings. In *Identity and the Life Cycle* Erikson considers the development toward self-objectivation as the crucial and climactic stage toward which all previous stages of identity formation must be referred.

While the end of adolescence thus is the stage of an overt identity *crisis*, identity *formation* neither brings nor ends with adolescence: it is a lifelong development largely unconscious to the individual and to his society. Its roots go back all the way to the first self-recognition: in the baby's earliest exchange of smiles there is something of a *self-realization coupled with a mutual recognition.* [pp. 133–134]

Erikson, at that phase of his work, modifies the traditional psychoanalytic ontogenetic approach, with its stress on the significance of the earliest experience of the child:

> We will not be able to make more definite the now very tentative designation ... of the precursors of identity in the infantile ego. Rather we approach childhood in an untraditional manner, namely, from young adulthood backward—and this with the conviction that early development cannot be understood on its own terms alone, and that the earliest stages of childhood cannot be accounted for without a unified theory of the whole span of preadulthood. For the infant ... does not and cannot build anew and out of himself the courses of human life, as the reconstruction of his earliest experience ever again seems to suggest. The smallest child lives in a community of life cycles which depend on him as he depends on them, and which guide his drives as well as his sublimations with consistent feedbacks. [p. 121]

Although Erikson has never modified this position, it is obviously not a complete statement of his ideas. It is instructive to contrast the above-quoted passage with Erikson's incisive description of the identity crisis of what he calls the "chosen young man," the young person who may, in one form or another, change the course of history.

> The chosen young man extends the problem of his identity to the borders of existence in the known universe; ... He acts as if mankind were starting all over with his own beginning as an individual, conscious of his singularity as well as his humanity; others hide in the folds of whatever tradition they are part of because of membership, occupation, or special interests. To him, history ends as well as starts with him; others must look to their memories, to legends, or to books to find models for the present and the future in what their predecessors have said and done. [1958, p. 261ff.]

This is a quite different approach to the emergence of identity.

It seems justified to assume the existence of a basic problem behind this ambiguity about the relative significance of self-objectivation (psychosocial identity) in contrast to the experience of "existential identity" and the uniquely personal identity of the "chosen young man." Obviously, the question touches upon the relative significance of "culture" versus the "biologism" of psychoanalytic theory. Erikson has frequently criticized psychoanalysts' neglect of the significance of the cultural and societal organization in which a human being grows up. One of his contributions has been his effort to add to psychoanalytic theory the analysis "of the individual's ego identity in relation to the historical changes which dominated his childhood milieu" (1959, p. 49).

In contrast to the neo-Freudian emphasis, however, Erikson has always fought a kind of two-front war: against those who are blind to the unfolding of man's existence in the historical process, and against those who forget that all "people and peoples begin in their nurseries," i.e., the biological condition of man (1959, p. 18). Thus, to equate the problems raised by Erikson entirely with the issue of "biologism" versus "culturalism" is superficial. His aim has always been the conceptual integration of these seemingly incompatible approaches to the human condition.

It is in the development of the concept of psychological epigenesis that Erikson expects the "dovetailing of psychosexual and psychosocial" developments (p. 121). In the words of Rapaport (1959), "This sequence of the phases of psychosocial development parallels that of libido development and goes beyond it, spanning *the whole life cycle.* This conception is the first in the history of psychoanalytic theory to encompass those phases of the life cycle which are customarily subsumed under the single concept of genital maturity, and to provide tools for their investigation" (p. 14). Erikson gives a most precise description of the epigenetic principle as applied to the psychological growth of a personality in his paper "Growth and Crises of the Healthy Personality" (1959, p. 52ff.).

The central ideas of the principle of epigenesis are: (1) the idea of a ground plan; (2) the development of the parts of the organism not as isolated occurrences, but as functionally related to the ground plan; and (3) the importance of the timing of the development of the parts, in such a way that a functioning whole can only emerge when each part evolves at its phase-specific, proper time. In its biological sense, the concept of epigenesis is clear. The ground plan refers to the known end stage of the fully developed organism, and the parts are, of course, the various organs which constitute the functioning whole of the organism. Only within an organism can true organs develop, and within a growing organism, each organ or biological system must develop at a phase-specific period if it is to develop at all. These biological concepts are applied analogously by Erikson to the growth of a personality. Following this analogy, we must find a definition for the ground plan of a personality.

While it is obvious that the ground plan for the developing chicken embryo is the fully developed chick, it is not equally obvious what the psychologically fully developed individual ought to be like. Should we assume that each individual has a "predestined" personality that is bound to come into being, or failing this, that the personality remains, as it were, malformed? Should we, for instance, assume that the ground plan of a van Gogh was to develop the personality of a painter, and must we look at van Gogh's early efforts to find fulfillment as a minister as deviations from the ground plan? Or should we rather reason along opposite lines: namely, that the ground plan is to be defined in terms of a traditional social role, so that following the ministry, in van Gogh's case, was the fulfillment of the ground plan, and his becoming a painter a deviation?

Both these possibilities would be compatible with the assumption of an epigenetic principle, but in each case the conclusion concerning the process of a personality development derived from such principle would be vastly different. In the first instance, the stages described by Erikson (1959, p. 53) as a *"progression through time of a differentiation of parts"* could not be uniform for all individuals because this progression would have to be different for the "born" musician when compared to those of the "born" political leader. Uniform applicability of Erikson's epigenetic principle would require that the ground plan be not defined in terms of the individual's unique fulfillment of a predetermined pattern of personality, but in terms of the development of the individual toward a culturally defined identity or social role. Such uniformity of the developmental pattern can have only a relative validity as a developmental principle, because it is applicable only to those individuals whose personality "fits" into certain social roles characteristic for a given culture. (See also Strauss's 1959 for its criticism of the concept of development in psychology.)

Erikson recognizes the fact that, applied to psychological development, the epigenetic principle must have a certain latitude. Thus, according to Erikson, during the stage of adolescence, "painful isolation" (opposed to the more healthy "self-certainty") may stimulate the creative potentialities of the individual (1959, p. 144). This implies that creative individuals may have a *differently* patterned ego epigenesis than those who are not creative (p. 144). In *Young Man Luther* Erikson makes this point even more emphatically. He adopts the term "once-born" in order to describe, following the terminology of William James (1902), "all those who rather painlessly fit themselves and are fitted into the ideology of their age, finding no discrepancy between its formulation of past and future and the daily task set by the dominant technology" (1958, p. 41). James differentiates the once-born from those "sick souls" and "divided selves" who search for a second birth, a "growth crisis" that will " 'convert' them in their habitual center of . . . personal energy" (p. 41). What Erikson has to say about the creative and historical role of these "sick souls" and "divided selves" is highly significant for the general applicability of the epigenetic principle to personality development:

> Some young individuals will succumb to this crisis in all manner of neurotic, psychotic, or delinquent behavior; others will resolve it through participation in ideological movements passionately concerned with religion or politics, nature or art. Still others, although suffering and deviating dangerously through what appears to be a prolonged adolescence, eventually come to contribute an *original bit to an emerging style of life*: the very danger which they have sensed has forced them to mobilize capacities to see and say, to dream and plan, to design and construct, *in new ways.* [1958, pp. 14–15]

This is vastly different from Erikson's claim in "The Problem of Identity" (p. 114) that the achievement of "psychosocial fittedness" marks the emergence of a young person's identity. At that time, Erikson considered it the culmination of identity formation (p. 113). In *Young Man Luther*, however, this concept of social fittedness is characterized as the mere fulfillment of one of "the departmentalized identities which [human beings] find prepared in their communities"

(p. 262). I conclude, therefore, that the epigenetic principle applied to personality development, at least in terms of the specific stages postulated by Erikson, describes only the development of the "once-born." That the phase-specific stages of ego development do not constitute the *universal* law of personality development is shown by Erikson's own profoundly searching investigations of the various dimensions of identity in his work on Luther.

In *Young Man Luther* Erikson boldly transcends the too narrowly conceived pattern of the epigenesis of the personality by his radical departure from the socially defined identity concept. This development of Erikson's concept of identity has three stages. In "Ego Development and Historical Changes" (1959), he characterizes the sense of ego identity as "a conviction that the ego is learning effective steps toward a tangible collective future, that is developing into a defined ego within a social reality" (p. 23). The second stage is indicated by Erikson's decision to change his terminology, giving up the original term ego identity in favor of "the bare term identity in order to suggest a social function of the ego which results, in adolescence, in a relative psychosocial equilibrium essential to the tasks of young adulthood" (1959, p. 150). The reason for this change in terminology was Hartmann's (1950) differentiation between ego and self. Following Hartmann's distinction, Erikson decided to use the "bare term identity ... until the matter ego vs. self is sufficiently defined to permit a terminological decision" (1959, p. 156). This self which can become an object for an ego constitutes what I have called identity as self-objectivation. It still refers to the social identity of the individual. Thus, the change in terminology does not yet indicate clearly a change of the identity concept. In *Young Man Luther*, however, a shift away from the emphasis on the social aspect of identity announces itself in a more complex definition of the concept of mutuality.

Mutuality, in Rapaport's words, "specifies that the crucial coordination is between the developing individual and his human (social) environment, and that this coordination is mutual" (1959, p. 15). In *Identity and the Life Cycle* Erikson uses the concept of mutuality in order to describe the relationship between the mothering adult and the child. Beyond that, the concept also characterizes the reciprocal relationship between the individual and his society. "Identity formation . . . is dependent on the process by which a *society . . . identifies the young individual*, recognizing him as somebody who had to become the way he is, and who, being the way he is, is taken for granted . . . the community, in turn feels 'recognized' by the individual who cares to ask for recognition" (p. 113). In *Young Man Luther*, on the other hand, the mutual relationship between society and the individual is described as follows:

> Each new being is received into a style of life prepared by tradition and held together by tradition, and at the same time disintegrating because of the very nature of tradition. We say that tradition "molds" the individual, "channels" his drives. But the social process does not mold a new being merely to housebreak him; it molds generations *in order to be remolded, to be reinvigorated*, by them. . . . In describing the interdependence of individual aspiration and of societal striving, we describe something indispensable to human life. [p. 254; my italics]

Here Erikson comes close to Ortega y Gasset's concept that the individual is "a vital program which . . . overpowers environment to lodge itself there" (1949). Erikson has always recognized that the individual is not only defined in terms of his social identity, but that society is also defined in terms of the emerging identities of individuals who impose themselves upon it (1950a, p. 368, n.).

But only in *Young Man Luther* does Erikson elaborate more fully on the nonsocial aspects of human identity. Talking about the early Christians Erikson speaks of the "horizontal of wordly organization" and "the vertical which [in the religious individual] connects each man's soul with the Higher Identity in heaven" (p. 179). With this distinction between the horizontal of wordly organization and the vertical of immediately perceived existential identity, Erikson returns to his earlier emphasis on the sense of identity. What he now describes (in religious terms) as the vertical that links man to a Higher Identity in heaven does appear, psychologically speaking, to be nothing else than the "immediate perception of one's selfsameness and continuity in time" (1959, p. 23). When he introduced this distinction, Erikson had claimed that these two ways of experiencing one's identity were simultaneous. Now, however, he allows for the fact that immediate perception of existential identity can become an alternative mode of identity maintenance after a total failure of any possibility for social definition of identity. For those who were truly *"disinherited in earthly goods and in social identity"* death became the highest identity on earth. Accepting death fully they could be sure of "the identity of knowing transcendence" (1958, p. 179). "Subjective" identity may be described psychologically as the experience of pure actuality of being. Identity experienced as pure actuality of being is incapable of any definition because it does away with the differentiation of subject and object, on which all definitions are based. Any attempt to give identity a content and a *definable* meaning must turn toward social identity, identity by means of self-objectivation: religion and metaphysics insist, therefore, that man, in so far as he claims "existential identity," must borrow it from "a Higher Identity [inhabiting] the great unknown" (1958, p. 177).

In his Luther book, Erikson describes several of the more important conceptualizations of the process by which man is thought to partake in the "pure actuality of being" of the Higher Identity. Such conceptualizations are described by Erikson as the mystic, gnostic, caritative or infused identity. All of them have in common the fundamental belief that man does not "have" an identity of this kind. "Augustine ... made no concession about the completeness of *perditio*, man's total lostness, nor is he less relentlessly convinced that only God has Being by Himself. ... Without grace [*infusio caritatis*], the identity of man is also one of the mere succession of men. But God gave him a mind and a memory, and thus the rudiment of an identity" (1958, p. 183). Psychologically, this religious conceptualization describes the dilemma of human identity. Identity as experience of the pure actuality of being remains indefinable, unworldly. Any definable identity requires that we perceive ourselves as objects, which means equating identity with the identity given to us as social roles, losing thereby the sense of identity as pure actuality of being.

A psychological study of the problem of human identity must accept this dilemma as the basic phenomenon of human identity. I believe that any effort to let "subjective" identity, as I shall briefly refer to it, emerge from the process of self-objectivation must lead to the unsolvable problem of trying to derive a "who" from a "what." It is my impression that Erikson has attempted to bridge this unbridgeable gap between the "subjective" experience of identity and the identity which emerges from self-objectivation by means of his application of the epigenetic principle to the development of the personality. Any such attempt seems to me to fall short of the epistemological insights already gained in the natural sciences. Science today is more willing to accept the principle of the impossibility of the simultaneous experience of mutually exclusive situations for the observation of certain phenomena in atomic physics than psychology is with regard to similar incompatibilities.

I am thinking here of the problems in modern atomic physics which led to the formulation of the concept of complementarity by Bohr (1948, p. 317ff.; my italics):

> The complementarity mode of description does indeed not involve any arbitrary renunciation of customary demands of explanation, but, on the contrary, aims at an appropriate dialectic expression for the actual conditions of analysis and synthesis in atomic physics. The epistemological lesson we have received from new developments in physical science . . . may also suggest lines of approach in other domains of knowledge where the situation is of essentially less accessible character. . . . Recognition of complementary relationship is *not least required in psychology, where the condition for analysis and synthesis of experience exhibits striking analogy with the situation in atomic physics.* In fact, the use of words like "thoughts" and "sentiments," equally indispensable to illustrate the diversity of psychical experience, pertains to *mutually exclusive situations* characterized by a different drawing of the line between subject and object. In particular, the place left for the feeling of volition is afforded by the very circumstance that the situations where we experience freedom of will *are incompatible with psychological situations where causal analysis is reasonably attempted.* In other words, when we use the phrase "I will" we *renounce explanatory argumentation.*

The relevance of these epistemological considerations to the problem of the relationship between human identity as self-objectivation and human identity experienced as ˙pure subjective actuality is made even clearer in Bohr's statement: "the approach towards the problem of explanation that is embodied in the notion of complementarity suggests itself in our position as conscious beings and recalls forcefully ... that ... it must never be forgotten that we ourselves are both actors and spectators in the drama of existence" (p. 318). When we deal with problems of human identity, we must, therefore, in the words of Bohr, "aim at an appropriate dialectic expression for the actual conditions of analysis and synthesis." The search for this appropriate dialectical expression for the actual conditions remains a task to be fulfilled. This task becomes obscured if we place a greater emphasis on identity as self-objectivation (socially defined identity) than on the experience of identity as pure actuality of being. Only if we give to each of these dimensions of human identity equal weight are we using a complementary mode of description which is characterized by the awareness that "in the contrasting phenomena we have to do with equally essential aspects of all well-defined knowledge about these objects" (1948, p. 317).

In both "The Problem of Identity" (1959) and *Young Man Luther* (1958), particularly in the latter, Erikson touches upon this dialectic relation of the two incompatible modes in which identity can be experienced in his discussion of the concept of ideology. Because of what appears to me to be an overemphasis on the aspects of self-objectivation in human identity, the conceptual clarification of the nature and function of ideologies remains, however, somewhat ambiguous and problematic. Erikson introduces the concept of ideology in the context of his discussion of the emergence of identity at the end of adolescence. He describes ideology as "the [unconscious] tendency at a given time to make facts amenable to ideas, and ideas to facts in order to create a world image convincing enough to support the collective and individual sense of identity" (1958, p. 22). Erikson is inclined to see an "ideological formula, intelligible both in terms of individual development and significant traditions" as essential for the establishment of psychosocial identity at the end of ·adolescence (p. 118). The matter is complicated by the fact that the historically available ideology does not always support the collective and individual sense of identity within a given culture. "Each historical period has its lacunae of identity and style; . . . Man never lives entirely in his time, even though he can never live outside it; sometimes his identity gets along with his time's ideology, and sometimes it has to fight for its life" (p. 221). And it is in the latter case that individuals arise who "sow ideological seeds into fresh furrows of historical change" (p. 221). The phenomenon of ideology can be shown to present most poignantly the dilemma of human identity in terms of self-objectivation versus the identity of pure actuality of being.

Erikson sees the relationship between identity and ideology as so significant that he characterizes his Luther book as "a book on identity and ideology" (p. 22). This is a recognition of the fact that identity in man leads necessarily to the emergence of a *historical* consciousness concerning his existence. The dilemma of man's historical existence can be understood as a derivative of the dilemma of "subjective" identity versus identity as self-objectivation: insofar as man is capable of self-objectivation, of a perception of himself as an actor in the drama of history, living a social identity within a historical context, he loses some of his capacity to "act historically." Historical consciousness is, in the most radical sense, incompatible with "making history." The reason for this incompatibility is that, in order to "make history," an individual must lose his socially defined, culturally supported identity. He must be so close to a catastrophic sense of loss of his "objective" identity that his only choice is a new self-definition, a groping toward a new identity. The more individuals in a given situation are confronted with such an inner necessity, the greater will be their determination to impose this new identity upon their contemporaries. This will imply a radical challenge to the culturally accepted world image and the cultural patterns and institutions that are based on it. This birth of a new identity constitutes one of those profound transformations of human identity which we have in mind when we speak of the historical process of human self-transformation. This transformation, I believe, presupposes a retreat, a narcissistic regression to the experience of the identity of pure subjective actuality.

Erikson refers to this phenomenon as the experience of "passive identity."

Meaningful implications are lost in the flat word *passivity*— among them the total attitude of living receptively and through the senses, of willingly "suffering" the voice of one's intuition and of living a *Passion*: that total passivity in which man regains, through considered self-sacrifice and self-transcendence, his active position in the face of nothingness and thus is saved. [1958, pp. 208–209]

Passive identity implies, then, a particularly radical form of the experience of pure actuality of being, in that it presupposes a complete shattering of all capacities of self-objectivation. Erikson elaborates on this concept of "passive identity" in his discussion of German mysticism, particularly of the mystic Tauler. "For Tauler God begins where all categories and differentiations end ... he is the Unborn Light. ... To reach him, one must be able to develop the *raptus*, the rapt state of complete passivity in which man loses his name, his attributes, and his will (1958, p. 189). To this description Erikson adds the following comment: "We are here confronted with a system which retreats far behind the gnostic position, and far below the trust position of infancy. It is the return to a state of symbiosis with the matrix, a state of floating unity fed by a spiritual navel cord. We may call it the *passive identity*."

In this extreme form of the experience of identity as a pure actuality of being, the objective social self is indeed sacrificed and the social reality, the "horizontal of worldly organization," is transcended. As Erikson insists, however, it is from this state of identity experience that man may regain his active position in the face of nothingness. The person who is capable of reaching this total eclipse of self-objectivation is approaching total loss of identity. But the possibility exists for the individual in such a crisis of regaining a new "active position" which is, however, not the activity of the workaday world of self-objectivation. It is a special type of activity that may be characterized as "historical action."

Historical action is based on a redefinition of human identity in the face of the danger of loss of all definable social identity. In the encounter with a most radical experience of identity as subjective actuality, it can lead to a new interpretation of the existing world and man's role in it. This is possible because the experience of "passive identity," as described by Erikson, is nothing but a regressive recapitulation of the stage of infancy when a "primary identity" is formed through the "imprinting" of an "identity theme" on the infant by the mother, as I have suggested in chapter 2. In the retreat to a "passive identity" this "primary identity" can be recaptured, and consequently a "new beginning" (Balint 1952a) becomes possible. This interpretation seems consistent with Erikson's claim that "an ideological formula . . . must do for the young person what the mother did for the infant: provide nutriment for the soul as well as for the stomach" (1958, p. 118). The adult who, in the despair of loss of his identity as self-objectivation retreats to his "primary identity," returns—if he returns at all—with a new interpretation of his "identity theme," which redefines his "instrumentality" toward his mother, i.e., the world. Such a new interpretation of man's instrumentality in relation to the world constitutes, if it becomes conceptualized, ideology.

It is therefore implicit in the concept of an ideology that it suspends the validity of the historical and social conditions which exist at a given time. These conditions appear to the new ideology as a denial of the "true" identity of man. Ordinary workaday activity of human beings, living in harmony with the prevailing, existing ideology of their age, appears to those "enlightened" by the new ideology at best as existing in a state of alienation from the ideal human condition, and at its worst, as wilful and malevolent challenge to his ideal identity: the challenger must be destroyed and "buried" by the disciples of the new ideology.

Here then is the paradox: a new ideology enables man to regain his capacity to "make history." But because of this very capacity, every new ideology is peculiarly lacking in "historical consciousness" in the ordinary sense of the word—an awareness of the historical condition-ing of the existing patterns of culture, an attitude which leads to their dispassionate understanding. The consciousness of the person who is engaged in "historical action," however, grandiosely and often destructively oversimplifies any given historical conflict as a struggle between the "children of light and the powers of darkness." This may well be the meaning of Goethe's remark that "the one who acts is always without conscience; nobody has conscience except he who contemplates" (1809–29). In describing the spirit of the early Christian church, Erikson vividly portrays the power struggle of a new ideology in its effort to impose a new identity upon an old culture.

The Roman church, more than any other church or political organization, succeeded in making an ideological dogma—formulated, defended, and imposed by a central governing body—the exclusive condition for *any* identity on earth. It made this total claim totalitarian by using terror. In this case (as in others) the terror was not always directly applied to quivering bodies; it was predicted for a future world, typically in such a way that nobody could quite know whom it would hit, or when. That a man has or may have done something mortally bad, something which may or may not ruin his eternal after-condition, makes his status and inner state totally dependent on the monopolists of salvation, and leaves him only the identity of a potential sinner. [1958, pp. 181–182]

This description seems to me to apply to *all* historic actions based on a redefinition of human identity: he who does not accept the new identity is persecuted and destroyed.

It can be see from the quotations from *Young Man Luther* that Erikson deals throughout this work with a particular aspect of the dilemma of human identity. It manifests itself in the incompatibility of "historical consciousness," based on a high degree of conscious self-objectivation, with the consciousness of those who "make history." The latter are imbued with a totally subjective experience of a new identity, recaptured from the wreckage of the social and cultural patterns of existing self-objectivations. In contrast, Erikson seems to believe that "historical action" can and should be derived from the existence of a "historical consciousness." To Erikson, if I understand him correctly, the awareness of the historical and cultural forces of an individual's era and their demands on him can lead to the conditions for the emergence of "historical action." He postulates some uniquely individual responses to these cultural demands of the era, such as "an overwhelming negative conscience . . . linked with a sensitivity and the power drive of a Luther." Given this personal psychological constellation, a "new positive conscience" might assert itself, which, in turn, may bring about a new ideology in common to ego qualities I have tried to circumscribe in this discussion" (1958, p. 221).

But guilt problems ("negative conscience" in Erikson's terminology), sensitivity, and power drive do not by themselves require the radical new departure that is implied in the "historical act." Erikson's own formulations regarding the individual's retreat to that "total passivity in which man . . . regains his active position in the face of nothingness" (pp. 208ff.) suggest that, whenever the available forms of self-objectivation in a given culture fail to provide a large group of individuals with the means of identity maintenance, there will be a return on the part of such individuals to the "passive identity" experience as the only way to recapture a new interpretation of their primary "identity themes." This experience will bring about a profound change of their world image and influence the institutions of the culture by means of a new ideology which thus becomes the pacemaker of historical change. An ideology will be effective when it offers a significant group of individuals a new and meaningful form of self-objectivation instead of the one that failed them. The individual can thus be reborn from the retreat to the state of "symbiosis with the matrix" into a world in which he can live and experience himself as an active partner of its mysterious, but dimly perceived designs.

The view presented here does imply that all identity in terms of self-objectivation is a translation or a variation of a primary, presocial, and precultural identity. It is therefore not compatible with Erikson's view that these earliest precursors of identity must be understood in terms of the later developing identity as self-objectivation, i.e., as a socially definable identity. My doubts concerning the possibility of making the social identity of adolescence the basis for the understanding of human identity are therefore reinforced by the difficulty of deriving an understanding of the transformation of identity in the historical process on the basis of such a premise. Self-objectivation can be understood only as a variation of a "primary identity." When dealing with the phenomenon of identity, we intuitively search for *"den ruhenden Pol in der Erscheinungen Flucht* [the continuum within the never ceasing transformations]" (Schiller 1795). Culture, society, institutions seem to offer, compared to the fleeting existence of single individuals, the appearance of a continuum. I believe, however, that the dilemma of human identity constitutes the continuum: society and culture arise from it as temporary systems of identity maintenance. The emergence, the dissolution, and transformation of these forms of identity maintenance we describe as the historical process.

The work of Erikson has opened up new dimensions of psychological awareness of psychoanalysis. In each successive contribution Erikson has transcended earlier, more traditional ways of thinking. Perhaps nothing is a greater tribute to the spirit of his work than the fact that in his latest work on Luther he has boldly transcended his own earlier conceptualizations. Without Erikson's contribution to psychoanalytic thought many problems that are germane to psychoanalytic psychology could not even be raised. It would be difficult, for instance, for a psychoanalyst to deal with the questions raised by Helen M. Lynd (1958) in her book *On Shame and the Search for Identity*. Because it illuminates particularly those aspects of the identity problem that lie beyond identity as self-objectivation, it appears as complementary to the work of Erikson.

Chapter 6

H.M. LYND:
IDENTITY AND METAMORPHOSIS

I shall confine myself to a discussion of those of Lynd's propositions that are pertinent to the problem under investigation, i.e., the dilemma of human identity. Lynd's book aims at a far more inclusive critique of the conceptial basis of the behavioral sciences, among which psychoanalysis occupies a place of special importance for her. This critique is part of an even broader reevaluation of the tradition of Western scientific thought and its philosophical foundations: Lynd, writing from a viewpoint close to existentialism, considers them as a hindrance for the development of a science of the human personality. This aspect of Lynd's book has been dealt with incisively by Coltrera (1962). In this essay I shall therefore concentrate on the contribution which Lynd makes to the phenomenology of the experience of shame, which I consider of great importance for psychoanalytic theory. I shall contrast her view with those of representative psychoanalysts who have dealt with this psychological problem.

Almost all psychoanalytic contributions to an analysis of the experience of shame see in it a reaction to the awareness of some form of moral wrongdoing, or to deviation from some ideal. In view of this widely held opinion, it appears to me a significant contribution to the psychology of shame that Lynd clearly and, I believe, convincingly demonstrates that such a close correlation between shame and moral wrongdoing does not exist. An indication of the complexity of the problem is the fact, emphasized by Lynd, that the experience of shame is not even necessarily related to one's own conduct: some of the most painful experiences of shame may be brought on by the conduct of others. I shall presently summarize the main characteristics of a phenomenology of the experience of shame as presented by Lynd.

All experiences of shame have in common the presence of indefinable imponderables which seem regularly to accompany its occurrence. According to Lynd, "the shameful situation" (p. 49ff.) can never be fully understood by focusing on the external circumstances under which it occurs. These external circumstances can be a most trivial matter, far removed from any moral significance, such as "an awkward gesture, a gaucherie in dress or table manners . . . a mispronounced word" (p. 40). But, "even more than the uncovering of weakness or ineptness, exposure of misplaced confidence can be shameful. . . . The greater the expectation, the more acute the shame" (p. 43ff.). This applies also to the revelation of one's love for another person. The explanation that this is always due to the danger of possible rejection is not convincing, because in may instnaces the opposite expectation is compatible with the experience of shame.

Lynd lists four basic characteristics which she believes are essential in any experience of shame: a sense of exposure, the element of unexpectedness, the feeling of incongruity or inappropriateness, and a unique feeling of confusion. Each of these four elements reflects, for Lynd, the *existential* character of shame. Thus, *exposure* does not refer to bodily exposure but to "exposure of peculiarly sensitive, intimate, vulnerable aspects of the self" which is only incidentally an exposure to others, but more fundamentally "exposure to one's own eyes " (pp. 27-28). Equally, *unexpectedness* "is more than suddenness in time; it is also an astonishment at seeing different parts of ourselves . . . suddenly coming together . . . with aspects of the world we have not recognized" (p. 34). *Incongruity*, or *inappropriateness*, is derived by Lynd from the sudden appearance of a sense of "discrepancy . . . between us and the social situation, between what we feel from within and what appears to us, and perhaps to others, seen from without" (p. 35). Finally, what Lynd describes as *confusion* is understood as a "loss of identity one thought one had" (p. 37). Thus, Lynd concludes that "shame is an experience that affects and is affected by the whole self. This whole-self involvement is one of its distinguishing characteristics and one that makes it a clue to identity" (p. 49). It follows for Lynd (p. 35ff.) "that aspects of the phenomenon of shame can be understood only with reference to transcultural values, and that this awareness of values beyond one's own society is one of the distinctions between shame and guilt." Lynd's existential analysis of shame invites a comparison with that of Sartre (1943). For this I must again refer to Coltrera's (1962) essay.

We recognize here a striking similarity between Lynd's understanding of the experience of shame and Erikson's concept of "passive identity" through which man regains his active position in the face of nothingness. Lynd attributes to shame, as Erikson to "passive identity," the capacity to "call into question, not only one's own adequacy and the validity of the codes of one's immediate society, but the meaning of the universe itself" (p. 57). Like "passive identity," the experience of shame is credited with the power of "revelation of the whole self" (p. 50) and of self-transcendence capable of effecting some change in the whole self. Lastly, like the German mystics whom Erikson quotes in connection with his discussion of "passive identity," Lynd sees in shame a revelatory, rapturous experience. This is in significant contrast to the traditional psychological interpretation of shame as an essentially agonizing, painful experience. While Lynd fully acknowledges this painful character of the experience of shame, she strongly emphasizes that the transformation of the whole self brought about by such experience could be described "in Plato's words, [as] a turning of the whole soul toward the light" (p. 51). Here the similarity to Erikson ends.

For Erikson, the experience of "passive identity" is indicative of a profound crisis, leading to a retreat "far below the trust position of infancy . . . [to a] return to a state of symbiosis with the matrix" (1958, p. 189). Lynd, however, sees in experiences of shame the crucial turning point through which the individual can realize the uniqueness of his individual existence. Thus we are told that

Experiences of shame . . . can lead in two different directions: 1) They can lead to protection of the exposed self and the exposed society at all costs—refusing to recognize the wound, covering the isolating effect of shame through depersonalization and adaptation to any approved codes. 2) If experiences of shame can be fully faced, if we allow ourselves to realize their import, they can

inform the self, and become a revelation of oneself, of one's
society, and of the human situation. [p. 71]

From these two directions to which experiences of shame can lead,
Lynd derives two basic personality patterns: those who live in terms of
a "guilt axis" are contrasted to personalities living in terms of a "shame
axis" (p. 204ff.). These two types are not essentially psychologically,
but existentially understood, comparable to Heidegger's (Coltrera
1962, Heidegger 1927) distinction of an "inauthentic" as against an
"authentic" way of existing. Here the fundamental difference between
Erikson's and Lynd's approach to identity becomes very clear: while
for Erikson identity tends to culminate in the self-objectivation of a
socially defined role, Lynd inclines to view self-objectivation as an
"inauthentic" identity that must be transcended in order for the
individual to discover his true, "authentic" identity. The latter is seen as
lying beyond all socially approved and approvable identities. Lynd
believes that the royal road to the revelation of an individual's
authentic identity is experiences of shame which, when unhesitatingly
confronted and accepted in all their agonizing ecstasy, give birth to an
identity beyond all culturally confined and confining roles. This
concept of identity revelation may, to the psychologically oriented,
sound indeed strange and rather mystical. The psychoanalyst can,
however, not deny that some descriptions of sexual ecstasy have a
similar quality. To illustrate this, I shall quote a passage from D. H.
Lawrence:

Though a little frightened, she let him have his way, and the
reckless, shameless sensuality shook her to her foundations,
stripped her to the very last, and made a different woman of her. It
was not really love, it was not voluptuousness. It was sensuality
sharp and searing as fire, burning the soul to tinder. Burning out
the shames, the deepest oldest shames, in the most secret places. It
cost her an effort to let him have his way and his will of her. She
had to be a passive, consenting thing, like a slave, a physical slave.
Yet the passion licked round her, consuming, and when the
sensual flame of it pressed through her bowels and breast, she
really thought she was dying. Yet a poignant, marvelous death.
[Lawrence 1928, p. 297]

I do not want to imply, by the choice of this passage from *Lady Chatterley's Lover*, that this ecstatic experience in which shame and the "triumphant" experience of transformation of the sense of identity are blended indistinguishably occurs only in sexual intercourse. I do believe, however, that phenomena as those described in this chapter raise questions concerning the relationship between sexuality, identity, dissolution of identity, and shame. These are the phenomena that I consider essential for any psychoanalytic study of the experience of shame, and I shall therefore depart temporarily from my discussion of Lynd's work in order to give a brief account of psychoanalytic thinking regarding the experience of shame. This will necessitate special attention to Piers and Singer's *Shame and Guilt* (1953).

The connection of shame with sexual exposure of the body is so obvious, at least in Western civilization, that it appeared to Freud (1905) that "shame was the force which opposes the voyeuristic drive and might be overcome by the latter." During latency, shame, like disgust, was erected as one of the barriers against the sexual drive and fortified by educational injunctions against exposure. Freud believed that "actually this development is organically determined, fixed by heredity and it is established occasionally entirely without the help of training" (1905, p. 583; Piers and Singer 1953, p. 8). Nunberg (1932) emphasizes that shame and guilt are not clearly distinguishable from one another. He postulates a common root for all such reactions to the manifestations of the drives, like shame, disgust, pity, anxiety, and guilt. He also emphasizes that shame becomes more and more a general response to any kind of immoral thought or immoral action even if no sexual content is involved. Fenichel (1937), while accepting the experience of shame as a defense against exhibitionistic and voyeuristic desires, felt that the sense of shame is a response to the notion of "ocular introjection," of being devoured by the other person's stare or nearing punishment for wanting to devour the love object through one's eyes. Erikson sees shame and doubt as specific dangers for the development of ego identity, to which the child passing through the phase of anal-muscular maturation is especially prone. This maturation should lead to a first sense of autonomy, but one that is still precariously balanced. Failure to succeed in this striving for autonomy will throw the child into the turmoil of shame and doubt (1950a, p. 223). This phase of "autonomy versus doubt and shame" is considered an important precursor of identity consciousness in adolescence.

> Identity consciousness . . . is a new edition of that original *doubt* which concerns the trustworthiness of the training adults and the trustworthiness of the child himself. . . . The obligation now to achieve an identity, not only distinct but also distinctive, is apt to arouse a painful over-all *ashamedness*, somehow comparable to the original shame . . . over being visible all around to all-knowing adults. [Erikson 1959, p. 143]

From these quotations one may deduce some correlation between shame, sexuality, particularly exhibitionistic and voyeuristic drive impulses on the one hand, and fear of loss of autonomy (being devoured), of being at the mercy of others on the other hand. Erikson goes a step further in postulating a definite correlation between shame and the "identity consciousness" of adolescence. Very different viewpoints are brought into the discussion of the experience of shame by Piers.

In their monograph, Piers and Singer (1953) aim at a decisive differentiation of shame from guilt. In order to arrive at such a differentiation between shame and guilt, expressed in structural terms, Piers introduces a sharp distinction between the superego and the ego ideal, in contrast to Freud's synonymous use of these two terms. For Piers, "the term Super-Ego [is defined] exclusively as stemming from internalizations (introjection) of the punishing, restrictive aspects of parental images" (p. 6). The ego ideal, on the other hand, represents, for Piers, the sum of the positive identification with the parental images: "Both the loving, the reassuring parent . . . and the narcissistically expecting parent and the parent who imposes his own unobtained ideals on the child, may be represented here" (p. 14). In addition, the "Ego-Ideal contains layers of *later identifications*, more superficial . . ., but of the greatest social significance. The 'social role' that an individual assumes . . . is largely determined by the structure of these developmentally later parts of his Ego-Ideal" (p. 14). Piers understands the ego ideal to contain the core of narcissistic omnipotence: it may lead to "pathological conditions with overinflated, grandiose or perfectionistic Ideals," or it may support "such healthy, integrative functions as self-confidence, hope and trust in others" (p. 14). He stresses the fact that "the Ego-Ideal is in continuous dynamic interfunction with the unconscious and conscious *awareness of the Ego's potentialities*" (p. 14). Piers postulates the existence of a "maturation drive" aiming at the realization of these potentialities. "It would signify a psychic representation of all the growth, maturation and individuation processes in the human being, beginning with the most primitive organizational functions made possible by the progressive myelinization of the nervous system in infancy up to those highly complex functions that strive for what is somewhat romantically referred to as self-realization" (p. 15).

Having thus developed his concept of the ego ideal, Piers defines shame as the completely internalized tension between the ego and the ego ideal.

> Shame . . . occurs whenever goals and images presented by the Ego-Ideal are not reached. If shame can reach such a degree that it appears as conscious anxiety, it must imply a severe unconscious threat to the Ego. . . . Behind the feeling of shame stands not the fear of hatred [by the superego], but the fear of *contempt* which, on an even deeper level of the unconscious, spells fear of *abandonment*, the death by emotional starvation. . . . We suspect, however, that the deeper-rooted shame anxiety is based on the fear of the parent who walks away "in disgust," and that this anxiety in turn draws its terror from the earlier established and probably ubiquital separation anxiety. . . . On a higher, social and more conscious level of individual development, it is again not fear of active punishment by superiors which is implied in shame anxiety, but social expulsion, like ostracism. [p. 16]

Piers's propositions are very far-reaching. I will confine myself to a single problem that seems to me inherent in his concept of an ego ideal. Pier suggests that the ego ideal represents all the growth, maturation, and individuation processes of the personality. It is against those "potentialities" that the ego measures its own state, and, if falling short of them, experiences shame. This proposition concerning the ego ideal raises theoretical problems similar to those inherent in Erikson's concept of an epigenetic principle of personality development. Like Erikson, Piers assumes the existence of a "ground plan" which constitutes the means by which we may measure the maturity accomplished by a personality.

I consider the notion of an ideal maturational stage a construction based on arbitrary standards of maturity. It appears to me characteristic of the development of the human personality that there cannot ever be any definable "goal" of psychological growth, for the reasons advanced in my discussion of Erikson's epigenetic principle. My first objection to Piers's theory of shame is therefore that it is based on the assumption of a predetermined developmental standard for the human personality. Moreover, Piers, when speaking of the ego ideal, implies that this ideal is constituted both by hypothetical maturational goals of the unconscious, and also by educational, i.e., social and cultural goals. To explain shame as a tension between the ego and the ego ideal would therefore presuppose that the maturational aim of Piers's "maturational drive" is always in harmony with the cultural ideals mediated by parents, educators, etc. I cannot believe in such a Leibnizian "pre-established" harmony between maturation and culture. The individual whose maturational potentialities would make him strive, for instance, to be a musician, while the educational goal would demand that he be a military leader, could, if I understand Piers correctly, exist only in permanent shame, because, whatever he chose to do, he would always fall short of one aspect of his ego ideal. Grinker, who also assumes a maturational ideal, is more consistent than Piers in that he clearly states "that there is a primary nuclear shame . . . before culture has exerted much influence" (1955, p. 251). Grinker is also aware that such an assumption raises many and difficult issues when he remarks that "primary shame must be related to the speed and completeness with which somatic and psychological structure-functions mature. Where is deviation registered? Are the discrepancies those of the organizer of pace-making functions inherent to the species or those of the individual's specific genic-determined growth-potential? Such questions have no current answer."

Finally, I cannot agree that shame is always and exclusively experienced in situations of personal shortcoming with respect to some normative ideal. I feel that Lynd has convincingly established the fact that there is no such simple correlation between shame and some sort of wrongdoing. I therefore propose to investigate alternative explanations of the experience of shame.

Feldman (1962) has extensively dealt with the symptom of pathological blushing. He, too, advances the proposition that shame is a response to failure to live up to a maturational goal. According to Feldman, "one is ashamed of not living up to one's biological task." This view is very close to Grinker's concept of nuclear shame. It also offers the same conceptual difficulties inherent in a concept of a predetermined ultimate aim of personality development. But Feldman's paper contains many important clinical observations that contribute relevant facts to our understanding of shame. Thus, he stresses the fact that the physiological symptoms of shame are those of sexual excitement. He also speaks of pathological blushers as displaying "frighteningly intense aggression. Such patients think that they could kill." They are also individuals "whose narcissism has been severely damaged." In this connection a passage from a paper by Hermann (1943), which Feldman quotes, seems significant: "He who is forced to be ashamed is not allowed to cling and is without support. He has no will. He is paralyzed and close to fainting. He is subdued like a slave and forced to serve. He loses ground, casts down his eyes, and wants to hide. The strong have dominance over him." Here again it is an equation of shame with loss of will, passivity, feeling like a slave, like a physical thing. It reminds us of Lawrence's passage quoted above.

In order to reconcile the fact that shame is experienced both as an agonizing, even overwhelmingly threatening emotion, and at the same time can have a close relationship to blissful self-abandon and ecstasy, a proposition made by Freud (1921, p. 130ff.) may prove helpful:

Each of the mental differentiations that we have become acquainted with represents a fresh aggravation of the difficulties of mental functioning, increases its instability, and may become the starting-point for its breakdown, that is, for the onset of a disease. Thus, by being born we have made the step from an absolutely self-sufficient narcissism to the perception of a changing external world and the beginnings of the discovery of objects. And with this is associated the fact that we cannot endure the new state of things for long, that we periodically revert from it, in our sleep, to our former condition of absence of stimulation and avoidance of objects. . . . It is quite conceivable that the separation of the ego ideal and the ego cannot be borne for long either, and has to be temporarily undone. In all renunciations and limitations imposed on the ego, a periodic infringement of the prohibition is the rule; this indeed is shown by the institution of festivals, which in origin are nothing less nor more than excesses provided by law and which owe their cheerful character to the *release* which they bring. The Saturnalia of the Romans and our modern carnival agree in this essential feature with the festivals of primitive people, which usually end in debaucheries of every kind and the transgressions of what are at other times the most sacred commandments. But the ego ideal comprises the sum of all the limitations in which the ego has to acquiesce, and for that reason the abrogation of the ideal would necessarily be a *magnificent festival* for the ego, which might then once again feel satisfied with itself. [my italics]

Freud postulates here that the relinquishing of a developmental acquisition may be perceived as celebration and triumph. Regression thus becomes a source of a special type of joyous, even orgastic ecstasy.

I believe that this Freudian proposition contributes an important consideration to our thinking concerning psychological growth and development. Instead of thinking of development as the attainment of a maturational plateau (see also Strauss 1959), Freud suggests, as I understand him, that the development of the personality has a dialectic movement of its own. Each new developmental acquisition approaches a certain limit, where it becomes an impediment rather than a stimulus to new growth. Instead of progressive psychological structuralization, Freud sees a growing pull toward an at least temporary relinquishing of the latest structure before new psychological growth can occur. My proposition is therefore that we do exist in constant tension between identity maintenance and the temptation to abandon our identity as humans altogether. When D. H. Lawrence describes Lady Chatterley as experiencing herself shamefully and blissfully as a physical thing, as a slave to her lover, or when Hermann compares being shamed to becoming enslaved and experiencing a loss of will, does this not imply a relinquishing of human identity to the point of yielding to the temptation of dehumanized "thing-ness"? This loss of the human quality of identity is acknowledged by Erikson in describing young people suffering from a severe identity crisis: "This rock-bottom attitude," as Erikson calls it, "is expressed *in a strange evolutionary imagery*. Total feeling becomes *dehumanized*, and eventually even *demammalized*" (1958, pp. 103ff.; my italics). This type of retreat to a nonhuman identity I have described as *metamorphosis*.

The concept of metamorphosis has recently received most valuable clinical support in the work of Searles (1960). I refer here to Searles's proposition concerning "phylogenetic regression." Searles defines this concept as follows: "This yearning to become nonhuman can frequently be viewed as a need, on the part of the patient, to regress phylogenetically, to 'return' symbolically to the nonhuman state out of which the human race emerged in the long course of evolution, in order to get a fresh start in the struggle to achieve individuation, and subsequent emotional maturation, as a human being" (p. 250). In the development of his propositions Searles discusses the role that the idea of metamorphosis plays in myths and fairy tales as well as in literature. Experiences of oneself as being nonhuman, or parts of oneself as being nonhuman, or treating others as if they were nonhuman are documented by the author's rich experience with psychotic and severely neurotic patients. Searles emphasizes that what we see in these pathological cases is only an extreme form of normal psychological states.

The phenomenon of metamorphosis requires the introduction of certain propositions concerning the nature of psychological processes. It suggests that all psychological processes occur as a kind of pendulum movement between identity and nonidentity or dehumanization. (See also Spiegel's [1959] concept of oscillation.) The difference between normal individuals and pathological cases seem to be not a difference in quality but one of the degree in the swing of the pendulum. The assumption of such a pendulum pattern of psychological development permits the distinction of yet another aspect of the dilemma of human identity. We might call it the dilemma of the *limits* of human identity. It implies that the establishment of identity gives rise to a movement of the pendulum in the opposite direction. Similar to Freud's idea that the acquisition of the superego brings about a yearning to "liberate" oneself from its yoke, human identity gives rise to both a yearning and a profound anxiety to abandon it. Such reaching out toward excesses of dehumanization seems to form an important aspect of the ecstasy of sexual orgasm.

We are now prepared to return to the discussion of the paradoxical character of the experience of shame that Lynd describes. Abandonment of identity produces profound confusion, bewilderment, and anguish. But it can also be experienced, as Lynd suggests, as liberation and ecstasy. For this *loss* of the *human* quality of identity a special term recommends itself, namely, the term *metamorphosis* which I have used to describe a uniquely *human* psychological phenomenon. I use this term not in its traditional biological meaning, as used, for instance, by Schachtel (1959), but in the tradition of myths, fairy tales, and literature. The term was used in this latter sense by Géza Róheim in a paper that appeared under the title "Metamorphosis" in 1948. I think, therefore, that my use of the term will not cause any confusion.

I believe that metamorphosis and identity are the two limits of human existence, incompatible with one another, but complementary in that human life exists in a movement between these two limits. The experience of shame becomes more understandable when seen in the context of this dilemma of identity and metamorphosis. Shame, according to this thesis, is a sudden, unexpected breakthrough of yearnings to yield to the ever-present temptation to abandon *human identity*, i.e., to accept metamorphosis as an alternative. Because it is a temptation, the response of the ego to the increase of this yearning is perceived as danger, and consequently anxiety is experienced. The physiological symptoms of blushing, warmth, palpitation, etc., which Feldman (1962) characterizes as indicative of sexual excitement, betray the powerful urge to yield to this temptation and indicate the lustful anticipation of the "marvelous death" of one's human identity. Feldman's assertion that "blushing begins with children at the time when they are expected to repress their polymorphous-perverse, exhibitionistic, voyeuristic, and genital drives" seems to support this proposition. Blushing appears at a time when the child is expected to have reached a firm perception and acceptance of its separateness, which is the prerequisite of all identity maintenance. It is only then that relinquishing of the rudimentary, just-established identity becomes tempting. Shame occurs in such situations where the burden of identity and separateness, the loneliness of autonomy has become unbearable: the temptation to abandon it, to give up one's will, to become a slave, a physical thing, triumphs over our defenses. I believe that the characteristic features of the "shameful situations" as described by Lynd can equally be understood in these terms.

By interpreting shame as a struggle against the temptation of metamorphosis it also becomes possible to understand why we correlate shame with the experience of wrongdoing. Piers (1953) has emphasized the fear of abandonment as characteristic of shame. Piers sees the abandonment as a punishment for a wrong act or, internalized, as tension between ego and ego ideal. I believe that fear of abandonment and painful separateness enhances the yearning for metamorphosis, the flight from human identity. Instead of seeing shame as a tension between ego and ideal, as Piers does, I interpret it as the breakdown of the capacity for identity maintenance, carrying with it the threat of metamorphosis. The feeling of being in communication with the world around him is endangered for the person who has committed an offensive act. He is suddenly cut off from the others; it is then that a yearning for a shortcut to a reunion with the matrix becomes overpowering. Shame thus betrays the latent willingness to abandon any pretense of individuality, autonomy, and human identity. This may well be the threat perceived by those "blushers" who, as Feldman (1962) says, "feel they could kill"; their aggression is proportionate to the intensity of unconscious desires to retreat from human identity. This danger will be greatest in those narcissistic individuals who, by their inability to establish meaningful object relations, yearn to return to a symbiotic union with a dominant parent figure.

I believe that the inner relationship between sex, love, shame, and abandonment of identity becomes clearer when we see each of these phenomena as aspects of the dilemma of identity, a dilemma that expresses itself in terms of identity versus metamorphosis. It is in the sexual union that the yearning to surrender one's identity is most powerful and indeed irresistible. Anna Freud (1952) has described patients in whom this feeling dominates their sexual life. Spiegel (1959) has spoken of the fear of sex as being due, in certain individuals, to their longing for "surrender of one's personality." In contrast, one could, paraphrasing Kris (1936), characterize "normal" sexuality as "metamorphosis in the service of identity maintenance."

At last, I can more precisely state my position with regard to Lynd's propositions concerning the experience of shame. Lynd's phenomenological descriptions of the "shameful situation" seem to me to be valid in their emphasis on the complex conditions under which experiences of shame occur. I share Lynd's view that shame cannot be understood fully as a response to moral wrongdoing nor as failure to live up to one's potentialities. I believe that Lynd perceives correctly an ecstatic quality in experiences of shame, which is particularly apparent in the "lustful shame" of sexual abandon. I cannot, however, follow Lynd when she goes on to claim that experiences of shame, fully faced, are the exclusive path which will invariably lead toward a revelation of the individual's "authentic" identity. If shame were nothing but a form of the experience of the pure actuality of being, it could be argued that no individual can reach the full range of human identity consciousness without the experience of his "subjective" identity. Shame, however, according to propositions developed in this essay, represents something quite different from the experience of the pure actuality of being, as contrasted to the self-objectivation of a socially defined identity. Experiences of shame, in spite of many similarities, must therefore be distinguished from Erikson's concept of "passive identity." Experiences of shame reveal the dilemma of the limits of human identity and metamorphosis. It is my belief that identity and metamorphosis do *not* constitute alternative choices open to man. As existential limits, they confront man with the necessity to exist *between* these limits—however precarious such balance may appear. It is always tempting to avoid the perplexities of human identity by forcing a choice in favor of one or the other of the aspects of these dilemmas. With regard to the dilemma of identity versus metamorphosis, this temptation has always been powerful: it leads to a cult of an "orgastic existence" for which spokesmen can be found in ancient and modern thought. Recently, it has been suggested by some authors, such as Norman O. Brown, that psychoanalytic theory, properly carried to its implicit conclusions, must advocate such a choice (Brown 1959). Against these seemingly radical positions, toward which, I believe,

Lynd in certain aspects of her book inclines, I want to set my conviction that any attempt to force a choice in favor of one aspect of the dilemmas of human identity as against the other may indeed let human existence "come to shame."

Chapter 7

ANSELM STRAUSS: HUMAN IDENTITY
VS. SOCIAL STABILITY

Chapter 6, dealing with the psychological meaning of shame, arrived at the conclusion that human identity has to be maintained against the temptation to regress to a state of nonidentity. This yearning to give up the mintenance of personal identity was described as the possibility of metamorphosis, implying the transformation of a person into a nonperson, be it an animal, a plant or an inanimate thing, or the transformation of something that is not a person into a person. Transformations of identity that include such radical possibilities are customary in fairy tales and myths, but are not taken into consideration by students of human psychology.

The recent attention to the processes that Mahler refers to as the "psychological birth of the infant" may permit the use of the concept of metamorphosis in human psychology, to characterize a yearning to give up separateness and personal identity for the sake of a return to the symbiotic oneness with the mother, the stage before one has acquired personhood. In this sense, to become a nonperson may become a powerful desire that may appear in numerous psychological disguises and that may well be characterized as a yearning for metamorphosis. This wish is, however, incompatible with the aims of human social organizations, whose existence depends on "stable" human identities and whose function is essentially the maintenance of such identities through socially supported, definable roles. In addition, social organizations must create systems of thought that make the transformation of individuals from birth to death meaningful and compatible with a sense of permanence within change. This task is accomplished in societies by means of religious or ideological interpretations of the position of human life in nature and history.

All these efforts at identity maintenance are, however, endangered by the temptation to yield to the desire to divest oneself of one's separateness and personal identity. This desire constitutes a danger to the stability of any social organization, and while it may be given an opportunity to express itself as part of religious rituals, it cannot be tolerated as an alternate option among other social roles. It is probably significant that deprivation of social identity is in many societies threatened as punishment to those who show unacceptable conduct, i.e., conduct that deviates from the prevailing definitions of social roles. It seems as if these punishments aim to exploit the link between the experience of shame and the yielding to the regressive desire to lose one's separateness and individuality. Punishments like setting a person into a pillory, or compelling somebody to wear a dunce's cap are obviously intended to impose a shameful state. Those that have failed to live up to the standards of their socially defined role identity are coerced to regress, and by their spontaneous shame reaction forced to admit their secret longings for regression. R. H. Williams (1942) refers to Max Weber's remarks that Puritanism created an "unprecedented inner isolation of the individual," which went together with a "value system and institutional norms of conduct [based on] an elaborate structure of universalist relations." The inner tension inherent in a social identity created by this particular social organization would make individual members of such a society especially prone to yield to the temptation of metamorphosis and shame.

The Williams paper came to my attention through a reference in Anselm Strauss's *Mirrors and Masks: The Search for Identity*. In this work, Strauss explores the role of social organization in the creation and maintenance of personal identity, and, in my opinion, contributes perhaps the most searching study available of the complexities of the phenomenology of personal identity, dealing with the transformations of identity, with the issues of change and continuity, and with the role of the historical past for the subjective experience of personal identity. I do not consider Strauss's work easy to read, because his arguments are very condensed, and they seem at times to convey the impression of containing self-contradictory statements. If I understand Strauss's main thesis correctly, he sees personal identity as the creation of human social organization. He seems, however, to hint that this is not entirely correct, though it is not clear which alternative he has in mind. Perhaps Strauss is aware that personal identity is neither a biological nor a psychological given, but consists of nothing more than a set of developmental possibilities which may or may not come into being; or they may come into being and be lost again. In short, to use one of Strauss's terms, identity in human beings is altogether "open-ended," and its specific configuration for any individual is unpredictable.

I consider this unpredictability as one aspect of the dilemma of human identity. I therefore see social organization as a response to the threat inherent in this human predicament. Social organization may be viewed as a collective effort to provide and maintain the semblance of "stable identities" for its members. "Social roles" are presented as if they were the "natural" or "given" condition of being human. Yet it appears that throughout history no social organization has succeeded in creating the universal human identity. Thus, the claim of social organizations to provide its members with a lasting identity might be no more than an illusion. I do not know, though, whether Strauss would agree with this position. I shall try to present his viewpoint as I understand it from his writings, which are, in his own words, not only open-ended, but at times "tentative, exploratory, hypothetical (and) problematic" (Strauss 1959, p. 91).

In the preface of his book, Strauss states: "I have been dissatisfied with much of the theory and research about self, ego and personality, because in this work the influence of social organization is so greatly underestimated, its role so insufficiently understood.... In sum: my essay ought properly to be regarded as an attempt to juxtapose and fuse symbolic interactional and social organizational perspectives into a workable, suggestive social psychology" (p. 11). Strauss refers to the symbolic interaction approach as "a point of view stemming from the pragmatists and from the work of several earlier sociologists." It stresses "the crucial role of language for human behavior. It also stresses a kind of open-ended, partially unpredictable, view of events: interaction is guided by rules, norms, mandates; but its outcomes are assumed to be not always, or entirely, determinable in advance. This indeterminacy need not be a stumbling block to scientific research, but has to be taken into account" (p. 10).

Strauss's discussion of transformation of identity, change and continuity, membership and history are all of great interest to the psychoanalyst who is attempting to understand the true complexities of the maintenance of human identity. One of the most cogent passages deals with the biological and psychological use of the concept of development. Strauss's position is stated as follows: "Presumably [development] refers to a progressive ment wherein the beginning, middle and end bear some discernible relationship to each other. But the notion of development is a trap for the unwary and a battleground for some centuries of philosophic contention. Precisely, what are the relationships that hold between the beginning, middle, and end? This is the nub of the argument" (p. 89). Strauss is of the opinion that "development . . . is commonly viewed either as attainment, or as a set of variations on basic themes. In neither case, you as the observer of the developmental pattern are omniscient: you know the end against which persons are matched, or you know the basic themes on which variations are composed. Neither metaphor captures the open-ended, tentative, exploratory, hypothetic, problematic, devious, changeable and only partly-unified character of human courses of action" (p. 91).[1]   Strauss's questioning of the notion of development corresponds in many respects to my criticism of Erikson's approach to development. I objected to the architectural imagery in such a metaphor as a "ground plan" underlying Erikson's idea of epigenesis. I believe that, when we are thinking of the development of an individual into a person, it might be more appropriate to use development as is used in music rather than in architecture; or, even more deterministically, in embryology. A musical theme is "developed" and can reach any stage of complexity without precluding a sudden return to the simple, unadorned theme. Music exists as thematic transformation in time, and its unfolding is a simultaneous disappearing. It is, in Strauss's sense, open-ended, tentative, exploratory and problematic. It is also communicative, a non-verbal language, and it would be difficult to imagine a listener to be omniscient. While he may know the "basic themes on which variations are composed" he cannot predict the possibilities that may happen to them and he is usually unprepared for the "course of action" that the composer might present him with. In my own concept of an "identity theme," its "development" or "variations" are so open-ended that they may encompass all the unpredictable fates of man, from ordinary to exceptional in terms of achievement, emotional stability or catastrophic self-destruction. In spite of its unpredictability, we cannot fail, however, to recognize, whatever course an individual's life may take, an inner continuity and sameness in change, without which there would be no sense of triumph or tragedy that we perceive as we are made to witness one person's fate. Strauss denies the reality of permanence in change. "Each person's account of his life, as he writes or thinks about it, is a symbolic ordering of events. The sense that you make of your own life rests upon what concepts, what interpretations, you bring to bear upon the multitudinous and disorderly crowd of past acts" (p. 145). Strauss concludes that "the awareness of constancy in identity ... is in the eye of the beholder rather than 'in' the behavior itself" (p. 147).

Strauss's denial of "constancy in identity" would be a contradiction in terms, since identity means sameness, and what we call "being the same" implies some form of constancy, such as in time or space, if we speak of inanimate matter. It is, of course, true that this spatiotemporal definition of identity cannot be applied to the identity of living beings, because "living" means constant change from beginning to end; if, then, we speak of identity in reference to a living being, the constancy must be based on something else. This is the problem Locke deals with in his discourse on identity and diversity. Strauss doesn't deny, of course, that there is a *subjective* awareness of a constant personal identity, but since it cannot be found 'in' the behavior of a person—as we might be able to find it 'in' the behavior of an animal— he concludes that it must be in the eye of the beholder, and nothing else. The fact that human or personal identity and the subjective awareness of it *cannot* be found in a "constant behavior," but *is* identity in the midst of change, is the very crux of the problem of personal identity. It can only be approached by the study of the emergence of the earliest or primary identity of the growing child, which is indicated by the child's discovery of an "I"—such as described by Lacan as the mirror stage *(stade du miroir)* and its verbal reference to himself as "I" or "me." This is a long time before a person can define his or her identity in terms of "social roles," and to equate social identity and personal identity does not seem to me supportable by what today is known about what Mahler has called the "psychological birth of the human infant." In spite of this disagreement, I believe that Strauss's observations and perceptive descriptions of transformations of identity, of change and continuity, of membership and history—to name but some of his topics—are of great value and make a significant contribution to the phenomenology of the dilemma of human identity.

It seems that Strauss would prefer to view identity as emerging from the social process. Such a clear derivation, if it could be proven, would establish a cause and effect sequence, which would reduce the complexity of the problem of human identity considerably. Strauss is, however, aware that this cannot fully account for the total range of identity phenomena because he himself makes certain reservations regarding the correlation between social process, personal identity, and identity transformation. "Some transformations of identity and perspective are planned, or at least fostered by institutional representatives; others happen despite, rather than because of, such regulated anticipation; and yet other transformations take place outside the orbits of the more visible social structure, although not necessarily unrelated to membership within them" (pp. 92-93). Strauss gives a most perceptive and detailed phenomenological description of the various ways in which transformations of identity may be experienced. He explores as especially significant for the understanding of the complexity of the problems of continuity in the midst of change experiences which he calls "turning points," i.e., "certain critical incidences that force a person to recognize that 'I am not the same, as I was, as I used to be!" (p. 93). He notes "the frequent occurrence of misalignment—surprise, shock, chagrin, anxiety, tension, bafflement, self-questioning—and also the need to try out the new self, to explore and validate the new and often fearful conceptions" (p. 93) which characterize turning points. He quotes Erikson's statement (1954) "that a sense of identity is never gained nor maintained once and for all. Like a good conscience, it is constantly lost and regained" (p. 109). Because of the profoundly disquieting quality of many transformations of identity—the threat of metamorphosis, in my own terminology—Strauss proposes that there are "institutional, cultural, as well as the more calculated personal means of minimizing change" (p. 145), especially profound change like that experienced as turning points. For example, "Insofar as careers can be visualized and implemented because of the relative stabilities of those social structures within which one has membership, the continuity and maintenance of identity is safeguarded and maximized, and methods of maintenance and restoration are more readily utilized and evolved" (p. 108). This would be an example of one way by which social organization serves the maintenance of identity. Strauss proposes that there are various methods which are used "to dull any sense of personal change even when the actual behavior associated with the status becomes altered" (p. 142).

Strauss's emphasis on the antithetical nature of the experience of turning points on the one hand, and "the institutional, cultural as well as . . . personal means to minimize change" introduces the issue of a sometimes basic incompatibility between the personal experience of transformation of identity and the aim of any social organization to maintain certain types of identities, defined in terms of institutionalized social roles. Transformation of identity and maintenance of identity are not necessarily antithetical. On the contrary, the coexistence, objective as well as subjective, of continuity *and* change is what defines personal identity. It is part of every one's identity to have been an infant, a toddler, a participant in kindergarten and in schooling, and finally a young adult. Undergoing all these changes, biologically as well as socially, and still being the same John or Joan, *is* human identity.

It is, however, true that the identity of social roles, as they are defined by social organizations, may indeed be incompatible with the sameness of a person. The social identity may be perceived as alien to an individual's personality by those who have known him closely, and it may be even more intensely incompatible with the private sense of identity of that individual. A college student drafted by the army for war service may consider the identity of his new role as a soldier to be incompatible with what he used to consider his "true" identity. Situations of this kind are especially disturbing for those who live under a social organization of a totalitarian character, but they are certainly not confined to these extremes. They are, in fact, not the exceptions but the rule that prevails in the conflicts concerning personal identity. It would seem that the existence of conflict and incompatibility between the social identity promoted and maintained by the social organization and the primary identity emerging from the processes and interactions between mother and child—Mahler's "psychological birth of the human infant"—makes it altogether impossible to view human personal identity as being essentially created by social organization (in the institutional sense).

This doesn't deny the significant function of social organization in stabilizing and maintaining personal identity, thus providing safeguards against the danger of abnegation of identity and metamorphosis. The threat of metamorphosis, indeed, constitutes the ultimate danger to personal identity, not the loss of socially defined identities. It can, furthermore, be said that an individual's ultimate commitment to personal identity is likely to come into being not from the loss of social identity, but from the possibility of yielding to the transformation which is incompatible with personal identity. Rather than yield, the person may choose to sacrifice his very life in an act of identity maintenance through death: *Antes muerto che mudado,* Rather dead than changed. This acknowledged by Strauss, although it seems to transcend the understanding of personal identity as inseparable from the roles assigned by social organization: "Self-sacrifice signifies often the firmest of identities and the most total of commitments" (p.42). Strauss goes on to elaborate on self-sacrifice: "The epitome of sacrifice, of course, is self-sacrifice or motive unto death. . . . The self-sacrificial act is supra-individual, it belongs to a larger and grander design which far transcends a person's own impure motive. . . . The thing at stake in self-sacrifice is an irrevocable statement as to what one's self *is*" (pp.42-43). Aside from implying an approach to the problem of personal identity that seems indeed to indicate an effort to "fuse—not merely juxtapose eclectically—something of the psychiatric and clinical perspectives with the more sociological ones" (pp.179-80) Strauss touches here on a most troubling, and very much neglected aspect of the dilemma of human identity. If the ultimate commitment to personal identity expresses itself in self-sacrifice or motive unto death, as Strauss claims—and, I think, rightly so—does this not also imply a motive for a "holy war" against those who constitute a challenge, and possibly represent the very antithesis to those "larger and grander designs" for which the truly committed one is willing to sacrifice his life? This tragic dimension of the dilemma of human identity confronts us in the cruel dramas of myth and of history.

Strauss is far more aware of these complexities and ambiguities inherent in the problem of human identity than most authors who have dealt with these issues. He touches upon them in his chapter on "Membership and History." It is not an easy chapter to condense, but I hope the following quotations will be sufficient to clarify the questions he raises. "Identities imply not merely personal histories but also social histories. . . . Individuals hold memberships in groups that themselves are products of a past. If you wish to understand persons . . . you must be prepared to view them as embedded in historical context." Since the relationship of the individual to the social group, and the group to the individual, confronts the researcher with "complexity [piled] upon complexity" (p.163), he who wants to study personal identity must realize that "persons can be conceived as taking some particular stance toward the historical, supra-personal past. They will be memorializing it, rejecting it, recreating it, cashing in on it, escaping, or in flight from it; these are but a few of countless possibilities" (p.169). Among these "countless possibilities" there are some that are of special significance both for the sociologist as well as for the psychiatrist. "There are further intricacies of membership, and hence of identity, that can be hypothesized if we take seriously the theme that group life is organized communication" (p.153). "Communication consists not merely in the transmission of ideas from the head of one person to that of another, it signifies shared meanings. 'Shared' means more than that terms are used in ways sufficiently alike so that persons understand each other; it also means that terms arise out of and in turn permit community action." (p.148). This leads Strauss to raise a question of special relevance to psychiatry, both in terms of clinical as well as sociological considerations:

When people possess those concepts basic to the functioning of a particular organization, then they can participate in it. If they do not—if they are somewhat, or completely, out of conceptual range so to speak—what then? Of course people who do not understand the purposes and the special languages of particular groups must learn these in order to participate: but there is a more profound sense in which outsiders may be beyond conceptual range. . . . A-mong those who are outside the boundaries of even ordinary public discourse are certain mental patients who suffer from impairment of certain thought processes (such as accompany aphasia and schizophrenia). It is said . . . that these patients cannot reason abstractly, or at least reason differently than before falling ill. Thus (they) lose the capacity to perform certain complex acts. . . . The relevance of such impairment of action to participation in social groups is that participation often requires high "levels of thought"; for instance, sustained attention, cognition about absent objects, and choices among projected lines of future behavior. [p. 155]

Strauss's emphasis on the incapacity of the "mental patient" to participate in the experience of "shared meanings" is an important contribution to the ongoing debate concerning the nature of mental illness. Strauss goes, however, beyond this particular psychiatric and sociological problem area, because his definition of those "who are outside the boundaries of social discourse" includes a wide variety of groupings. There are, for instance, "countless social relationships into which young children cannot enter" (p. 155). There are limits of communications between members of different social classes: "Different populations conceptualize somewhat differently, and therefore can cooperate (within the social organization) only in limited or in special ways." If you include "those abstract groupings called in popular parlance 'worlds': the world of drama, of art, fashion, crime, the radio, the homosexual, of baseball and of medicine" (p. 161), it is easy to see why Strauss would conclude that "different conceptions of what communication is, what conversation is, and what information is, are held by different populations. These conceptions condition the ways, and extent that these populations can communicate with each other" (p. 156), although Strauss holds that "people can cooperate even when their conceptions of the cooperative act are quite different" (pp. 157–58). Summarizing, Strauss states that "the central feature of social worlds is not their tightly knit nor extensive organization; just the opposite, for they are characterized by their looseness or diffuseness" (p. 162). Nevertheless "however difficult it may be to talk of memberships in such abstract groupings, and however transitory such memberships may be," Strauss considers them "immensely relevant to personal action and identity" (p. 161).

If this is true—and I am inclined to agree with Strauss that it is—it is hard to reconcile these facts marshaled by Strauss on the basis of his own and others' sociological studies with the central significance of social organization for the creation and maintenance of human identity. If it is true that there are countless groups who are, more or less, "outside the boundaries of social discourse," among them young children, whom one would expect to be the most malleable members of social organizations, it is hard to see that human identity is predominantly shaped by social organization especially, as bstrauss demonstrates, if most social groupings are characterized by their "looseness and diffuseness." How can such differences explain that personal identity has the power to create "the most total of commitment" for individuals, for which they are willing to sacrifice their lives, as Strauss states so emphatically, particularly when such self-sacrifice is often motivated by a profound disillusionment with the social organization in which they claim membership and in whose "historical context they view themselves as embedded" (p. 164).

In chapter 14 I touch upon similar issues. I hypothesize there that the widening gap between the generations may be due to the inability of social organizations, especially those of Western civilization, to create a consensus—a "standard meaning" in Struass's terminology—regarding what is real. Since there seems to be a basic link between reality perception and the senses of identity which the individual develops, the breakdown of the consensus about what is real has led to a situation where each generation's sense of identity is threatened by that of the other. One could probably say the same about the communicational breakdown that has created an ever widening gap between the industrial nations of the West and the so-called underdeveloped or formerly colonial countries. In this situation, too, there is no consensus of what is real, and consequently Western identity in itself is perceived as a threat by non-Western nations, and Western nations feel menaced by the implications of the emergence of new individual and national identities which seem to negate Western civilization's "firmest . . . identities and . . . most total . . . commitments"(pp. 42–43).

Strauss is very keenly aware of the deadly confrontations of irreconcilable commitments, but he does not view it as one of the destructive aspects of the dilemma of human identity. Toward the end of his book, he introduces an especially gripping example of the tragedies which so often arise out of a clash between equally committed members of social groups whose sense of identity is by both groups perceived as the very negation of the reality of their being. Strauss quotes at length a passage from the classic report by Rebecca West (1940) on Yugoslavia after the break-up of the Austro-Hungarian hegemony. In the quoted passage, two friends, a Serbian poet and a Croatian intellectual, confront each other in a discussion of the new political realities and, to their pain and horror, discover that they have become enemies, because of their incompatible perception of the new facts of their national lives. Strauss claims that he is offering nothing more than an example in the analysis of personal styles in dealing with the historical, supra-personal past. It seems to me that Strauss does an injustice to his own achievement, which deals with something much deeper than a difference of personal styles. As I read his quotation from Rebecca West, she describes the destructive aspect of a total commitment to a sense of identity which requires "self-sacrifice or motive unto death" (pp. 42–43) as the "irrevocable statement as to what one's self *is*" (p. 43). The clear implication of the discussion of the friends is that those who refuse this total commitment, will be treated as enemies and might well deserve death, unless they do unconditionally surrender their commitment to their own identity.

This supports the thesis that there exists a very intimate link between human identity and human destructiveness, constituting perhaps the most disturbing aspect of the dilemma of human identity. Thus, the Serbian poet pleads with his one-time Croatian friend that "a true human being is a Slav, he knows that to be a Slav is important, for that is the shape God has given him, and he should keep it" (p. 170). The Croatian is reluctant to agree wholeheartedly. He finally admits that he considers the position of Serbs and Croatians in the new Yugoslavia as unequal: "It is as if the Serbs were the elder brother and we Croats the younger brother, under some law . . . which gives the older everything and the younger nothing." The Serbian does not deny that inequalities exist, but argues that under the old regime "You got also Germanization and Magyarization, you got the violation of your soul. But now you are part of Yugoslavia, you are a part of the kingdom of the South Slavs, which exists to let you keep your soul, and to guard that kingdom we must have an army and a navy . . . and we must give Serbia many things she did not have." But the Croatian keeps on pointing to other inequalities, always to be told by the Serbian that they are part of the struggle for a truly independent Yugoslavia. Finally, the Croatian, trembling by now, makes his final point: "You would say we are well governed here? . . . You would say that nobody is arrested without cause and thrown into prison and treated barbarously? You would say that nobody has been tortured in Croatia since it became Yugoslavia?" The bitter argument goes on, with the gap between the one-time friends widening until it is irreversible: "What is so horrible in this conversation is that you are never wrong, but I am always right," the Serb states with hopeless disgust. "And we would go on talking like this forever, till the clever way you are never wrong brought death upon us." To which the Croatian replies: "Some have died already." I believe that Strauss could not have chosen a more poignant example to demonstrate one of the tragic predicaments inherent in personal identity: human identity is not only, as Strauss defines it, "an irrevocable statement as to what one's self *is*" (p. 43), but a simultaneous, equally irrevocable disavowal of what one is *not,* and must never be. In this dilemma lies the root of both personal and social disintegration. Social organizations offer protective structures that are expected to minimize this risk of being human. It seems, however, that they are unable to eliminate it altogether.

NOTE

1. For a discussion of the concept of development see also Werner (1957) and Wolff (1960). As much as I agree with Strauss's critical comments concerning the dangers hidden in the concept of development, I cannot avoid the impression that Strauss assumes that he is taking psychoanalysis, perhaps Freud himself, to task for saddling psychiatry with an untenably deterministic concept of development: "One premise underlying psychiatric accounts of development might well be abandoned—or at least held in abeyance. This premise is that there are certain steps through which the human organism

must pass to become more or less healthy, adapted to reality, and adjusted to social life. This seems, of course, a very reasonable premise; but its assumption ties development to bodily maturation, to inevitable and hidden premises about the nature of healthy functioning, and very probably to culture-bound norms as to this functioning" (p. 139). The theory as presented by Strauss has little to do with Freud's thinking. As early as 1910, in his essay on Leonardo da Vinci, we find (1910, p. 135) the following remarks—and they are only one example of other similar statements in Freud's writings: "But even if the historical material at our disposal were very abundant, and if the psychical mechanisms could be dealt with with the greatest assurance, there are two important points at which a psycho-analytic enquiry would not be able to make us understand how inevitable it was that the person concerned should have turned out in the way he did and in no other way. In Leonardo's case we have had to maintain the view that the accident of his illegitimate birth and the excessive tenderness of his mother had the most decisive influence on the formation of his character and on his later fortune, since the sexual repression which set in after this phase of childhood caused him to sublimate his libido into the urge to know, and establish his sexual inactivity for the whole of his later life. But this repression after the first erotic satisfactions of childhood need not necessarily have taken place; in someone else it might perhaps not have taken place or might have assumed much less extensive proportions. We must recognize here a degree of freedom which cannot be resolved any further by psychoanalytic means. Equally, one has no right to claim that the consequence of this wave of repression was the only possible one. It is probable that another person would not have succeeded in withdrawing the major portion of his libido from repression by sublimating it into a craving for knowledge; under the same influences he would have sustained a permanent injury to his intellectual activity or have acquired an insurmountable disposition to obsessional neurosis. . . . The apportioning of the determining factors of our life between the 'necessities' of our constitution and the 'chances' of our childhood may still be uncertain in detail; but in general it is no longer possible to doubt the importance precisely of the first years of childhood. We all still show too little respect for Nature which (in the obscure words of Leonardo which recall Hamlet's lines) "is full of countless causes ('ragioni') that never enter experience." It would seem to me that the concept of development, even at such an early stage of Freud's career, is far more open-ended and problematical than it might appear from Strauss's rendering of the theory. Nor is it difficult to show that among the factors influencing development, Freud specifically refers to societal conditions.

Part III

Metapsychology of the Self

Chapter 8

NARCISSISM AND
PRIMARY IDENTITY

Few concepts are as pivotal in psychoanalytic theory as the concept of narcissism. It serves simultaneously as the conceptual support for a new departure in the libido theory, and for the study of the development of object relations, with far-reaching consequences for the clinical approach to the psychoneuroses and the psychoses. In addition, it is the anchor for the new ego psychology, and, last but not least, on it rests, as a basis, the structural reformulation of metapsychology. It is not surprising, therefore, that a concept which must support such a multitude of theoretical edifices is at once indispensable and yet exposed to an extraordinary degree of "conceptual stress." In this sense narcissism can still be spoken of, as Jones (1955) did, as a "disturbing" concept. As a consequence, there have been numerous attempts to redefine it, make it handier by eliminating some of its original, Freudian connotations, replace some of its uses with new, more specific terms, etc. (Balint 1960, Bing et al. 1959, Jacobson 1964, Kaywin 1957).

This paper endeavors to contribute to these efforts at obtaining a clearer view of what is implied in the concept of narcissism. It hopes to accomplish this result, however, by a somewhat different approach to the problem. This approach consists of the somewhat paradoxically sounding attempt to differentiate between a variety of psychological phenomena that are all condensed in the one concept of narcissism, and simultaneously to pay close attention to the underlying truth which justifies Freud's insistence on uniting all the phenomena under one single concept. To make such an approach possible, I shall take the liberty of dealing with narcissism not so much as an abstract concept, but as a kind of ideogram, i.e., a pictorial symbol or a "word in its visual, not in its auditory, form, the mere tracing of which evokes the whole group of ideas or notions that it connotes" (Etiemble 1954).

It is, I believe, no coincidence that in Freud's treatment of narcissism visual images abound. One of these is, of course, the mirror; another, the amoeba and its pseudopodia (Jones 1955). I believe it is justifiable to add a third visual image, although it does not occur in the context of any discussion of the concept of narcissism. I am referring here to Freud's (1911) use of the bird's egg as a model of a closed psychological system. Freud says: "A neat example of a psychical system shut off from the stimuli of the external world and able to satisfy even its nutritional requirements autistically . . . is afforded by a bird's egg with its food supply enclosed in its shell; for it, the care provided by its mother is limited to the provision of warmth." The closest approach to the shell-enclosed bird's egg in human psychology would be the condition of the embryo during the intra-uterine phase and that of the individual during sleep. To both of these Freud refers specifically as narcissistic states, as in the passage in the *Introductory Lectures* (1916–17) where he says that

> The likeness we see in the condition which the sleeper conjures up again every night to the blissful isolation of the intra-uterine existence is thus confirmed and amplified in its mental aspects. In the sleeper the primal state of the libido-distribution is again reproduced, that of absolute narcissism, in which libido and ego-interests dwell together still, united and indistinguishable in the self-sufficient self.

I believe that it is helpful to be aware of the analogy between these models of narcissistic states and the reference to the bird's egg. Not only does Freud's use of the bird's egg as a model of a closed psychic system bring to our mind Freud's nearness to embryological thinking, but it also illuminates one of the conceptual dilemmas surrounding narcissism. Defining this dilemma as a psychological version of the old problem concerning the priority of the chicken or the egg is intended as more than a mere manner of speaking. In this case the question takes the form: What is first, object cathexis or ego cathexis? These questions are usually formulated in terms of primary narcissism versus primary love. Primary narcissism implies that in the earliest stages of development no objects are cathected and all libidinal cathexis rests in the ego. This theory, as proposed by Freud, has been criticized because of certain logical contradictions. At this early stage, the argument goes, there is no ego that could be cathected, consequently we should relinquish the concept of primary narcissism. "Primary narcissism might be thought of as the primary state of energy distribution not truly narcissistic, since no sufficient ego structure exists for cathexis of a self-representation. The energy in this primary state seems much more of a physiological nature" (Bing et al. 1959). Jacobson's (1954) reasoning also implies that the concept of primary narcissism in the sense in which Freud applied it is not compatible with our present concepts of ego development. In this view, the ego must first develop before there can be any object cathexis.

In contrast to this position, Balint (1960) "makes the assumption that the cathexis of its environment by the foetus must be very intense." For Balint such a primary cathexis does not necessarily imply a true primary object cathexis. "This environment . . . is probably undifferentiated; on the one hand, there are as yet no objects in it; on the other hand it has hardly any structure, in particular no sharp boundaries toward the individual." Thus Balint can postulate that the child has a primary love relation to the mother which then becomes the condition under which the ego can develop. For the ego psychologist this view is as self-contradictory as the concept of primary narcissism is for Balint. Kanzer (1961), obviously referring to Balint's views, states that "in his later works Freud indicated with sufficient clarity the need for distinctions between objects and their psychic representatives, so that it should not be possible today to speak of any primary object love that is not filtered through the perceiving apparatus of the ego." Behind this logical dilemma we can easily recognize the problems inherent in the concept of *development* that find their expression in that paradox about the chicken and the egg. Developmental theory demands that everything living originate from another living organism. Consequently if we know that the presence of a primordial cell is required to give rise to new life, it is logically necessary to assume the previous existence of this primordial cell. On the other hand, we also know that such primoridal cells, like the egg, can develop only in the organism of a living system. Consequently both statements, that the chicken must be first or that the egg must be first, are equally the consequences of developmental logic.

The extent to which the genetic approach to psychic phenomena has been influenced by theories developed from embryological experiments has recently been re-emphasized by Spitz (1959). Spitz distinguishes between congenital equipment, maturation, psychological development, and biological development. While there are obvious differences between the concept of biological development as used by embryologists and the psychoanalytic concept of psychological development, all these concepts have one idea in common: that of a progressive process of change and growth which leads from a very simple, almost unstructured primary configuration to a very complex, highly individualized, and highly structured end-condition that we equate with the idea of maturity. The whole process is *irreversible* in the sense that any kind of backward development would be implying some form of disintegration of the organized structure which had been achieved by the developmental process. I believe that it is this concept of development, with some modifications, that is implied in the genetic approach of psychoanalysis.

With the introduction of the concept of narcissism, however, Freud introduced an altogether different concept of development: one which permits the notion of reversibility of the developmental process. This reversibility is from now on understood as an essential aspect of psychological development. It may *sometimes* be equivalent to regression in the sense of disintegration, but not always, as Freud's frequent reference to the phenomenon of sleep indicates. Ernst Kris (1935) recognized this implied developmental reversibility when he spoke of regression in the service of the ego. It is my belief that Freud's insistence on distinguishing between a primary and a secondary narcissism is due to his need of a concept that implied the dimension of developmental reversibility. The concept of narcissism introduced a developmental concept incompatible with earlier concepts borrowed from embryology, symbolized by the image of the bird's egg. This new concept of development required a new image, and Freud found this new image in his famous simile of the amoeba. As the amoeba can send forth pseudopodia to external objects and then retract them again, in a similar manner libido can be cathected to objects and be again withdrawn. Under certain conditions this may be a pathological process, but it has a normal aspect too. Thus Freud (1925) envisages a rhythm of libidinal object cathexes and ego cathexes: "All through the subject's life his ego remains the great reservoir of his libido, from which object-cathexes are sent out and into which the libido can stream back again from the objects. Thus narcissistic libido is constantly being transforned into object-libido, and *vice versa.*" In the *New Introductory Lectures* (1932) Freud states:

> We must understand that the ego is always the main reservoir of libido, from which libidinal cathexes of objects proceed, and into which they return again, while the greater part of this libido remains perpetually in the ego. There is therefore a constant transformation of ego-libido into object-libido.

I do not agree with those, such as Kanzer (1961), who look upon the simile of the amoeba essentially as an abstraction to describe libidinal forces in a strictly mechanistic and quantitative manner. While it is true that Freud repeatedly refers to the ego as a reservoir of narcissistic libido, I believe that the central concept illustrated by the amoeba is that of constant libido transformation throughout life. This assumption of a back-and-forth movement requires an entirely different concept of development as applied to psychic phenomena. I have suggested the analogy of thematic development, borrowed from musical theory. A musical theme is developed as it undergoes variations. But the variations may revert to the original, undeveloped theme without destroying the structure of the composition. We could refer to the musical theme as a primary configuration and consider its variations as secondary elaborations. If narcissism implies a thematic configuration, it would then be necessary to juxtapose a primary configuration to secondary transformations, or, as we are accustomed to say, developments. Since I am aware that this musical analogy has its limits, I shall later on try to replace it with a more abstract formulation of this different concept of development.

First, however, I want to raise the question whether there is any clinical evidence that the concept of narcissism implies the emergence, in Freud's thinking, of new phenomena demanding a new approach to the problem of psychic development. An indirect evidence for such an assumption I see in the fact Freud gave the new concept he was introducing into analytic theory the name "narcissism." Freud (1914) claims that he simply adopted the terminology of P. Näcke, who had described under this name a perversion consisting of the use of one's own body as the only sexual object. In the *New Introductory Lectures* Freud (1932) puts it, however, somewhat differently when he states: "We have borrowed the name of *narcissism* from the Greek legend." I believe that the implications of the Greek myth must have been significant enough to Freud to move him to choose this particular term. It appears to me striking that in many contributions to the theory of narcissism it is customary to speak of Narcissus as a youth who died after falling in love with himself. This, however, is not what the story of Narcissus claims. Narcissus, as we all know, fell in love with his mirror image in a pond. There is, of course, a considerable difference between being in love with oneself and being in love with one's mirror image, as has been noted by Lacan, Greenacre, Elkisch, and others. The image in the mirror is not real in the same sense in which the ego or the self are real. Somebody who is in love with his mirror image loves a picture or a phantom which he can never possess and reach. This inability ever to reach the object of his love or even touch it was, according to the Greek myth, the cause of Narcissus' death.

If the phenomenon of narcissism refers to the love of one's mirror image, it seems important to deal with the psychological meaning of the mirror and mirror images. The mirror introduces a *third* element between the lover and his object; What, or who, is symbolically represented by the mirror? Finally, he who looks into a mirror does not see only himself. A mirror reflects a great many more things than the person who looks into the mirror. The mirror includes the room, and possibly other persons—in short, a part of the world in which the individual exists. Someone who sees in the mirror nothing but himself has apparently a very special kind of looking that suppresses everything else except his own picture in the mirror.

These are only some of the implications that enter into a concept derived from the myth of Narcissus. I believe it is impossible to rid narcissism of the mirror hidden in the concept. I derive support for this belief from the fact that only five years after Freud's paper on narcissism, in 1919, Géza Róheim published a volume entitled *Spiegelzauber* ("Mirror Magic"). In this work he examines in great detail everything that has been reported about customs and rituals involving the mirror. Róheim aims to show that the concept of narcissism, as Freud has just introduced it, could explain the immensely varied and complex mirror rituals, mirror tabus, mirror superstitions that exist apparently all over the world. It is, however, difficult to suppress the feeling that Róheim was keenly aware that mirror magic also contributed something to our understanding of narcissism. This seems implied in the motto given of the book, a quotation from one of the Upanishads, which reads as follows: "The Self, indeed, one must see, one must hear, one must understand, one must reflect upon; indeed he who has seen the Self, has heard the Self, has understood and recognized the Self, to him the whole universe will be known." Does this motto not appear to contradict the psychoanalytic notion that narcissism, the libidinal involvement with the self, destroys the capacity to relate to the world? Róheim does not see any contradiction, perhaps because he paid so much attention to the meaning of the mirror and its psychological implications.

I must confine myself to listing the contents of Róheim's book to give an approximate idea of the richness and ramifications of mirror rituals and customs. Róheim first discusses the relationship of child and mirror, in both negative and positive rituals. He goes on to describe the role of the mirror as a means of predicting the future. Another chapter discusses the magic powers given to kings and rulers by means of the mirror. Róheim then gives an extensive description of the many forms of love magic that involve the use of a mirror. To give one example of such magic: in certain rituals the mirror enables the girl to see her future husband. Róheim discusses, furthermore, tabus concerning the use of the mirror; superstitions with regard to the broken mirror; the custom of covering mirrors at certain occasions. And in the last chapter he deals with the equating of the heavenly bodies, particularly the sun, with the mirror. This mere listing of the themes of Róheim's book on mirror magic confirms Elkisch's (1957) assertion that "whenever we deal with the mirror phenomenon we are dealing with something enigmatic, uncanny, with a thing that has been made the screen for man's projections of the mysterious and the uncanny."

Elkisch points out that, aside from the role of the mirror in mystical religion, folklore, fairy tale, and myth, poets and writers of all times "have used the mirror symbolically or allegorically in various meaningful ways." She sees the reason for this wide use of the mirror as a symbol of the mysterious and the uncanny in the fact that it appears to reflect man's soul or inner self, making thus exactly the same point as is implied by Róheim's motto to his book. According to Elkisch, the mirror may either refer to the possibility of man's losing his self or his soul, and thus become a symbol of death, or it may become a means of retrieving the lost self. For this latter reason, Elkisch believes the mirror is "so fascinating to psychotic patients." "The very activity of mirroring whereby, according to animistic thinking, one loses his soul, (appeared) in . . . psychotic patients as an intriguing attempt to rescue the lost. . . . Each of (my) patients was gazing at his image as if through such mirroring he might restore his self-identity." Similar conclusions have been reached by M. L. Miller (1948) through the analysis of mirror dreams, which have also been investigated by Kaywin (1957) and Eisnitz (1961).

Greenacre (1958a), discussing the early physical determinants in the development of the sense of identity, devotes a lengthy discussion to the relationship between confusion of sexual identity in twins or pseudotwins of the opposite sex and the Narcissus myth. For Greenacre the various versions of the myth, and the role in it of the nymph Echo, refer to the bisexual identification and the confusion of identity in the development of twins: "Such is the beautiful condensation of the myth that it emphasizes also the two-facedness of identity—not only the contrast with the opposite, but also the need to look at the self-image as though from the outside, apparent in the repetition of Echo and the reflection of Narcissus."

I believe that these examples from psychoanalytic literature suffice to support the conclusion that the concept of narcissism has suggested to many authors problems transcending the issues of ego cathexis versus object cathexis. The mirror and the act of mirroring introduce problems of the emergence of a primary identity, and of identity maintenance as well. I believe that the concept of narcissism compels us to investigate the relationship between the experience of mirroring and the emergence of a primary identity on the one hand, and the relationship of such a primary identity to the development of the ego on the other hand.

Rollman-Branch (1960), in an interesting study, examines the question of primary object need. Her extensive studies of the ethological and animal-experimental literature lead her to the conclusion that there may be some human need which could be compared to what in animals is described as the need for companionship, a need apparently independent of feeding. "If the critical period to form attachment to an object passes unused, a fear and flight reaction sets in (in animals)." Rollman-Branch compares this animal "attachment behavior" to certain observations of infants. "Infants need a certain . . . amount of human contact aside from the satisfaction of their physical needs. Deficiency in this contact with mother or mother substitute around the age of six months may lead to marasmus and death."

In chapter 2 above, the existence of something akin to primary object need as described by Rollman-Branch is proposed. I view the phenomenon as a mirroring experience—a description referring to the libidinal cathexis of the mother with regard to the child which I see as necessary for the infant's survival and further development. I follow the terminology of Elkisch (1957), Greenacre (1958a), Mahler (1958) and others in emphasizing the mirroring quality of the infant's sensory responsiveness to the mother's libidinal attachment. This mirroring cannot, of course, be understood in terms of any visual perception, but a reflection through touch, smell, and other primitive sensations. What is dimly emerging in this mirror is, at least in the beginning, not a primary love object, but the outlines of the child's own image as reflected by the mother's unconscious needs with regard to the child. In this first, archaic mirroring experience of the child a primary identity emerges which may be called narcissistic. It is not as yet a sense of identity, for that presupposes consciousness. I see in it rather a primary organizational principle without which the process of developmental differentiation could not begin.

Perhaps this first basic orientation may be described as a psychological version of the tropism of primitive biological systems. Insofar as it is understood as an organizational principle making possible the process of psychological development proper, the primary identity of the child is comparable to the concept of organizers of the psyche in the terminology of Spitz (1959). Spitz assumes that in the earliest stage of non-differentiation the infant is not capable of differentiating between incoming stimuli. This is certainly true if compared to the stage where the child is capable of responding with the smiling response, which is an indicator, as Spitz has shown, of a perception of a Gestalt. But in order to arrive at the smiling response, must we not attribute to the libidinal stimuli emanating from the mother a specific effect different from that of other stimuli impinging on the child? I am inclined to assume such a specific effect in view of the lack of instinctual direction in the human infant. In the human organism this turning toward the source of libidinal stimuli provides the only direction, a direction which must exert an organizing effect on all later development.

I have found some confirmation and support for this view in the work of Spiegel, particularly in his paper "The Self, the Sense of Self and Perception" (1959). From this very rich study I shall select a few propositions which seem to me to have an important bearing on the question of the emergence of a primary identity and ego development on the one hand, and the relationship of narcissism and primary identity on the other. Spiegel investigates patients who suffer from disturbances in the feeling of personal identity and of reality of one's own person. He re-examines psychoanalytic concepts of the self. He states that

it may be advisable to stress the basic distinction between the self just described and self-feeling. Self-feeling is an ultimate, not further describable clinical fact, but the self is *not a clinical* fact in the same sense that self-feeling is. It is a conceptualization or a construct which we invoke to clarify clinical phenomena, just as we use the constructs of the ego, superego, id, and defence mechanisms for the same purpose. But while the distinction between clinical fact and construct is usually maintained in these examples, in the area we are now interested in self and self-feeling are treated as one.

Spiegel attributes to the self a biological function similar to that of the frame of reference for visual perception. Quoting the Gestalt psychologist Koffka (1935), Spiegel gives the following example of the relationship of the frame of reference to perception:

If a train goes up a steep mountain, the trees and telephone poles will appear as oblique—not vertical. . . . But after we put our head out of the window the trees will soon appear vertical. In the first instance we accepted the car window as the source of our cues for horizontality and verticality. Therefore the tree had to appear as if it were oblique against the assumedly vertical car window frame. Once we put our head out of the window the tree appears vertical against the true verticality of the external world.

Spiegel continues:

> I would extend this concept of the frame of reference . . . to include what Freud calls "innere Wahrnehmung" (internal perception). The orderly perception of these internal states requires a frame of reference that possesses a continuity in time. I believe it may prove profitable to consider the self . . . as a frame of reference or zero point to which the representation of specific mental and physical states are referred, against which they are perceived and judged.

Summarizing, Spiegel states: "The operational significance of the concept 'self' is its function as framework." He proposes that "perceptions having to do with self-feeling result from the ego's relating of a single or small number of self-representations to the self considered as framework." Disturbances in the development of the self as a framework have, in Spiegel's view, a special relevance for those patients with a chronically shaky sense of personal identity. Alterations in the sense of personal identity can be explained, he thinks, by a rapid oscillation between self-representation and object-feeling:

> For example, the genital is an aspect of the self that frequently receives the greatest cathexis. Its representation in states of sexual excitement is consequently more vulnerable to the oscillation just described and therefore tends to become a source of alterations in self-feeling, as . . . in orgasm, an extreme example of altered self-feeling.

It is very difficult to condense the closely reasoned arguments of Spiegel without making them appear obscure. I have been trying to bring into focus two important points made by him: first, before there can be any kind of *sense* of self there has to be a framework, a zero point which must precede all other mental developments. This framework or zero point Spiegel calls the self. For reasons which I cannot here enumerate, I prefer to call it a primary identity. Secondly, according to Spiegel, there exists a close connection between the constancy of this frame of reference and sexuality. He sees sexuality as simultaneously contributing to intense self-feeling and also threatening it by what he calls oscillation. I believe that his work supports the view that the emergence of an organizing principle has to precede psychological development. This framework or organizing principle has a close and demonstrable relationship to the development of the sense of personal identity.

Spiegel's postulate of a close correlation between sexuality and the constancy of self-representation lends support to my proposition that the outlines of a primary identity become delineated through the processes stimulated by the maternal libidinal cathesis to the child. The child, while not capable of perceiving the maternal object or of possessing a sense of self or of identity, experiences its existence as reflected by the libidinal cathexis of the mother. The mother, in contrast to the nonhuman environment, reflects back to the child a configuration of its own presence. I have suggested (chapter 2) that this primary identity has the form of an identity theme, i.e., the specific reflection received from the mother conveys to the child a primary identity defined as instrumentality in relation to the mother. This thematic identity will be "developed" in the course of life as an infinite variety of identity transformations, as a simple musical theme is developed into a symphony. This development is reversible, so that we are entitled to speak of a primary and a secondary method of identity maintenance.

The primary identity is always based on a mirroring experience. It does not enable the individual truly to cathect an object. Instead, it uses the object as a mirror in which to reflect the outlines of its primary identity. Since this primary method of identity maintenance originated during a phase when there was no differentiation between the subject and the object, this narcissistic libidinous mirroring reinforces the identity delineation through magnification and reduplication (echo).

Seeing the reflection of one's own figure on a cloudbank under certain conditions of lighting while climbing a mountain makes one's person seem like a giant shadowy configuration which mirrors every move. This type of mirroring is a well-known form of narcissistic object relation in which the object serves as a mirror for a faltering or undeveloped identity. As Erikson (1959) has said "For where an assured sense of identity is missing, even friendship and affairs become desperate attempts at delineating the fuzzy outline of identity by mutual narcissistic mirroring." We can see here the narcissistic omnipotence as a result of the pattern of identity maintenance through mirroring in the object.

But a different form of identity maintenance develops when the pure reflective mirroring experience is replaced by an increasing significance of eliciting a corresponding *action*, thus replacing mirroring by a pattern of *acting* and *reacting* to one another. Only now can we speak of a *sense* of identity maintained by the capacity to select types of actions which will bring a corresponding reaction from the other. This form of identity maintenance implies an everextending capacity to elicit reactions to one's own *actions* in an ever-widening social group. But as we leave the early group of love objects, people no longer react to our individuality, but to the particular function we may represent for them. Thus the danger arises that instead of *maintaining* a sense of identity the reaction to a *depersonalized* social role may empty the sense of identity and create the danger of alienation.

Under such circumstances a return to the earlier, mirroring experience will again become necessary. Such mirroring experiences will most likely be intensely libidinal and narcissistic, leading even to a temporary object loss. But in such experiences the identity theme of the individual will be reinforced, so that in the normal person he can again return to the more adult pattern of acting and expecting supporting reaction from the others. Such fluctuation from narcissistic mirroring of one's own identity in the object to rediscovery of the other as a partner in a configuration of mutual interaction is the phenomenon to which Freud refers when he speaks of the fact that there is a constant transformation of ego libido into object libido and vice versa. It may be more precise today to speak of rhythmic changes in the pattern of identity maintenance. In the adult such return to the primary identity maintenance by mirroring may sometimes indicate regressive phenomena, at other times it may indicate a second birth in the sense in which Erikson (1958), following William James, has used this term.

Here we return to the problems implied in the concept of psychological development. At the beginning of this paper I suggested that the imagery of narcissism, such as the amoeba and the mirror, imply a new concept of development, different from the developmental processes which we usually conceptualize as progressive and irreversible. I shall recall my discussions elsewhere (see chapter 4) of the mathematical concept of transformation and invariant (Keyser 1922). I would then describe the concept of a primary identity as an invariant the transformations of which we could call development. Not being a mathematician, I cannot be sure whether such direct application of the mathematical theory of groups is allowable for the solution of problems of psychological development. I want to emphasize, however, the logical necessity for the concept of an invariant to which all transformations are related, as the basic difference between the psychoanalytic and the biological perception of development. I admit that the problems inherent in this distinction between biological and psychological development must wait for future clarification.

Let me then summarize the propositions of this paper. The introduction of the concept of narcissism was an attempt on the part of Freud to follow the analogy of embryological thinking consistently, leading to the concept of a closed psychic system comparable to a bird's egg. But the concept of narcissism became a kind of catalyst that opened up entirely new theoretical horizons. These are implicit in the imagery of the amoeba as well as in the mirror of Narcissus. They introduce problems of human identity and indicate their relationship to the development of psychic structure. These identity problems, though never explicitly stated, exerted their influence in that they gave rise to a completely different concept of development. Freud's insistence on retaining the distinction between primary and secondary, when speaking of narcissism, does not constitute just a flaw in Freud's thinking. I believe that in some of his seemingly self-contradictory formulations, in which the theory of narcissism abounds, we must see the breakthrough of new insights. These new insights, hidden behind the imagery of narcissism, are problems of identity emergence and identity maintenance. They foreshadow the necessity for a new concept of development which may be tentatively described in terms of an invariant and its transformations. If these propositions prove tenable, the concept of narcissism contains as radical a revolution of Freud's thinking as does his reformulation of early dynamic psychoanalytic theory in terms of the structural concepts.

Chapter 9

TOWARD A METAPSYCHOLOGY
OF THE SELF

THE CONCEPT OF ADAPTATION
IN THE CONTEXT OF EVOLUTIONARY THEORY

The Aristotelian evolution was the development of the so-called "form," the nature of the thing, which was already present. It presupposed the existence of the form as something that was there. In this conception a metaphysical entity was thought of which existed in and directed the development of form. The species—which is the Latin word for the Greek term "form"—was actually conceived of as a certain nature that supervised the development of the seed of the embryo into the normal adult form. Under the conception of Christian theology this form was thought of as existing first in the mind of God, then as appearing in the plants and animals and various other objects that he created, and finally as arising in our minds as concepts. . . .

The difference between that conception of evolution and the modern conception is given . . . in the very title of Darwin's book, *The Origin of Species*, that is, the origin of forms. What this theory is interested in is the evolution of the nature of the object, of the form, in a metaphysical sense. It is this which distinguishes the later theory of evolution from the former, namely, that the actual character of the object, the form or the nature itself, should *arise* instead of being *given*. [George Herbert Mead 1936; my italics]

Thirty-five years ago Heinz Hartmann's *Ego Psychology and the Problem of Adaptation* appeared in printed form. I want here to reflect upon some of the questions raised in his 1939 paper.

By approaching his investigations of ego-psychological problems in terms of the more general problem of human adaptation, Hartmann has confronted psychoanalysis with the necessity of having to deal with the basic problems underlying any theory of evolution. It is certainly true, as Hartmann says, that

> We may not yet fully appreciate how fruitful it is that the foundation on which Freud built his theory of neurosis is not "specifically human" but "generally biological," so that for us the differences between animals and man (whether they be characterized as insight for action, or speech, or use of tools, or whatever) are relative. [1939, p. 28]

But this broad biological approach to the problem of mental functioning demands answers to certain questions inherent in the theory of evolution as a philosophical doctrine. If, as George Herbert Mead formulates it in the above-quoted passage, any modern evolutionary theory must give an answer to the question how "the actual character of the object, the form or the nature itself, should *arise* (in the process of evolution) instead of being *given*" we immediately understand the evolutionary logic of Hartmann's ego-psychological emphasis. For Hartmann (1939) "the problems of autonomous ego development, of the structure and rank order of ego functions, of organization, of central regulation, of self-suspension of function, etc. and their relations to the concept of adaptation and mental health" had to be faced and accounted for by psychoanalytic theory if that theory rightfully claimed the title of an evolutionary approach to human mental development. This is so, because the specific problems listed by Hartmann as "having a just claim on our attention" are dealing with the very heart of the problem of the origin of "forms," i.e., the structural aspects of the mind within a process of evolution. In contrast to earlier theories of evolution, modern, i.e., Lamarckian, Darwinian, or Freudian, evolutionary theory has no concept of a *pre-existing* form, conceptualized as Aristotelian entelechy or a Kantian a priori to explain the natural forms, be they biological species or mental structures. Consequently, for every emerging form the evolutionary theorist has to prove its emergence in the process of becoming, of arising in the process of development itself. This central fact motivates Hartmann's approach to ego psychology.

Hartmann considered a radical rethinking of the psychoanalytic approach to mental development necessary because he did not accept as satisfactory Freud's (1911) original explanation of the emergence of mental structures as a result of the impact of reality on an organism dominated by instinctual drives which, in turn, were regulated by the pleasure principle.

> How the pleasure principle was, so to speak, forced to modify into the reality principle has still not been explained unequivocally. We understand that the mental apparatus must search the external world for pleasure possibilities as soon as its needs exceed a certain measure and can no longer be satisfied by fantasy . . . But what we call the reality principle implies something essentially new, namely the function of anticipation. [Hartmann 1939, p. 42]

Hartmann then quotes Freud's statement: "A momentary pleasure, uncertain in its result, is given up, but only in order to gain in the new way an assured pleasure coming later" (Freud 1911). To this Hartmann comments:

> The ability to renounce an immediate pleasure-gain in order to secure a greater one in the future cannot be derived from the pleasure principle alone; not even memories of painful experiences suffice alone to explain it. [p. 42]

Because of this failure, in Hartmann's view, on the part of Freud to explain unequivocally the emergence of a new structure (the ego function of anticipation) Hartmann considers it necessary to introduce the notion of "ego development . . . as an independent variable" (p. 43).

From the postulation of ego development as an independent variable to the formulation of the concept of the primary autonomy of the ego is only a short step, but a step of paramount importance for psychoanalytic theory. Almost the whole of modern structural theory has been a logical consequence of these conceptualizations of

Hartmann's. They include besides the basic new concepts of primary (hereditary) and secondary (acquired) autonomy, such concepts as the conflict-free sphere of the ego. Hartmann's assumptions concerning the instinctual energy of the mental apparatus (libido and aggression in various degrees of neutralization) are an integral part of the conceptual edifice of structural theory. Hartmann's derivation of primary ego autonomy from inherited biological ego propensities has been subject to criticism. I myself have expressed certain conceptual reservations about the entelechtic and aprioristic implications of such concepts (see chapter 2). More recently other authors have raised questions about the validity of Hartmann's "biologism" (Apfelbaum 1962, Furstenau 1964, Glover 1961).

In this paper I want to concentrate on a largely neglected aspect in Hartmann's insistence on an independent variable—independent, that is, from the instinctual drives and the forces of physical reality. Hartmann (1952) states:

> Those inborn characteristics of the ego and their maturation could then be a third force that acts upon ego development, besides the impact of reality and of the instinctual drives. We may call autonomous factors the elements on the side of the ego which originated in this hereditary core (primary autonomy). Their development is, of course, not independent from the development of other elements, but they enter this development as an independent variable.

I believe that today we are beginning to see a third force which acts as an independent autonomous variable in mental development. As we are beginning to trace the outlines of the "third force," this independent variable of mental development, they seem to me to point toward new psychoanalytic propositions that may lead to significant revisions and expansions of our current ego-psychological concepts.

THE RELATIONSHIP OF PSYCHIC STRUCTURES
TO THE CONCEPT OF THE "WHOLE PERSON"

The development of the human mind confronts us with the problem of the evolution of form (structure) on two different levels of inquiry.

These two levels are indicated in Hartmann's (1950) distinction of the self from the ego:

> In analysis a clear distinction between the terms ego, self, and personality is not always made. But a differentiation of these concepts is essential if we try to look consistently at the problems involved in the light of Freud's structural psychology. But actually, in using the term narcissism, two different sets of opposites often seem to be fused into one. The one refers to the self (one's own person) in contradistinction to the object, the second to the ego (as a psychic system) in contradistinction to other substructures of personality. [p. 127]

These distinctions lead Hartmann to differentiate "object cathexis from cathexis of one's own person, that is self-cathexis; in speaking of self-cathexis we do not imply whether this cathexis is situated in the id, the ego, or superego." Hartmann thus defines narcissism not as libidinal cathexis of the ego, but the self, and he suggests that it might be useful to distinguish self-representation from object representation. Hartmann's important distinction between the ego, as a concept defining a psychic system, and the self, as a concept referring to one's own person, raises the question of the developmental order in which psychic structures (systems or aspects of systems, such as various ego functions, like thought, memory, etc.) stand in relation to the concept of the person.

The latter also conveys the idea of a "form" or structure. What is not clear are the characteristics that distinguish the concept of the "whole person" as form (Gestalt, configuration) from psychic structures in the usual psychoanalytic sense. Does the "whole person" constitute nothing but the synthesis of the psychic structures—the id, the ego, and the superego? Or do we have to regard the "whole person" (the self) as quite distinct both in origin as well as in function from the other psychic structures, for instance, as an organizing principle (Spitz 1959) guiding the development, the utilization, and the intersystemic relationship of the psychic structures that psychoanalysis has described and studied?

Jacobson (1964) has devoted a monograph to the development of the self, as it evolves through processes of psychic differentiation and synthesis of the psychic systems. The term "self" is employed by Jacobson "as referring to the whole person of an individual, including his body and body parts as well as his psychic organization and its parts." This implies a parts-to-whole relationship of psychic structures to the Self or the "whole person." A parts-to-whole relationship can be descriptive of spatial or functional coordination. The former would be exemplified by a statement such as "Gaul is divided into three parts," the latter by "The heart is a part of the human body." We cannot consider it self-evident that either of these types of parts-to-whole relationship is applicable to the relationship between psychic structures to the "whole person" or to the Self.

This raises the question: What is the appropriate concept to characterize the relationship between psychic structures, either in the sense of systems (id, ego, superego) or substructures (ego functions, for instance) and the "whole person"? The issue centers upon the fact that the "whole person" cannot be, strictly speaking, an object of *observation*. Neither can we observe such constructs as the id, the ego, the superego, but we can, as Hartmann, Kris, and Loewenstein (1947) have pointed out, observe and describe certain characteristic *functions* which permit us to define the psychic systems.

Observation of the "whole person" does not yield any specific functions of the "whole person." Observation of the "whole person" confronts us with the infinite sequence of bodily and behavioral *transformations* during the whole life of the individual. Only these changes can we observe and describe in detail. The *perception* of the "whole person" means the process of abstracting an invariant from the multitude of transformations. This invariant, when perceived in our encounter with another individual, we describe as the individual's "personality." Insofar as we are perceiving such an invariant as a characteristic of our own inner world (Hartmann), we tend to refer to it as the *experience (Erlebnis)* of our Self. We are merely able to point to a phenomenon, but we cannot appropriately define it. Such definition could indeed be a task transcending the conceptual dimensions of psychological discourse as it is known to us today. Psychoanalysts might find themselves compelled to follow the example of Piaget (1953), who has not hesitated to use the method of an algebra of logic "to specify psychological structures, and to put into calculus form those operations and structures central to our actual thought processes," because of his awareness of "the relative imprecision of psychological theories."

The desirability of such a calculus for proper understanding of complex psychological phenomena becomes apparent when we realize how inadequate our psychological tools are in an attempt to render accurately the phenomenology of such an important, and yet elusive, mental configurations as the Self. Self has a *time dimension*, in that the term encompasses the Self of the changing phases of our childhood, our adolescence, through all the phases of our adult lives. Beyond that, we include into the experience of our Self the life that is still ahead of us. The description brings to our attention the immense variations of our personality, which differ so vastly from one another under the perspective of experienced time that the perception of an invariant element, the self, has seemed to some observers (Strauss 1959) as a bold and arbitrary claim. During each of the phases of our lives our mental structures are discernible through their specific functions, but it seems impossible to derive from them as parts the invariant Self as a whole. This impossibility becomes even more striking if we take into account another, it seems to me undeniable, fact of self-observation. I refer here to our inclusion, when thinking or speaking of our self, of those aspects of our personalities which were at some phase possible—potentialities that existed, but were not actualized. This contrast between our potential and our actualized selves is stronger in some individuals than in others, but it seems always recognizable, and the relationship of the potential to the actualized selves during a lifetime constitutes perhaps what we refer to as the *uniqueness* of personality. The relationship of potentiality and actuality to the psychic structure and substructures cannot be described at all in terms of parts to wholes. When we turn to psychopathology, the relationship of self to psychic structures becomes even more complex. In multiple personalities (Thigpen and Cleckley 1957) and in some cases of amnesias and fugues (Geleerd et al. 1945) the intrapsychic systems and important ego functions are maintained, while the self-perception is profoundly altered. The reverse phenomenon of a tenuously maintained self-perception in an individual whose ego functions and intersystemic balance are grossly disturbed has been described by Winnicott (1952, 1954) as that of a

defensive "false self" preserving the possibility of a "true self." Khan
(1963) has recently demonstrated the capacity of a self-experience to
survive failure of the synthetic function of the ego.

If in view of all this perplexing evidence we cannot accept the
concept of the "whole personality" or of the Self as the "end product"
of the developing intrapsychic structures, or as an aspect of the
synthetic function of the ego, what alternative views are open to us? I
shall attempt to show that the pursuit of these questions leads to the
postulation of an independent variable. It is my contention that in the
exploration of the relationship of psychic structures to the "whole
personality" Hartmann's pioneering search for a "third force" can be
considered as the beginning of a new chapter in psychoanalytic theory
which may yet lead to dimensions of mental functioning not
encompassed by structural theory.

RECENT TRENDS TOWARD
A CONCEPTUALIZATION OF THE "WHOLE PERSON"

The extension of the psychoanalytic "discussion of ego-pathology
. . . to the larger issues of identity formation . . . and the establishment
of self" (Khan 1964) has for more than a decade focused the theoretical
interest of many psychoanalysts on the task of arriving at a coherent
view of such phenomena as identity, whole person, and Self. To deal
with such problems within the developmental frame of psychoanalytic
theory had long been delayed because it required the previous
development of structural theory.[1] The renewed impetus to extend
psychoanalytic theory beyond ego psychology to a psychology of the
whole person and the self can, therefore, be traced to Hartmann's
formulations, especially his concept of primary autonomy. Rapaport
(1959) recognized this clearly when he speaks of one of the most
significant extensions of structural theory, namely Erikson's (1950b)
introduction of the concept of epigenesis, as the beginning of a
theoretic direction "to particularize Hartmann's concept of autonomous ego development." Erikson's ego epigenesis, in Rapaport's (1959)
words,

parallels that of libido development, and goes beyond it, spanning
the whole life cycle. This conception is the first in the history of

psychoanalytic theory to encompass those phases of the life cycle which are customarily subsumed under the single concept of genital maturity, and to provide tools for their investigation.

It is significant that Erikson (1950b) clearly differentiates the epigenetic principle, as the concept of an organizing growth pattern or "ground plan," from the structures that will arise within this plan, "each part having its time of special ascendancy, until all parts have arisen to form a *functioning whole.*" In addition to the parts-whole relationship Erikson here stresses *time* as a vital dimension. It should also be noted that Erikson's epigenetic principle is seen as analogous to the growth of the embryo, an analogy that we will also encounter in the efforts of other authors trying to define more precisely the relationship of psychic structures to the "whole personality." The reason for this recourse to embryological analogies is understandable: embryology seems to provide a clear instance of maintenance of "form" through a series of transformations. But the form maintained in the embryological growth-processes is that characteristic for the species, the genotype. In contrast, when we are dealing with mental development of the human individual, we are confronted with the problem of the maintenance of the "form" that constitutes each person's unique self throughout the transformations of his inner experience. In trying to conceptualize this invariant, we seem to encounter an independent variable not identical with the structures and substructures that we can define in terms of their mental functions. A brief reference to the views of Spitz (1959), Spiegel (1959), and Sandler (1960) will demonstrate how the formulations of authors differing considerably in their individual approach to problems of mental development converge toward the concept of an independent variable affecting as an organizing principle the functioning of the psychic structures of the mental apparatus.

Spitz (1959) refers specifically to the teachings of embryology. In applying Spemann's (1938) term *organizer* to early mental development, Spitz quotes Needham's (1931) definition of this concept:

An organizer is thus a developmental pace maker for a particular axis.... It accounts in all probability for the phenomena described by experimental biologists under the name *Wirkungs-*

feld, Organizationfeld, and *Determinierungsfeld.* It is not yet possible to draw preliminary conclusions concerning the fundamental nature of its dominance.

Needham's further elaboration of the concept of organizer as a "relational factor in development" and as "a centre radiating its influence" is emphasized by Spitz. With regard to the propositions of psychoanalytic theory Spitz states:

All this adds up to the picture of a far reaching organization, a process of crystallization in the psyche. A variety of discrete components, some of them maturational, some of them developmental (that is, specifically psychological), have been integrated and will from here on operate more or less as a unit. [1959, p. 24]

Pointing to basic similarities between his own formulations and Erikson's epigenetic principle, Spitz notes the "gratifying convergence of conclusions based on dissimilar research approaches" (p. 44). This convergence toward the concept of an organizing principle acting upon the development and the functional actualization of psychic structures is also apparent in the propositions of Spiegel (1959). Spiegel defines the self as a frame of reference or zero point, a term borrowed from Gestalt psychology. Significantly, the frame of reference or zero point has farreaching effects on the ego function of perception, as has been shown by Koffka (1935). Spiegel (1959) extends this concept of the frame of reference

to include what Freud (1940) calls *"innere Wahrnehmung"* (internal perception). The orderly perception of these internal states requires a frame of reference that possesses a continuity in time. I believe that it may prove profitable to consider the self . . . as a frame of reference or zero point to which representations of specific mental and physical states are referred, against which they are perceived and judged. [pp. 95-96]

It would appear then that in Spiegel's view the self does not emerge from the psychic structures as their synthesis, but that it constitutes an independent organizing principle which makes the interaction of these structures possible. From the study of superego functions in the child Sandler arrived at the very interesting concept of an *organizing activity* in mental development. According to Sandler (1960), "organizing activity embraces those activities grouped by Piaget (1936, 1937) under the headings of 'assimilation' and 'accommodation,' by Hartmann (1939) as 'fitting together' " and other similar concepts. Sandler states:

> Organizing activity is much more than the mere taking in of impressions from the outside, but is intimately connected with the development of all organized ego functions and secondary processes. It includes the construction of frames of reference, schemata, and all the technique by which the child controls his perceptions (arising from the id or the outside world) and activities. It includes also the development of ego functions such as memory, thinking, imagination, and the capacity for purposive action. . . . Part of the child's inner world consists of models of his objects . . . and of the self. [p. 147]

Sandler also emphasizes that

> organizing activity begins to occur extremely early in life . . . from the moment that differential cathexis of aspects of the child's world can be said to occur. Clearly, it is those experiences which are directly concerned with need satisfaction that are first organized by the child, under the dominance of the pleasure principle.

I believe that Sandler's concept of an organizing activity beginning extremely early in life is closely related to Erikson's epigenetic principle, to Spitz's "organizers of the psyche," Spiegel's concept of a frame of reference for internal perception and the "primary identity" suggested by me (chapter 8). I cannot, however, agree with Sandler that organizing activity is "a reflection of the synthetic function of the ego." It would appear from Sandler's own description that organizing activity precedes the development of such a relatively advanced ego function as the synthetic function. Rather, organizing activity seems to establish the possibility of the orderly development of various ego functions. In describing so clearly the organizing activity, Sandler appears to me, like Spitz and Spiegel, to move in a direction beyond ego psychology—a direction which he seems suddenly to abandon by subordinating the concept of organizing activity under the synthetic function of the ego. At the same time, Sandler links his concept of organizing activity with Hartmann's "fitting together." With this I fully agree, because I do indeed believe that this is one of Hartmann's basic concepts that transcends the ego-psychological frame of reference.

HARTMANN'S APPROACH TO THE PROBLEM OF ADAPTATION AS ANTICIPATION OF A PSYCHOLOGY OF THE WHOLE PERSON

I suggested above that Piaget's (1953) attempt to formulate psychological theories in the algebra of logic might advance the task of clarifying the implications of psychoanalytic propositions. In the absence of such a rigorous procedure it is gratifying to see the many serious efforts to examine the logical relationship of basic psychoanalytic assumptions to one another. The contributions of Rapaport and Gill (1959), Gill (1963), Arlow and Brenner (1964) exemplify this trend. I shall follow the example set by Rapaport and Gill by attempting to state some of the ideas advanced by Hartmann in a propositional form in order to separate more clearly the general assumptions from the more specific propositions. I must confine myself to just a few of the hypotheses Hartmann has contributed to psychoanalytic theory. I shall begin with the concept of primary autonomy of the ego, as quoted above in this paper.

When Hartmann speaks of the inborn characteristics of the ego as a third force acting upon ego development, besides the impact of reality and the instinctual drives, we may distinguish between several assumptions contained in this proposition:

a. In order to understand the observational data of ego development, the impact of reality and of the instinctual drives is insufficient to account for many phenomena. We must hypothesize the existence of a third force which is not identical either with environmental influences or with the instinctual drives. It must, therefore, be considered as an autonomous factor in ego development.
b. The third force is an aspect of the ego.
c. The third force represents the inborn characteristics of the ego, its hereditary core, and their maturation.

It would appear that the assumption (a) is a very general one, implying a different order of abstraction from either (b) or (c). Its validity does not depend on the validity of (b) and (c). Rapaport and Gill (1959) formulate the assumptions underlying both Hartmann's primary autonomy as well as Erikson's ego epigenesis as follows: "All psychological phenomena originate in innate givens, which mature according to an epigenetic groundplan." It seems to me that this formulation does not do justice to the generality of assumption (a). It is thinkable, for instance, that the "third force" is not an *innate* given. This would apply to Sandler's concept of organizing activity. Nor is the concept of an epigenetic ground plan a necessary derivative of assumption (a). As I have suggested in chapter 5, the relationship between the "third force" and the emergence of psychic structure might be more analogous to that of a musical theme to its variations rather than to that of a blueprint to the finally emerging object. The difference between a ground plan and a theme lies in the degree to which individually possible patterns of development, such as Greenacre (1957, 1958a) has demonstrated for the personality of the artist, may vary. Hartmann's assumption in its generalized form (a) raises new questions and suggestions for investigation of such phenomena as identity, self, of the specifically human aspect of work and man's historical existence. All of these problems touch upon the issue of an autonomous third force in man, an independent variable which profoundly affects the "shape of the representational world" (Sandler and Rosenblatt 1962) for the individual. In other words, it is this autonomous "third force" which transmutes man's adaptation to reality into the actuality of his historical existence (Erikson 1962) by opening up for the individual the one and only perception of "reality" accessible to him. In a similar manner pressures of needs and drives appear as manifestations of personal will. This was recognized by Hartmann (1939) when he predicted "that the psychology of will-processes is destined to play a role in the psychoanalytic ego psychology of the future" (pp. 74-75). We may therefore say that Hartmann's concept of an autonomous third force, while formulated to meet the exigencies of psychoanalytic research at a certain stage of theory development, contained a vision of the psychoanalytical psychology of the future. The exigencies of the historical moment were met by assumptions (b) and (c) (Fuerstenau 1964). Assumption (a), however, opens up areas of problems which only recently have come into closer view.

It would not be difficult to demonstrate in many of Hartmann's formulations the same coexistence in a single proposition of assumptions to meet present conceptual emergencies with assumptions to indicate future developments.[2] I shall confine myself to two more examples because of their significance in the context of this paper. One of Hartmann's (1939) most original conceptualizations is his use of the term "fitting together" *(Zusammenpassung)* which is contrasted with adaptation, *(Anpassung)*, although both are interdependent. Hartmann borrows from biology the concept of an "organization of the organism" and quotes Parr's (1926) definition of this term as "the lawful correlation of the organism's individual parts," which does not seem far removed from Needham's (1931) reference to a "relational factor in development," as mentioned by Spitz. Hartmann states that "this correlation also includes psychophysical relation and its psychological expression is the synthetic function which is thus a special case of the broader biological concept of fitting together" (p. 40). Hartmann thus terms "fitting together" a concept "above adaptation":

> If we encounter—as we do in man—a function which simultaneously regulates both the environmental relationships and the interrelations of the mental institutions, we will have to place it above adaptation in the biological hierarchy: we will place it above adaptive activity regulated by the external world, that is, above adaptation in the narrower sense, but not above adaptation in the broader sense, because the latter already implies a "survival value" determined both by the environmental relationships and the interrelations of mental institutions. [pp. 40-41]

If we apply Gonseth's distinction (1948) of the two horizons of reality, we would have to say that in terms of the "apparent horizon" fitting together is a description of the condition for the possibility of adaptation, both on the biological as well as—in man—on the psychological level. Since man is not adapted to a specific environment by means of instinctive behavior patterns, like the animals, we must consider his mental apparatus as his "organs of survival." In the absence of a preadaptedness to a specific environment based on behavior patterns like those in the lower animals, man is able to survive *only insofar* as he has an integrated mind. Thus, in terms of the "apparent horizon," to speak of an adaptive function above adaptation to reality seems to introduce a dichotomy between biological and psychological survival in man: an implied assumption that man could somehow biologically survive even without integrated mental functioning; only the latter, however, would raise this narrow biological adaptation to the human level.

But it is obvious that this is not the reason for Hartmann's introduction of the concept of fitting together. There is a second reason, *l'horizon profond*, which reveals itself in this thesis of a function "above adaptation." This is the awareness that survival in man must refer to survival as a unique person, an individual capable of living his life in possession of his "true self" (Winnicott 1952) who has been able to develop a sense of his own identity and has been capable of maintaining it. Seen in this way, the postulation of a mental functioning aiming at a fitting-together above and beyond adaptation for survival raises our sights beyond ego psychology and charts a course for further exploration of the human mind as a manifestation of an invariant self.

"I have totally separated," wrote Goethe to a friend,

> my political and social life from my moral and poetic one and in this way I feel at my best. . . . Only in my innermost plans and purposes and endeavors do I remain mysteriously self-loyal and thus tie my social, political, moral and poetic life again together into a hidden knot. [quoted by Eissler 1953, p. 118]

To survive the dangers of ego-multiplicity (Fairbairn 1944) that threaten everyone with some degree of dissociation, the function of fitting together will enable some people (like Goethe) to tie even the most diverse latent potentialities into a hidden knot. This capacity is more likely to depend on that independent variable, the autonomous third force which Hartmann postulates, rather than on the synthetic function of the ego, which does serve the adaptation in the narrower sense—survival. The capacity of the independent variable, i.e., its function and effect within the "whole person" might greatly vary according to the mysterious way in which the "hidden knot" is tied.

There is another formulation in *Ego Psychology and the Problem of Adaptation* where Hartmann reaches out beyond present-day structural theory, in this case the theory of the superego. According to Hartmann, Luther's "Here I stand—I cannot do otherwise" is not pathological behavior, because, as Hartmann puts it, "the normal ego must be able to control, but it also must be *able* to *must*" (1939, p. 94). Here again, it seems to me, Hartmann lays the foundation for a theory of what Jones (1947) called the sense of "oughtness," not on the basis of identification with parental images alone, but as an aspect of identity maintenance ("self"-preservation). While Hartmann's remark about man having to be able to "must" is almost inserted as an aside into his discussion of preconscious automatism, it deserves a fuller treatment within a reconsideration of a theory of the superego. Since I have attempted to deal tentatively with these problems elsewhere (see chapter 12), I shall not pursue them any further in this paper.

THE SELF AS
A "METAPSYCHOLOGICAL FOURTH DIMENSION"

Like all things in a universe in which time is definitely established as a fourth dimension, life is, and only can be, a size of evolutionary nature and dimension. Physically and historically it corresponds with a coefficient X which determines the position of every living thing in space, in duration and in form. [Teilhard de Chardin 1955]

Glover (1961) in a recent review, has critically discussed Spitz's concept of "organizer of the psyche." Because of the pertinence of Glover's argument for the questions raised in this paper, I shall summarize its main line of reasoning. Glover introduces his critique with the following statement:

If it should appear niggling to pass new terminology through the metapsychological mill, it must be said that . . . the onus is on the coiner of terms to justify their introduction, in particular to show that they constitute improvements on or useful expansions of existing terminology.

This is a stern but wise admonition. It encourages me to conclude this paper with some metapsychological reflections of whose tentative and fragmentary nature I am keenly aware.

"An organizer," says Glover, "has more dynamic implications than a state or stage or phase or organization. As a regulator it must represent in each instance an integrated pattern." In the case of Spitz's organizer of the psyche, Glover feels it combines structural, dynamic, and economic elements so that

> the term "organizer" is itself a synthetic product, a unifying caption which can readily be broken down into its metapsychological constituents. . . . Unless therefore one is prepared to postulate a fourth metapsychological order, a "something else," a metapsychological fourth dimension . . . the term "organizer" is useful mainly in highlighting "phases" of development of increasing complexity, a suggestive concept which however must dance attendance on clinical observations and their clinical interpretation. [Glover 1961, p. 97]

Since I have throughout this paper used Hartmann's concept of an autonomous third force, of an independent variable, in a sense that links it to a number of ideas that I consider related to, though not identical, with my own formulations of a primary identity (see chapters 2 and 8), I accept the inference drawn by Glover that such concepts do postulate a metapsychological fourth dimension.

Rapaport and Gill have included in "the assumptions constituting metapsychology proper" both the genetic as well as the adaptive point of view, in addition to the classical dynamic, topographic, and economic criteria. Glover does not agree with this thesis: for Glover, neither genetic nor adaptional viewpoints deserve to be called metapsychological assumptions "although essential for the evaluation of psychic events, developmental and adaptional measures are complex serial interpretations, not basic (irreducible) postulates." It seems to me that this disagreement has more than a semantic significance. It illustrates the very issue of the psychoanalytic theory of the "whole person" and the limitations of structural theory. Glover seems to regret that neither Hartmann nor Spitz have conceptualized a fourth metapsychological dimension, because

> the chaos that exists in characterological classification cries out for attention; and since the therapeutic field of psychoanalysis is sometimes alleged to have shifted from symptom formation to character disorders, Dr. Spitz's diagrammatic field formula would at least afford *Lebensraum* for practical (clinical) classification..

This would be true, according to Glover, "even if these assumptions (i.e., organizers, dependent differentiations, directional development) were only approximately applicable to the mental apparatus." The "characterological classification" would, I assume, include borderline cases indicating ego multiplicity (Fairbairn 1944), identity problems, disturbances of the self-experience, ego distortions, among others. What Glover seems to imply, then, is that for the time being our theoretical understanding of these phenomena is "chaotic" because a metapsychological fourth dimension for their appropriate conceptualization does not exist.

> The reconstruction of normal mental development and the establishment of psycho-analytic aetiologies calls for a *sequence* of correlations, combinations, and permutations of the three metapsychological criteria in both progressive and regressive directions. But this historical reconstruction is not a fourth metapsychological dimension: it is rather a cautionary *Masstab* based on the direct interpretation of clinical data. And it is in this sense that the concept of an "organizer" might prove of some heuristic utility. [Glover 1961, p. 98]

In contrast to Glover's conceptual reserve, Rapaport and Gill, aware of the same necessity to go beyond the limitations of structural theory, have extended the range of metapsychological assumptions. Because they intend to include in psychoanalytic psychology the total dimension of the "whole person," in the actuality of the social and historical experience of man, they have not hesitated to give genetic-epigenetic as well as adaptive propositions the dignity of metapsychological assumptions. In this way, they seem to feel, classical structural theory can be made to approximate Hartmann's aim of psychoanalysis as a general psychology.

Since I am inclined to share Glover's scepticism concerning the metapsychological status of genetic and adaptive propositions, I shall present for theoretical consideration a number of assumptions aimed at establishing an independent variable that is not identical with the metapsychological postulates of psychological forces, psychological energies, and psychological structures in the classical sense, and might therefore constitute a fourth metapsychological dimension. Referring to the last quotation from Glover concerning the reconstruction of mental development, I propose a rewording of Glover's statement as follows: The reconstruction of normal mental development and the establishment of psychoanalytic etiology calls for a *constant* correlation[3] of the three metapsychological criteria whose combinations and permutations constitute *transformations* of this constant correlation such that in normal mental development each transformation can be understood as function of the invariant correlation.

From this abstract formulation a number of deductions could be derived. In chapter 8 I suggested that the infant, in its early contact with the mother, establishes a primary identity. This primary identity I considered an invariant whose transformations would provide the developmental sequences with an unchanging inner form or core (Keyser 1922). This formulation might permit one to add that what occurs in the earliest mirroring experience is the establishment of a constant correlation between basic metapsychological elements. This constant or invariant correlation was previously described by analogy with the musical theme in which not the notes but their relationship to one another remains constant in the thematic transformation.

At the beginning of this chapter I asked how we define the relationship of the psychic structures to the whole person, to the self. It seems that the psychic structures are not appropriately conceptualized as constituting parts in relationship to the *whole* person. Instead, an alternative view might define the self as the sum total of all transformations which are *possible* functions of an early-formed invariant correlation of the various basic elements of the mental apparatus. This definition seems to be compatible with the observation that the self-experience includes all the past selves of one's life and the not-yet-lived future. It also seems consistent with the fact that in the self-experience the potential selves that we could have been are merged with the actualized selves that we were and are. It is important to clarify the meaning of the term "possible functions" in the context of mental development and psychological reality, because from the concept "possible functions" we might derive a theory of psychoanalytic etiology based on the formulations I have suggested.

I hope that I shall not tax the patience of the reader by again using a mathematical analogy to illustrate my point. There are "nonsense" algebraic problems such as the following: *A father is three times as old as his son. In ten years' time the son will be twice as old as his father. How old are they now?* Titchmarch (1959), from whose book this example is taken, adds:

> This problem is obviously an idiotic one; but the algebra goes along quite happily. If the father's age now is x and the son's is y, the two statements are represented by the equations
>
> $$x = 3y, \; y + 10, \; = 2(x + 10)$$
>
> and the solution is x = –6, y = –2. . . . As we have forgotten to mention that there cannot be negative ages, the data are actually quite consistent, and the answer, though absurd if related to real life, is perfectly correct mathematically.

I believe that this example is not a mere flippancy. If we assume that a constant correlation between basic psychological element constitutes an invariant in mental life, changes that occur in one element would bring about corresponding changes in the other correlated elements. These changes would be dependent on two entirely different factors. The one factor would be defined by the formal characteristics of the correlation *only*, regardless of whether or not the change thus induced is "translatable" into the realities of biological and mental life. The second factor, determining what may possibly happen in the actual *life* of the individual, depends on the chances of what in a person is capable of being "translated" into the concrete terms of his life. Such a notion as "negative ages" might sound biologically "untranslatable." But is it not at least thinkable, given the propensity of mental life for the creation of abstract and symbolic realities, that under some circumstances an individual may "invent" a way to become "older" than his father, perhaps by becoming the "creator" of his own father as an artist painting the father's picture, or by achieving a goal that father had been striving for, but had been forced to abandon—such as a son of a peasant becoming his father's "father" as a priest?

Whether or not a certain mental development is possible or impossible is not decided, according to this thesis, exclusively by the maturational or adaptive processes. There would, in addition, exist the organizing function of an autonomous factor, defined by the necessity to maintain a constant correlation between the basic metapsychological elements, definable as a "primary identity." The development that *actually* occurs would be the resultant of (a) the possible transformations of the existing invariant correlation and (b) the possibility for a given individual to "translate" the "organizing directions" emanating from (a) into actualities corresponding to the potentialities of his psychological structures and the opportunities given by the *Umwelt* in which he happens to exist. The possibilities (a) and (b) are of a quite different order. The former represent an "oughtness" (Jones, 1947) that is indifferent to existing realities, while (b) is the totality of "available" psychic structures which may or may not become actualized by the individual depending on whether or not they enter the organizing radius of (a). Thus, developmental crises or breakdowns may occur either because of particular complexities of the invariant correlation, or because the structures capable of development do not "fit" the psychological task which the individual, in order to live as a whole person, must fulfil. Under both circumstances role-diffusion, disturbance of self-experience, ego distortion, etc., will indicate the failure of identity maintenance. In man, then, it is the necessity for identity maintenance, i.e., for self-preservation, which forms the psychological basis for the possibility of inner continuity of the whole person throughout life, and for the possibility of dissociation and disentegration as well.

I shall, in concluding, mention only briefly one more area of problems that might be interesting to consider in terms of the propositions advanced in this paper. I am referring here to the problems of "energy transformation," such as neutralization, defusion of instincts, of free aggression, etc. These concepts have been indispensable because they alone can give account of many important transformation phenomena both in mental development as well as in pathology (Rapaport and Gill 1959). The proposition of formal transformations of a constant correlation of forces, energies and structures might permit a different approach to some of these problems.

In my attempt to trace the influence of Hartmann's hypotheses (primary autonomy, independent variable, fitting together), first formulated in *Ego Psychology and the Problem of Adaptation,* on problems of the psychoanalytic approach to the person and the self, I have arrived at propositions of which I could only give a very abstract presentation. Whether they have any usefulness will be decided by their applicability to clinical observation. I would probably not have dared to engage in the kind of theoretical exploration presented in this paper if it had not been for the example set by Hartmann, who has taught us not to be afraid of ideas that are tentative, complex, and incomplete.

NOTES

1. The attempt to deal with these problems seems to induce many authors to abandon the evolutionary approach to mental development in favor of one reinstating preexisting, entelechtic forms or spiritual entities. This is especially true of Jung's concept of the self (see Perry 1953; also Moustakas 1956).

2. One could express this also in terms of Bohr's (1948) concept of complementarity in that Hartmann often includes in one proposition two assumptions that are complementary to one another. The elaboration of the concept of complementarity by F. Gonseth (1948) is especially applicable to Hartmann's formulations: "Nous allons donc imaginer deux horizons succesifs de réalité, le premier devant être appelé l'horizon apparent ou l'horizon A et le second l'horizon profond ou l'horizon P. Conformément a ces dénominations, nous supposerons que l'horizon profond se dévoile par un approfondissement de l'horizon apparent, comme l'horizon quantique se dévoile par un approfondissement de l'horizon classique ou, de façon encore plus marquée, de l'horizon naturel. . . . En psychologie, par exemple, l'horizon A pourrait être identifié au theatre de la conscience, donnant figure au traces de l'horizon profond P que serait ici le subconscient."

3. Spiegel (1959) sees a "constant ratio" in the distribution of cathexes as the basis for "constancy of self-feeling."

Chapter 10

IDENTITY CONFIGURATION
AND DEVELOPMENTAL ALTERNATIVES

THE PROBLEM OF DEFINING A SPECIFIC INDIVIDUAL
BY THE USE OF PSYCHOANALYTIC TERMINOLOGY

The concept of identity is defined in this chapter[1] as invariance within change, or invariance within a process of transformation. This identity concept is quite abstract, as indicated by its usage in mathematics, but its pertinence for the psychiatrist is evidenced by the fact that when we deal with human development in ontogenetic terms, we are actually speaking of an invariant whose transformations we can observe. When we describe such genetic phases as the psychosexual development, the emergence of ego functions, of object relations, we describe, in fact, nothing but the transformations, while our perception of the invariant is not based on simple observable givens. We assume nevertheless the existence of such an invariant in human development as if it were a given fact. When we speak of phases of infantile development we postulate that, though the phenomena presented in each phase may vary radically, we are dealing with the same, identical individual. This assumption is for us so basic and self-evident that we would consider the absence of "sameness" in a person as a sign of severe pathology. The same holds true for the subjective experience of our own sameness and continuity throughout the various phases of our lives, and here again an absence of this sense of inner continuity or even a doubt concerning it we would not hesitate to characterize as pathological. I may add that our observations of the transformations of the human individual which we describe as following a normal or abnormal pattern of development could not even be made without the concept of an invariant individual frame of reference: we could not speak of development, but could only describe a random pattern of changing behavior.

In psychoanalysis, the origin and nature of the invariant in personality development is rarely investigated per se. The absence of a definition of the invariant, the incapacity to obtain a conceptual hold upon what constitutes the uniquely personal quality of an individual's identity maintained against the changes and vicissitudes which we are able to observe and describe, confront us with a curious incompleteness in our grasp of personality development. This incompleteness manifests itself in the fact that, on the basis of the dynamic, structural, economic, genetic and adaptive theories that we may apply to our understanding of the personality of a patient, we cannot reconstruct the actuality of personal identity, the invariant continuity that would enable us to recognize from such analytic description the uniqueness of the person referred to in our clinical descriptions.

Let me give you an example from the recent literature. Meyer (1964) has published a series of excellent papers dealing with the personality of Joseph Conrad. Let me quote two passages from the last of them:

> Conrad lived most of his life in a condition of precarious mental balance. A chronically depressed man who was morbidly attracted by the specters of sickness and death, there is good reason to believe that . . . Conrad at one time attempted to take his own life. . . . This self-destructive urge was but one manifestation of a singular deformation in the make-up of his character in which a fuzzy sense of personal identity, a sado-masochistic conception of love, fetishism, and allied distortions of reality were distinct components in a highly obsessional individual caught in the grip of an intense castration problem.

One might consider this a condensed, but fairly complete psychoanalytic conceptualization of the personality problems of Joseph Conrad. But does this combination of deviant developmental patterns permit us to arrive at the uniqueness and actuality of Conrad as a living person?

Obviously not, as becomes even more strikingly evident when we read on in Meyer's paper:

> In seeming flight from the threatening furies of madness, and in a headlong pursuit of that elusive prize—the unquestioned establishment of his own unique and unambiguous identity—Conrad wandered over the four corners of the earth, masquerading, as it were, in the temporal vestments of personal and traditional heroes. Adventurer in Latin America, partisan of a deposed king, sailor upon the high seas, skipper of a river boat in the Belgian Congo, and finally English man of letters, the Polish-born Teodor Josef Konrad Korzaniowski sought in action and in art a shield by which he might ward off the mad devils leering at him behind the draperies of his unguarded mind.

Many people might be able to guess from the latter quotation that this could only be Conrad, even if his name were not mentioned, but I am sure that nobody could arrive at this conclusion from the first quote. What I am saying here is, in fact, uncontested: Nobody *claims* that we can arrive, from the most complete psychoanalytic description, at a recognition of the individual in his uniqueness and invariant identity. This basic incompleteness of even the most painstaking psychoanalytic description of a personality raises questions which seem to me worthwhile pursuing, even though it will confront us with more unresolved problems than with any final answer.

THE UNCERTAINTY OF PREDICTING INDIVIDUAL DEVELOPMENT ON THE BASIS OF PSYCHOANALYTIC OBSERVATIONS

Greenacre (1957), in a most thought-provoking study on "The Childhood of the Artist" arrived at a number of conclusions concerning the basic characteristics of the personality endowed with creative talent. According to Greenacre, one can describe these basic traits under four headings: "first, greater sensitivity to sensory stimulation; second, unusual capacity for awareness of relations between various stimuli; third, predisposition to an empathy of wider range and deeper vibration than usual; and fourth, intactness of sufficient sensorimotor equipment to allow the building up of projective motor discharges for expressive functions." Greenacre elaborates on these points later on as follows:

> If we think . . . of the potentially gifted infant as possessing a conspicuously greater than average sensitivity to sensory stimulation, this may mean both an intensification of the experience and also a widening of it to include not only the primary object . . . but more peripheral objects which are related in some degree or fashion to the primary one in their ability to arouse somewhat similar sensory responses. . . . Thus we can conceive of the fact that for the potentially gifted infant the primary object which stimulates certain sensory responses to it is invested with a greater field of related experiences than would be true for the infant with lesser endowment.

This expansion of the sensory stimulation to a field of related experiences leads, according to Greenacre, to the formation of "collective alternates" for the primary sensory stimulation. With this term "collective alternates" Greenacre describes "the range of extended experience which may surround or become attached to the main focus of object relationships." Thus, Greenacre concludes, "the relationship between the forces of the individual cathexes and those of the collective alternate ones would appear to exist in varying balances . . . and this balance would influence very much the outline and organization of the incipient ego development; especially the growth of any self-image or self-representation; and even of perception of the self." Thus, from an extended study of autobiographical and biographical material of outstanding talents in numerous fields, as well as from her clinical experience, Greenacre has tried to abstract certain basic qualities of sensory experience which she considers typical for the potentially gifted infant. Given such basic characteristics, she has conjectured what the consequences of this type of response to sensory stimuli might be for the development of object relations, for libidinal cathexes, for the emergent ego structure and for the perception of the self.

Making use of the criteria developed by Greenacre for the psychoanalytic understanding of the personality structure of the potentially gifted infant, it would still be impossible to *predict* with certainty that an infant displaying this personality structure would indeed become a person of creative talent and achievement. This has been proven by direct observation of children whose personality structure corresponded strikingly to Greenacre's criteria for the potentially gifted infant. I am referring here to the well-known paper by Bergman and Escalona (1949) on "Unusual Sensitivities in Very Young Children" which forms a fascinating counterpart to Greenacre's study of "The Childhood of the Artist." Bergman and Escalona report in their paper "a number of observations in children who very early in life, possibly from birth, showed unusual sensitivities." These sensitivities manifested themselves "in several, if not all sensory modalities (visual, auditory, tactile, etc.). . . . These children were 'sensitive' in both meanings of the word: easily hurt, and easily stimulated to enjoyment. Variations in sensory impression that made no difference to the average child made a great deal of difference to these children. They were also characterized by a certain precocity. . . . The first impression . . . was that of unusual giftedness such as might be observed in the budding of a genius." Here, then we seem to find a close enough parallel to Greenacre's postulates. But the authors continue: "Further observation, however, suggested comparison with individuals suffering from a traumatic neurosis, or a psychosis, and even with feeblemindedness. Closer study and follow-up made it appear that childhood psychosis was the fate of these children." The authors add, however, that they are not sure yet "that all children of the type . . . described eventually develop a clear psychotic picture."

In the children they observed the similarity of the personality structure to that suggested by Greenacre for potentially creative individuals is indeed very striking. Not only did they display a heightened sensitivity to sensory stimuli. The authors also felt that these children showed signs of a precocious ego organization which they consider responsible for the early breakdown of ego functioning. There were sufficient indications of artistic tendencies, especially an early interest in music, which lead Bergman and Escalona to raise the same question that Greenacre has treated in her paper on the childhood of the artist; "Can we find apparently normal persons, persons who can stand a fair amount of frustration, and who show average or better 'ego-strength' . . . but who show in some ways that stimuli reach them with unusual intensity? . . . Could just this be the case in individuals of high sensitivity and great gifts who show adequate or superior ego functioning, to take extreme examples, in persons like Goethe, Rubens, Titian?" In an attempt to answer these questions, Bergman and Escalona hypothesize "that there may be two types of stimulus barriers, one constitutional, organic and a second one making use of these higher functions ... which we ascribe to the ego and which—through attention, apprehension, symbolization ... contribute the second protective layer (of the stimulus barrier)." The authors conclude, that their observations on children with unusual sensitivities "indicates a number of questions that might be answered by future research."

ON PERSONAL IDENTITY

The questions raised by Bergman and Escalona (1949) and given a new impetus by the studies of Greenacre (1957, 1958b) are still with us. In their most general formulation, they are questions concerning developmental alternatives.[2]

The papers I have quoted seem to lead to the conclusion that we must assume the existence of alternative developmental paths in individuals whose early personality structure displays striking similarities. Nevertheless, from these similar constellations some children will develop a childhood psychosis, some may show feeblemindedness, and others may give rise to creative talent. It is especially remarkable that the latter is quite compatible with any of the former. According to Greenacre, the English poet Thomas Chatterton showed the behavior of a dull child before his remarkable poetic gifts asserted themselves. The fact that he ended his life, before the age of eighteen, by suicide, indicates the coexistence of high talent with emotional instability of almost any degree. The examples of this among men of genius are too well known to be listed here. I shall only briefly refer back to the quotations about Joseph Conrad to underline how little we know about the things that determine whether an individual may through a creative effort maintain a sometimes temporary, sometimes permanent mental balance, whether he becomes an artist manqué, or whether a progressive disintegration of the personality structure will mark his life as that of a chronic mental patient. Nor do we know what determines the development of many a gifted person into a capable, well-functioning and integrated individual who seems throughout his life remarkably stable—even though psychoanalysis may discover a personality structure not dissimilar to that described for the artist by Greenacre. I now propose to approach this issue of developmental alternatives with the help of the concept of a primary, invariant "identity theme" or "identity configuration" that I have attempted to develop in earlier chapters (2, 4-9).

There I postulated that human identity is acquired very early in life as a thematic configuration, arising in the earliest, most primitive contact of the infant with the mothering adult. Borrowing from ethology, I thought of this earliest identity theme as an imprinted configuration which from then on constitutes the invariant in the development of the individual.

I am now raising the question how this hypothesis of identity as an early, acquired, invariant configuration might contribute to our understanding of the problem of developmental alternatives. For this purpose I shall once again introduce the distinction of "possible" and "impossible" identity themes that, in a different context, I discussed in chapter 9. If you conceive of the identity theme as a kind of imprinted demand or command on the part of the mothering one, expressing what, unconsciously, she wants the infant to be for her, you can assume that there are themes that are capable of concrete implementation and others that are not. It is, for instance, likely to be possible for an infant to fulfill the unconscious expectations of a mother that he safely grow up into a man like his father so that, in time he may become a father himself to his children. In contrast, let me give you an example of an "impossible" identity theme. I am using for this purpose Greenacre's (1957) biographical sketch of the poet Thomas Chatterton. He was, we learn, a posthumous child, born three months after his father's death in 1752. His mother was a young woman, barely twenty years old. The other members of the household were a two-year-older sister and the paternal grandmother. Thomas Chatterton was thus the only male in a household of women.

What might be the unconscious expectations of so young a widow with regard to her infant son? We cannot be sure, of course. But if you permit me to use my own imagination, it is at least thinkable that one could paraphrase these unconscious maternal expectations as follows: I wish that this son of mine would take the place of my dead husband

and also be a father to me. What encourages me to postulate such an attitude on the part of the mother are the data which we have about the development of the child Thomas Chatterton.

Chatterton was in his first years of life an obviously disturbed child that was considered too dull to go to school, given to violent tempers and infantile depression. Then, suddenly, he began to develop precociously when the mother gave him a song book which had belonged to his father. In the mother's words, he fell in love with the Gothic script of the songbook. Soon he learned to read letters, then, began to read words and finally could read the songs in a way, that, according to Greenacre, showed extreme precocity and absorption. He developed an infatuation with the church building in which his father had been a teacher and singer in the choir. Thomas Chatterton went, however, further than that. At about fourteen years of age he invented an imaginary monk, Thomas Rowley, who was alleged to have lived in the fifteenth century and who had belonged to the circle of men around the important figure of the fifteenth-century mayor of Bristol, the very man who helped to build the church with which Thomas Chatterton's father had been so closely affiliated during his life time. Chatterton attributed poetry that he himself had written to this imaginary monk, and his attempt to present the poetic manuscript as his discovery earned him the reputation of a perpetrator of a literary forgery. After this disastrous beginning he had only scant and irregular employment. Finally, he was to have an interview with the mayor of London, in the hope of improving his position, and, as Greenacre suspects, of finding in the mayor a present-day version of the good father mayor of Bristol. On the eve of his anticipated interview, the mayor died. From then on Thomas Chatterton seemed gradually to disintegrate, and four months later he commited suicide by arsenic poisoning. Only after his death was his once repudiated manuscript attributed to the imaginary Thomas Rowley rediscovered as the work of a poetic genius.

I have allowed myself this digression because I believe that it may serve as an example of the influence of an "impossible" identity theme on the development of a personality. In what sense could one call an identity theme "impossible"? If my paraphrasing of the mother's unconscious expectations for her infant son approximates the truth, we can state that in a realistic, concrete way a son cannot be his mother's father and her dead husband. Since I have compared the identity theme or the identity configuration to an imprinted condition for the establishment of an invariant identity of the person, the impossibility of implementing the identity theme realistically and literally would seem to indicate that such a child could not ever establish a livable identity, and thus the essential frame of reference for the development of ego functions would be missing. We would, therefore, expect the child to show signs of dissociation and possibly final disintegration of his ego structure.

But this is obviously a gross oversimplification, on several scores, of the interaction between identity configuration and personality development. First of all, the unconscious expectations of the mother are not conveyed or communicated to the child in the verbal form in which I paraphrased them. I believe that the child is responsive to the mother's *unconscious* expectations, transmitted to the child by non-verbal manifestations of maternal attitudes.[3] I have tried to describe these earliest interactions with the help of the concept of mirroring experiences. In whatever way we attempt to account for the conveying of maternal unconscious fantasies regarding the child, we must assume that they are characterized by a measure of indeterminacy,[4] leaving open a multiplicity of meaningful implementations. Perhaps one could compare what a child perceives of the mother's unconscious wishes to the strange indeterminacy of the ancient Delphic oracles which never precisely indicated what was going to happen and how it was going to happen, but who nevertheless had that ring of fatefulness to them from which there was no escape.

Identity themes, then, are definable as conditions under which the child will perceive himself as responded to by the mother in a specific and constant manner, contributing in this way to the constancy of the child's emerging self-image. The child has, however, considerable leeway *how* to elicit this maternal response. Thus, what I have called an "impossible" identity theme taxes the ingenuity of the child in his efforts to elicit a mirroring response, but it does not foreclose the possibility of an integrated development. Thomas Chatterton, we could reason, failed at first to obtain the maternal responses needed for the development of a constancy of his self-image. Thus he was dull, depressed and had outburst of violent tempers. But with his first show of interest in the father's song book he might have perceived a different, affirmative response on the part of the mother which from then on guided his development toward a precocious and imaginative identification with his dead father.

Let me now elaborate on the other danger of oversimplification when we use such distinction as "possible" and "impossible" identity themes. Not only must we beware of thinking of identity themes as conveyed in some verbal, explicit manner, we must also clarify the implications of the concepts "possible" and "impossible" in terms of personality development. It is, as I said, realistically impossible for the child to become the mother's husband and father. But as I understand the life story of Chatterton, this is exactly what he set out to do by "inventing" or "creating" a father and an ancestor that he could become, as we would perhaps say, in spirit, though not in the flesh. Thus the child, imprinted with an "impossible" identity theme, may actually create the terms under which the realistically impossible might become, on a higher level of abstraction or symbolization, possible.

This is, I think, the type of correlation we may surmise between "impossible" identity themes and the emergence of creative talent. It is also I believe, the reason why there are so many interesting connections between the personality of the artist and the impostor, another theme that Greenacre (1958d) has written about extensively: both are compelled, by the configuration of an "impossible" identity theme, to invent their own conditions for its fulfillment. In the case of the artist, this is done through symbolizations, while the impostor invents a fictional reality that fits his inner needs. But when we return to the question what is "impossible" for a given child, we encounter problems for which there is, for the time being, no answer. Whether a child may succeed in transforming the impossible identity configuration will depend, first, on how extreme maternal expectations are, and secondly, on the child's capacity to mobilize suitable symbolic translations of these expectations.

We know little about the first, and less about the second. What we do know is that under certain conditions children develop prematurely "symbolic aspects of themselves," to quote James (1960), who describes an infant that he observed during the first three months of life.

In psycho-analytic terms . . . instead of a phase-adequate access to instinct and physical function, so to say a body ego relish leading through need satisfaction to object relations, this infant cathected and developed a narcissistic "thought action" which also fulfilled a need satisfaction, but in a different way. On the one hand such infants miss something, and on the other they acquire a quality that others do without. That is, they develop non-muscular and symbolic aspects of themselves which are yet active responses. This is a special kind of ego development with its own potential advantages, no doubt, as well as disadvantages. We should only evaluate reluctantly. They may even come to have survival value in later life.

James elaborates this general description as follows: "This child from the time of first walking and expressive gesturing showed a subtle disorder of motility which seemed to be linked with her unusual mental plasticity and activity. . . . Her ideas ran away with her, and if she thought of a thing she was liable to act as though through magic it had already happened." This child, in spite of showing many schizoid mechanisms, was judged by James to be in no way psychotic, even though he points out the great similarity with the children described by Bergman and Escalona. When we try to account for such differences in development, we usually have to hypothesize various degrees of ego strength, of adequate protection by the stimulus barrier, etc. Without wanting to argue the importance of such factors, I suggest that there may be another way to account for the existence of developmental alternatives.

ON POSSIBLE AND IMPOSSIBLE IDENTITY THEMES

I am proposing that the decisive factor making either for success or failure of integration is the patient's ability to find the appropriate terms to implement the invariant identity configuration. In patients confronting an "impossible" identity theme, the finding of the appropriate terms may be a never-ending search throughout the patient's life. A great variety of implementations are tried and rejected, and new levels of symbolic implementation are discovered, which may lead to a surprising new integration, without, however, a guarantee of lifelong stability. For instance, Joseph Conrad experimented with numerous identity implementations, of which his identity as a British novelist, writing in a foreign tongue, came closest to permitting him a balanced existence. As the studies of Meyer (1964) indicate, however, his mental balance remained always precarious, greatly depending on special emotional conditions, such as close relationships to selected friends.

In chapter 9, I quoted the mathematician Titchmarsh (1959) as noting that certain problems "though absurd when related to real life, (are) perfectly correct mathematically.[5] This dilemma we face very definitely as we try to translate "impossible" identity themes into the language of human relationships. The expectation of becoming older than one's father, which I suggested as an aspect of the identity theme of Thomas Chatterton, is realistically absurd, but it may be permissible to go beyond the strictly biological concept of age, when we deal with *symbolic realities* of the "inner world" of human experience: Thomas Chatterton did perhaps invent a way to become older than his father when he created the imaginary Thomas Rowley and spoke through him to his contemporaries.

We do not know, of course, whether an individual possesses the specific propensity that will permit him to find the appropriate symbolic transcript of his identity theme. The person who can implement an identity theme by making use of the realistic possibilities of life might have a better chance toward the development of an integrated personality than the one who must, as it were, create a noneuclidian space in which his individual identity theme may find the conditions of successful translation. It has been my impression that this process of identity implementation usually takes place, particularly in the more complex developmental situations, on several levels simultaneously.

We may observe a search to implement the identity theme in a very realistic and sometimes too concrete way which may, particularly in adolescence, lead to experimentation with very extreme possibilities. At the same time there may be attempts to resolve the dilemma of identity configuration symbolically, and that again may take place on several levels of symbolization and abstraction. The process might involve artistic efforts such as acting, painting, writing. Or the search may go on on levels of highest abstraction, perhaps in the form of mathematical or philosophical creativity. This struggle can coincide with many forms of psychopathology, including psychotic episodes. Such efforts towards symbolic implementation of an "impossible" identity theme, occurring on several levels of concreteness and abstraction simultaneously, create in the individual a multitude of potential personalities. In extreme cases this condition might come close to a state of dissociation, akin to what Fairbairn (1944) has described as ego multiplicity. This dissociation corresponds to Greenacre's (1957) finding that "It is evident in studying the lives of markedly creative people that splits in the self-presentation, going over into even a split in the sense of identity, do occur and relatively frequently—sometimes developing along parallel lines and sometimes alternating, one emerging from cover of the other. This division into the two or more selves may be experienced in childhood with some distress and with the wish to deny the creative self in favor of the social stereotype. . . . Under many circumstances, this struggle continues into adult life." It seems likely that every individual is endowed with multiple developmental alternatives, and not just one self, which by definition excludes all other potential selves. I think of the self as the sum total of all developmental alternatives that are compatible with the individual's invariant identity configurations, (chapter 9). If you permit me another reference to mathematics, I conceive of the pattern of human personality development in terms of what is called a diophantine equation, which, as I understand it, describes a type of equation having more than one unknown, and having therefore an infinite number of valid solutions, and not just one correct one.

I have neglected until now to emphasize the importance of the historical situation for the implementation of any human identity configuration, i.e., the historical setting which the infant enters at birth and which will be the world in which he will exist during his lifetime. This is a problem of great significance and complexity. It appears related to the question of the availability of certain socially recognized identities within a given culture. I am envisioning culture, here, as a collective effort to provide workable—i.e. possible—identity configurations to as many of its members as possible, enabling a majority to deal with the major existential crises and predicaments that can be considered "expectable" in a certain era. I do not consider human identity as derived from the demands of culture. Rather, I see the necessity of culture for human beings originating from the fact that man alone does not have an innate identity as the animals can be said to possess. Only humans are, therefore, compelled to acquire, or to create identities. This can only be done collectively, because without specific institutions for the maintenance of identity, human identity would remain unreal. Cultures are storehouses, collectively maintained, for the accumulation of available identities. The storehouse offers to most but not all individuals within a given culture realistic or symbolic options of identity implementation. If the number of individuals for which the available supply of identity configurations is out of reach or inapplicable increases, sooner or later a great cultural crisis tends to occur. Such a crisis may lead to the emergence of culturally available identity implementations, or to the decay of the culture. Thus, there remains the fact that for each individual it is the historical situation in which he lives that will either provide or fail to provide the real or symbolic prerequisites which could enable him to find an implementation appropriate to his personal identity theme.

THE IMPLICATIONS OF THE CONCEPT
OF AN IDENTITY THEME FOR THERAPY

My presentation of the complex interaction between identity configuration and personality development has led me far afield, into areas not strictly within the realm of psychiatry. Thus, it is proper to return to the questions that concern the psychiatrist. Is there, we must ask, any tangible value for the clinician in the hypotheses I have been presenting?

I believe there are several dimensions of clinical significance that the theories as outlined touch upon. To view individuals as being engaged in a constant search for an appropriate implementation of their personal identity themes and to see this search as a process taking place on several levels of mental life (realistic, symbolic, abstract) simultaneously introduces an important therapeutic guideline through its recognition of developmental alternatives. It appears to me to permit a better understanding of the unity of often widely divergent affective states and behavior patterns than is offered by the modern structural theory. For instance, a compulsive sexual acting-out pattern coexisting with a search for the creative expression of an individual's perception of self, of interaction with others within a shared world, can be compatible with a sense of the unity of the person within the theories developed here. Where I formerly would have seen only signs of increasing personality disintegration and dissociation, I can now recognize the basic unity of the total person, struggling for a meaningful translation of a unique identity configuration. Since the personal identity theme is an invariant, the individual must succeed or fail on his own terms: it is not possible to replace the identity theme with another one that might appear to the therapist more realistic, safer, or culturally more acceptable. These principles have influenced my prognostic judgement. I feel more concerned today about individuals who are fixated to what Winnicott (1954) has called a false self, than those who are seemingly showing signs of considerable dissociation of the personality.

The understanding of personality development as an expression of the need to implement a basic identity configuration can be important for the prevention of serious damage to the growing child. In the previously quoted paper by James (1960), he makes this comment: "It is important to note how hard it may be for parents to resist the pressure and seduction of one-sidedness in favor of all-around development. It is easy for the parent to take credit for having a 'forward' child, and not to notice at the time the loss of later ego-integration from narcissistic developments not achieved through object relations." What James describes as the parent's response to one-sidedness, I would understand as a manifestation of the unconscious expectations of the mother with regard to the child. In cases like the infant observed by James, the mother may have burdened the child with a damaging restriction upon the means acceptable in its search for its own appropriate implementation of its identity configuration. James describes how successful handling of the situation, once the tendency of the mother toward such one-sided responses had been recognized, can modify and mitigate the child's developmental difficulties. Thus, the interpretation of developmental crisis in terms of difficulties arising from the child's effort to translate its identity theme in the only way available to it may have clinical value for the prevention of developmental failure.

Finally, I believe that certain problem areas within psychoanalytic theory may be approached more constructively with the help of the propositions presented here. For instance, the emphasis on the infinity of developmental alternatives, as well as the important role that historical circumstances play in the process of finding an appropriate implementation of an individual's identity configuration may be helpful in achieving a more satisfactory understanding of the important, but somewhat imprecise concept of sublimation.

To summarize: the theories and often speculative possibilities considered here are based on the conviction that psychoanalytic theory is far from needing radical conceptual reconstructions because its base is altogether too narrow. On the contrary, the heritage that Freud left to posterity is fragmentary because it is based on a vision of human life so wide and sweeping that only gradually are we becoming aware of its true dimensions. The hypotheses presented here are an attempt to explore some of these dimensions that have been left to us to struggle with, because of their implications for the human condition and its possible future.

NOTES

1. I have been reluctant to have this essay published because of its wide-ranging and speculative character. I have come to believe, however, that in the crisis of certainty which characterizes our era, it is justifiable to raise basic questions, even though it is impossible to provide answers based on verifiable evidence. This is happening right now in the very model of science, mathematics. I am referring here to the recent introduction of "catastrophe theory" by the French topologist René Thom, which raises questions of great importance for many sciences, since it deals with new models for the understanding of phenomena of "discontinuous change." There can be no doubt that such a theory would be of great significance to a psychology based on psychoanalytic assumptions. The following quotation from Thom's *Structural Stability and Morphogenesis* (New York: W. A. Benjamin, 1975) seems indeed to fit the problems raised by Freud's theory of mental processes: "Many of my assertions depend on pure speculation and may be treated as day-dreams, and I accept this qualification—is not a day-dream the virtual catastrophe in which knowledge is initiated? At a time when so many scholars in the world are calculating, is it not desirable that some, who can, dream?" It is with full awareness of the impossibility of furnishing verifiable proof for many of the propositions presented in this essay that I offer it, with minor changes from the original manuscript, as a contribution to the ongoing debate concerning psychoanalytic theory and metapsychology.

2. Greenacre's concept of "collective alternates" offers a hypothesis for the explanation of such alternatives in the case of the potentially gifted infant.

3. See also Spitz's description (1964) of the early mother and infant "dialogue," which he sees as consisting entirely of nonverbal action exchanges. A disturbance of this "dialogue" is called by Spitz "derailment" and considered by him of great importance for the future development of the child.

4. Spitz refers to "stochastic progression."

5. The usefulness, perhaps necessity, of turning to mathematical models for the development of a scientific approach to the complexities of human mental life has quite recently been emphasized by E. C. Zeeman (1976) in his description of mathematical "catastrophe theory." Here he states: "The seemingly incomprehensible terms in which some (psychiatric patients) describe their illness turn out to be quite logical when viewed in the framework of the catastrophe surfaces. The advantage of a mathematical language in such applications is that it is psychologically neutral. It allows a coherent synthesis of observations that would otherwise appear to be disconnected."

Chapter 11

THE CHANGING CONCEPT
OF PSYCHOSEXUAL DEVELOPMENT

In his paper "Inhibitions, Symptoms and Anxiety: Forty Years Later," Waelder (1967) stresses the fact that there are suggestions in that essay whose relevance for psychoanalytic theory has not yet been given sufficient thought. This seems to be true with regard to most of Freud's writings. Thus, in Freud's (1905) *Three Essays on the Theory of Sexuality* we find a footnote, added in 1910, whose implications for the theory of psychosexual development deserve our attention. It reads as follows:

> The most striking distinction between the erotic life of antiquity and our own no doubt lies in the fact that the ancients laid stress upon the instinct itself, whereas we emphasize its object. The ancients glorified the instinct and were prepared on its account to honour even an inferior object; while we despise the instinctual activity in itself, and find excuse for it only in the merits of the object. [p. 149]

This footnote appears remarkable for several reasons. First, it focuses our attention on issues that are most acute in the moral and intellectual crisis through which we all are living. Secondly, Freud's juxtaposition of the glorification of the drive itself in antiquity and the idealization of the object in the Judeo-Christian civilization implies that both of these opposing attitudes toward the erotic life are fully compatible with the highest intellectual, artistic, and philosophical achievements of man. If this is so, it raises as yet unanswered questions concerning many traditionally held psychoanalytic assumptions. The very concept of genital primacy, for instance, implies the existence of a correlation between the capacity for stable object relations on the one hand, and the achievement of optimal performance in terms of the individual's potentialities for creative work. Freud's footnote in the *Three Essays* clearly states that some of the highest creative accomplishments in antiquity were not impeded by an erotic life in which "the nature and importance of the sexual object recedes into the background" (p. 149).

How can we reconcile our understanding of psychosexual development with such independence of ego function from mature object relations? In order to clarify some of the problems involved in this seeming contradiction between our psychoanalytic assumptions and the historical and, often enough, clinical facts of observation, I shall approach the problem by dealing first with the psychological function of sexual experience, secondly with the classical assumptions of psychoanalytic theory concerning psychosexual development and their transformation under the impact of ego psychology. I shall then, thirdly, sketch tentatively certain reformulations of the theory of psychosexual development which might permit a resolution of the contradictions that Freud's footnote of 1910 would seem to imply.

THE PSYCHOLOGICAL FUNCTION OF SEXUAL EXPERIENCE

In order to illuminate the difficult problem of the psychological function of the erotic experience, let me quote from the introductory passage of the first volume of the autobiography of Bertrand Russell (1967):

I have sought love, first, because it brings ecstasy—ecstasy so great that I would often have sacrificed all the rest of life for a few hours of this joy. I have sought it, next, because it relieves loneliness—that terrible loneliness in which one shivering consciousness looks over the rim of the world into the cold unfathomable lifeless abyss. I have sought it, finally, because in the union of love I have seen, in a mystic miniature, the prefiguring vision of the heaven that saints and poets have imagined. [p. 3]

Of the three aims for love that Bertrand Russell distinguishes in this passage, psychoanalysis has come close to conceptualizing the last two, the relief from loneliness and the yearning for union with the loved one. They express that kind of relation to the love object that Freud (1905) has in mind when he speaks of the "exact convergence of the affectionate current and the sensual current, both being directed towards the sexual object and sexual aim" (p. 207).

Bertrand Russell can be said to describe in powerful, poetic imagery the psychoanalytic utopia of genitality, which comprises, according to Erikson (1950), "mutuality of orgasm... with a loved partner... of the other sex... and with whom one is able and willing to regulate the cycles of work, procreation, recreation... so as to secure to the offspring, too, a satisfactory development" (pp. 230ff.). The less understood, though perhaps the most important of the aims of love is the desire for ecstasy. While it is well recognized that ecstasy is the affective experience of the orgastic climax in sexual intercourse, its psychological function has not yet found a precise definition in psychoanalytic psychology. This is true even though the function of orgasm has been investigated extensively. One just has to think of the work of W. Reich (1927), Ferenczi (1924), Balint (1938), and, more recently, Keyser (1947) in this respect. What is particularly difficult to reconcile with the classical concepts of psychosexual development from orality to full sexual maturity is the fact that the experience of ecstasy does not show an invariant correlation to the capacity for stable object relations. In fact, it often seems to contradict the concept of the utopia of genitality, in that ecstasy might be found under conditions where, to use again Freud's (1905) words, "the nature and importance of the sexual object recedes into the background" (p. 149). Under such circumstances we may even observe the glorification of the sexual drive itself in a manner similar to that which Freud found characteristic for the erotic life of antiquity.[1] The phenomenon of ecstasy without stable object relations is, of course, well known to psychoanalytic observation. It is usually conceptualized in terms of infantile fixations, regression, narcissism—in short, as a vicissitude of a deviant psychosexual development.

Freud (1916-17) attributes the hostility toward all forms of perverted sexual pleasure to "a quite special ban": "as though people felt them as seductive, and had at bottom to fight down a secret envy of those who were enjoying them.... In reality perverts are poor wretches, rather, who have to pay extremely dear for their hard-won satisfaction" (p. 321). Psychoanalytic insistence on the basic unhappiness of those who experience ecstasy in circumstances other than the conditions of the utopia of genitality seems to stem from this assertion of Freud's. I believe that such cases, where ecstatic experiences do occur without any stable or mature object relationship, are only *seemingly* contradicting psychoanalytic theory. They *appear* to be contradictory because the psychological function of the experience of ecstasy is very poorly understood, and without such understanding the relationship between ecstasy and the maintenance of a sense of self and of one's own reality as a person remains obscure. Eissler (1958) has made an important beginning toward the investigation of these problems. Discussing the treatment of perversions, he states:

> I am convinced that research in this field is hampered by our ignorance about the psychology of orgasm. The phenomenon of genitality is fairly well investigated in biological terms and man's intense longing for the orgastic experience is easily understood because of the pleasure it affords and the awareness of deprivation in its absence. But biological knowledge has little value when it is observed that the pleasure premium is unconditionally tied to a rigid individual pattern.... Despite many other available channels for gratification the physical demand remains ungratified... if reality withholds the particular conditions they require. This finding surprisingly demonstrates that orgasm (aside from the biological aspect) when viewed in its relationship to the ego must contain a meaning and function beyond the attainment of physical pleasure and the reduction of tension. [p. 236ff.]

Within the context of my own attempts (chapters 2, 8, 13) to reach a better understanding of the psychological function of sexuality, I find Eissler's formulations especially valuable. Eissler hypothesizes an "ego function" of orgasm. He arrives at this proposition by differentiating between two modes of arriving at the conviction of truth. One mode is exemplified by the truth concept of science, which is based on logical principles, best represented by mathematics. The other mode by which we arrive at a conviction of truth is called by Eissler "emotional conviction," exemplified by conviction of truth based on belief in the Bible. Eissler goes on to say: "it is obvious that the former [i.e., mathematical truth] is correlated with the secondary process and the latter [i.e., emotional conviction] with the primary" (p. 238). According to Eissler (1958):

> it becomes reasonable to assume that there are still other even more archaic forms which provide man with the conviction of truth. Descartes' famous *cogito, ergo sum* ... is after all the genetic product of a long development. The infant, if it had the power to verbalize, would never base incontrovertible truth on such flimsy evidence. Rather, it would say: "I experience pleasure, hence I exist." Since the greatest pleasure available to the human organism is orgasm, I hypothesize that one of the ego functions of orgasm is to ascertain an incontrovertible truth. [pp. 238-239]

Eissler's thesis appears to me to imply that there is a special correlation between the power of orgasm "to create or confirm conviction" and a unique function of sexuality in the establishment and reaffirmation of the "incontrovertible truth" of the reality of personal existence. I propose that sexuality is the most archaic mode, closely related to the primary process, that is capable of conveying—to use Eissler's term— the "emotional truth" of personal existence, and that only in the course of development other modes, such as expressed in the Cartesian *cogito, ergo sum* take over the function of "creating or confirming" the conviction in thought that one does, in fact, exist. From this viewpoint, psychosexual development can be understood as the genetic pattern of changing modes of establishing and supporting the conviction of one's personal existence. If the more advanced, more cognition-based modes of confirming such conviction are poorly developed or break down, the archaic forms are regressively revived, and the conviction of one's existence becomes dependent on orgastic experiences, while the significance of the object, through which this orgastic confirmation is obtained, recedes. This correlation will become clearer by a brief review of the changes that have taken place in our understanding of psychosexual development in general and the concept of genital primacy in particular under the impact of ego psychology.

In Freud's (1905, 1908, 1923b) original conceptualization of psychosexual development, the independent variable in the complex processes of human individuation was unquestionably sexuality as it unfolded through the various libidinal stages. Today sexuality or libidinal development is seen as only one among several variables. This change has come about mostly as a result of the impact of ego psychology. The fact of this change in the role of sexuality is taken for granted, but the question of its implications concerning the psychological function of sexuality in the process of individuation is far less clear, if it is asked at all. I shall very briefly sketch the changes in the understanding of the process of psychosexual development that have taken place as a result of the formulation of the structural theory and the development of ego psychology. Freud (1908) claimed that "The sexual behaviour of a human being often *lays down the pattern* for all his other modes of reacting to life" (p. 198). Peller (1965), in a recent review of Freud's changing views concerning libidinal organizations in child development, comments as follows on Freud's (1908) concept of the "exemplary function" of sexuality: "To a certain extent, ego and superego functions and the forces of the id exert a mutual influence upon one another; yet drive developments prompt and dominate the unfolding of all the other functions" (p. 746). Peller (1965) quotes in this context Anna Freud's (1949) statement that "Analytic psychology... ascribes to the innate instincts the main role in shaping the personality. It is the claim of the instinctive urges on the mind which results in the development of new functions, the so-called ego-function."

It was Hartmann (1952) who took the radical and theoretically decisive step of introducing into the developmental sequence several independent variables of a nonsexual nature:

One aspect of ego development can be described as following, in several respects, the lead of the drives. We are used to speaking of an oral and anal ego, and so on, and trace specific ego attitudes to specific libidinal characteristics of the correlated phase. This aspect shows the phases of ego development in close connection with the sequence of libidinal phases . . . . But to describe ego formation only in terms of its dependence on instinctual development is to give only part of the picture. . . . While describing the development of the child in terms of libidinal phases, we are today very much aware of the fact that cross sections of development cannot be completely described in referring only to libidinal aims—not even if we include the corresponding object relationships in our description. We have to describe them also with respect to . . . two other series of factors: the vicissitudes of aggressive drives and the partly independent elements in the ego. It might well be that even the timing and the individual formation of the typical phases could, to some extent, be traced to individual variations of ego development, e.g., to the precocity of certain of its functions. [p. 12ff.]

In Hartmann's approach to psychosexual development, sexuality is clearly no longer the independent variable. It is one among three or perhaps five variables. Hartmann's introduction of these variables does more justice to the intricacies and complexities of the processes of human development. But it is also clear that the cause-and-effect relationship between the sexual phases and the shaping of the personality has become quite blurred with the introduction of these new variables. It appears questionable whether the Freudian notion of the "exemplary function" of sexuality can be applied to the pattern of psychosexual development as outlined by Hartmann. But if it *cannot* be applied, what psychological function should we ascribe to sexuality in man? If we stress too exclusively the development of object relations as the prerequisite for complete sexual gratification, we have avoided the issue that sexuality, as the longing for ecstasy, can exert a unique power over the human personality, in spite of a high degree of independence from genuine object relations. This is the issue raised by Freud when he contrasted the erotic life of anitquity with that of Judeo-Christian man, though he did not pursue its implications for the theory of sexuality.

The extent of the changes in classical psychoanalytic assumptions about the role of sexuality in psychosexual development becomes especially clear when we examine the consistent application of ego-psychological principles by Jacobson (1964) in her presentation of psychosexual development. To begin with a seemingly formal difference between Jacobson's work and earlier treatments of psychosexual development, it seems to me significant that Jacobson's book does not contain any of the traditional ontogenetic diagrams or charts. Fenichel (1945) could still reprint, with slight modifications, Abraham's original diagram, which related stages of libidinal development to stages in the development of object love, and both of these were correlated to the pathology anticipated in case of libidinal fixation at specific phases of sexual development. Fliess's Ontogenetic Table of 1948 is already vastly more complex, having, among other refinements, added stages of ego development and their relationship to pathology. More recently, Erikson (1950a, 1959) in spite of his many reservations concerning overemphasis on the biological factors in the process of human development on the part of psychoanalytic theorists, nevertheless made use of modified charts of psychosexual developments by introducing the concept of stages of identity formation. Jacobson completely dispenses with any attempt of any graphic representation of psychosexual development. I believe that the reason for this omission is by no means arbitrary. It seems highly doubtful whether any two-dimensional diagram of Jacobson's developmental model could be designed with even approximate accuracy, for Jacobson pays close attention not only to partly independent ego elements as independent variables, but to the superego stages as well. Furthermore, she traces the vicissitudes of aggressive drives with equal emphasis as the phases of libidinal development. Following the suggestion of Hartmann, she treats not only the stages of object representations, but also the representations of the self, and their interaction with all the other variables. And last, but not least, Jacobson does not stop the description of the developmental processes after reaching a hypothetical final stage of genital maturity, but follows the complexities of interacting variables into adulthood, including the process of aging. There is, then, no place in her model for a final genital stage that would be correlated, as in the older ontogenetic tables, to postambivalent love and to an ideal mental balance, assuring a state of mental health. As a matter of fact, it is significant that Jacobson, while referring extensively to the oral, anal, phallic, and genital stages, never uses the term "genital primacy." This can only imply that the balance between the various independent variables shaping the human personality remains throughout life unstable, depending on the vicissitudes not only of the intrapsychic forces, but also on the interaction of these forces with the fateful determinants of the individual's life situation. The concept of "genital primacy," implying a guarantee of mental health once it has been successfully reached, has indeed no place in this ego-psychological view of human mental development. Thus, identity problems, so frequently encountered in adolescence, may reappear, according to Jacobson, in the adult "under the onslaught of . . . narcissistic assaults" (p. 199).

Compared to the classical description of psychosexual development, attributing to the vicissitudes of sexuality an "exemplary function" in shaping the human personality, we are now offered a picture of numerous independent variables that may, under favorable circumstances, reach, but only temporarily, a stable equilibrium. While this new model has the merit of doing more justice to the facts of observation as they are now available to us, we must also face the fact that the very multitude of independent variables makes it nearly impossible to establish any regular correlation between certain regressive fixations of libidinal development and a particular pathology. It is striking, indeed, how similar Jacobson's descriptions of certain types "of fluid interplay between primary- and secondary-process functioning" (p. 185) in creative individuals, are to the dynamics of those who will develop a psychosis. The main value of the classical model of psychosexual development seemed to lie in its establishment of definite correlations between certain vicissitudes of development and pathology, serving thus not only as a means of prognosticating the likely course of events, but also as a model of preventive psychiatry. It also gave us a guide for our therapeutic intervention in that the study of the fate of the libido, which is relatively accessible to clinical observation, seemed to alert us to specific dangers as well as reassure us about likely areas of ego strength. The very refinement of the new model of psychosexual development, as demonstrated so convincingly by Jacobson, makes us aware of so many intangibles—all independent variables—that both the theoretical and practical value of the classical assumptions concerning psychosexual development, especially the thesis of the "exemplary function" of the vicissitudes of sexuality, appears questionable. If the development of sexuality is just one among numerous other independent variables, should we not admit that classical psychoanalytic theories have vastly overestimated its role for both normal and pathological development? I do believe that the development of ego psychology compels us to raise these questions. Such questioning leads me to conclude that the emphasis placed by ego psychology on the multiplicity of variables understates the unique psychological function of sexuality among the other variables. This seems to be particularly true with regard to the psychological function of orgasm, i.e., the experience of ecstasy, which has not received the attention it deserves as a developmental factor.

THE NEED FOR AFFIRMATION OF THE REALITY OF ONE'S EXISTENCE AS A UNIQUELY HUMAN PROBLEM

Jacobson (1964) states the problem most poignantly when she asks:

Why do we find embedded in the adolescent's conspicuous and unique emotional manifestations such characteristic, disturbing fluctuations in his feelings for others and in his self feelings, his feelings of identity? Why does he at one time show a close relatedness to the world, to people, to nature or art or God, in conjunction with rich experiences of "I am I, I live, and the world is mine and will be mine," while at other times he has painful doubts about the meaning of life and the world . . . and is convinced of the nothingness of his existence, of life, of his own life and future? [p. 160]

Jacobson furthermore points out that adults too, under the impact of particular life situations, may despair of the meaning of life and become convinced of the nothingness of their existence. Such observations can only lead to the conclusion that the experience of the "I am," the conviction of the reality of one's existence as a person, is *not* a simple given of psychological life, but is itself the product of complex developmental processes. Even at best, the experience of the "I am" remains forever precarious, because clinical observation shows that, under the impact of regressive developments, the conviction of the reality of one's existence may cease to be felt as an "incontrovertible truth" in the sense of Eissler's description. This condition of man's basic and irremediable uncertaintly concerning the conviction of his existence was poignantly stated by Ortega y Gasset (1939) when he spoke of "the tremendous fact that, unlike all other beings in the universe, man can never be sure that he is, in fact, a man, as the tiger is sure of being a tiger and the fish of being a fish. . . . Being man signifies precisely always being on the point of not being man, being a living problem, an absolute and hazardous adventure" (p. 174).

But it has been Freud who has given us the conceptual tools to study the emergence of man from a state of not-being-man, and it is through Freud's developmental approach to psychology that the hazardousness of being man can be subjected to investigations and the specificity of each individual's way of being a living problem be brought closer to our understanding. Freud, in his theory of psychosexual development, applied the phylogenetic and ontogenetic viewpoint to the process of human individuation. He stressed that sexuality in man can only be understood in developmental terms, the general pattern of which permits us to speak of typical sequences, though details differ in each individual. He applied the same developmental principles to the development of the ego and the superego. Even though we have come to take Freud's developmental approach to human individuation for granted, we have perhaps been inclined to take the experience of the "I am" as *implied* in the very concept of the ego. We now discover that a functioning ego is in no way a guaranty for the conviction of the "I am" as an incontrovertible truth. The ego functions of the adolescent, which Jacobson describes so impressively, may not show any signs of developmental pathology, and yet he may be convinced of the nothingness of his existence and betray gross fluctuations in his self feelings. The psychological difficulties of modern "alientated" youth can hardly be attributed to disturbances of ego and superego development alone. Their outstanding symptom is a precariousness of the conviction of the reality of their existence. It does, however, appear as if a feeling of "I am I, I live and the world is mine and will be mine"—to quote Jacobson (1964) again—is a prerequisite for a full integration of ego functions, superego functions, as well as of a capacity for object relations. Only man, in contrast to all other living beings, seems to depend for the conviction of the reality of his existence on specific experiences of affirmation, experiences the nature of which is as yet poorly understood. I believe that there is a basic correlation between the psychological functions of sexuality, and, under certain circumstances, of aggression, and the experiences of feeling affirmed in one's existence.

We can now return to Eissler's (1958) thesis that "orgasm is the strongest affirmation possible to man . . . . The truth that is affirmed by orgasm is not represented by words and not necessarily by explicit fantasies . . . orgasm is endowed with the power to confirm, create, and affirm conviction" (p. 242). This permits us to draw some conclusions which are pertinent to our present-day understanding of the role of sexuality in psychosexual development and the meaning of the concept of genital primacy. Since the capacity to experience orgasm is reached relatively late in an individual's development, one must assume that there are functional precursors of the orgastic experience that create and affirm the conviction of one's existence. It seems to me a logical extension of Eissler's thesis that the experiences of libidinal gratification during the stages of psychosexual development (i.e., the oral, the anal, the phallic phases) constitute preorgastic methods of creating and affirm the emotional conviction of the individual's existence. This is not meant to diminish the significance of the various known developmental steps that have been shown to be specific for each of the stages of psychosexual development. It rather is meant as an attempt to reconcile Freud's (1908) insistence on the "exemplary function" of sexuality in human development with the equally insistent claim of modern ego psychology that sexuality is only one among numerous independent variables in the process of individuation.

Such an attempt requires a certain measure of revision of our traditional views. I propose that Freud's concept of the "exemplary function" of sexuality, defined as the principle that sexuality lays down the pattern of behavior, should be revised, because it does not conform to the findings of ego psychology as demonstrated by the work of Hartmann, Jacobson, and many others. I do not conclude from this, however, that Freud's original concept of a *unique* role of sexuality, i.e, of the libidinal drives, in human development should be replaced in favor of a view that considers sexuality as just one variable among a number of equally important ones. I believe that Eissler's thesis of orgasm as being able to "confirm, create, and affirm conviction" points the way in which Freud's concept of the "exemplary function" of sexuality should be revised. I suggest that we attribute to sexuality an "affirmative function" and that we define this term as the principle that sexuality contitutes the primary, most archaic, and nonverbal mode through which the conviction of one's existence is affirmed as an incontrovertible truth. I would like to emphasize the terms "primary and most archaic," because it is obvious that in the course of development other modes become available, exemplified by Eissler's concept of the truth capable of securing logical, rather than emotional, conviction.

This proposition would imply that sexuality has a *special position* among the other variables of development, because the very core of a person's being fully himself profoundly depends on the affirmation of the conviction of his existence as an incontrovertible truth. In chapter 13 I have undertaken to demonstrate that failure of this affirmative experience regarding one's existence during the early stages of development has important consequences with regard to the later emerging pattern of adult sexuality. It appears that under such circumstances adult sexuality is placed in the service of the need for affirmation of the reality of one's existence. The object becomes the means by which the individual compulsively and often coercively attempts to be affirmed in his existence through orgastic experience. This pattern interferes with the development of a relationship of mutuality between the individual and the object, insofar as the object is valued only to the extent to which it serves the orgastic and ecstatic needs of the individual. In the most extreme types of this kind, sexuality takes on a sadistic character in that the suffering, the anguish, of the object becomes the only way to feel affirmed in one's existence. These observations would indicate that aggression is *not* an independent variable, as the assumption of two basic drives, libido and aggression, implies. It rather would appear that the manifestations of aggression are dependent on the affirmative function of the libidinal drives in such a way that only if the affirmative function of pregenital and genital libidinal satisfaction fails, is aggression of various intensity used to coerce the subject to serve as a means for the experience of being affirmed.

This proposition seems to me compatible with Freud's (1905) assumption that the erotic life of antiquity glorified the sexual drive as such, while "the nature and importance of the sexual object receded into the background." This seems to be confirmed by Hanns Sachs's (1933) scholarly essay on the sexuality of antiquity in his comments on "The Delay of the Machine Age." This form of sexuality did not interfere with the achievement of the highest forms of intellectual and artistic life, but it created a civilization, as Sachs documents in his essay, compatible with the total use and abuse of human beings as a means to serve the needs of the few. Slavery was the very basis of both Greek and Roman civilizations. Thus, Freud's footnote of 1910 implies that our view of psychosexual development as culminating in mature object relations as a prerequisite for complete orgastic experiences on the one hand, and as the precondition for the full utilization of an individual's creative potential on the other is open to serious questioning. It is particularly dubious when it holds out a kind of promise for the security of a stage of postambivalent object relations that guarantees not only full orgastic fulfillment but the secure possession of mental health ever after as well.

What is at issue is our understanding of the dynamics and the metapsychology of the state of maturity. The concept of maturity is equated in psychoanalytic theory with that of the genital character. With the achievement of genital primacy an ideal state of balance between man's instinctual drives, the adaptive pressures of the ego, and the demands of the superego is postulated by psychoanalytic theory.[2] The attainment of this balance is considered to be a prerequisite for the development of stable object relations and the capacity for "full satisfaction through genital orgasm" (Fenichel 1945). That maturity in this sense may be a relative balance, weighted heavily in favor of ego and superego demands, implying an unavoidable imbalance in other respects, has been stressed by Novey (1955). Novey states that while the "mature individual gains in integrative capacity [he] suffers another kind of loss." This loss, according to Novey (1955), "has to do with a decrease in sensitivity, at an unconscious level, to unconscious motivations within himself [the mature individual] and as he may experience them from others" (p. 90). In contrast, Novey points out, impairment of the integrative functions of the mature level can manifest itself in "periodic exceptional insights," such as occur in both the child and the psychotic. "In the mature adult there would seem to be a decreased capacity to communicate with one's own unconscious process or with the unconscious process of another, as compared to ... less integrated groups, but an increased capacity for organized conduct performances" (p. 90).

Novey's relativistic concept of maturity, as compared to the traditional, absolute one, is supported by the findings of the "relative balance" that appears to be characteristic for creative individuals. According to studies by Kris (1952), Greenacre (1957, 1958b, d), and Eissler (1967), for instance, there seems to exist in such personalities a high degree of correlation between lack of stable object relations, "immature," i.e., deviant, sexual patterns, regressive tendencies on the one hand, and high artistic achievement on the other hand. Novey's view may also account for the often observed clinical fact that there is no invariant correlation between "maturity," enabling the individual to establish stable object relations, and capacity for "full satisfaction through genital orgasm" in the sense of genital primacy as defined by Fenichel (1945). If indeed, as Novey claims, the mature individual suffers from a decrease in sensitivity to unconscious motivations in himself and in others, this may very well impair the capacities essential for orgastic fulfillment. Under these circumstances, it seems simplistic to postulate a "stage" of genital maturity. This does not exclude the occurrence of moments or phases in a person's life where, without sacrificing the capacity for integration which characterizes maturity, he may also be "in communication" with his own as well as with the love object's unconscious life, and thus reach an ideal balance enabling him to achieve the union between stable object relations and full orgastic fulfillment. We might refer to such experiences as the climax of maturity, without postulating that its occurrence establishes a permanent stage that will safeguard the individual against the dangers inherent in being, in Ortega y Gasset's (1939) words, "a living problem, an absolute and hazardous adventure." The reason for this "permanent lability" is man's unique need for being affirmed in the conviction of his existence, and that this need, if it becomes overpowering, can at any time make him possessed by sexual and aggressive drives aiming at this affirmation of his existence at all costs, even that of the destruction of the love object.

The recognition that sexuality and aggression may serve man's urgent need to be affirmed in his existence would reconcile Freud's insistence on a unique function of sexuality in human development with the insights of ego psychology that stress the multidetermined influences on this development. What we know least about seems to refer to the total range of experiences affirmative of the conviction of existence beyond the archaic forms of sexuality and aggression. Eissler speaks of the logical conviction of truth, but the logical conviction that affirms the uncontrovertible truth of one's existence must simultaneously have the character of an emotional conviction in Eissler's sense. Perhaps phenomena similar to what Greenacre (1957, 1958b, d) describes as the development of "collective alternates," a term used to describe the "range of extended experience which may surround or become attached to the main focus of object relationships" (1957, p. 57), exist in some form in the normal process of individuation as well and not only in the artistic personality. When Greenacre speaks of the artist's "love affair with the world," or of "cosmic emotional conceptions" (1958b, p. 11), she might in fact describe experiences affirmative of the conviction of existence which transform the experience of emotional conviction by freeing it from its captivity within the subjectivity of one's "personal truth." In some such way the individual's conviction of his existence might be affirmed through "the development of a creative relation to the world" (Milner 1952, p. 194), which, because it can be shared with others by means of language and thought, enables him to perceive the reality of his personal existence *(esse)* as convincingly reflected in the mirror of communicable thought *(cogitare)*.

I believe that only if we learn more about these less primitive modes of experiencing affirmation and their genetic vicissitudes will our knowledge of psychosexual development reach the point where it will help us to find access to the most burning psychological issues of today: the alienation of our youth, the despair of the black minority, the threat of violence that hangs over our world today. It is my belief that what all these issues have in common is the problem of how to affirm human beings in the emotional conviction of their existence.

NOTES

1. Russell confirms this experience in a poem placed at the opening page of his autobiography, which reads:

I found ecstasy, I found anguish,
I found madness,
I found loneliness.

The poem goes on to tell us that only late in his long life has he, at last, found both ecstasy and peace.

2. See for a definition of the genital character, Fenichel (1945, p. 496), especially the passage quoted in Novey's (1955) paper.

Chapter 12

POSTSCRIPT: SUPEREGO FUNCTION
AND IDENTITY MAINTENANCE

The notes presented here express my theoretical reservations about
many aspects of the present approach to superego development and
superego functions. I am inclined to agree with Ricoeur's (1970)
comment: "Is not the transition from infancy to adult life sufficiently
accounted for by a psychology of personality, or by what the various
neo-Freudian schools have called ego-analysis? I make no secret of my
distrust of these corrections that transform psychoanalysis into an
eclectic system. . . . They certainly mask theoretical problems that
Freud himself was clearly aware of" (p. 462). Ricoeur specifically refers
to "the concept of identification . . . that remains unharmonized with
the metapsychology" (p. 478). He furthermore claims that Freud was
"puzzled" by this concept, which Ricoeur considers "more of a
problem than a solution" (p. 479). He quotes, to support this view,
Freud's statement "I myself am far from satisfied with these remarks
on identification: but it will be enough if you can grant me that the
installation of the superego can be described as a successful instance of
identification with the parental agency" (Freud 1932). The derivation
of the superego, or, to be more exact, of a sense of morality, from
identification with the parents or other adults is being taken almost as
an established fact in the structural theory of psychoanalysis, a
position about which I have considerable theoretical misgivings. In the
following remarks I am presenting the traditional view, represented by
a quotation form Hartmann (1960) followed by quotations from an

almost neglected thesis by Jones (1947). These quotations form the basis of a discussion of the various reasons that have made me view the derivation of the origin of a sense of morality from identification with parental authorities as highly problematic. In part IV of this outline I propose an alternate approach to the problem of the development of a sense of morality and, finally, in a last part I offer suggestions for additions to a theory of superego function.

I. From H. Hartmann (1960)

In the development of the superego, demands from the outside are transmuted into inner imperatives—the character of a command is preserved, and the tension between demand and fulfillment. Not only the prohibitions of the parents, but also their love survives in the relation of the superego to the ego. In the course of the same development the experience arises of being responsible to oneself (p. 27). . . . What we have actually to deal with in judging the moral stability of a person clinically, as well as more generally, is certainly not only the genetic question. . . . Practically and theoretically, the most relevant aspect is the constancy or dependability of morality vis-à-vis reality, mostly social reality, and vis-à-vis opposing pressures from within. That is its "autonomy," which is in some ways comparable in its definition to the secondary autonomy of the ego. A transvaluation of moral values takes place in the development of every individual. On the long way form interiorization of parental demands after the oedipal conflicts to the more elaborate codes of the adult, another factor becomes decisive. That is a process of generalization, of formalization, and of integration of moral values. It would be difficult to attribute what I have in mind here to the superego itself. It rather corresponds to what we know of the functions of the ego. One can say, I think, that in what one may call the moral "codes" the influence both of the superego and of the ego, particularly of the integrating and differentiating functions of the ego, are traceable. [pp. 29, 30, 31]

II. From E. Jones (1947)

In Hartmann's view the adult superego represents the precipitate of outside demands which have become transvalued by a series of complex inner processes. Hartmann's is essentially a more elaborate restatement of Freud's (1923) definition of the superego as the heir of the Oedipus complex, seen in the light of modern ego psychology. In contrast, there exists in psychoanalytic literature an approach to the problem of superego genesis and function that emphasizes the decisive role of an inner factor, not derivable from transvalued outside demands. The following quotation from Ernest Jones (1947) seems a particularly lucid and articulate statement of this position:

> The conscience is plainly the guardian of morality in the fully developed sense of that term. . . . Now the superego is certainly not moral in that sense. . . . and yet it possesses an important attribute that closely mimics it. That is the sense of urgent "oughtness," a categorical imperative. Actually, this "oughtness" in the superego may yet get attached to attitudes that are either moral or immoral as judged by our reason and conscience, although in both cases it is at least as strong and compelling as any corresponding dictate of the conscience. . . . When . . . Freud says that the superego gains its power of affecting the ego from its representing reality demands, one certainly has to add "and unreality demands as well": more accurately, the demands of psychical reality as well as those of physical reality."

I wish to limit my considerations to the following question: If it could be shown that the experience of "oughtness" cannot in its entirety be derived from outside demands, is there any intrapsychic source that could account for it?

III. Three Unresolved Problems Concerning Identification

1. I see three reasons that make it difficult to trace the sense of urgent "oughtness" to outside demands, emanating essentially from parental demands. First, I see a logical and psychological non sequitur in the postulate that identification with parental demands must lead to the development of self-imposed, basically autonomous moral rules. For this sequence to occur, one would have to demonstrate the possibility of drawing compelling inferences from specific demands made by the parents in a concrete situation that would be leading to general principles of human conduct applicable to infinitely varying situations that are unpredictable in their implications. I do not see how

it follows from the demand "Eat slowly and chew your food well" that it is morally wrong to waste food. Rather it seems more likely to deduce from the principle that wastefulness of food is wrong, that one should make the most of the food that one eats, by eating slowly, etc. The derivation of urgent "oughtness" from outside demands does, in other words, fail to make understandable how the human mind is capable of conceiving of general principles of conduct applicable to unforeseen, concrete situations, not by relying on precedent, but by respecting the quasi-logical principle of moral consistency. It is pertinent in this context to quote Piaget's (1932) definition that "Logic is the morality of thought just as morality is the logic of action."

2. I see a second difficulty concerning the derivation of moral conduct from internalized outside demands in the fact that, typically, great moral decisions involve a conscious suspension of values based on outside demands, internalized by upbringing and tradition. The founding fathers of the American republic, by signing the Declaration of Independence, consciously set aside the demand of obedience to the king of England, in order to honor a moral principle applying to mankind itself, even though they risked their lives in the very act of giving precedence to the urgent "oughtness" of their consciences. These historical acts—many examples could be cited—do not seem to make sense in terms of the understanding of morality as internalized outside demands. This interpretation of morality can only apply to young children, to whom Piaget (1932) attributes a primitive sense of what he calls "the morality of constraint": "The child accepts from the adult a certain number of commands to which it must submit whatever the circumstances may be. Right is what conforms to these demands; wrong is what fails to do so." (p. 335) A theory of the development of a moral code based on the transmutation of outside demands may account for the "morality of constrainst" in the sense of Piaget. It fails to make understandable the development of the sense of morality of the adult.

3. There is a third difficulty in tracing the development of the "oughtness" that characterizes the adult morality from identification and internalization of outside demands. This is the problem of the individual selectivity of identifications. When we speak of the child identifying with the parents and their values, and later on accepting cultural values presented by important figures in its life, we must

account for the principle of selectivity, which makes one child identify with a great sports figure, another with an explorer, and a third one with the hero of a story. Erikson (1947, 1950) touches upon this fact of selectivity and its inherent complexity when he points out that "the historical era in which (an individual) lives offers only a limited number of socially meaningful models for workable combinations of identification fragments. Their usefulness depends on the way in which they, simultaneously, meet the requirements of the organism's maturational stage and the ego's habit of synthesis." Such factors are clearly indicating inner principles of selective identification not explainable by the direct impact of outside demands.

IV. The Relationship of the
Superego to Identity Maintenance

1. I shall now attempt to formulate what I consider the basic theoretical problems posed by the concept of the superego. I shall define the problem by borrowing from mathematics (Keyser 1922) the concepts of the invariant and its transformations. We can then say that a human individual implies the coming into being of an invariant, the growth and development of which can be understood as its transformations. Since I define personal identity as the maintenance of invariance in the midst of constant change, the superego could then be defined as the principle of identity maintenance becoming increasingly important during the oedipal and postoedipal stages of development. These developments include what we may call—paraphrasing Freud— the vicissitudes of the ego. In their totality, these transformations form the content of a person's autobiography, encompassing everything from the beginning of our lives, through the phases of the child that we became, the stage of separating from our identity as a child (i.e., the phase of adolescence) leading to the numerous and often dramatic changes of our adult lives. Even though they make us aware of the various roles that we have lived, of changes of aims, goals and values, there is—with certain exceptions—never a doubt for the majority of individuals that all these transformations are an unfolding of an invariant. It is this that gives us the sense of being always the same person. In the words of Strauss (1959) "Each person's account of his life, as he writes or thinks about it, is a symbolic ordering of events. The sense that you make of your own life rests upon what concepts, what

interpretations, you bring to bear upon the multitudinous and disorderly crowds of past acts. If your interpretations are convincing to yourself, if you trust your terminology, then there is some kind of continuous meaning assigned to your life as-a-whole. Different motives may be seen to have driven you at different periods, but the overriding purpose of your life may yet seem to retain a certain unity and coherence."[2]

2. The changes of the personality throughout life may involve more or less radical revisions of moral codes and convictions. It is noteworthy that it is taken for granted that several moral codes can coexist side by side in the same person throughout life. The individual will act on the basis of one code or another code according to his social role. He is expected to be able to slip from one moral code to another, seemingly incompatible one, without any sense of disruption of his sense of inner unity as a person. A young person, for example, is expected to adhere to a peacetime code of conduct as a college student. If he is drafted into the armed forces, and sent to the front, he is assumed to be able to abandon his peacetime code of morality for a wartime code. After the war, his return to the peacetime code is by and large taken for granted. Should he continue to behave according to the wartime code, this is considered a symptom of serious personality disturbance, and judged to be an exceptional phenomenon. We might say that in such situations the superego has failed to maintain the sense of continuity in the midst of change. It might seem as if the person has lost an autonomous superego and regressed to the pattern of Piaget's (1931) "morality of constraint."

3. I believe that Freud (1923) was aware of the relationship between the function of the Superego and the maintenance of inner coherence and continuity of the person. Discussing the superego in *The Ego and the Id*, he digresses in order to direct our attention to the problem of the so-called "multiple personalities." After referring to what appears in such cases as a severe disruption of the sense of inner continuity, he remarks: "Even if things do not go so far as this, there remains the question of conflicts between various identifications into which the ego comes apart, conflicts which cannot after all be described as entirely pathological." I understand this to mean that the unity and cohesion of the person was not taken for granted by Freud: without a unifying

principle, the person is in constant danger of coming apart into a multiplicity of identities—"identifications" in Freud's terminology.

4. Both the capacity of the normal personality to maintain its inner continuity, as well as the not infrequent failure of this capacity, deserves our clinical as well as theoretical attention. I believe that only with the help of the notion of an invariant as an inherent aspect of the human personality does it become possible to account both for the inner changeability of them (the person as a civilian and the person as a soldier), and, finally, the possibility of failure of "identity maintenance." Since the very coherence of the ego seems to depend on the function of "identity maintenance," the latter cannot itself be another ego function, such as the synthetic function.

5. In an effort to account for the function of "identity maintenance," I have attempted to establish where, in postnatal existence, there may come into being an invariant, the transformations of which we can trace as the individual development of a person throughout a lifetime. In chapter 8, I postulated that with "the first archaic mirroring experience of the child (mediated by its awareness of the mother's response to its being) a primary identity emerges. ... This primary identity is not yet a sense of identity, for that presupposes consciousness. It is thought of rather as a primary organizational principle without which the process of developmental differentiation could not begin." I defined "primary identity" as the actualization in the infant of one particular potentiality of being, namely the child for this particular mother, attuned to her unique and individual unconscious expectations with regard to the child. "Primary identity" can be seen as akin to Spitz's (1959) concept of "organizers in the psyche." It also can be considered as related to Spiegel's (1959) idea of a "frame of reference" or "zero point," implying an invariant to which all later developments must stand in the relationship of transformations.[3] It is this invariant that enables the individual to maintain identity and continuity in change. This description does not imply a specific content, but a form, permitting infinite variations, just as the geometrical form of the triangle does not have just one, but infinite, equally valid configurations. I believe that this abstract definition of an invariant as an organizing principle of developmental transformations can be helpful in our understanding of the function of the superego for identity maintenance and preservation of inner continuity of the person.[4]

V. Suggestions for an
   Alternate Theory of Superego Function

1. The propositions presented here seem to me to permit an understanding of the central phenomenon of the superego, namely the "urgent oughtness" which Jones (1947) considers the quality characterizing the superego. The assumption of a primary identity, constituting an invariant, introduces an organizing principle into the process of development. It could be compared to a gravitational field which defines the range within which the complex maturational and developmental processes unfold. The phenomenon of "urgent oughtness" may well indicate the subjective consciousness of the directing power of such an organizing principle, a kind of inner command, distinctly differentiated from the experience of outside demands and prohibitions. The inner contradictions that are encountered if the experience of "oughtness" is derived from internalized outside demands are thus resolved. The far-reaching independence of adult morality from parental moral values becomes understandable, and the selectivity of identification, which appeared difficult to explain, may be shown to be based on a principle derived from the overriding importance of "identity maintenance": the choice of persons with whom an individual may or may not identity could depend on the question whether a particular identification is or is not compatible with its perception as a valid transformation of its primary identity.

2. I have previously emphasized the formal, nonspecific character of the concept of primary identity as an invariant undergoing many possible kinds of transformations. The primary identity is not in itself a guide to meaningful human action, be it with regard to relations with other people, nor within the experience of a shared world. The parents, however, are encountered as real people who act in a specific way, doing certain things, while abstaining from others. The child is thus provided by the parents with a working model of action. Thus, what the child may predominantly identify with in the parents is their capacity of translating a formal identity theme into a concrete action-model within a real world. This will help the child to translate his own identity theme into a way of being a person, living within a world shared with others. He may turn into a different kind of person from his parents, but without their example the child might never discover

any form of a livable identity in a real world. The parents' actions will also convey to the child that they maintain their own continuity as persons in the midst of change. Identity and a sense of inner continuity would be gravely endangered in a setting of random activity in which every kind of action is equally possible. Identity maintenance implies a choice between actions that do and those that don't feel compatible with a person's sense of inner continuity. Moral codes are socially fostered systems supporting certain types of workable identities for certain types of individuals and groups. To this they both owe their power and their perishable quality. If they fail to fulfill their function as support systems of identity maintenance for a plurality of persons, they are likely to be replaced by other socially supported systems.

3. Summarizing, the superego seems to combine a very early and some rather late developmental acquisitions. Freud (1914) believed that the early narcissistic ego ideal was a forerunner of what later developed into the complex structure he called superego, a point stressed in Strachey's (1957) introduction to the "Narcissism" paper. I see this earliest, narcissistic layer in terms of a primary identity acting as an organizing principle and constituting an invariant making the inner continuity of the person possible. It is the source of the experience of "urgent oughtness." What the superego tests is the compability of the individual's potentially infinite ways of being a person with regard to their validity as transformations of the person's unique "identity theme." In this way, it is the guardian of the individual's sense of inner continuity of himself as a person.

NOTES

1. The notes presented here are a restatement of a contribution to the Panel "Current Status of the Theory of the Superego," which took place at the Annual Meeting of the American Psychoanalytic Association, Los Angeles, May 1964, under the chairmanship of Martin H. Stein, M.D. The Panel Discussion has been reported by Dr. Stanley Goodman, M.D., in the *Journal of American Psychoanalytic Association* 13:172-180.

2. Riezler (1950), whom Strauss (p. 33) quotes, states: "The Me can mean many things: The Me of yesterday, today, or tomorrow, or the Me of everyday, the Me in this particular action or situation, or the Me in all actions or situations."

3. Spiegel attributes to the concept of self a biological function similar to that of the frame of reference for visual perception: "I would extend this concept of the frame of reference ... to what Freud calls 'innere Wahrnehmung' (internal perception). The orderly perception of these internal states requires a frame of reference that possesses a continuity in time. I believe it may prove profitable to consider the self ... as a frame of reference or zero point to which representation of specific mental and physical states are referred, against which they are perceived and judged." Since I see the concept of self as a developmentally later acquisition, I would prefer to consider the very earliest organizing function—primary identity—as the framework or zero point in the sense of Spiegel. See also chapter 9.

4. See also Piaget's (1931) use of the concept of a "developmental a priori": "One may say ... that in a certain sense neither logical nor moral norms are innate in the individual mind.... This does not mean that everything in the a priori view is to be rejected. Of course, the a priori never manifests itself in the form of ready-made innate mechanisms.... Yet to speak of directed evolution and asymptotic advance toward a necessary ideal is to recognize the existence of something which acts from the first in the direction of this evolution.... Such is the a priori: it is neither a principle from which concrete action can be deduced, nor a structure of which the mind can become conscious as such, but it is the sum-total of functional relations implying the distinction between existing states of disequilibrium and ideal equilibrium yet to be realized."

Part IV

Human Identity
and Cultural Change

Chapter 13

THE MALIGNANT NO: INSTINCTUAL DRIVES AND THE SENSE OF SELF

PROLOGUE

The reader should note that this chapter was written at a moment of contemporary history very different from that of the present. While the late months of 1966 belong to a relatively recent past, the "revolution" had yet to occur. Neither the student uprising in Paris, nor those at Columbia, Harvard, and elsewhere had taken place. The flood of publications on the Counterculture, the New Morality, and the like, which constitutes a library in itself, was just beginning to emerge. The various commissions on violence were still in the process of gathering material which has since been published in a variety of reports. The author is fully aware of the fact that since the formulation of this paper both events and their sociological and psychological interpretation have gone rapidly beyond its original frame of reference. The writer has nevertheless decided to let the text stand. Any attempt, he feels, to bring it up to date would shift the emphasis from the basic psychoanalytic propositions which form its nucleus to a psychoanalytic study centering on the psychohistorical dimension for which the time, in the writer's opinion, has not yet come.

In the foreword to Max Schur's (1966) monograph, *The Id and the Regulatory Principles of Mental Functioning*, the editors credit Schur's work with "reflecting the *Zeitgeist*," insofar as it constitutes a "reappraisal of basic psychoanalytic concepts in the light of recent advances in our discipline" (p. 7). Characteristic for this reappraisal is Schur's emphasis on the "concept of a continuum ... between the structures 'ego' and 'id' " which, as he goes on to say, "is part of the problem of the *mutual* influences in the development of ego and id" (p. 48). The acute awareness of the importance of the continuum between ego and id, together with his stress on Freud's concept of the complementary series, does reflect indeed the Zeitgeist in psychoanalytic thinking in the last decades, representing a dialectical understanding of the interdependence of "the differentiation of psychic structure and relation of the self to external objects" (Hartmann, Kris, and Loewenstein 1949, p. 27). Here I attempt to study the dialectic relationship between the ego function of negation and the sense of self and their mutual influence on the manifestations of the instinctual drives. I introduce an hypothesis correlating a specific deviation of the ego function of negation and the predominance of aggressive patterns of object relations. This deviation of the function of negation is referred to as the "malignant No." It is defined as the experience of feeling negated in one's existence as an individual. "The malignant No" not only affects the individual's object relations, but also influences his perception of reality. Some contemporary social phenomena which might be understood as reflecting this dialectic interaction will be discussed briefly.

THE DEVELOPMENT OF THE NO-CONCEPT

The development of the no-concept, of negation, constitutes an important aspect of psychoanalytic ego psychology. In discussing the special characteristics of the system Ucs., Freud (1915b), states: "There are in this system no negation, no doubt, no degrees of certainty: all this is only introduced by the work of the censorship between the Ucs. and the Pcs. Negation is a substitute, at a higher level, for repression. In the Ucs. there are only contents, cathected with greater or lesser strength." This proposition is several years later taken up and elaborated by Freud (1925b) in a paper exclusively devoted to the concept of negation. Freud declares: "With the help of the symbol of negation, thinking frees itself from the restriction of repression and enriches itself with material that is indispensable for its proper functioning" (p. 236). Instead of repression, according to Freud, the individual has now acquired the intellectual function of judgment, by means of which we are able "to affirm or deny the subject matter of thoughts" (p. 236). He sees the intellectual function of judgment as depending genetically on the acquisition of the no-concept: "The performance of the function of negation has endowed thinking with a first measure of freedom from the consequences of repression and with it from the compulsion of the pleasure-principle" (p. 239). Insofar as freedom from the compulsion of the pleasure-principle would appear a prerequisite for nonambivalent interactions between individuals, it comes as a surprise to read that Freud correlates the function of negation to the destructive instinct: "The polarity of judgment appears to correspond to the opposition of the two groups of instincts which we have supposed to exist. Affirmation—as a substitute for uniting—belongs to the Eros; negation—the successor to expulsion—belongs to the instinct of destruction" (p. 239). If the incapacity to negate characterizes the primary process, indicating the domination of thought processes by the id, is then unlimited affirmation not a sign of ego defect? And if negation ushers in the freedom from domination by the id, is then negation not the prerequisite for an integration of the personality on a higher level of adaptation?

One is inclined to reject Freud's correlation of affirmation and negation to Eros and the destructive instinct as inconsistent with the whole argument in his paper on negation. Freud gives us, however, some clue to what might have motivated him to postulate a correlation between negation and aggression when he refers to the negativism of the psychotics. The aggressive and destructive quality of psychotic negativism has impressed many observers. Insofar as negation may lead to a frustration of needs, it has been singled out as the most important motivation for aggression (Dollard et al. 1939). Sullivan's (1953) concept of malevolence postulates a correlation between denial of tenderness to the child and the malevolent transformation, i.e., aggressive behavior. Negation, it seems, is Janus-faced: one of its faces looks toward the liberation of the individual from the compulsive pressures of the pleasure principle and thus toward the possibility of genuine object relations; the other face, however, appears to menace the very basis of object relations in that it expresses the aggressive potentialities of man. It seems, therefore, justified to investigate the phenomenon of negation and its role in human development. With this in mind, it become imperative to review the important studies of infants that have been undertaken by Rene Spitz (1957) concerning the genesis of human communication.

THE GENESIS OF HUMAN COMMUNICATION
AND THE ACQUISITION OF THE "NO"

In the monograph "No and Yes" Spitz (1957) explores the acquisition by the infant of the "No" and "Yes," as word as well as gesture, from evolutionary, ontogenetic, and clinical viewpoints. Following Freud's ideas on the acquisition of the function of negation, Spitz quotes Freud's (1925b) distinction concerning what a negation negates: "The function of judgement is concerned in the main with two sorts of decisions. It affirms or disaffirms the possession by a thing of a particular attribute; and it asserts or disputes that a [mental] presentation has an existence in reality" (p. 236). For Freud (1925b), these two types of decision indicate important steps in ego development. The first type of judgment is, according to Freud, a more primitive type of decision, indicating a dominance of judgement by a wish. "The original pleasure-ego wants to introject into itself everything that is good and to eject from itself everything that is bad...." The judgment concerning the existence of a mental presentation in reality is seen as an indication of more advanced ego development:

> The other sort of decision made by the function of judgement...is a concern of the definite reality-ego, which develops out of the initial pleasure-ego.... In this stage of development regard for the pleasure principle has been set aside. Experience has shown the subject that it is not only important whether a thing...possesses the "good" attributes but whether it is there in the external world. [p. 237]

This affirmation or negation of the reality of a thing Freud considers genetically to constitute a step forward because it "offers a further contribution to the differentiation between what is subjective and what is objective" (p. 238). Spitz (1957) reformulates these ideas of Freud concerning negation as follows: "The acquisition of the 'No' is an indicator of a new level of autonomy, of the awareness of the 'other' and of the awareness of the self; it is a beginning of a reconstruction of mentation on a higher level of complexity; it initiates an extensive ego development, in the framework of which the dominance of the reality principle over the pleasure principle becomes increasingly established" (p. 129). Spitz dates these developments "somewhere around fifteen months of age" (p. 129). Beyond the significance for ego development, Spitz emphasizes the importance of the acquisition of the "No" in terms of its impact on the patterning of object relations: "The child, as an independent person, with a will of his own, confronts the 'other,' who is equally independent, also a discrete person with a will of his own. ... This raises object relations from the level of instinctual drive to the level of social relations" (p. 132). Spitz uses this as a turning point in the evolution of man, in that "it established man as a species different from all others in regard to the level of his social relations" (p. 145).

How, then, does the child acquire the "No"? Freud (1925b) does not elucidate this question beyond implying that it is the result of the child's interaction with the love object. Spitz (1957) is more specific. He suggests several theoretical possiblities, but the one that he singles out for detailed discussion is based on Anna Freud's (1936) concept of the child's identification with the aggressor. The aggressor is "the frustrating object against whom his own [the child's] 'No' is hurled" (Spitz 1957, p. 47). Thus, we are again confronting the ambiguous, Janus-faced nature of the function of negation. Just as Freud's postulated correlation of aggression and negation, Spitz's derivation of the acquisition of the "no" through identification with the aggressor seems incompatible with his claim that the function of negation transforms instinctual responses into specifically human, i.e., social relations. It is difficult indeed to consider aggression as the matrix of social relations. Spitz (1965) is not unaware of this conceptual dilemma, when he says that "it should be clearly understood that when I speak of the aggressive drive or of aggression I do *not* mean hostility" (p. 178).

The seeming dilemma can be removed, according to Spitz (1957), if we understand the aggression set free in the child by the "No" of the frustrating adult as a trigger mechanism that sets in motion *thought* processes in the child: "Imitation, turning of the affect against the adult, thought process—present energy transformations on a large scale. In this transformation of energies the motor expression of the affect 'against' has been subjected to the control of the ego and modified, with far-reaching consequences" (p. 52).

This is a very interesting and ingenious hypothesis. It is based on a hypothetical transformation of aggressive drive energies into ego functions—a metapsychological alchemy by means of which the leaden weight of the aggressive drives is transformed into the pure gold of higher ego functions. It is possible that such transformations do occur. They are, however, very difficult to validate. Spitz's own observations contain possibilities of another approach toward the dilemma of the relation between negation and aggression when he says "the adult mental processes and the possible rational reasons for his 'No' are completely beyond the fifteen-month-old's capacities of understanding. He cannot understand whether the adult prohibits because of concern for the child's safety or because of anger when the child does something forbidden" (p. 50). This is certainly correct as far as the rational reasons of the adult are concerned. But is it really self-evident that the affective implication of a "No" might not be perceived, even by a young child, as more meaningful than the verbal articulation of it? In the adult the effect elicited by the "No" seems to vary greatly according to the experiential context in which it occurs. The possibility that this may also be true for the child cannot be ruled out without further evidence to the contrary.

THE PERCEPTION OF THE "NO" IN ADULT INTERACTION
AND THE CONCEPT OF DIALOGUE (SPITZ 1963)

One example shall suffice to illustrate that the meaning conveyed by a "No" is derived from the human context within which it occurs. If a motorist stops a stranger to ask him whether the road straight ahead leads to Xville, he may receive the answer: "No, you must take the next turn to the right." In this context, the "No implies neither aggression nor frustration. Rather it indicates that the stranger is *sharing a common world* with the motorist: he understands that the motorist wants to reach a certain place, his identification is with this particular aim, and his "No" protects the motorist from losing his way. It is in acknowledgment of this sharing identification that the motorist expresses his thanks to the stranger. This type of "No" may be described as the "coaching No."[1] It is proposed that the "No" with which a mother confronts the child is—in an ideal, conflict-free relation—intended to be a "coaching No" and is perceived as thus by the child. The mother who tells the child, "Don't play with matches," is coaching the child in how to deal with a shared world that is complicated and often dangerous, and about which she knows more than the child. It is not unreasonable to assume that the child, even if he feels frustrated by such prohibition, is more affected by the sense of being coached in finding his way in this strange and new world, shared by him and the mothering person, than by an aggressive implication of the word "No." As a result of this coaching, the area of the world that the child can share with the parental persons is enlarged and enriched. This is true as long as mother and child partake in the "dialogue," as defined by Spitz (1963). This important concept denotes in Spitz's (1965) terminology an essentially nonverbal communication between mother and child, a "specific sector of reciprocity between mother and child" (p. 173) which is described more fully as a "dialogue of action and response which goes on in the form of a circular process within the dyad, as a continuous, mutually stimulating feedback circuit. Actually, it is a *precursor* of the dialogue, an archaic form of conversation. In the human it leads eventually to the acquisition of verbal communication, of speech" (p. 173). Because this is the earliest form of communication, the consequences of a breakdown of the dialogue are considered especially grave by Spitz (1964) insofar as "the deviation will become evident in increasing measure from phase to phase eventuating in a skewed personality" (p. 765). This breakdown of dialogue is not identical with maternal deprivation, maternal rejection, or other tangible forms of maternal neglect. One consequence of such a breakdown might well be the inability on the part of the child to perceive the mothering person's "No" as an aspect of the ongoing dialogue, i.e., as a "coaching No." In other words, the undiscriminating perception of every "No" as aggression on the part of the parental person might be considered an early manifestation of a damaged ego. Only by such children, it is suggested, will the "No" be perceived exclusively as frustrating. Referring back to Freud's (1925b) distinction between the negation (or affirmation) of a particular attribute of a thing, and the negation (or affirmation) of the existence of a thing in reality, it is proposed that there are individuals who perceive the parental "No," not as a verbal negation to them of a particular thing (for instance a piece of candy); rather, they interpret the verbal "No" as expressing a nonverbal negation by the other one of their own existence. Because this interpretation has a disruptive effect on the pattern of the object relations of the individual, it is referred to as the "malignant No." The "malignant No" does, in more severe cases, not only distort object relations, but affects the individual's total interaction with his social environment as well. It is the perception of the verbal "No" as a nonverbal "malignant No" that establishes a correlation between negation and aggression. The nature of this correlation will be investigated further, but it is necessary to state here that it was described decades ago by Erikson (1950a), when he declared: "Deprivation of identity, not frustration, leads to murder" (p. 212). It seems indeed likely that the transformation of the "coaching No" into the "malignant No" indicates a damage to early processes of identity formation in the child. It also appears probable that such damage is specific for a certain pathology of the mother-infant dialogue.

THE MANIFESTATION OF THE EXPERIENCE OF
"BEING NEGATED" IN CLINICAL OBSERVATION

The experience of "being negated in one's existence" remains unconscious, although affective aspects of it enter the individual's conscious perception. Its unconscious reality is hypostasized on the basis of certain characteristic modifications of the individual's object relations. They consist of an inability to deal with a temporary or permanent denial of their needs, i.e., negation in the sense of nonfulfillment of a desire, regardless of whether this negation emanates from another person, from the social order, or, in the most extreme cases, from the conditions of life itself. Coexisting with the unacceptability of negation, one observes in these individuals a characteristic manifestation of their instinctual drives, which ranges from a coercive sexual approach to varying degrees of aggression in their object relations. A definite correlation exists between the severity of the response toward negation and a shift from a sexual to an aggressive approach in their object relations. While it is not claimed that patterns of sexuality and aggression are *exclusively* determined by the perception of negation, the latter appears to be one determinant of drive manifestation that deserves attention. The following clinical observations attempt to illustrate these points.

Robert, a twenty-seven-year-old unmarried male patient, complained about his profoundly unsatisfactory relations with girls and about the difficulties in dealing with his associates at work. In both situations he encountered a rejecting, if not outright hostile attitude toward him, an attitude he could not understand because he tried hard to please both his girl friends as well as his employers and coworkers. His feelings about the cold and hostile responses he met with assumed at times a paranoid coloring, but generally left him dejected and depressed about his failure to establish satisfactory relations. In spite of good looks, intelligence, and other assets, he suffered repeated rebuffs from girls he was interested in, and lack of success and advancement in his chosen career.

During the treatment, it became clear that this patient expected an instantaneous and unconditional affirmative response to his verbalized and even to his unverbalized wishes. If he called a girl in order to make a date with her for a certain evening, he expected her to accept his invitation immediately and enthusiastically. If he wanted her to sit very close to him in the car, he was profoundly disappointed, if not angry, if she did not conform to his wish. This same expectation applied to every aspect of the girl's behavior: he wanted a girl to dress the way he liked it, enjoy the same things that he enjoyed. Otherwise, he perceived coolness, rejection, or hostility on her part. His own reaction would fluctuate between anxiety, depression, and rage against the particular girl or girls in general. These emotions reached their climax when a girl did not give in to his sexual advances. He justified the intensity of his disappointment (a disappointment that seemed especially keen when the girl was a casual date) by elaborating with great eloquence and vigor his philosophy of male-female relationships. He believed in total sexual freedom between the sexes, quoting extensively proponents of these views, stressing that any relationship between a man and a woman ought to be consummated sexually without hypocritical moral or religious restraints. A girl who accepted a date, according to his view, had implicitly consented to have sex relations with a man. To refuse the sex act was, therefore, a kind of a breach of contract.

In striking contrast to these programmatic statements was his actual behavior in his relation with girls. The almost fanatically held views appeared oddly dissociated from the actually felt affects in a real contact with a girl. What he was trying to do was to enact a fantasy in which the girl was responding to his verbalized and unverbalized wishes like an automaton who had no spontaneity and no desire of her own, but was "coming to life" only through his own directions. He would tell the girl that they were going to his apartment to have sexual intercourse. He sometimes prescribed to the girl how she should dress to excite him sexually, even indicate how she should react to his advances. If the girl refused to cooperate with his instructions, he was disappointed, resentful, and often angry. If, however, the girl was willing to have sexual relations with him, he was disappointed too, because the reality of her spontaneous responses did not correspond to his anticipations in fantasy. He consequently had a letdown feeling even if he was successful, his sexual excitement was not very intense, and at times he had difficulties in performing adequately. Occasionally he met a girl who was just as eager to have sex relations with him as his theories postulated a girl should be. With an especially responsive girl, he admitted feeling bored if not somewhat disgusted. He explained this by saying that this girl just enjoyed sex but did not really respond to *him*. There were, however, exceptions which were all the more remarkable because they did not fit his theories at all, nor did they correspond to his fantasies. There were a few occasions when he met girls with whom he became genuinely emotionally involved. These he described as "always cooperative," in the sense that they enjoyed whatever he offered them in terms of entertainment, and were also tolerant of his sexual advances. They did not, however, fulfill his desire for complete freedom from any sexual restraint. These girls, whose company he enjoyed genuinely and for a long time, did not, in fact, consent to have sexual intercourse with him, one girl because of religious scruples, the other because of an unsettled marital status. Although he regretted their reluctance, it did not affect his fondness for these particular girls; in fact, he even contemplated marriage with either of them.

While his relationship to girls appeared thus very complex and full of emotional contradictions, his relationship to his superiors and coworkers was consistently strained. It seemed indeed true that he was thoroughly disliked both by his colleagues and by the people that worked under him. Ideas which he had contributed and developed were handed over to someone else because people expressed unwillingness to work on a project under his direction. Apparently the same coercive approach that estranged most of his girls alienated his coworkers, his secretaries, etc. He displayed an imperious and dictatorial manner, expecting instant execution of any order. This attitude expressed itself in many other situations as well. When required to wait, for instance, in a physician's office, he told the doctor's secretary that his time was as valuable as the doctor's, and that he would be back some day when the doctor could see him. Similar situations occurred when he had an appointment with a person with whom he had to discuss some matter pertaining to his work projects and whose cooperation was important for its success. He often held forth on the subject that certain rules, such as traffic laws, should not be applied to him. He referred to the immunity of diplomats and other high-ranking public officials with regard to speeding, and expected, though he was just a junior executive with a prestigious organization, that such immunity should also be extended to him. When his tactless manner antagonized people, the negative responses puzzled him, made him anxious and depressed, as if he was unable to see the obvious connection between his approach to people and their reaction to him. The theoretical implications of the reported case for the thesis of this paper shall be stated briefly. In this connection, a quotation from Sandler (1960) seems pertinent:

The problem of what it means to "feel loved," or to "restore narcissistic cathexis," is one which has as yet been insufficiently explored. What the child is attempting to restore is an affective state of well-being, which we can correlate, in terms of energy, with the level of narcissistic cathexis of the self. Initially this affective state, which normally forms the background of everyday experience, must be the state of bodily well-being which the infant experiences when his instinctual needs have been satisfied (as distinct from the pleasure in their satisfaction). This affective state later becomes localized in the self, and we see aspects of it in feelings of self-esteem as well as in normal background feelings of safety. The maintenance of this *central affective state* is perhaps the most powerful motive for ego development, and we must regard the young child (and later the adult) as seeking well-being as well as pleasure-seeking; the two are by no means the same, and in analysis we can often observe a conflict between the two. [p. 149n][2]

The conflict between seeking well-being and seeking pleasure is most obvious in the case of Robert. It is this conflict that seems to account for the inconsistencies and contradictions concerning the patient's coercive sexual and aggressive behavior on the one hand, and the actuality of his relations with girls on the other hand. We think of the sexual drive as a means to experience lust, joy, or ecstasy. In contrast we link the experience of well-being with inner harmony and security. For the gratification of such aims we need a sense of self-esteem based on the acceptance and respect of others and the internalized representations of important love objects in the superego. Well-being in this sense would be a function for the "loving and beloved superego" (Schafer 1969). This patient appeared bereft of a sense of well-being as a central affective state which only under special circumstances gave way to a more comfortable feeling concerning himself.[3] His efforts to secure a sense of well-being consisted of quixotic attempts to coerce others into the role of a loving superego by means of sexuality and aggression. The function of this coercive sexuality and his aggressive manipulations was not primarily to enjoy sexual pleasure, but to obtain an unqualified and unconditional affirmative response to any kind of desire. This included not only sexual desires, but many nonsexual desires as well, such as the permission to drive at high speeds at will. A loving superego, in the interpretation of this patient, was one that said "yes" to whatever he demanded.

This superego was not fully internalized, but remained attached to a real person who could provide this affirmative, yes-saying attitude toward him. If he found such an individual, he experienced a sense of well-being that changed his total behavior. This was the case with the girls of whom he grew extraordinarily fond. They were affirmative in their response to him as a total person, able to overlook the peculiarities by which he alienated most people. The striking fact under these circumstances was the disappearance of the coercive sexuality and of aggression as a response to this experience of feeling affirmed by these individuals. In the transference, he displayed a similar attitude toward the analyst, whom he apparently perceived as an affirmative figure. Since, however, none of these experiences became truly internalized, he needed, when such relationships came to an end, a new person to take over the affirmative function on which his well-being depended. His method more often than not had the very opposite effect of confronting him with mildly to extremely negative responses to his coercive approach, leading to a vicious circle, in that the increase of his emotional malaise made his approaches ever more aggressive, with the expectable negative result. That he failed to understand these predictable responses shows a definite disturbance of his reality testing, since he seemed unable to learn from experience.

The use of coercive sexuality and aggression rather than pleasurable gratification in order to bring about well-being appears thus as a defense against the possibility of encountering negation, instead of affirmation. What is perceived as negation in these individuals is so all-encompassing that they appear incapable of distinguishing between shades of negation. What is not considered unconditional affirmation is easily perceived as a total negation—a negation not of *a* a specific desire, *a* particular need, but, as became clear from the response of the patients, a negation of the reality of their existence. It is this unusual response to negation that led me to hypostasize the concept of the experience of the "malignant No." The instinctual drives are placed in the service of eliminating the possibility of the dreaded negation of existence, and it is this striving for the elimination of such possibility that maintains their coercive and aggressive force. This pattern proved to be especially destructive in its effect on psychoanalytic therapy.

THE EXPERIENCE OF "BEING NEGATED" AND ITS EFFECT ON THE PSYCHOANALYTIC SITUATION

It should be emphasized that the coercive sexuality or aggression of individuals who have experienced the "malignant No" does not invariably lead to acting out of sexual coercion or aggression recognizable in the individual's manifest behavior. This can be the case, but there are many other outcomes of the coercive sexuality and aggression that depend on numerous factors, for instance, on the anxieties aroused in the ego by the pressure of sexuality and aggression. Thus, the actual behavior of these individuals may range from subtle but pervasive seductiveness, with anxious withdrawal when this seductiveness meets with response, to a pattern of "sexual addictiveness," where the consummation of the sexual act is experienced as the only means of feeling affirmed. If the individual feels, however, that the sexual partner is interested in his or her own sexual pleasure only, and does not feel responded to as a total person, the ecstatic quality of sexual experience may give way to an even greater sense of having been negated in his or her existence. Such disappointment may be followed by a new attempt to find affirmation with another sex partner. Thus a vicious circle may develop, with all kinds of destructive results, including psychotic withdrawal.

These consequences of the experience of the "malignant No" manifest themselves in a characteristic way in the transformation of the transference into a battle for total affirmation, in which the affirmation is acceptable to the patient on his or her terms only. This type of transference may prove unmanageable because the therapeutic process in itself implies to some of these patients a repetition of the experience of "being negated," in that the abstinence which is inherent in the psychoanalytic process is perceived as a negation of their reality.

The perception of the therapeutic process as an experience of being negated was most poignant in some women patients who responded with an initial development of a seemingly intense, at times clinging, transference. This positive transference coexisted with a violent rejection of the analytic process. On the contrary, the more positive the feeling toward the therapist, the more negative the reaction to interpretations that were offered. They were belittled as mere empty words, or worse, as criticism or even insults. It was very clear, however, that it was not the particular content of the interpretation that these patients found so unacceptable, but the disappointment in not having obtained a total affirmative response to them as individuals. It was quite obvious that an acceptable response implied to them unconditional affirmation.

Mrs. N., for instance, became very abusive and vehemently criticized the stupidity of the interpretations. She would then become very distraught, anxious, and depressed, sometimes leaving the session abruptly with the remark, "You do not perceive me at all." Sometimes she returned, or telephoned, apologizing for her intemperate language.

Such sessions often left her anxious and depressed for many hours afterwards. She denied most emphatically that she expected anything from the therapist beyond help with her personal problems. She wished that the therapist would take the initiative, start talking, not wait for what she had to say, not just listen and give interpretations. This she interpreted as lack of communication. References to statements that she herself had made, and which appeared meaningful in a certain context, she perceived as negative comments; "Now you are throwing this up at me," was one of her remarks on such an occasion.

Mrs. G. had a tendency to respond to every interpretation with an almost automatic "No." The suggestion that her marital difficulties were due to a particular type of interaction between her husband and herself, one which was very threatening to both of them, she saw as intolerable criticism. When the point was illustrated by reference to certain specific situations which she had mentioned, she could only conclude that she was blamed for everything that had happened. In one such context she burst out: "You always negate me. I cannot endure to be negated." Both of these patients, after many years of treatment, came to the conclusion that the total affirmative response on their terms was not forthcoming. It led in both to a most conflictual ending of the treatment, an ending neither of them truly wanted. For both of them, the treatment implied a degree of feeling negated in their existence which they perceived as intolerable.[4]

In male patients, extreme fluctuations in the relationship to the therapist are common too, as was the case with Frank, a young business executive. He had consulted several psychiatrists before entering psychoanalytic treatment; for both of them he felt an unrelenting loathing because of certain questions they had raised. In one case the question pertained to the patient's emotional capacity to deal with his managerial responsibilities under the pressure of his often intense anxiety. This he perceived as a total negation of his competence, his intellectual abilities, and his personal qualities. He devoted himself to endless tirades on how one day he would "fix that guy," followed by streams of invective, which were probably intended to intimidate the therapist. In a similar manner he would talk about business associates, employees and customers who had in one way or another differed with his judgment or displeased him by not cooperating with him. He was in business with many relatives, among them a brother who was his favorite. Nevertheless he had frequent fits of rage that led to repeated threats of physical violence. In college, he had once threatened his brother with a knife because of a disagreement between them. At the same time, he could be very solicitous and almost fawning when he aimed at being "recognized" by a person whose good opinion and respect were important to him.

With girls, he was aggressively seductive, passionate in his love-making, which once he described as the "only moments of happiness" in his life when he felt free of anxiety. It was all the more striking that after he married a girl who was most responsive to him as a sexual partner, he felt uneasy about their frequent sexual relations and particularly about the fact that his wife seemed to enjoy sex so much. His verbalizations suggested that total affirmation—in this case expressed as willing surrender—was giving him happiness only when he could interpret it as affirmation of himself by someone he perceived as a potential "negator," someone he had, at least in fantasy, coerced— by seduction, or, as in the case of his business affiliates, by aggressive threats—into affirming his existence. He was at first very pleased about his experience in analysis. He was rather fulsome in his praise. How much better analysis was than the treatment he had before. As the treatment progressed, however, he was often profoundly bored with it, expressing the desire to cut the hour short, or to end the treatment altogether, or complaining that he had to come to his appointment when he was really too busy. It seemed he had anticipated being negated as a person, was at first delighted to feel "affirmed," but when the affirmation lost the quality of having been "won" from the therapist by coercion or seduction, he felt depressed, bored, fatigued, and often extremely anxious. He did continue treatment in spite of great fluctuations in his sense of relatedness, of self-esteem. He, like the patient Robert, appeared to use the anlyst as a "loving superego" which he needed to sustain him. His fear of "feeling negated" in his existence functioned in him also as a challenge to which he would often rise, in his own aggressive way, by performing successfully. This was also true of Mrs. N., whose dread of feeling negated—"I shall never want to live as one of those grey people of whom nobody is ever aware"—acted as a constant stimulus to achieve success in her chosen field.

There are certain striking similarities among the patients who, according to the thesis of this paper, had experienced the threat of the "malignant No" in their early life. None of these patients could be said to have suffered gross emotional deprivations. Not one of them came from a broken home. Neither were they only children, a number of them were middle children. Some of them came from affluent families, with parents trying to give them many advantages such as private schools, summer camps, expensive clothing, etc. None of them came from poverty-stricken backgrounds. All of them, however, remembered their childhood as a period of profound loneliness and inner isolation, even though they often remembered having been a favorite child. Mrs. N. spoke of her childhood as "endless periods of silence." She spoke with great warmth of her father, who never failed to hug her, but added: "I cannot remember, though, that he was ever talking to me or I to him. My closest companions were my pets." Frank was sent each year to an exclusive camp. He remembers his loneliness there and the conviction that nobody would come and bring him back home. The same was true of Robert. He never felt that anybody communicated with him, although he was given many material and education advantages. These facts must be taken into consideration in an attempt at a genetic reconstruction of these patients' development.

GENETIC RECONSTRUCTION OF THE EXPERIENCE OF "BEING
NEGATED" IN ONE'S EXISTENCE

In view of the absence of any gross emotional deprivation in these patients, it seems appropriate to apply Spitz's (1963, 1964, 1965) concept of the derailment of dialogue to a genetic reconstruction of the pathology. The concept of the derailment of dialogue is suggested here as constituting at least a major contributing factor to pathological development, but a factor within a "complemental series" (Freud 1916–17, p. 347). This must be emphasized particularly with regard to the development of the instinctual drives, where it is known that other genetic and maturational factors cannot be neglected. Important as the concept of derailment of dialogue is, its exact nature is not yet fully known. It is likely that Spitz's (1964) theory of the stimulus overload is true for some cases. Brodey's (1965) description of the image-pattern of mother-child relationship can also lead to a derailment of dialogue, but perhaps of a different type than that which Spitz (1964) observed. The disturbance in mother-child communication which is referred to in this paper as the "malignant No" may not be identical with either of these situations.

In the cases reported here, there are so many variations in the degree of pathology that the disturbance of dialogue must be assumed to occur in varying degress of severity. They have, however, in spite of great differences, certain common characteristics, such as the tendency to respond to negation in the previously described intolerant way, culminating in the coercive-aggressive drive pattern. There thus remains enough specificity to justify a proposition concerning the particular developmental origin of this disturbance of dialogue. The strong sense of being alone and isolated in their childhood, as well as the transference phenomena encountered in the psychoanalytic treatment of these patients, makes it particularly suggestive that they suffered a disturbance of their "mirroring experience" (see chapter 10): "The child, while not capable of perceiving the maternal object or of possessing a sense of self or of identity, experiences its existence as reflected by the libidinal cathexis of the mother. The mother, in contrast to the non-human environment, reflects back to the child a configuration of its own presence." Insofar as this mirroring experience was considered essential for the later development of a sense of self, it would be consistent with this hypothesis to assume that the patients who perceive the verbal "No" as a nonverbal negation of their existence suffered from some disturbance of the mirroring experience.[5]

This hypothesis, if confirmed, could have interesting implications for certain assumptions of psychoanalytic theory. In a restatement of Freud's thesis (1900), Gill (1963, p. 63) has postulated that a "mental content can stimulate the sense organ [consciousness] only if it possesses ... 'quality,' and that 'quality' can be derived only from perception or from sensations of pleasure and pain from within." But, as Gill points out, Freud considered the possibility that contents possessing great sensory intensity may also excite consciousness directly. Freud (1900) considered the sensations of pleasure and unpleasure as directly expressing the state of instinctual drive tension (see also Schur 1966). In Sandler's (1960) previously quoted opinion, the sensations of pleasure-unpleasure and those of "well-being" should be distinguished from one another. Does this perhaps imply an additional "quality" of mental contents (Gill 1963) or primitive thought processes (Schur 1966) which is capable of stimulating consciousness directly, a consciousness of "well-being" rather than one of pleasure or unpleasure?

The subjective consciousness of the patients who, according to the hypothesis presented in this paper, have experienced the "malignant No" seem to lack a basic sense of "well-being." It was suggested this could be due to their not having experienced the subjective affirmation of their reality by a disturbance in the "mirroring" experience. This would make it probable that "mirroring" i.e., the experience of one's own reality as affirmed by the other one, endows mental contents with a "quality"—we may call it "subjective affirmation"—which becomes conscious as the affect of well-being, which, for Sandler (1960), is the underlying experience of being loved on the part of the child. If this were so, we would have to consider the possibility that affirmation and negation do not primarily, as Freud (1925b) thought, confirm or deny whether a thing has the good or bad attribute, but whether there is an experience of feeling subjectively affirmed or negated. The develop-ment of the judgement of affirmation and negation, as Freud (1925b) describes it, would differ according to whether the child has previously experienced himself affirmed or negated in his existence. Because the ego functions of negation are important aspects of reality testing, it would be understandable that the hypostasized experience of the "malignant No" affects this function to a remarkable degree in the patients described previously. But the most striking feature in the symptomatology of the patients was the coercive pattern of their sexuality and the tendency toward aggression in their object relations. This would speak in favor of the assumption of a genetic independence between the drive tension of the individual and his capacity for the affective state of well-being due to the experience of subjective affirmation by the other one. A shift toward coercive sexuality or aggression would occur as a result of the absence of that "quality" in their mental processes which brings about the conscious affective state of well-being. This suggests that the instinctual drives might serve, in case of absence or deficiency of the experience of subjective affirmation, as an alternative means constituting a kind of reserve against the threat of feeling negated in one's existence.[6] Through this regressive use of the sexual or aggressive drives, the aggressor manages to perceive the object's response to them as an affirmation of his existence.

With the last remarks, we return to the question of a correlation between negation and aggression. It does not appear that the ego function of negation is genetically derived from the aggressive drive as Freud had suggested (1925b). Rather, there seems to exist a correlation between the experience of feeling negated in one's existence (a disturbance in the "mirroring experience") and the dominance of aggressive drives in the individual's object relations. Most generally stated, both sexuality and aggression can be employed to *ward off* the "dreadful" affect of feeling negated in one's existence. Sexuality and aggression thus appear as the means of ultimate resort for undoing the very possibility of negation and for assuring instantaneous, total, and unconditional affirmation of one's existence from the object that is sexually or aggressively pursued. This implies that sexuality and aggression are perceived as capable of establishing object relations which, in contrast to all other forms of object relations, are exempt from the possibility of negation. According to Spitz (1957), the acquisition of the "No" which enables each individual to affirm or negate, is the developmental prerequisite to raising "object relations from the level of the instinctual drive to the level of social relations" (p. 132). The capacity to affirm or negate—making possible the acquisition of the function of judgement (Freud 1925b)—leads to the emergence of thought, separation of I and Not-I, autonomy, and awareness of self, all of which form the developmental prerequisite for object relations on the human level.

The implication here is that human object relations are dependent on a functioning ego. It is the ego that has acquired the capacity to negate, but the id remains beyond negation. Insofar as the instinctual drives are an aspect of the id, they can only affirm, but not negate. An individual able to stimulate by his sexuality or aggression the sexuality or the fear of another individual perceives instantaneously a response to his existence from the other one that constitutes an unconditional affirmation of his reality. The individual who reacts to the sexual desire or the aggressive threat of the other person may mobilize his ego and superego defenses. These defenses can restrain his own sexual responses from being expressed or acted upon. The individual cannot, however, *negate* having been sexually stimulated or threatened by the perception of an aggressive threat. If one would paraphrase the nonverbal dialogue between two such individuals, one would have to say that it leads to an answer on the part of stimulated object of "Yes, but . . ." The "yes" would imply that there has been an affirmative response, the "but" would be a negation made possible by the ego and superego defenses that enable the individual to refrain from action such as sexual intercourse.

Nothing, however, can transform the affirmative response of the instinctual drives into a negation. The affirmation may become apparent to the sexual pursuer or the aggressor by blushing on the part of the person to whom the sexual message has been communicated, or by trembling, as a response to aggression, and by numerous other "affirmative" somatic manifestations. It is, therefore, possible to undo by means of sexuality or aggression all the developmental steps that have been acquired by the emergence of the capacity to negate. The more coercive the sexual approach and the more violent the aggression, the more obvious will be the affirmative response—affirming, that is, the existence of the aggressor—on the part of the chosen object. Everybody's capacity to negate, with all its developmental consequences, will indeed collapse under threat of violence and aggression. Even heroic individuals cannot conceal their pain in the face of torture. Thus, the individual who insists on coercing another one to respond to him with instantaneous and unconditional affirmation will always triumph by the use of coercive sexuality or aggression. What he will not obtain by aiming at the inherent psychic vulnerability of the other one is a genuine object relation on a human level; this can only be obtained by two individuals permitting each other to affirm or negate the uniqueness of their individualities, in an act of autonomous choice. One could paraphrase Kris' (1935) formulation of "regression in the service of the ego" by speaking of a regression of object relations in the service of clinging to the certainty of one's existence. Thus, the triumph that coercive sexuality or aggression may achieve, in terms of unconditional affirmation of an individual's existence by another one, is always a Pyrrhic victory. The victory has been won at the price of losing the free acknowledgment, by another person's total personality, of one's own individuality. This is the tragedy of the individuals who have suffered the experience of the "malignant No": their victories always end up in a more profound sense of feeling negated in their existence.

Nevertheless, there exist forms of feeling negated in one's existence that reach such extremes of dread that only the most violent aggression affords them the means to compel the other one to recognize their existence as real. Edward Albee (1959) has powerfully presented a variation of this theme—in that the victim coerces the murderer to acknowledge his existence—in one of his plays. But in order to fathom the full implications of the fateful interdependence between the experience of feeling negated in one's existence and the malignant transformation of the instinctual drives, one has to turn to the writings of the Marquis de Sade (1740–1814). Psychiatry has failed to acknowledge any debt to de Sade beyond its appropriation of his name in the adjectival sense. What de Sade has to say about the relationship between the experience of feeling negated in one's existence and the recourse to unlimited sexual coercion and murderous violence constitutes, however, one of the most lucid and intellectualy forthright confrontations with the problems of human relations whose primary aim has become the unconditional affirmation of one's existence by the other one. It is impossible to do justice to the implications of de Sade's ideas within the limits of this paper. The remarks which follow can therefore only aim at demonstrating the relevance of de Sade to the work of the psychoanalyst who attempts to deal with the emotional problems of "the age of alienation."

THE USE OF SEXUALITY AND AGGRESSION AS A DEFENSE AGAINST THE EXPERIENCE OF "FEELING NEGATED" IN DE SADE

Since their appearance, the writings of the Marquis de Sade have been considered as among the most notorious examples of pornographic literature. De Sade's claim that they were didactic treatises expounding a revolutionary philosophy of the human condition was taken seriously by few in the last part of the nineteenth century. A philosophical re-evaluation of de Sade on a large scale has been in progress only in our own era. Among the outstanding contributions by philosphers is a study by Simone de Beauvoir (1951–52), on which the following remarks are based. The direct quotations from de Sade are taken partly from de Beauvoir's essay, and partly from an American selection of his writings (Dinnage 1953), which appeared together with the English translation of de Beauvoir's study.

"The curse which weighed upon Sade" de Beauvoir characterizes as his "autism," which she defines as his incapacity for "ever forgetting himself or being genuinely aware of the reality of the other person" (p. 33). What de Beauvoir calls de Sade's autism is interpreted here as the affective state of an individual who has, in a most extreme way, experienced the sense of being negated in his existence, i.e., the experience of the "malignant No." This proposition is derived entirely from statements found in de Sade's writings. In these writings one of the recurrent themes is de Sade's horror at the silence and total indifference of Nature. For de Sade, as an eighteenth-century atheist and mechanist, Nature is the only reality, but he perceives Nature, which he calls "the mother of the human race" (p. 31), as truly murderously hostile and destructive to her creatures. "Man is isolated in the world," he asserts (p. 66), and he conceives as man's greatest torment "the impossibility of offending Nature" (p. 70). When de Sade describes the atrocities that his protagonists commit, he lets them express again and again their impotent rage against Nature's indifference and silence. "We have reviled, dared and defied Nature. . . . Oh, rest assured, no crime in the world is capable of drawing the wrath of Nature upon us" (p. 198). It is obvious that by describing Nature as indifferent, cruel, and murderous, even attributing to her "concealment of motives" (p. 70), de Sade anthropomorphizes Nature. This is logically incompatible with his mechanistic view of Nature, which he emphasizes repeatedly. Reading these resentful, bitter tirades hurled against Nature—"I abhor Nature . . . I loathe her" (p. 70)—one is reminded of Sullivan's (1953) concept of the "not-me," which is marked by the breakthrough of "uncanny emotions," consisting of "awe, horror, loathing and dread" (p. 163).

It appears justifiable to interpret all this bitterness and hate as the response of an individual who desperately attempts to establish a dialogue with someone who refuses to answer. It is proposed that de Sade responds to the silence of Nature as if he has encountered a cosmic "malignant No." It is not surprising then to find that his reaction to this "malignant No" shows a most striking resemblance to that of the patients previously described. De Sade's reply to Nature's "malignant No" is his proclamation of a new morality, in which the most violent forms of coercive sexuality and the most destructive methods of aggression toward any potential love object are hailed as the only means to establish genuine contact between two individuals. Thus, de Beauvoir states, "Eroticism appears in de Sade as a mode of communication, the only valid one" (p. 79). But this eroticism is characterized by coercive sexuality and aggression: "At the basis of de Sade's entire sexuality, and hence his ethics, is the fundamental identity of coition and cruelty" (p. 31). "What the torturer demands is that ... the victim recognize ... that his destiny is the freedom of the tyrant. He is then united to his tyrant by the closest of bonds. They form a genuine couple" (p. 78). The "freedom of the tyrant" is nothing other than the total, instantaneous, and unconditional acknowledgement of the existence of the torturer as the only person who is real for the victim. In the name of this freedom, de Sade demands the total elimination of any possibility of negation in the relationship of the individual and the object of his sexual or aggressive desires. The "new citizen" must be "free to vent (on the objects of his desires) all those passions prescribed in him, without ever being restrained by anything. ... The lightest refusal (of complete subordination) will be punished immediately" (pp. 132–33). By becoming thus the victim's destiny, possibly his death, the torturer has gained his "freedom," i.e., he is no longer negated in his existence, he is, for that one moment, totally real.

In de Sade's words: "What does one want when one is engaged in the sexual act? That everything about you give you its utter attention, think only of you, care only for you" (p. 16). This total acknowledgement of one person's existence by the other one is for de Sade incompatible with giving pleasure to the sexual partner. "If the objects who serve us feel ecstasy, they are then much more often concerned with themselves than with us, and our own enjoyment is consequently impaired" (p. 33). For individuals who have not suffered the experience of being negated, the ecstasy of the partner enhances their own gratification. De Sade's objection to the sexual pleasure felt by the partner is almost verbatim the argument used by the patient Robert to explain his annoyance with a girl who gave every indication of enjoying intercourse with him. De Sade, however, takes one more step: the sexual object must not enjoy the sexual act, but must submit to it while suffering, because "No kind of sensation is keener and more active than that of pain; its impressions are unmistakable" (p. 34). In the terminology of this paper, no acknowledgement of their existence for individuals afflicted with the dread of being negated, no "affirmation" is more convincing, more "unmistakable" than the evidence that the other one is reacting to the pain caused by the aggressor. It should be noted, however, that not only the aggressor, if he suffers from the sense of being negated, feels confirmed absolutely in his existence by becoming another person's destiny. The victim too, if he has suffered from the experience of the "malignant No," may perceive it as an acknowledgement of his existence if he is able to coerce the other one into a frenzy of violence directed toward him, as in the Albee play mentioned earlier.

In summary, de Sade's writings seem to support the thesis proposed in this paper that "feeling negated" in one's existence interferes with the development of a sense of well-being and makes the individual prone to an affective state of dread or horror. Against this dread the individual mobilizes the instinctual drives as a means of obtaining total and unconditional affirmation of his reality from another one. The more severe the sense of "feeling negated," the more aggressive become the means of obtaining unconditional affirmation. The writings of de Sade would be remarkable if they did nothing else but state this interdependence in a most explicit manner. De Sade is important, however, for numerous other reasons that are relevant for psychoanalysts who attempt to deal with the psychological complexities of our present age. De Sade is perhaps *the* philosopher of alienation. For him, alienation is a new, radical, philosophical, and moral position, the only one that modern man, existing in a godless universe, could support with intellectual honesty.

DE SADE ON THE NEW MORALITY
AND NEW FREEDOM FOR ALIENATED MAN

It would be a fallacy to understand the outrageousness of de Sade's philosophy as nothing but a rationalization of the personal sexual aberrations of an individual who had suffered a severe disturbance of his sense of self. It is true enough, as de Beauvoir says, "that his vices condemned him to solitude. He was to demonstrate the necessity of solitude and the supremacy of evil" (p. 65). What makes de Sade important as the most articulate representative of a new ideology is the fact that "he ascribed to his situation the value of a metaphysical inevitability" (p. 65). "His situation" does not only refer to his sexual perversions. Rather, it defines his existence within a universe which is perceived as indifferent if not hostile toward life, and within a social order that is seen as inherently opposed to the interests of the individual. He had no illusions about the oppressive character of the old aristocratic order into which he was born. He had hoped that the new order, brought about by the French Revolution, would integrate him into a collectivity. But the Terror, which he was to witness "with the guillotine before my eyes" (p. 26), convinced him that the "body politic . . . considers men a mere collection of objects" (p. 26). His new morality, which has been referred to as the Ethics of Criminality, is based on the conviction that crime (i.e., destruction) is the supreme Law of Nature and therefore the only natural law of conduct, and that every society is criminal (destructive) in its relation toward the individual. Therefore "In a criminal society one must be a criminal" (p. 75). This is not meant as a submission to society, but as a refusal "of any complicity with the evils of the given situation" (p. 76).

Thus, total alienation from society is the only way to assert one's existence as a person: "The most perfect being we could conceive would be one who would depart most radically from our conventions and consider them most hateful" (p. 202). We are confronted here, therefore, with a *threefold* sequence of the experience of feeling negated in one's existence. In this paper, only the first psychological layer of these experiences has been considered. It was assumed to have its roots in a miscarriage of the processes of individuation. Now, however, we discover in de Sade experiences of feeling negated in one's existence by a malevolent conception of Nature and Society. Neither of these can be said to have its roots in the vicissitudes of individual psychological development. Conceptions of nature are shared aspects of the sense of reality in a given society. The same is true to a large extent of the concepts an individual forms about the society to which he belongs, or about the role of any social organism. While in the latter case different classes have greatly varying conceptions of the society in which they live—an individual belonging to the underprivileged class will have a vastly different conception of society than one belonging to an affluent or a ruling class—it is nevertheless true that these conceptions are shared by a group so that they too partake in the formation of the sense of reality of the individual.

The interdependence between the *individual* experience of feeling negated—the "malignant No"—and the *shared* experience of feeling negated by Nature or Society is a complex one. In the era of de Sade, he was isolated insofar as his social and moral philosophy was concerned—so much so that the new Republican Society confined him to a mental hospital. His conceptions of Nature were, however, shared by many philosophers of the age. His critique of Society, although more extreme than most, was not unique in that period. But no other contemporary philosopher arrived at an Ethics of Criminality comparable to that of de Sade, nor at the concept of total alienation from any social organization as the only true form of individual freedom—the new freedom of the libertine and criminal—thus consciously promoting "an apocalyptic condition which constrains all individuals to ensure their separateness, and thus their truth, in a state of constant tension" (de Beauvoir 1953, p. 76).

Does this imply that only when all three experiences of feeling negated—the individual one of the "malignant No" and the shared ones of feeling negated by Nature and Society—coincide in the total experience of an individual, that only then a radical transformation of the personality results in which the freedom to engage in coercive sexuality and aggression characterizes the individual's object relations because there is no other way to be certain of one's reality? For the answer we have to turn from de Sade to the contemporary world, because de Sade's apocalyptic vision has become the existential truth for a whole generation of intellectuals, artists, writers, and "alienated youth" (Keniston 1965). While not all of them would accept all of de Sade's theses, they all share essential aspects of his ideology. The relationship between de Sade and the contemporary mode of experience has not escaped the attention of other observers. Thus, Steiner (1965) states: "There may be deeper affinities than we as yet understand between the 'total freedom' of the uncensored erotic imagination and the total freedom of the sadist. . . . Both are exercised at the expense of someone else's humanity, of someone else's most precious right—the right to a private life of feeling" (p. 76). In the context of this paper, one might say: someone else's right to affirm *or* negate. Susan Sontag (1966) defines the sensibility of the modern artist as one "which disclaims ideas, which situates itself *beyond negation*" (p. 229, italics added). In its more extreme forms, this new freedom is encountered in the cult of sex and violence by such groups as the Hell's Angels (Thompson 1966) and in many of the radical revolutionary ideologies which extoll violence as the only means of countering threat of "existential negation" (Fanon 1963).

These themes can only be hinted at within the limits of this paper. They raise more questions about the condition of man in a technological society than it is yet possible to answer. It might well be possible that it is modern technology itself which creates conditions under which the psychological experience of the "malignant No" becomes a dangerous factor in child development. Perhaps this is the result of radical changes in the pattern of family life, as Mitscherlich (1965) has suggested. Keniston (1965) has raised the question of the effects of the "technological ego" on personality development. Together with modern man's perception of existing in an impersonal universe and feeling threatened as an individual by a depersonalizing social system, the sequence of a threefold negation of personal existence may thus be a far more universal experience than in previous ages.

If it should be borne out that this threefold sequence of existential negation is able to bring about a profound change in the structure of modern man's personality, the study of the hypothesis of the "malignant No" has more than a theoretical significance for the understanding of human individuation. It would raise issues of relevance for our age of violence and existential despair, urgent issues that the psychoanalyst least of all can shirk. When Freud discovered the unconscious as a dynamic concept, embodying for him, at first, the instinctual drives, he laid the foundations for a new science of the human mind. His ideas were, however, relevant beyond the field of psychiatry. They contributed to a new self-knowledge of an era. As psychoanalysis developed and was amplified by the discovery of the unconscious aspects of the ego and the superego, it became a general psychology whose influence has touched profoundly the social sciences, the moral climate, and the arts of a whole generation. Today, psychoanalysis appears to many to have lost touch with the problems and agonies of the technological and social revolution through which we are living. This revolution which touches all aspects of human life has, to use the language of St. Augustine, made man a question to himself. By raising the issue of the unconscious aspects of the human self and their dialectic relationship to the possibility of man's relatedness to the other one, within the context of nature and the society of which he is a part, psychoanalysis addresses itself to the phenomenon of modern man's alienation. The hypothesis of the "malignant No" is an attempt to uncover the roots of a regressive, dedifferentiating process that deserves to be called a malignant transformation of the human potential.

NOTES

1. The term *coaching* is borrowed from Anselm Strauss (1959). In this paper the concept of coaching is, in contrast to Strauss, limited to interpersonal relations based on a protective identification of the coach with the needs of the learner.

2. See also Nelson (1967). Referring to experiences that "will condition the young organism toward different patterns of feeling 'alive' and 'engaged,'" she stresses the importance of "[S]uch primary modes of awakening of the sense of self . . . in character formation and the individual's underlying perception of the world" (p. 6).

3. Kubie (1963) has described, under the name of Central Affective Potential, a latent affective state to which he ascribes the decisive formative influence on personality development, object relations, patterns of sublimation, etc. Kubie stresses the diversity of Central Affective Potentials in different individuals. This concept appears applicable to the patients described here. Their underlying Central Affective Potential, as will be discussed more fully later, is a specific form of dread.

4. See also Schur's (1966) important discussion of certain patients whose resistance is impervious to working through. Especially pertinent in the context of this chapter are Schur's comments on patients with "masochistic character disorder with a tendency to depression" (pp. 188-189).

5. The mirroring experience of the child through its reflection in the mother may be the genetic precursor of the Mirror Stage described by Lacan (1953).

6. The absence of the experience of subjective affirmation can become conscious as an affect of dread. This affect has been described by various authors differently, in accordance with the theoretical approach of the author. Jones's (1927) concept of aphanisis should be mentioned here, as well as

Eidelberg's (1957, 1962) concept of "narcissistic mortification." Sullivan's (1953) "personification of not-me," characterized by the break-through of "uncanny emotions," which he lists as awe, horror, loathing, or dread, and of which he furthermore says that they are "practically beyond discussion in communicative terms" (pp. 163–64), seems to refer to the same class of experience.

Chapter 14

REALITY PERCEPTION, PSYCHIC STRUCTURE
AND THE GENERATION GAP

THE VOICE OF THE "ENEMY"

A recording by the Jefferson Airplane (Kantner 1969), a rock group, puts forth the following challenge:

> All your private property is
> Target for your en-em-y
> And your enemy is
> W-e-e-ee.

Who is this self-declared enemy, this "We" with whom the singers identify themselves? They don't leave any doubt about it: the "We" are the young—and they proudly announce that they are all outlaws in the eyes of America. Without hesitation, they declare to all those who are *not* young that they are themselves "obscene lawless hideous dangerous dirty violent." They also claim that whatever they are and whatever they do ("We steal cheat lie forge—hide and deal") they must be and must do "in order to survive." One may question whether the survival values—or antivalues from a traditional viewpoint—that these young have adopted do not imply a far more radical target than just "private property" in the sense of "what money can buy." After all, they too own property, such as cars, television sets, musical instruments, possibly even houses. I am inclined to think that the real target of these self-declared enemies of mine is not my material possessions, which I may lose for any number of reasons, but the one true private property without which I would cease to be me: that is, my identity as a person, my sense of self.

It is my sense of identity that has determined my values, my choice of a profession, my social consciousness, my way of relating to others. It is, however, not possible to separate the acquisition—and I deliberately use this proprietary term—of a sense of identity from the issue of reality perception. They are certainly closely related, in that personal identities can only exist within a certain structure of shared reality perception. The fact that such articulate representatives of the young generation as the Jefferson Airplane challenge the identity that is my "private property" must therefore imply that the reality perception which formed my identity poses a threat to them, a threat to their very survival. Their self-perception as "outlaws in the eyes of America" demands a full psychoanalytic inquiry into *their* perception of reality. This is all the more true in view of the fact that our definitions of the psychic structures—the id, the ego, and the superego—rest on their differentiated functions with regard to "adaptation to reality." Should we not expect that these functions will be very different for those whose perception of reality has been shaped by experiences vastly divergent from the ones that led Freud to the psychoanalytic concept of "external reality"? These speculations were not triggered primarily by the bellicose words of the Jefferson Airplane. Rather, they reflect my psychoanalytic experience over the last few years with youthful patients, young people who, insofar as they came to me for help, most obviously did not look on me as their enemy.

The question of what the term "external reality" means in psychoanalysis was raised by Novey (1966, p. 492). When we, rather loosely, speak of "external reality," we mean, according to Novey, "to infer that a common consensus could be established within a specific culture that a given event or situation has or has not transpired." It is my thesis in this paper that the assumption of the possibility of such a common consensus is far more problematic in our present stage of human history than in the earlier periods that saw the development of psychoanalytic theory and therapy. I shall describe what I consider the effect of this transformation in reality perception as it manifests itself in certain observable clinical phenomena. I shall then outline the implications of such observations for our traditional psychoanalytic conceptualizations. I shall finally raise some questions concerning the relevance of this situation for the future of psychoanalysis within a changing world (see also chapter 15).

THE DISINTEGRATION OF A COMMON CONSENSUS

As early as 1937, Hartmann (1939) in his classical study, *Ego Psychology and the Problem of Adaptation,* stressed the relativity of the concept of external reality in his formulation of the "average expectable environment." Let me quote just a few passages from Hartmann's essay: "Waelder . . . rightly said that mental health cannot be considered a product of chance. One of its premises is preparedness for *average expectable* internal conflicts" (p. 55). An aspect of the average expectable environment is the social environment of which the individual becomes a part as he is maturing. In Hartmann's words,

We should not underestimate the importance of these value hierarchies among those socially determined hierarchies which the child must come to terms with. . . . The child, by accepting these values, may find an appropriate way to cope with his libidinal and aggressive impulses, and his acceptance thus may amount to a synthetic achievement. . . . This form of adaptation, like any other, is suitable only in average expectable situations. The social norms which the child adopts only partly coincide with the rewards and punishments he will actually receive from society in later life. Nevertheless, these value hierarchies may serve as switching-stations or crystallization points of human behavior. [pp. 75–76]

Although Hartmann's words were written only a little more than 30 years ago, we cannot help feeling that the reality he describes is already far removed from the one that we, and particularly our children and grandchildren, would consider an average expectable environment.

We may, in fact, wonder whether the concept of an "average expectable environment," with the exception of the first years of life when the parents *are* the child's environment, is still applicable today. For an answer, we must turn to the social scientists. Bennis and Slater,

for instance, in *The Temporary Society,* devote their studies to the
realities of the modern industrial society and chart the future
development of this reality on the basis of currently existing trends.
They characterize this experience as one "of temporary systems,
nonpermanent relationships, turbulence, uprootedness, mobility, and,
above all, unexampled social change" (1968, p. 124). They go on to
describe the psychological consequences of these developments in
terms of "concomitant feelings ... of alienation, of anomie, of
meaninglessness." To counteract such feelings, they claim, "It will be
increasingly necessary to take people as one finds them—to relate
immediately, intensely, and without traditional social props, rituals,
and distancing mechanisms" (p. 86). They predict that "internalized
controls of a fixed kind rapidly become irrelevant to a changing social
environment" (p. 87). "If one must make and break relationships
rapidly then it becomes increasingly important that people be as
interchangeable as possible" (p. 83). The authors are fully aware of the
unprecedented demands that these conditions are making on human
adaptation. "Interchangeability is a threatening concept. It violates
every principle of association known to man and conjures up an image
of social chaos. Yet it is only the logical extension of the evolution of
associational principles up to this moment" (p. 83). Underlying all
these momentous changes is the

> force of technological change and unlike the earlier ones [i.e. the
> force of the great immigration, the frontier, etc.] it has no natural
> limits. ... Like the earlier colonists, frontiersmen and non-
> English speaking immigrants, *all* Americans of the present
> century must face the irrelevance of their knowledge and skills for
> the world into which their children will mature. And this is an
> accelerating trend. ... Parents cannot define the parameters of
> the future for their children—cannot even establish the terms of
> possible change or a range of alternative outcomes. They are
> therefore useless and obsolete in a way that rarely befell parents of
> any previous century. [p. 43; see also Mead 1969, Roszak 1969,
> Parsons 1970, Reich 1970]

The authors refer to the concept of "age cohorts," introduced by
Ryder (1965, p. 23), which defines "classes of individuals who have
simultaneously experienced some new set of social conditions at an

important period of their lives." This concept has supplanted the older term of "generation," which implied groups of people about 25 years apart. But, the authors state "the rate of social change has increased so much that we can identify many different cohorts within any twenty-five year period." Again they quote Ryder, who speaks of the "experiential chasm" between age cohorts under conditions of overwhelming social change in the social environment. While this "experiential chasm" can be considerable between age cohorts, it is particularly deep between parents and children, "for the parents have not even experienced what is of central importance to the child, or at least have not experienced it in the same way, at the same time in life" (Ryder, p. 23).

I believe these quotations suffice to demonstrate the point that concepts like Hartmann's "average expectable environment," or "average expectable conflicts," have lost their meaning. It is true, of course, as Bennis and Slater point out, that under the prevailing circumstances of life in a technological age, change itself has become a chronic experience and represents a condition that becomes an expectation. This means, however, that the average *expectable* environment has been transformed into an average unpredictable one. It is obvious, as Bennis and Slater emphasize, that these changes are not felt uniformly in all existing societies, and that even within American society there are areas of very rapid change coexisting with others that have not been touched to the same extent by the impact of change. Consequently, there are "experiential chasms" not only between the young and the old, but also among varying segments of the population. If, as Novey emphasized, the concept of external reality is based on the possibility of a common consensus about any given event or situation, the divergence of exposure to the characteristics of the technological age drives deeper and deeper "experiential chasms" between more and more people, all of whom live within the range of the same cultural pattern.

THE TRANSFORMATION OF "REALITY" SINCE FREUD

At this point, it seems imperative to look back to Freud's classic formulations concerning reality perception. In his "Formulations on the Two Principles of Mental Functioning," Freud states:

We have long observed that every neurosis has as its result, and probably therefore as its purpose, a forcing of the patient out of real life, an alienating of him from reality. . . . Neurotics turn away from reality because they find it unbearable—either the whole or parts of it. The most extreme type of this turning away from reality is shown by certain cases of hallucinatory psychosis. . . . But in fact every neurotic does the same with some fragment of reality. And we are now confronted with the task of investigating the development of the relation of neurotics and of mankind in general to reality, and in this way of *bringing the psychological significance of the real external world into the structure of our theories.* [1911, p. 218; italics added]

According to Freud, then, the experience of alienation, of turning away from reality or certain aspects of reality, is the result or possibly the aim of all neurotic and psychotic manifestations. The psychoanalyst is therefore inclined to interpret such phenomena as the alienation of modern youth as a neurotic symptom or, at times, a psychotic withdrawal from external reality in the sense in which Freud uses the term. This interpretation presupposes, however, that the psychoanalytic assumptions regarding psychic structure are applicable without modification to individuals whose perception of reality has undergone a radical transformation. Freud's definition of the two principles of mental functioning, with its differentiation of pleasure principle and reality principle, foreshadows in a most condensed way the structural theory and its postulation of a differentiation of the mental apparatus into id, ego, and superego. Underlying these conceptualizations is, however, the postulation of a uniformly definable, or, to use Sullivan's (1953) terminology, consensually validatable, reality perception. Freud is very specific in the above-quoted passage in pointing out that the structure of our theories cannot be independent from our experience of the real external world.

During the years in which psychoanalysis developed as a theory, many changes in man's perception of external reality did in fact take place. Scientific advances and their technological application began to transform many aspects of external reality. Freud (1917) himself traced the blow that human narcissism suffered through the

Copernican Revolution and its impact on our cosmological perception, through Darwin's discovery of human evolution from animal ancestors, and, finally, through the discoveries of psychoanalysis itself, which revealed the limits of power of man's reason in controlling the forces shaping his life. Although the impact of these changes in the perception of reality on human self-perception was acknowledged, the possibility of a more radical shift in the functions by which the structure of the mental apparatus are defined, as a possible result of the transformation of reality perception, was not taken into consideration. This may possibly be due to what Novey (1955, p. 89) called "man's need to structure his environment so as to give him a feeling of security, which is often based, in a sense, upon a delusion. He needs to believe . . . that his life is a meaningful thing and that that which he looks upon as his self is a purposeful unitary thing." Novey also saw in natural science this need to structure our perception of the environment in the interest of our sense of security. Scientists say "that they seek for order in nature and that the guiding principle shall be that such order is inevitable. The logical extension is that there is order in man's existence as a part of nature." Although this view of order as delusion might have appeared to be an extreme position in 1955, today it is accepted as a simple statement of fact by many of the most advanced scientists.

Jacques Monod (1970), for instance, head of the Department of Cellular Biochemistry at the Institut Pasteur in Paris, winner of the 1965 Nobel Prize in medicine and physiology, published in the fall of 1970 his book *Le Hasard et la Necessité* (Chance and Necessity), with the subtitle "An Essay on the Natural Philosophy of Modern Biology." The following remarks are based on a discussion of Monod's impact in France by Dubois (1971). In this book, Monod asserts that life is the result of accident, and so, therefore, is man himself. "The universe was not pregnant with life, nor the biosphere with man." A product of chance, man must wake up "from his thousand-year-long dream and become aware of his complete solitude, his fundamental strangeness. He now knows that he is a kind of gypsy, on the fringe of the universe in which he must live. A universe which is deaf to his music, indifferent to his hopes, his sufferings, and his crimes." Monod has stated in his inaugural lecture as Professor of Biology at the Collège de France,

November, 1967: "It is by chance that man has no importance in the universe, that he counts for nothing: even his emergence is a result of chance; this, the principle result of science, is also the most unacceptable." Monod's thesis invalidates any vision of the world which sees in man and nature the ordered realization of a plan. This includes the Christian vision, of course. But he also dismisses just as coolly the dialectical materialism of Marx and Engels, and other ideologies. Science has destroyed all the old value systems. "It ruins all the mythical and philosophical ontogenies on which rested all the values, morality, rights, duties and prohibitions . . . of the tradition."

For Monod, just as for Novey, to derive from science any principle of order in nature, and, by extension, in man's existence is, indeed, a delusion. Novey felt that man could not exist without some such delusion, because its absence would burden him with a degree of insecurity that he could not endure. Monod feels, on the contrary, that man cannot afford any more delusions if he is to survive on this planet. Aside from the effects of ever more rapid technological change as described by sociologists, science itself has brought about a radical change in the perception of reality. It is not necessary to assume, however, that the change in perception we have been observing in the younger generation is based on a systematic study or even an acquaintance with modern science. Like all revolutionary changes that pertain to man's way of perceiving himself in the world, man's complete solitude, his fundamental strangeness, his gypsy experience on the fringe of the universe has been the universal experience of twentieth-century man long before Monod. For many decades such perceptions have been the dominant vision in all the arts, in literature, in music, and, last but not least, in the art film (Roszak 1969, Lifton 1970, 1971). The themes reiterated in the contemporary arts—the sense of the absurd, of meaninglessness, of chance—reflect this fundamental change in the perception of reality. And in turn it is through the medium of the arts and their reflection of the disintegration of the social order that this change has become an integral part of the experience of the younger generation, especially the educated young. They do not have to read Monod to learn about man's gypsy existence on the fringe of the universe. They live this gypsy existence, and many of them feel that it is the only life that they can live without participating in the official "delusions of order" that Novey spoke about. (For a recent fictional treatment of these issues, see Rhinehart 1971.)

STRUCTURAL THEORY AND CHANGING REALITY PERCEPTION

How radical this change in reality perception has been within the last half-century becomes apparent when we listen to Freud (1911) describing the ascendancy of the reality principle over the pleasure principle—certainly one of the fundamental conceptualizations of psychoanalytic theory. External reality, according to Freud, imposes frustrations upon the growing individual. But while the reliance on hallucinatory wish-fulfillment had to be abandoned, this sacrifice was in fact more apparent than real: "Actually, the substitution of the reality principle for the pleasure principle implies no deposing of the pleasure principle, but only a safeguarding of it. A momentary pleasure, uncertain in its results, is given up, but only in order to gain along the new path an assured pleasure at a later time" (Freud 1911, p. 223). Freud could thus approvingly quote George Bernard Shaw's dictum—"To be able to choose the line of greatest advantage instead of yielding in the direction of least resistance"—as an apt expression of the superiority of the reality ego over the pleasure ego.

These quotations illuminate the extent of the transformation of the perception of reality that has taken place since Freud's time. Science and its technical application have had consequences even more radical than the speeding-up and unpredictability of change that Bennis and Slater describe. Science raises the question whether we can indeed be sure that by giving up the "momentary pleasure" the pleasure principle might hold out for us, we will gain an "assured pleasure" at a later time. Does not the concept of an "assured pleasure" postulate an orderly, lawful, not chance-dominated (in other words, trustworthy) reality? How trustworthy is a reality that is controlled by chance? And what assurance can anyone have that there will be any pleasure, as Freud holds, "at a later time?" Today we wonder: will there be a "later time." It is hard, indeed, to be alive today and not ask such questions.

For Freud, however, pessimist that he was with regard to the human condition, nature, the "external reality," was not in doubt: it would be there to fulfill basic human needs if man was willing to accept limitations. It also was reasonable for Freud to assume there would be a "later time." These were premises that no scientist of Freud's generation would have doubted, and they form a part of Freud's most basic conceptualizations. It was the successful substitution of the pleasure principle by the reality principle from which originate, according to Freud, consciousness, attention, memory, and such ego functions as judgment and thought. All these changes in the functioning of the mental apparatus are traceable to the impact of external reality. They are adaptive functions acquired, in Freud's (1911) words, "to form a conception of the real circumstances in the external world and to endeavour to make a real alteration in them.... what was presented in the mind was no longer what was agreeable but what was real, even if it happened to be disagreeable" (p. 219). This assumption especially underlies the psychoanalytic approach to sexuality (see also chapter 12): here the emphasis throughout is on the superiority of real satisfactions obtainable only through the development of stable (i.e., potentially lasting) object relationships in comparison to which immediately available gratifications involving unstable (i.e., here-and-now-oriented) object relationships are judged to be immature and basically unsatisfactory, insofar as they can only provide "a momentary pleasure, uncertain in its results"—in short, a satisfaction lacking the enduring quality of reality. Neurotic and psychotic individuals, in Freud's (1926) view, are unable to perceive reality as capable of granting the possibility of lasting gratification. They distort reality, in that they see dangers where there are none. They "remain infantile in their behavior in regard to danger and do not overcome determinants of anxiety which have grown out of date" (p. 148). The neurotic, in Freud's (1926) words, "behaves as though the old danger-situations [such as castration, abandonment, etc.] still existed" (p. 147). Thus, Freud (1911) can say that "An essential part of the psychical disposition to neurosis thus lies in the delay in educating the sexual instincts to pay regard to reality and, as a corollary, in the conditions which make this delay possible" (p. 223). In all these formulations is an implication that reality, properly perceived, is *less* threatening than the fantasy world of the infant and the child, and, furthermore, that the dangers man faces are not so overpowering as to jeopardize the possibility of meaningful gratifications on many levels of human existence. It is precisely this assumption that the changes of reality perception have radically undermined. The psychoanalyst is therefore confronted with the challenging question whether a profound change in reality perception has not brought about equally profound changes in the functions of the psychic structures that Freud postulated and finally conceptualized as the id, the ego, and the superego—and which we still tend to take for granted so far as their functions are concerned. Can we still say, without qualification, as Hartmann, Kris, and Loewenstein did in 1946, that *"Functions of the id* center around the basic needs of man and their striving for gratification. . . .[and that] *Functions of the ego* center around the relation to reality. . . .[and] *Functions of the superego* center around moral demands"* (p. 15)? It is my thesis that we can observe in younger patients, in varying degrees of extremeness, striking functional shifts regarding these patterns of mental activity. I have repeatedly observed that id functions, especially sexuality, center around an urgent need to support a sense of one's own reality as a person as well as to discover in sexual experience the reality of another. Ego functions seem, in younger patients, to center on defensive maneuvers against vast areas of reality experience (school, jobs, and the like) that are perceived as threatening one's survival as a person, areas that formerly did not have these threatening connotations. ("In order to survive we stealcheatlieforge—hideanddeal.") Superego functions center around the effort to maintain a sense of personal integrity and continuity (see also chapter 12) in the face of the speed-up of environmental change. But, most importantly, superego functions seem to support extreme efforts to retain a sense of being uniquely human against the pressure of overpowering dehumanizing forces. These dehumanizing forces are usually equated with "the" culture, "the" establishment. For instance, resisting the pressures of these forces to accede to any form of participation in "the" culture by choosing a life work, such as a profession, can be a powerful superego demand.

The introduction of theoretical propositions implying reformulations of established psychoanalytic concepts demands a justification of the necessity for such far-reaching re-evaluation of basic psychoanalytic assumptions. This justification can only be found in the therapeutic process itself, in the actuality of the "psychoanalytic situation" (Stone 1961). In the Freud Anniversary Lecture bearing this title, Stone concludes his re-examination of the nature of the psychoanalytic situation as follows (p. 111):

In the classical psychoanalytic situation, we have an instrumentality of unique scientific productiveness, also of tremendous
psychodynamic range and power. It can, however, be improved,
not only as a therapeutic instrument, but in a genuinely scientific
sense, if we accept confrontation with certain ineluctable, if not as
yet well-formulated, psychological realities. For these are always,
by common agreement, more important than formulations as
such, however convincing the latter may seem in primary logical
encounter, and however valuable their actual historical contribution may have been, and may indeed continue to be. Their
continued, perhaps increasing, value may indeed rest on the open-
mindedness with which they are repeatedly tested against our
realities, and brought into conformity with them, as opposed to
their arbitrary preservation as ideal standards, to which exigent
realities must somehow be adapted.

The following clinical examples are reported with the intent to test
our traditional concepts of id, ego, and superego functions against
what seemed "ineluctable psychological realities" with which some
young people today are confronted and to which they respond in new
and often hazardous ways.

THE CHANGING FUNCTION OF THE ID (A CASE HISTORY)

Ronnie is twenty-six years old, an only child of middle-class parents.
He is finishing his education by acquiring an advanced academic
degree. He is, therefore, no dropout, nor is he at odds with his parents.
Though he feels that he cannot communicate with them, he has a sense
of loyalty to them. He had always been regarded as a good son; he had
had good grades in school, and had never really been in trouble.
Ronnie came to me because of what he called his "sex problems." He
was also taking drugs—anything except heroin—including some
rather rare forms of hallucinogenic drugs which he injected
intravenously. This, however, he considered not a problem, but rather
a sort of research project. Ronnie's sex problem had several aspects.
He had been sexually involved with girls rather early, by the time he
was in high school. There had always been girls in his life, and,

although sometimes he had lost out to other boys, he could be described as really quite successful in that most of the girls he was interested in were quite responsive, and apparently none refused to have sex relations with him. Some of the girls were strikingly beautiful, had appeared as cover girls on magazines, and had had previous involvements with rather well-known public personalities. Nevertheless, Ronnie felt that he was sexually inadequate. He thought he might be homosexual and had tried some homosexual relationships with very virile-looking men. This, however, did not make him happy either

One rather striking aspect of Ronnie's relations with girls was the fact that Ronnie was anything but casual about the numerous girls he was involved with—often several at the same time. But he was not a woman chaser, not a Don Juan type aiming at conquests. He was very serious about each girl who came into his life: yet he was always disappointed in himself. He was looking for some supreme experience of ecstasy in which he would reach an orgasm that would make him feel blissfully happy, simultaneously with the girl, whom he would thus initiate to the same ecstatic happiness, a happiness she supposedly had never experienced before. Then, and only then, would he feel adequate. Most of the time, he felt dejected and depressed. It was the same yearning for ecstasy that motivated his elaborate drug experiments. These, too, left him disappointed, even though he experienced many extraordinary, long-lasting highs. Sex and drug experiences finally joined, in that he wanted any girl that he was involved with to take drugs together with him, in the hope that they both would reach that ultimate state of bliss which was his aim. These experiments were especially disappointing to him because the drugs very frequently had the opposite effect: they made him and the girl feel estranged from one another. In some respects, one could say that, in the terminology of Bennis and Slater, girls were interchangeable for Ronnie. But that was only true in part. Actually, Ronnie did care about one girl especially for a long time. She was the only girl he talked about in terms of marriage. She was also the girl with whom he felt particularly inadequate, because he could not reach a simultaneous climax with her. This he perceived as the absolute proof of human failure.

I have sketched this patient's dilemma as he saw it because I believe that it implies a shift in the function of sexuality. Ronnie was a bright young man and could have done better in his studies had he not been so preoccupied with his problems. But the possibility of academic success meant absolutely nothing to him. For Ronnie, sexuality was the only experience that could convey a sense of conviction concerning the reality of himself as a person and the reality of another person. He experimented with drugs for the same reason. Ronnie was not a political activist. Rather, he was something of a chronically depressed Hell's Angel, insofar as his one great passion aside from girls and drugs was his motorcycle. He loved this Hell's-Angel image of himself, and he roamed through the United States and Europe, an Uneasy Rider in search of a reality that would suddenly be revealed to him.

Ronnie's case seems to relate closely to a suggestion of K.R. Eissler's (1958), dealing with problems of adolescence. Eissler proposes "that orgasm . . . when viewed in its relationship to the ego must contain a meaning and function beyond the attainment of pleasure and the reduction of tension" (1958, p. 237). According to Eissler "it becomes reasonable to assume that there are . . . archaic forms [of experience] which provide man with the conviction of truth. . . . I hypothesize that one of the ego functions of orgasm is to ascertain . . . truth" (p. 239). Eissler asserts "that orgasm is the strongest affirmation possible to man. . . . The truth that is affirmed by orgasm is not represented by words and not necessarily by explicit fantasies. . . . Orgasm is endowed with the power to confirm, create and affirm conviction" (p. 242). I would add to this last statement: conviction of one's own reality and the reality of another. What Eissler suggests here touches upon some very archaic, nonverbal ways to affirm what he calls "truth." It does not seem unlikely that a profound change in reality perception, characterized by a failure to develop a consensual sense of truth and falsehood—by means of more conceptualized formal thought processes and verbal expressions—compels the individual to use the sexual experience in the service of a desperate effort at affirmation of the reality of the self and the other, thus reactivating, in Eissler's words, archaic forms of ascertaining truth. This is what I consider a shift in the function of psychic structures.

Lifton (1970, 1971) has approached some of these phenomena with a slightly different emphasis. Rather than focusing on the change in function of the psychic structures under the impact of a change in reality perception, he concentrates on the tendency of modern individuals to use a variety of identities as interchangeable masks. Here the concept of interchangeability turns up once more, but Lifton does not mean the interchangeability of persons with whom one establishes temporary relationships, as Bennis and Slater describe it, but the interchangeability of identities of the same individual. He calls this the "Protean style" which, in his words, "is characterized by constant shifts in identification and belief, and results from such broad factors as the velocity of historical change, the revolution in mass media, and the effects of the 20th-century holocaust. The self can no longer be considered a fixed concept in psychiatry, and the term self-process is preferable" (1971, p. 298).

There are aspects of Ronnie's personality that bring to mind Lifton's Protean life-style. Ronnie maintained a kind of traditional identity insofar as he aimed to become a professional person after finishing his studies. But he enjoyed as well the Hell's-Angel image, into which he could slip with ease. Because he was quite good with his hands, he also liked the role of a kind of master craftsman. He mostly thought of himself—these were his words—as a kind of guru who could, by a process of sexual gnosis, initiate others to a discovery of their true selves. That his various ways of defining himself were often in conflict with one another was to be expected.

If we attempt, however, to evaluate the total psychodynamic balance in Ronnie's seemingly impulse-ridden efforts to establish a meaningful life for himself, we must be mindful of Stone's previously quoted admonition to "accept confrontation with certain ineluctable . . . psychological realities." We will then give due weight to the fact that a young contemporary like Ronnie cannot but perceive himself as living in a world offering only temporary and uncertain gratifications, a world whose very existence in the future appears questionable. It is in this context that Ronnie's sexual promiscuity and compulsive experimentation with drugs, as well as his shifting self-definitions have to be understood. What would have appeared, in the classical psychoanalytic situation, as a clear indication of ego defect and impairment of reality adaptation, we must now acknowledge as a shift of the adaptive function to the id in the face of a radically altered perception of reality. Sexuality becomes a search for an "alternate reality," a search aiming at an affirmation of the reality of one's own existence in relation to another person who is capable of sharing the ecstatic bliss of mutual affirmation. It thus becomes an act of faith in the possibility of one's own and the other one's humanity, a faith in the possibility of meaning—a possibility that is cruelly questioned by the scientific vision of nature and by the inability of the social organization to create a human order capable of averting the self-destruction of mankind, if not of life itself.

THE CHANGING FUNCTION OF THE SUPEREGO: A CASE HISTORY

These very same "ineluctable psychological realities" (Stone 1961) led another patient, Joan, to an even more radical and more desperate struggle to maintain a sense of continuity of herself by means of shifting the function of her superego from the traditional representation of the demands of the social and cultural environment to the very negation of these demands: only through that extreme shift in superego function did she manage to cling to a precarious sense of her own identity in the face of an overwhelmingly threatening perception of a potentially-destructive "external reality." Joan was twenty-eight when I first saw her. She was unmarried, and in dress, speech, manner, and beliefs she seemed to be an intelligent and articulate representative of the counterculture (Roszak 1969). The oldest of three siblings, she is the daughter of affluent parents. Joan's father is a self-made man, proud of having achieved affluence and status in his small community. He is intolerant, given to fits of rage when his wishes are not obeyed. Joan has had a violently ambivalent relation with her father from an early age. In spite of a deep involvement, their relation has been characterized by fierce clashes that began when Joan was only a schoolgirl. Her father insisted on shaping Joan in the image of the "ideal" daughter, whose life would culminate in her marriage to a successful young man from an established family.

Having a similar temper to that of her father, Joan rebelled in every possible way. In adolescence, she antagonized her father by choosing her boy friends from among ethnic groups and social classes that were anathema to him. When she was sixteen, she hid in the home of a boy with whom she had a passionate romance that lasted for several years. She was, of course, soon discovered in her hideaway, and more violent scenes followed. She was a good student, even though she did not study very hard. After graduation, she went to a university that had her father's approval because it was considered acceptable by many of his social peers. She felt very different from the average students. In her own words, she was a hippie before the concept became fashionable. The young men she befriended were outsiders too, and even though she had the opportunity to marry a young man who would have been acceptable to her family, she broke her engagement because the idea of settling down in marriage profoundly frightened her.

During her college years, she developed severe anxieties pertaining to her work for the first time. While she had never had any trouble with her studies in high school, in college she became frightened about tests, term papers, and participation in class. She nevertheless obtained her bachelor's degree and settled for several years in New York City. She worked for the Welfare Department, getting first-hand impressions of the ghetto, the poor, and the world of the drug addicts. It was at this time that certain attitudes toward the social order that she had never before clearly formulated became conceptualized. She had for many years rejected her parents', especially her father's, social values. She perceived them as unreal and false and had refused to identify with them. Now she became consciously opposed to the establishment, although this did not lead to active political militancy. She made friends among artists, writers, theater people. They seemed to her to be in touch with what was real and meaningful. She had always had artistic inclinations, especially in music. She soon became intensely involved with all the avant-garde movements in the arts—the mixed-media experiments, light shows, experimental theater, electronic music, etc.

But by far the most important influence was the group around Timothy Leary, in whose home at Millbrook, New York, she was a frequent guest. Here were people who, like her, were convinced that the traditional reality was meaningless if not dead, that the true reality was accessible only through consciousness expansion. It was here that she was introduced to smoking pot and, after long hesitation, to LSD. Her first LSD trip was an unforgettable experience. She perceived it as a revelation of what was truly real, and it seemed to confirm to her what she had dimly felt all her life. She became aware that there are really no objects, that everything is force, energy that flows through what is living, as well as through inanimate objects, in unbroken waves or vibrations. She began to read articles on modern physics in *Scientific American,* which bore out her feeling that there was no objectivity, no mechanistic laws and that the ordinary reality of every day life represented only one limited dimension of what was real. She liked to quote Timothy Leary as saying that men must learn to live on all dimensions of reality at once and not be confined to the so-called objective reality. She took LSD for a limited time only, because further attempts did not reach the same meaningful intensity that she had experienced the first time. Rather, she felt that further experimentation might confuse her. With her psychedelic experience she had gained a sense of confirmation of a truer reality than the reality to which she was expected to adapt herself and in which she knew she should be able to live.

This, however, posed a formidable problem for her. Although she had a profound yearning for emotional closeness to others, none of her numerous love affairs helped her to overcome her fear that any lasting relationship would imprison her sooner or later in a world of things which would stand between her and what for her was real. She encountered the same problem in all her efforts to achieve a place for herself in some field, preferably the arts. While she had the highest respect for people who were able to create and to achieve, she was overcome with anxiety whenever she attempted, even with authoritative encouragement, to give her creative ideas objective expression. This conflict she has not been able to solve. On the contrary, it has deepened as the years have gone on. She spent nearly two years in various European countries, especially in an artists' colony in the Mediterranean. Here she was among people who shared her reality perception. Some were able to translate it into structured work, while others were not. In the end she panicked, feeling that she was losing touch with everything, and she came back to the United States.

Joan can be very coherent, rational, and persuasive when talking intellectually about the issues that she sees as essential. She is well read and is familiar with existentialist philosophy, the writings of Antonin Artaud, and, last but not least, R.D. Laing. She, is however, unable to bridge the inner gap between a reality perception that absorbs her, as she calls it, into an inner space, and the competitive world around her. She feels temporarily at peace when she can be in touch with nature, but she yearns for a shared life with others, emotional contact, and meaningful communication, and this, more and more, evades her.

This is a fragment of an extraordinarily complex psychological dilemma. It would not be difficult to use well-known psychiatric labels for Joan's condition. But what seems to me pertinent in the context of this paper is the fact that Joan's experience is one shared by many young people today. The central issue is a fundamental change in reality perception. Once this change has been experienced, the function of the ego is to defend this new perception against falsification by the so-called objective reality. At the same time, a way has to be found to live with the new reality perception without losing oneself entirely in one's private world. The new reality perception demands a new shared world, a task that seems in many cases to be taxing the resources of the individual to its breaking point. What the ego is challenged to accomplish in this situation is fundamentally different from what Hartmann could define as adaptation to an average expectable environment. Especially, we see that the function of the superego in Joan's development is to maintain her personal sense of integrity against the pressures of a value system, represented by her parents, which she considers destructive to her sense of self. The difference between the schizophrenic process, as we are used to applying the term, and Joan's dilemma is that an unambiguous, universally shared meaning of reality is today evading us, thus forcing the individual to choose among a multitude of contradictory realities. Some of the most sensitive young people are being destroyed by this predicament.

PSYCHOANALYSIS AND THE CHALLENGE OF THE FUTURE

My presentation of Ronnie and Joan are obviously mere fragments of much richer and far more complex life stories. I have focused on certain themes that seem to me typical of conflicts in young patients. These conflicts differ in my opinion, from those that are presented by older people undergoing therapy. I attribute the difference to a radical transformation of reality perception. Due to this transformation, the perception of danger is also changed and thus different patterns of defense are elicited. To conceptualize these struggles in terms of the classical conflict situation of ego aims versus id pressures, or of superego demands versus ego interests is likely to be misleading, because the reality of the dangers for these young people is thus misconstrued, and their often very desperate defense efforts are completely misunderstood and misinterpreted as, for instance, a flight from mature adult responsibilities. The range of conflicts with which the young of today must deal, is, however, compounded by a kind of double-take effect concerning reality perception. This is due to the fact that the young child today, as in the past, is prepared for a reality that is relatively stable, predictable, and, for most children, trustworthy. This is caused not so much by what parents tell their children, but by the way children perceive their parents: as powerful, omniscient, just, and, hopefully, loving. We have noted Hartmann's (1939) observation that the rewards and punishments which the child learns to expect in his interaction with his parents will only partly coincide with those he will actually receive from society later. In today's world, however, the expectations awakened in the child by his parents are in irreconcilable conflict with the realities of nature and society as perceived by the young adult. The discrepancy between the reality presented by the parental environment and the later experienced reality does more than make parental perceptions, beliefs, and values obsolete. Rather, it causes them to appear fictitious, fraudulent, and evil. And thus the possibility of a shared reality based on a consensually validated experience breaks down, and with it the possibility of shared moral values. What emerges as value from an earlier reality perception becomes an antivalue for those who cannot help but perceive reality in a radically changed way. Defiantly they sing that "we are all outlaws in the eyes of America" and proudly they proclaim that in order to survive they "stealcheatlieforge," are "obscenelawlesshideousdangerousdirty-violent," and, of course, *young*. Yes, they say, we are your enemy—and thus the war is on. Facing this radical challenge to their deepest, most cherished convictions, those whose lives have been built upon an older, more hopeful reality perception, feel bewildered, enraged, and often ready to kill when they are confronted with what must feel to be a sacrilegious, satanic force. Yet, as we study the dynamic forces that compel young people to adopt extreme and dangerous methods of living in today's world, it becomes clear that they are indeed making a desperate effort to survive, to find a way to adapt to the new and threatening reality as they perceive it. The powers of the id, the ego, and the superego are quite recognizable, but they have undergone a radical modification of function.

To the psychiatrist, these young people might appear on the verge of personality disintegration, but that might well be deceptive. These extreme experiments of reordering existential priorities are often recognizable as a mobilization of new adaptive possibilities. We, as psychiatrists, must accept the fact of indeterminacy as we evaluate a person's or a group's adaptive balance. This is not a time for schematic diagnostic labeling of phenomena that are as strange and disquieting to us as is the new reality that is gradually closing in on all of us, young and old alike. I think it is dangerous, however, to minimize the depth of the abyss that separates the young and the old. It is not really just a gap, but often enough it is an unbridgeable chasm. Radical changes in reality perception have hardly ever, so far as I know, been settled by compromise in human history. The world of antiquity disintegrated under the impact of the Christian vision of reality. And the Christian reality perception, as open to compromise with science as it has been, seems in great danger of losing its capacity to provide even Western man with a consensus as to what is real. Thus I am unable to share the messianic hopefulness of Reich (1970) for a renaissance of human life, born without as much as even a birth pang, by a sudden burst of youthful enthusiasm. I think we should be aware that, however sympathetic we might be with the desperate struggles of the young, we, whose personality development has been shaped by a different perception of reality, cannot replace our own values with others that would find more sympathy with the young. It is our reality perception that determines our deepest sense of identity, and even if we wanted to, we could not will ourselves another identity.

This poses a grave problem for the psychoanalyst whose work is founded on meaningful communication based on the use of language. But, as the linguists tell us, language is the precipitate of old and mostly unconscious ways to perceive reality. In his film *Le Gai Savoir* Jean-Luc Godard (1969) goes far beyond the Jefferson Airplane singers: For him it is not our property that is the target; the "enemy" is language, because words imprison us in fixed ways of seeing the world. Godard wants us to believe that *no* new *shared* reality perception can be built without first systematically destroying language, destroying words, and all their old associations. The revolution must build an entirely new language that will shape a new man. These are disturbing thoughts. I believe, however, that psychoanalysis, having itself contributed so much to destroy old and dead ways to perceive reality, has a special obligation to confront the dangerous, the inevitable necessity that Freud liked to call *Ananke* (1930). It is the very ethos of psychoanalysis that comples us to be aware of all the realities that shape the human condition—not just those of the past, as is often charged, but equally those of today and those of tomorrow.

Chapter 15

PSYCHOANALYSIS CHALLENGED

There can be no question that psychotherapy, especially psychoanalytic psychotherapy, is at present in a state of crisis and that its future is in doubt. Supporting this statement are not only the ever more strident voices of criticism raised against psychoanalytic theory and practice (Agel 1971) but the words of our most outstanding psychoanalytic theorists and practitioners, such as Eissler (1969):

> Psychoanalysis is not able to provide the tools with which to combat the majority of forms in which drug addiction is now making its appearance among the younger generation in the United States. It seems that, just as psychoanalysis is, with few exceptions, not the method of choice in acute conditions, so it is not prepared to stem the tide of that form of psychopathology that is provoked by anomie. The dissolution of societal structures does not travel solely the path of lessening the strength of institutions and finally abolishing them entirely... but also the path of reducing structure in individuals. The structure of the ensuing psychopathology seems to be quite different from the pathology whose treatment led to the evolvement of psychoanalysis.... It is my impression that the field of psychoanalytic therapy is diminished during periods of latent or manifest revolutions.

The problems raised by Eissler are by no means confined to psychoanalysis; they make themselves felt in other forms in any mode of psychiatric treatment, be it community psychiatry, drug treatment, or, last but not least, psychosurgery. This is because the revolution that Eissler speaks of raises basic issues concerning the *raison d'être* of the field of psychiatry itself—a theme recently treated by Mandell and Schuckit (1972):

> Professors of Psychiatry and their [politically] committed new students are currently engaged in a struggle concerning the meaning of the field itself. I think the first year residents...are asking in a far more formidable way than ever before, what is psychiatry? And they have added a question or two: Why is psychiatry? Should there be a psychiatry?

The conceptual and educational predicament of psychiatry in general and psychoanalysis in particular, to which the above quotes refer, has its roots in a phenomenon that virtually defines a "world in crisis." A world is in crisis when it is nearly impossible to establish a rather generally accepted consensus—at least within a given culture—of what is real (Novey 1966). While there is never a complete consensus among all people living within a certain culture as to what is real (what for one group of people might be a well-established causal correlation between events may be for their contemporaries elsewhere an obvious case of "superstition"), today the perception of what is real is no longer shared even by groups who have a comparable educational background. The chasm of opinion dividing people in the United States concerning the reality of what happened in Vietnam is just one obvious example of this fact. This lack of consensus applies to the most vital issues of every person's life: about being male or female, a success or a dropout, on drugs or not on drugs, sexually "liberated" or "uptight," white or black or nonwhite. The list could be continued. In each of these areas of nonconsensus—different age groups, different career groups, different sex groups—not even a semblance of agreement about what is real can be established.

It is therefore not at all surprising that psychiatry in general and psychoanalysis in particular (for which the issue of *what is real* is thematic in the same sense in which the question of what is artistic is thematic for those professionally committed to the arts) should feel the pain of anomie and the breakdown of communication more keenly than almost any other group or professionals. Superficially it seems rather clear why this crisis condition has arisen in the world of today. During the last few hundred years the Western world started to rely on certain criteria of what was to be considered "real." These criteria were defined in terms of "scientific proof" that A was real and B was not, because B could not be validated according to the principles of scientific validation. The inherent dangers to a consensus concerning reality based on scientific evidence soon became apparent to the philosophers because the most basic aspects of reality, on which meaning and order in life depend, are not capable of being proved scientifically.

Kant's *Critique of Pure Reason* (1781) was perhaps the most encompassing effort to limit the area of science in order to prevent the faith in meaning from being destroyed by science. But Kant's work did not stop the conquest of the human realm by the process of applied scientific reasoning. Kant could argue that reason itself compelled us to set limits to its applicability because Kant equated knowledge and consciousness. This equation of consciousness with knowledge was, however, soon to be challenged.

According to Ricoeur (1970), there were three challenges that made Western man suspicious of the trustworthiness of human consciousness. These three challenges are tied to the names of Marx, Nietzsche, and Freud. Marx showed that human consciousness reflected man's economic self-interest. Nietzsche, the prophet of nihilism, revealed that man's religious and moral consciousness served the need to interpret reality as essentially man-centered. Freud discovered that human consciousness protected man from the awareness that more often than not he was using reason to conceal from himself profoundly irrational and amoral strivings.

Thus, the problem of what is real—if all knowledge is based on interpretation of experience from a specific viewpoint—invaded the totality of our thinking just as inexorably as the application of science in the form of technology not only conquered the Western world but became the fate of mankind, regardless of the cultural tradition that had prevailed before. It is against this background that psychiatry and psychoanalysis are criticized for defining what is real under the disguise of science in such a way as to give aid and comfort to whatever the ruling classes may consider expedient in defense of their own economic and political self-interest.

It is against the same background that we must understand the breakdown of the possibility of a consensus concerning the definition of what is real. Today everyone has an equal right to claim that his perception of what is real is the only valid one because, in the absence of any agreed upon criteria for demonstrating what deserves to be considered "real," individuals as well as groups rely on what Eissler (1958) called the "emotional conviction of truth." Should we, then, in the face of such relativeness of the experience of what is real, accept everybody's emotional conviction of truth as equally valid? Should we, in order not to give offense, consider every human experience that carries conviction as equally authentic? Or possibly consider the experience that carries conviction as equally authentic? Or possibly consider the experience that is especially inaccessible to us more authentic than that whose perception of reality we may be able to share? Should we, because the social order—any social order— imposes its special kind of distortion on our sense of what is real, see it as our task to prepare our patients to engage in combat with that particular order that has distorted their self-images and thus contributed to their sense of isolation and alienation? There are psychiatrists who have advocated some or all of these alternatives. They misjudge, in my opinion, the radical implications of the insights of psychoanalytic psychology concerning the perception of what is real.

I think that there can be no doubt, on the basis of clinical experience and studies of the development of the sense of reality in children, that human beings do not have an inherent consensus of what is real. I believe that for each child what is real would be an individual, not shareable experience, were not a consensus regarding what is real *imposed* on the growing child. This consensus is imposed by the parents, by the tribe, by the social structure. The most important means of imposing a shared sense of what is real among human beings is to teach children the language of the group in which they are reared. Human beings are not provided with an innate sense of what is real, as animals, in order to survive, apparently are. It is obvious that the survival of any group of living beings depends on its ability to share a sense of what is real. Thus, human beings are existentially endangered because of the individuality and privacy of their sense of what is real.

We know that children go through a stage of magic thinking which implies a very special sense of causality that differs profoundly from the "adult" concept of causality. But even within the magic reality of a child's world there are highly individual differences. Not every child fears horses, as Little Hans, or feels to the same degree compelled to avoid certain thoughts, or fears touching certain parts of his body or his environment. For each of these children there is a separate sense of what is real, what is dangerous, what is safe. It is only because the adults impose a consensus regarding what is to be considered real— this is what education is all about—that most children develop a capacity to perceive what is real in accordance with the consensus prevailing in their environment.

The neurotic child or adult can say, "I ought not to be afraid of ghosts; I know they are not real," but the severe phobic patient, in the throes of phobic anxiety, responds to an "unreal" danger with a terror that makes the personal danger totally and convincingly real to him. The more the sense of what is real remains an unshareable, private experience, the more excluded the individual becomes from the life of his group and the more endangered is his existence in a human world that is based on the sense of being a part of and a partner in the *collective* experience of living. The most extreme private and unshareable experiences of what is real for a given individual form the basis for the concept of mental illness because (and this is the meaning of *illness*) his chance of survival is impaired or foredoomed.

Contrary to what Szasz (1961) claims, having "problems of living" constitutes exactly what individuals *share* with one another, it defines them as healthy since they partake in the consensus of what is real. To experience an unrequited love and to grieve about the loss of a close relationship are problems of living that, because they can be shared with others, make an individual more, and not less, like the rest of his peers.

The inability of the individual to share in the consensus of what is real can be not only a matter of survival for the individual but also a threat to the survival of the group. It is for this reason that in human beings a consensus about what is real must be imposed and strictly enforced by the group, especially if it is small. The first political act, then, would be to impose on a group of individuals that depend on each other for survival a consensus of what is to be considered real. Man is a "zoon politicon" because he is not given, as innate endowment, a naturally shared perception of what is real. He is able, by complex methods of learning to speak and learning to think, to acquire a shared sense of what is real, which is the foundation for his possibility to survive as an individual within a larger group. It is this unique psychological complexity of human development—the process of individuation, uncovered first by psychoanalysis—that requires a social structure for the individual's and the group's survival.

A society is essentially an instrument for the imposition and maintenance of a consensus among a group of individuals of what they are to consider real and what to consider as not real. If the consensus disintegrates—if the traditional sense of what a group has been taught to consider real is no longer shared by large and powerful subgroups of a social organism—a new group whose perception of what is real serves the survival of a *majority* of the members of the social structure will by persuasion or force impose on society a new sense of *what is real*. This process we call revolution. A revolution means the replacement of one consensus of what is real by another one. In order to be successful, the new consensus must prove itself superior to the older one in terms of the survival needs of the majority of the society.

These considerations might appear farfetched in a paper devoted to psychoanalytic psychotherapy in a world in crisis. I believe, however, that they are fundamental for an understanding of the problems psychoanalysts face today, particularly with many of their younger patients, but also in terms of critical issues concerning psychoanalytic theory itself. Last but not least, they are essential if we are to enter into a dialogue with the radical young therapists who, as Mandell and Schuckit (1972) point out, insist on raising the very question of the meaning of psychotherapy, of psychiatry itself, in a most urgent manner.

THE RELATIVITY OF THE ID, THE EGO,
AND THE SUPEREGO FUNCTIONS

In chapter 14, I proposed that profound changes in reality perception, which occur in a great many patients in their late teens, twenties, and even later, have taken place due to rapid technological and social changes which form a basic new experience of the younger generation. Concepts like Hartmann's "average expectable environment" make little sense to a generation for which the only expectable element of their environment is its unpredictability. It is also argued that the permanence and immutability of nature, expressed by its lawfulness and order, have been a basic concept in Western European thought, shared by Kant as well as by Freud. The perception of what is real for the young generation, even as it applies to nature and the cosmos, is far less reassuring, if not outright menacing. These perceptions touch on deep fears of an earlier stage of development, especially the magic stage of experience, but they also reactivate powerful fears of abandonment and desertion by caring and loving persons only to find oneself all alone in a cold, indifferent, and potentially hostile world. As a matter of fact, it is difficult to speak of *fantasies* of desertion and abandonment. The expectation of love and caring, being part of any child's early experience if he is lucky enough to have a "good mother" in Winnicott's sense (1948), is rather more brutally disappointed in today's technological and mass society than it used to be in earlier stages of history, when relatively small communities tended to maintain a sort of parental interest for any member throughout his life.

In chapter 14, I proposed that under these circumstances there are significant shifts in the functions of the id, the ego, and the superego. It appears that the id, particularly the sexual strivings of the id, serves to support a very endangered sense of one's own reality against the threat of annihilation (one might think of Jones's concept of aphanisis, 1927) by a world perceived as hostile to a life of feeling. Sexual contact seems to support, albeit on a primitive level, a sense of being real, by being touched or held, by feeling another's body as a reassurance against the cold impersonality of the environment. Ego functions, in classical psychoanalytic theory, serve the adaption to "external reality." In the new perception of what is real, ego functions serve as a defense against being overpowered, fragmentized, deprived of one's sense of being a person—by an impersonal and destructive "reality" that often is equated with "the system," meaning, of course, the social forces that tend to be seen as evil powers by the young generation. The superego, far from internalizing parental and societal demands, seems to function as the defender of one's sense of integrity and authenticity against degrading parental and societal pressures. It is a superego that bears resemblance to the superego of the inmate of a concentration camp: its function is to resist the temptation to give in, in order to gain material or materialistic advantages, to fight for one's integrity in the face of an overpowering death machine.

It is obvious that these profound changes in the functions of id, ego, and superego must profoundly influence the therapeutic approach of the analyst. The phenomena referred to are obviously a common psychoanalytic experience today. I believe Eissler (1969) is calling attention to the same issues when he says that psychoanalysis has to deal today "with a kind of psychopathology that could be referred to—in accordance with modern trends in philosophy and literature—as existential."

Eissler goes on to state that "it seems that an increasing number of people have now taken to questioning human existence *per se*" While Eissler does not consider the raising of this issue as an indication for the treatment, he does, however, feel that

> quite frequently it appears in a distorted, twisted form, devoid of any constructive implication, and then it takes on forms that may be described as "dislocations and restrictions" of the ego—terms that Freud used to describe those alterations of the ego that cause great obstacles to psychoanalytic treatment.

Eissler adds, however, "that the deepening of our insight into the structure of the ego has made for a better prognosis in such cases."

These quotations from E ssler throw into sharp focus what I consider a central issue in psychoanalytic theory as well as therapeutic technique today. I believe, if I understand him correctly, that Eissler is speaking of the same manifestations that I have described above as *shifts* in the functions of the id, the ego, and the superego. He describes them, however, as distorted, twisted forms of dealing with existential issues and, more specifically, compares them to the dislocations and restrictions of the ego that Freud saw as a certain type of severe ego pathology.

The difference between the two formulations implies a theoretical problem, which deserves as precise a conceptualization as is possible at this stage of psychoanalytic theory. To me, the problem is whether, when we speak of functions of the id, the ego, and the superego, we are referring to absolutes, to givens of a general model of a human mind—comparable to speaking of functions of the respiratory, circulatory, and nervous systems in physiological terms. We assume that, physiologically speaking, they will be differentiated and definable in the same terms for any member of the human species at any place in the world, and at any stage in history. Do we imply an analogously absolute identity of function of id, ego, and superego for any thinkable pattern of "human mind"? I do not think we do—and many psychohistorical studies support this—but I also think that we should be more precise about what the functions of these structures are relative to. My proposition is that the functions of the id, ego, and superego are relative to the individual's perception of reality. According to Novey (1966), the concept of "external reality," as we use it in psychoanalysis, implies "that a common consensus could be established within a specific culture that a given event or situation has or has not transpired." We might find Novey's relativistic definition of the concept of "external reality" plausible, but I doubt that Freud would have considered it acceptable.

For Freud, as for any scientist and philosopher of his generation, external reality was not a matter of consensus but "a given fact," an ordered universe that was, due to its eternal laws, the ultimate measure to which all living things, including man, had to abide. It was the clearest manifestation of the Ananke that ruled all living existence. It might be considered stern and austere, but it was certain and reliable, so that bowing to the demands of reality was yielding to a superior order. Therefore the ascendency of the "reality principle" was a vast advance over the rule of the "pleasure principle," whose aims were, compared to the laws of reality, ephemeral and deceptive.

If we concede, as I think we must, that this view of "external reality" is no longer the accepted conceptualization of science (which today gives probability and chance a much greater range than earlier generations of scientists, including Einstein, could have been comfortable with), must we then not concede that our structural definition of id, ego, and superego functions, as formulated by Freud, is relative to a very specific, historically conditioned perception of reality? And if that is the case, are the "distorted and twisted" forms in which an increasing number of people deal with what Eissler recognizes as existential dilemmas, only 'distorted" because they are measured against a perception of "external reality" as an absolute principle of natural order?

This has been my impression in dealing with members of the younger generation, who accept as a matter of course that they live in a physical universe governed by randomness and about which nothing is certain that would matter to human beings. The very question whether man as a phenomenon has a future is part of their perception of the reality in which they live. Consequently, to experience themselves as real they must be capable of responding with instantaneous feelings to somebody else's feelings. To forego, in Freud's words (1911), a "momentary pleasure" for an "assured pleasure" in the future, is tantamount to foregoing something *unquestionably* real for something uncertain and therefore perceived as unreal.

The unconscious, Freud said, does not know any negation (1915). For Freud, this characteristic of the unconscious was its limitation because, in order to survive, man must acknowledge a reality even if it implies a negation of wishes and of needs. To be able to differentiate between what is real and not real is more important than to suffer the unpleasure of negated gratification. For Freud the experience of certainty, of safety (Sandler 1960), was the reward for acknowledging a trustworthy reality, even at the sacrifice of pleasure.

But for the new generation what reality negates is not pleasure, but existential affirmation. Many spokesmen of the counterculture postulate a spiritual universe, against the reality of which the "external reality" of science is irrelevant and represents the loss of man's existential roots (Roszak 1972, Weil 1972, Castaneda 1968, 1971, 1972). In contrast, the nonnegatable experience of wish-fulfillment, the yielding to feelings and desire, to sex, to drugs, to anything that provides an instant emotional contact with the individual's inner reality, is—as Eissler (1958) has pointed out—the most powerful affirmation of the experience of *existential* reality.

It is true that such reliance on the forces of the id to achieve an affirmative sense of being real can be described as a regression. It is not, in Kris's sense, a regression in the service of the ego, but rather a regression in the service of maintaining a sense of humanness. Thus, while there can be no doubt of the danger to human integration even if such regression is called forth as a defense, I would hesitate to deny it any constructive implication. Nor would I be inclined to equate it to those dislocations and restrictions of the ego, observed by Freud in certain patients, to which Eissler (1969) referred. There is a shift in the functions of id, ego, and superego (see chapters 11, 13, 14). One might say that the forces of the id assume a more adaptive existential function than previously attributed to them; the ego serves as a guardian against the dangers emanating from what is felt as a dehumanizing reality; and the superego represents the moral claim to the right of one's own perception of what is real. Thus, the superego is more often than not in opposition to parental and societal moral attitudes, which are likely to be based on an historically earlier perception of what is real.

A good example of this last point is the women's liberation movement, whose power and persuasiveness undoubtedly derived from its moral appeal to existential values. This appeal, based on a new way of perceiving what is real, makes the "old way" of reality perception tantamount to a distortion of the existential priorities for the sake of power relations.

Thus, we are again confronted with the problem of the relativity of the functions of id, ego, and superego. They are relative, not primarily to cultural patterns or political attitudes, but to changes in the perception of what is real. "Culture" and "political preconceptions" are themselves nothing but ways to impose, within a social group, a consensus of what is real.

This relativity of the functions of intrapsychic structures poses formidable theoretical problems, not only for psychoanalysis but for many more general "humanistic" concerns, such as the question of the priority of some values over others. Perhaps these latter, vaster problems—raised with such fervor today in regard to the value of psychotherapy and of psychiatry in general—will become more accessible after exploring the narrower issue of the pertinence of the relativity of those functions traditionally assigned to psychic structures.

THE PERCEPTION OF REALITY AS "A DELUSIONAL PROCESS"

Freud's discovery that the human mind encompasses processes of which the individual is not conscious, but which nevertheless exert a powerful influence on his beliefs, values, and motivations, especially the loves and hates that determine his actions, can be seen as a blow at the Cartesian tradition in Western European thought. No longer could one maintain, after Freud, that the reality of one's thinking and the reality of one's being were related in such a way that the former was the sole and exclusive condition for the truth of the latter. As psychiatrists we know that the reality of the experience of one's thought processes is compatible with doubt regarding the reality of one's existence. The depersonalized individual may be quite aware of his thought processes, but nevertheless have a sense of not being real. We are also familiar with the experience of perceiving one's thought as emanating from outside one's person.

Freud taught us that there is a *me* that is under the sway of drives, passions, and overwhelming needs that are not "in my interest" in the way my rational, reasoning thought processes would interpret "my interest." We have learned that this other *me* exists in a world of magic interaction between people, a world that is not experienced in terms of the "starry heavens above me" of Kant,[1] but as a universe of human bodies and minds interacting with one another, where all the manifestations of our and other's physical reality—the experience of touching, smelling, eating, urinating, defecating, being touched, being smiled at, being held—carry much more conviction and power concerning what is real than any logical thought, any "disembodied" inanimate reality.

The chance of survival of this primitive *me* is endangered because of its total subjectivity and the completely personal quality of its experience. It does not yet exist in a world that can be meaningfully shared by a group of other persons constituting a social universe, because there is no differentiation between others as a means for wish-fulfillment and others as coexisters in a world that represents far more than a potential source of gratification. The pleasure-ego is, as Freud emphasized, the weak spot in the organization of the human mind, because it is essentially not adapted for survival.

Freud answered the question of how the developing individual advances from the pleasure-ego to the reality-ego in slightly different ways at various stages of his theory building. In the "Two Principles" (1911) the pleasure-ego yields to the reality-ego because the gratifications which are real are, in the long run, more satisfying than those that are based on the mere wish for fulfillment. Reality triumphs in the end over the most tempting fantasy.[2]

Later, in "Instincts and Their Vicissitudes" (1915), Freud postulated a primary reality-ego based on the narcissism of the infant, who is capable of autoerotic gratification. If this condition were capable of prevailing, there would be no interest ever in the external world. But not all the needs of the child are capable of autoerotic satisfaction, and thus the child has to turn to caring adults for the gratification of such needs. He thus enters a stage of dominance by a pleasure-ego which ties him for a long time to the early love objects, until he emerges, according to this version, with a final reality-ego that permits him to seek satisfactions that are independent from the response of adults. This Freudian hypothesis is based on the assumption that biological needs—drives—propel the human infant toward reality, because reality, not the primary love objects, can satisfy those needs.

It may be worthwhile to note that these formulations were conceptualized at a stage in Freud's theoretical thinking when he differentiated between sexual and self-preservative drives. Ego-psychological thinking would stress that, in addition to the role of the drives in promoting the replacement of the primitive pleasure-ego by the adaptive reality-ego, we have to consider the maturation of many cognitive structures—such as perception, abstract thought formation—which are all aspects of the conflict-free sphere of development.

We need not deny the role of biological needs, nor can we underestimate the maturational processes in the ego development. Nevertheless, due to anthropologic linguistic studies (Levi-Strauss 1966) and to greater knowledge of severe thought disorders, such as in schizophrenia, neither the original Freudian model concerning the replacement of the pleasure-ego by the reality-ego nor the ego-psychological modifications can be considered the complete answer to the problem of how the perception of reality is formed, and why it asserts itself over the primitive pleasure-ego.

In a remarkable paper Novey (1955) questioned in a most searching way the capacity of man to be "objective" about himself as well as about his external environment:

The inquiries in psychoanalysis into the development of a sense of reality have essentially been based upon observing and speculating as to what the human infant experiences and what phases can be detected in the process of establishing its own boundaries. . . . There has been little consideration given to what the eventual characteristics of these boundaries are in the adult human whom we describe as mature.... We are apt to assume that the mature adult has attained an ultimate appreciation of reality, but this appear to be far from the facts.

Novey went on to raise questions that seem to anticipate problems raised by psychoanalysts such as R. D. Laing (1967) in recent years:

The development of a clear delineation between self and not-self has its advantages in establishing man's integrity as a separate being and in increasing his functional capacities in certain directions. An example of this is presented by man's capacity to advance beyond an animistic concept of the environment external to himself. At the same time, this differentiation of self and not-self has grossly distorted other phases of the observable relationships of man. It has tended to abstact him, in his thinking, too much from the world around him. The sense of self can only have subjective reality.... We assume a sense of self essentially similar to our own in other humans only through and because of an inner conviction of the reality of this sense experience within ourselves.

Having stated this, Novey was not afraid to draw conclusions that, in a true sense of the word, deserve to be called radical:

Man is prone, in his more usual process of thinking, to assume that his observations of both internal and external events are "objective" in character. By this I am referring to an essential unawareness of the impact of his own emotional bias on his capacity of observation. The urge to assume this position of "objectivity" depends upon man's need to structure his environment so as to give him a feeling of security, which is often based, in a sense, upon a delusion. He needs to believe, whatever the facts, that his life is a meaningful thing and that that which he looks upon as his self is a purposeful unitary thing. I propose to use the word"delusion," since this is a construct on man's part based upon no conceivable provable grounds, but one to which he feels compelled to cling to with the greatest tenacity—"as if his very life depended on it," and so I believe it to be. ... If one chose to look at this process from another viewpoint it would appear that man is "creating" meaning, purpose, and security for himself, but insofar as he does this at the expense of denying observable facts it appears to me to be a delusional process, however efficacious it may be.

Finally, Novey placed these theoretical problems of psychoanalysis into the broad context of Western European philosophical thought:

The parallel in modern science and in psychoanalysis to the concept of LOGOS in ancient philosophy would appear to be very great and serves as a good example of this delusional process. This concept advances the idea of an "immanent reason" in the world, giving order and regularity to the universe and thus to man. ... It is here, however, that the threat of perceiving man as being controlled by a "tyranny of circumstances" becomes too great and the flight begins into the thesis of the special destiny of individual man.

Yet again and again, Novey stressed that what he calls the "delusional process" is part of the human condition, an existential determinant of being human which is "esential for the full integration of the individual." Thus there is the dilemma that only at the cost of impairment of the integrative functions, such as in the child and in the psychotic, a capacity for "periodic exceptional insights" remains intact. On the other hand, the mature individual must pay the price of a decreased "capacity to communicate with one's own unconscious process or with the unconscious process of another." But this deficit on the part of the mature adult Novey recognized as the prerequisite of social relations. The child and the psychotic:

experience stress in social relations because they cannot enter into a tacit conspiracy with others as to the meaningfulness and purposefulness of living and relatedness. In the fable (of The Emperor's New Clothes by Hans Christian Anderson) the adults are allowed to engage in a *conscious* conspiracy; in actual living it is an *unconscious* conspiracy. [italics mine]

Novey's propositions cannot help but strike us as paradoxical. The equation of the "sense of reality" with a "delusion" does not seem to make sense, since we define a delusion as a system of convictions which is totally incompatible with "the reality" of the person's life situation and the conditions considered real by his contemporaries. In other words, a delusion conveys the conviction of a reality which is absolutely unsupported by the shared reality of the delusional individual's peers. This argument, however, does not deal with the essence of the problem that Novey raised, because it limits itself to the *terminology* that Novey used.

As I see it, Novey recognized in what we refer to as the sense of reality a selective process, by which some aspects of what is real are given a preferential status in contrast to others which are also real, but are actively excluded from perception—we might say repressed. The sense of reality is not formed by an "objective" reality impinging upon the mind in its totality, but by a mental process which permits very specific elements of the totality of possible experiences to be singled out and therewith to become "real." Those elements that have not been singled out either don't become real or are not permitted (by what one is tempted to describe as an "unconscious intent") to attain the quality of a reality of equal status.

This "unconscious intent" appears to be aiming at the possibility of "giving man a sense of fitting into a mosaic in which he is an integral part. I cannot overemphasize the importance of this since it is unthinkable to man not to conceive of himself as participating in forming the mosaic" (Novey 1955). Novey referred to this active exclusion of some experiences that are, in principle, possible as "impairment" of the identity of the individual, but this "impairment" "makes for the sense of oneness of man among men."

Such seemingly arbitrary exclusion of some aspects of what is real and the resulting "impairment" of the individual's identity are also recognizable in a state that we call delusional. Even the aim of such "reality-manipulation"—"giving man a sense of fitting into a mosaic in which he is an integral part"—could well be applied to the delusional person. The delusional individual fails, however, to achieve "the sense of oneness of man among men." On the contray, the delusional person is bound to lose that perception of reality that is shared with others.

What Novey contributed is an awareness that the psychoanalytic use of the concept of "objective reality," "external reality," does not take into account that this "reality" is the product of a complex process of actively "fitting" reality to the given circumstances of one's existence—namely, to make possible for the individual "the sense of oneness of man among men." It is, in other words, a "tendentious" perception of reality, fitting the need of those who "promote" it at a given time and place. It is "tendentious" even if we acknowledge that only by this "shaping" of the sense of reality are we enabled to live as humans.

Novey also made us aware of the fact that, for a certain sense of reality, a complementary type of "being human" is proclaimed as *the* way of being human. The historical configurations of human identities cannot be isolated from their "sense of realtiy."

Psychoanalysis has tended to treat the Western European sense of reality as if it were "the objective reality" for all and has consequently defined *the* sense of identity as if it were universal. This is probably the reason why psychoanalysis, in Eissler's previously quoted statement, appears to be diminished in its applicability during times of latent or manifest revolution. Psychoanalysis, faced with a breakdown of a shared sense of reality, lacks the theoretical basis required in that predicament. This has nothing to do with the failure, so often attributed to psychoanalysis, to stress the cultural factors or to be aware of the economic conditioning of human consciousness.

On the contrary, the possibility for the development of culture would seem to depend on the emergence of a shared sense of what is real. This consensus constitutes the prerequisite for any system of order in human relations, for the establishment of a hierarchy of values, and thus acts as a stimulus to communicate the shared perception of reality (Freud 1913, pp. 188-189). Language obviously cannot develop unless there is a shared sense of what is real. But since there are numerous, if not infinite, ways that can be said to constitute a "sense of reality," which one will be shared and which one will remain a private and isolated experience? Must we not say that it requires an act of power to impose one particular "sense of reality" on others and thus make them share a common sense of what is real? Insofar as this would lead to the emergence of a shared language—in contrast to the possibility of private languages—the prevailing sense of what is real in a given historical situation would be codified in the language. It is through language that a political and social order is imposed, which derives from the shared sense of what is real among those whose "language" prevails. Property relationships would be the consequence of a particular sense of what is real, and it may not be coincidental that the property on which one lives is referred to as "real estate."

But the sense of what is real changes throughout history and thus the established political and social order eventually no longer reflects what is real to ever-increasing numbers of individuals. Under those circumstances the spoken language reflects a sense of reality out of touch with the experience of those who have discovered a different, a new way of perceiving what is real. These are the times of anomie, of latent and open revolution, of attempts to impose another sense of reality which would introduce a new and different order of human relationships, of power relationships and property relationships.

Only one thing would not change. What is considered real, even if shared by many, would still be, in Novey's terms, as delusional, as conspiratorial as the previous accepted reality, except it would be shared by a different group of people. There can never be an "objective sense of reality," only one selectively chosen by "unconscious intent"— one which excludes other aspects of reality experience and defines identities in its own specific way, as every *shared* sense of reality must do. The new sense of reality would, according to Novey, equally "impair" the individual's identity—differently, but just as effectively.

Individuals and groups, whether nations or smaller units of humanity, react with fear and hate toward those whose sense of reality is different enough to threaten their own sense of being at home in a shared world. No individual or group voluntarily gives up its own sense of what is real and its own definition of what it is to be human. It is always a matter of winning or losing, of life or death. The most radical social and political upheavals must insist on the "objectivity" of their sense of what is real just as vehemently as the representatives of the "old order," whatever they may have stood for. This cannot be changed, because every sense of what is real must insist, in Novey's words, on "giving man a sense of fitting into a mosaic in which he is an integral part."

Only as an individual permits himself to confront the "unconscious conspiracies," the secret denials of the excluded "reality" whose effects on his life he experiences as anxieties, can he approach a sense of self that is relatively "unimpaired." It will temporarily take away "the sense of oneness of man among men," but it will enable him to be more radically himself, even as he sees the necessity to share a common sense of what is real with his contemporaries. This has been the aim of psychoanalysis; it still is the only way to diminish one's delusions and one's impairment as a person. Because we are living in a crisis, due to the many competing claims—of nations, of groups within nations, and of the sexes—as to what is real, the psychoanalyst insists on every person's right to discover, in the privacy of the therapeutic relationship, the true dimension of his "reality." The psychoanalyst enables the individual, instead of yielding to the sense of reality that is imposed on him, to chose a reality that he can share with others by intent, without negating the uniqueness of what he knows to be real only for himself.

A CHALLENGE TO PSYCHOANALYTIC THEORY
AND THERAPY— THE ANALYSIS OF REALITY

To claim that psychoanalysis has always understood itself as a way to question the prevailing, historical sense of what is real; that it is the only means by which each individual can decide what aspects of reality he can genuinely share with his contemporaries, without "impairing" his own perception of what is real; that it is the only way to discern the degree to which one has lived with a false self (Winnicott 1952) would indeed be a self-congratulatory statement. On the other hand, it is equally false to go to the other extreme—to depict psychoanalysis as nothing but a retrogressive force, aiming in a surreptitious way to support the "established" sense of reality in the interest of law and order. The Freudian questioning of the validity of what we consciously consider to be real was a radical step that did more to change the world we live in than can be said of many attempted changes of the social order.

In every psychoanalysis there are possibilities of radical break-throughs in a person's perception of the world as he confronts his inner reality that he considers to be *the* reality. But it is also true that psychoanalysis has failed to supplement the critique of consciousness with an equally searching critique of what we perceive to be real. We are still too often hearing and reading references to "reality," as if it were an unambiguous, objective fact, accessible to anyone who made an effort to acknowledge it. Now we are becoming aware that what anyone perceives to be real is the result of, to paraphrase Sullivan, selective attention plus selective inattention. But *inattention* is too neutral a term; rather we should speak of unconscious negation in the interest of affirmation of our identity in a world shared with others. What is unconsciously negated is profoundly threatening to our specific sense of being human.

This negation does not only apply to aspects of the "external" reality (as an example, the idea of a miracle threatens a modern intellect's conception of an ordered world); it also includes aspects of our inner reality, such as aspects of human sexuality, with which other eras felt more at ease than we do. What we must negate externally and what we must negate internally are complementary: a certain type of perception of what is real externally fits a specific definition of what we are as persons. It seems that these mutually exclusive perceptions of what is real play a decisive role in what is described as prejudice.

To state these propositions does not imply a failure of psychoanalysis as a theory. Rather, psychoanalytic theory needs to apply its very own principles to the analysis of the unconscious determinants of reality perception—not just of an individual, but of the shared reality of one's historical existence. If it is hard to become aware of the unconscious aspects of our perception, of our relationship to other individuals, especially those who are emotionally meaningful to us, it is even harder to become aware of the unconscious biases that shape our perception of what is real in the contemporary shared world. Our very sense of objectivity is a nearly insuperable obstacle to our awareness of how we are "screening" reality to comply with our own need to fit into a "mosaic in which [we] are an integral part" (Novey 1955).

Such a theoretical endeavor would require a reconsideration of the interaction between the development of a specific "sense of reality" and the function of the drives, the ego and the superego. The traditional conceptualization that the id represents the pressures of the drives, that the ego serves the function of adaptation to "reality," and that the superego represents the demands of morality can already be seen as a preanalytic statement—preanalytic in the sense that it uses an "unanalyzed" concept of reality.

Obviously, this is a difficult conceptual task. It seems to me, however, that it is a task that only the psychoanalytic approach to the phenomenon of man can be expected to undertake, because it has the conceptual tools and the technical means to do so. If psychoanalysis fails in this task, other, far more uncritical theories of man will not wait, because the awareness that our sense of reality needs a restructuring is becoming more urgent and more widespread all the time. These other approaches, lacking the theoretical discipline of psychoanalysis and its experience in the process of "making aware the hidden," will proudly proclaim their new perception of reality as the the only objective one. They will impose it, without regard for its implicit "impairment" of the total dimension of human perception, as the only valid and legitimate one. Thereby the individual will lose the right to choose between the totality of what he knows to be real for himself and what he must acknowledge to be those aspects of reality that he can share with others in order to create a common world.

Psychoanalysis sprang from psychiatry. From psychiatry it inherited a critical concern with the question of what is real for a particular person. Psychoanalysis has, however, gone beyond this strictly clinical interest toward a general concern with the psychological fundamentals of the human condition. This is its revolutionary aspect, its claim to ask more radical questions concerning man than any activist theory.

Other theoreticians have become aware of this pivotal role of psychoanalysis in today's crisis of the traditional order. To mention only one example, I shall quote a passage from a searching and profound work by Kilian (1971) which does not hesitate to confront the issues of our times in an uncompromising and radical manner:

Psychoanalysis and Marxism can be viewed as two complementary halves of an unfinished attempt to overcome a subject-object split of consciousness, a split reflecting a specific power structure of society. In both of these coordinative systems the denial of the four-dimensional extensity of the process of being human has been revoked only halfway: Karl Marx made conscious the "objective" process operating in the social structure and in history. Sigmund Freud lifted the "subjective" process of individual developmental history into the visual field of critical knowledge. At most, one can say that both thinkers initiated a "Copernican Revolution" of the Science of Man. The model of reality underlying Karl Marx's system, insofar as it juxtaposes the organized conditions of production to the suppressed antithetical forces of productive energies thrusting toward freedom, remained hemianopic. The same is true concerning Sigmund Freud who saw the organized conscious confronting the suppressed forces of the unconscious drive energies pressing toward liberation. Neither thinker was able to undo the subject-object split of consciousness. The attention of the one remained exclusively directed toward the object aspect of the process that is man, while the other concentrated on man as subject only. Sigmund Freud had, as it were, only one eye open to do justice to man as a subject. With this one eye he could see the growth of every individual tree. But it did not permit him to see the connectedness of the individual with the forest of society, nor could he see the historical development of the forest to which the tree belonged. Karl Marx never transcended the perspective of one eye trained on the objectively describable facts, which permitted him to grasp the process of the developing forest, but not the growth and development of individual trees. If we place these thinkers next to one another, it becomes possible to see them as representing a condition characterizing the social consciousness of our era throughout—and that means notwith-standing all differences of specific philosophies and ideologies. Human self-awareness in the present time remains one-eyed in a twofold way, even though it has at its disposal both eyes. Since our self-perception is diplopic, it remains, even with the best intention, one-sided. It must close the eye that keeps us informed concerning subjective reality, whenever it wants to be open to what is objectively given. Or, it blocks out the vision for what is objective, in order to focus on subjective reality. The bipolar foundation of Cartesian consciousness does not succeed in achieving, figurative-ly speaking, binocular synthesis of human reality: a synthesis able to provide self-knowledge with a spatial *and* temporal depth perception founded on an apperception, appropriate to the four-dimensional totality of the System Man extended in history. This is the reason why the Cartesian consciousness in its manifestation as societal consciousness is impotent to transcend the class division inherent in the pattern of a social structure based on a ruling class. The Cartesian consciousness is suffering from diplopia, in that it looks upward to an autonomous subject and simultaneously squints downward with the aim of control over the objects. Thus it remains identified unconsciously with the structure of class division characteristic for a ruling class civilization, even when it aims to overcome this division through revolution, or by means of an illusion which feigns to have achieved it in fact. [*The Expropriated Consciousness,* pp. 44-45, my translation from the German]

The essence of Kilian's reasoning seems to me to be that a true social revolution or reordering of human relationships requires a radically different consciousness. It is my conviction that such a change of self-awareness requires the insights of psychoanalysis, extended toward an analysis of the perception of reality in all its ambiguousness and complexity. One cannot change the world, as Marx aimed to do, without knowing that our world perception is constituted by unconscious processes that more likely than not will deceive us into believing that we know *the* reality as it objectively is. In a time of crisis, psychoanalysis should be on the firing line. It will never be popular, not because it is too complacent, but because in its true implications it is too radical and uncompromising to please those who want their radicalism without prior questioning of their own unconscious bias and distortions. Self-criticism has long been an established instrument of revolutionary movements. Properly understood, psychoanalysis is a critical examination of all the assumptions about oneself and about reality that we all too easily consider self-evident.

NOTES

1. "Two things fill the mind with ever new and increasing admiration and awe, the oftener and the more steadily we reflect on them: The starry heavens above and the moral law within. I have not to search for them and conjecture them as though they were veiled in darkness or were in the transcendent region

beyond my horizon; I see them before me and connect them directly with the consciousness of my existence" (Kant, I., *Critique of Practical Reason,* 1788).

2. After the completion of this paper I had the privilege to attend the presentation of Dr. Robert S. Wallerstein's plenary session address, "Psychoanalytic Perspectives on the Problem of Reality," in New York on 2 December 1972 at the fall meeting of the American Psychoanalytic Association. I greatly regret that I therefore have been unable to do justice to Dr. Wallerstein's brilliant development of his thoughts concerning the problem of reality.

REFERENCES

Adler, F. (1947). Operational definitions in sociology. *American Journal of Sociology* 52:438–444.

Agel, J., ed. (1971). *The Radical Therapist.* New York: Ballantine.

Agoston, T. (1946). Some psychological aspects of prostitution: the pseudopersonality. *International Journal of Psycho-Analysis* 26:62–67.

Albee, E. (1959). The zoo story. In *The American Dream and The Zoo Story: Two Plays.* New York: New American Library.

Alexander, F. (1921). Metapsycholgische Betrachtungen. *Internationale Zeitschrift für Psychoanalyse* 7:283.

Allport, G. W. (1957). European and American theories of personality. In *Perspectives in Personality Theory,* ed. H. P. David and H. von Bracken, pp. 3–26. New York: Basic Books.

Angyal, A. (1956). A theoretical model for personality studies. In *The Self: Explorations in Personal Growth,* ed. C. E. Moustakas. New York: Harper.

Apfelbaum, B. (1962). Some problems of contemporary ego psychology. *Journal of the American Psychoanalytic Association* 10:526–537.

Arendt, H. (1959). *The Human Condition.* New York: Doubleday.

Arlow, J. A., and Brenner, C. (1964). *Psychoanalytic Concepts and the Structural Theory.* New York: International Universities Press.

Bak, R. (1939). Regression of ego-orientation and libido in schizophrenia. *International Journal of Psycho-Analysis* 20:64–71.

Balint, A. (1949). Love for the mother and mother love. *International Journal of Psycho-Analysis* 30:251–259.

Balint, M. (1938). Eros and Aphrodite. *International Journal of Psycho-Analysis* 19:199:213.

———(1949). Early developmental states of the ego: primary object love. *International Journal of Psycho-Analysis* 30:265–273.

———(1952a). New beginning and the paranoid and the depressive syndromes. *International Journal of Psycho-Analysis* 33:214–224.

———(1952b). On love and hate. *International Journal of Psycho-Analysis* 33:355–362.

———(1955). *Primary Love and Psychoanalytic Technique.* London: Hogarth.

———(1960). Primary narcissism and primary love. *Psychoanalytic Quarterly* 29:6–43.

Barag, G. (1937). Zur Psychoanalyse der Prostitution. *Imago* 23:330–362.

Beauvoir, S. de (1951–52). Must we burn Sade? In *The Marquis de Sade,* ed. P. Dinnage, pp. 9–82. New York: Grove Press.

Bellak, L. (1959). Conceptual and methodological problems in psychoanalysis. *Annals of the New York Academy of Science* 76:971–1134.

Benedek, T. (1949). The psychosomatic implications of the primary unit: mother-child. In *Psychosexual Functions in Women.* New York: Ronald Press, 1952.

Bennis, W. G., and Slater, P. E. (1968). *The Temporary Society.* New York: Harper and Row.

Bergler, E. (1949). *The Basic Neurosis.* New York: Grune and Stratton.

———(1951). *Money and Emotional Conflicts.* Garden City, N.Y.: Doubleday.

Bergman, P., and Escalona, S. (1949). Unusual sensitivities in very young children. *Psychoanalytic Study of the Child* 3/4:332–352.

Bergson, H. (1888). *Time and Free Will.* New York: Macmillan, 1910.

Bernfeld, S. (1937). Zur revision der Bioanalyse. *Imago* 23:197–236.

Bernfeld, S., and Feitelberg, S. (1931). The principle of entropy and the death instinct. *International Journal of Psycho-Analysis* 12:61.

Bettelheim, B. (1960). *The Informed Heart: Autonomy in a Mass Age.* New York: Free Press of Glencoe.

Bibring, E. (1941). The development and problems of the theory of the instincts. *International Journal of Psycho-Analysis* 22:102–131.

———(1943). The conception of the repetition compulsion. *Psychoanalytic Quarterly* 12:520–540.

———(1947). The so-called English school of psychoanalysis. *Psychoanalytic Quarterly* 16:69–93.

Bing, J. F., McLaughlin, F., and Marburg, R. (1959). The metapsychology of narcissism. *Psychoanalytic Study of the Child* 14:9–28.

Bohr, N. (1948). On the notions of causality and complementarity. *Dialectica* 2:312–319.

Bonaparte, M. (1952). Some biophysical aspects of sado-masochism. *International Journal of Psycho-Analysis* 33:373–383.

Bowlby, J. (1958). The nature of the child's ties to his mother. *International Journal of Psycho-Analysis* 39:350–373.

Boyer, L. B. (1956). On maternal overstimulation and ego defects. *Psychoanalytic Study of the Child* 11:236–256.

Brodbeck, A. (1961). Values in the lonely crowd: ascent or descent of man? In Lipset and Lowenthal (1961).

Brodey, W. M. (1965). On the dynamics of narcissism. *Psychoanalytic Study of the Child* 20:165–193.

Brown, N. O. (1959). *Life Against Death: The Psychoanalytic Meaning of History.* Middletown, Conn.: Wesleyan University Press.

Brun, R. (1951). *General Theory of Neuroses.* New York: International Universities Press.

———(1953). The biological aspect of Freudian psycho-analysis. *International Journal of Psycho-Analysis,* Supplement, pp. 83–94.

———(1953–54). Ueber Freuds Hypothese vom Todestrieb: Eine kritische Untersuchung. *Psyche* 7:81–111.

Buber, M. (1961). *Tales of the Hasidim: The Later Masters.* New York: Schocken, 1961.

Butler, Joseph (1896). *The Works of Joseph Butler,* ed. W. E. Gladstone. Oxford: Clarendon Press.

Cannon, W. B. (1932). *The Wisdom of the Body.* New York: Norton.

Claparede, E. (1911). Recognition and me-ness. In *Organization and Pathology of Thought,* tr. and ed. D. Rapaport. New York: Columbia University Press.

Cohn, F. (1928). Aus der Analyse eines Falles von Strassenangst. *Internationale Zeitschrift für Psychoanalyse* 14:387–400.

Colby, K. E. (1955). *Energy and Structure in Psychoanalysis.* New York: Ronald Press.

Coltrera, J. C. (1962). Psychoanalysis and existentialism. *Journal of the American Psychoanalytic Association* 10:166–215.

Dahrendorf, R. (1961). Democracy without liberty: an essay on the politics of other-directed man. In Lipset and Lowenthal (1961).

Descartes, R. (1955). Discourse on method *and* The principles of philosophy. In *The Philosophical Works of Descartes,* tr. E. S. Haldane and G. R. T. Ross. New York: Dover.

Deutsch, H. (1929). The genesis of agoraphobia. *International Journal of Psycho-Analysis* 10:51–69.

———(1942). Some forms of emotional disturbance and their relationship to schizophrenia. *Psychoanalytic Quarterly* 11:301–321.

———(1944). *The Psychology of Women Vol. 1.* New York: Grune and Stratton.

———(1955). The imposter: contribution to ego psychology of a type of psychopath. *Psychoanalytic Quarterly* 24:483–505.

Dinnage, P., ed. (1953). *The Marquis de Sade: An Essay by Simone de Beauvoir, with Selections from his Writings.* New York: Grove Press.

Dollard, J., Miller, N. E., Doob, L. W., Mowrer, D. H., and Sears, R. R. (1939). *Frustration and Aggression.* New Haven: Yale University Press.

Drucker, P. (1957). The new philosophy. *Harper's Magazine,* August, p. 36.

Dubois, J. (1971). Man the accident: Jacques Monod's views on man's origin and destiny. *Realités,* No. 248, pp. 34–37.

Eidelberg, L. (1957). An introduction to the study of the narcissistic mortification. *Psychoanalytic Quarterly* 31:657–668.

———(1962). On narcissistic mortification. *Journal of the American Psychoanalytic Association* 10:593–605.

Eisnitz, A. J. (1961). Mirror dreams. *Journal of the American Psychoanalytic Association* 9:461–479.

Eissler, K. R. (1953). The effect of the structure of the ego on psychoanalytic technique. *Journal of the American Psychoanalytic Association* 1:104–143.

————(1958a). Notes on problems of technique in the psychoanalytic treatment of adolescents: with some remarks on perversions. *Psychoanalytic Study of the Child* 13:223–254.

————(1958b). Problems of identity (abstract). *Journal of the American Psychoanalytic Association* 6:131–142.

————(1967). Psychopathology and creativity. *American Imago* 24:35–81.

————(1969). Irreverent remarks about the present and future of psychoanalysis. *International Journal of Psycho-Analysis* 50:461–472.

Elkisch, P. (1957). The psychological significance of the mirror. *Journal of the American Psychoanalytic Association* 5:235–244.

Ellis, A. (1959). An operational reformulation of some of the basic principles of psychoanalysis. In *Minnesota Studies in the Philosophy of Science,* ed. H. Feigl and M. Scriven. Minneapolis: University of Minnesota Press.

Erikson, E. H. (1947). Ego development and historical change. *Psychoanalytic Study of the Child* 2:359–396.

————(1950a). *Childhood and Society.* New York: Norton.

————(1950b). Growth and crises of the healthy personality. In *Identity and the Life Cycle.* New York: International Universities Press, 1959.

————(1954). Wholeness and totality. In *Totalitarianism,* ed. C. J. Friedrich. Cambridge: Harvard University Press.

————(1955). Freud's "The Origins of Psychoanalysis." *International Journal of Psycho-Analysis* 36:1–15.

————(1956). The problem of ego identity. In *Identity and the Life Cycle.* New York: International Universities Press, 1959.

————(1958). *Young Man Luther: A Study in Psychoanalysis and History.* New York: Norton.

————(1959). *Identity and the Life Cycle: Selected Papers,* with a historical introduction by D. Rapaport. New York: International Universities Press.

————(1962). Psychological reality and historical actuality. In *Insight and Responsibility.* New York: Norton, 1964.

Etiemble (1954). New China and the Chinese language. *Diogenes* 8.

Fairbairn, W. R. D. (1944). Endopsychic structure considered in terms of object relationships. In *An Object-Relations Theory of the Personality*. New York: Basic Books, 1954.

———(1952). *Psychoanalytic Studies of the Personality*. London: Tavistock.

Fanon, F. (1963). *Wretched of the Earth*. New York: Grove Press, 1966.

Federn, P. (1952). *Ego Psychology and the Psychoses*. New York: Basic Books.

Feldman, S. S. (1962). Blushing, fear of blushing, and shame. *Journal of the American Psychoanalytic Association* 10:368–385.

Fenichel, O. (1926). Identification. In *Collected Papers*, vol. 1, pp. 97–112. New York: Norton.

———(1935). A critique of the death instinct. In *Collected Papers*, vol. 1, pp. 363–372. New York: Norton, 1953.

———(1937). The scoptophilic instinct and identification. In *Collected Papers*, vol. 1, pp. 373–397. New York: Norton, 1953.

———(1945). *The Psychoanalytic Theory of Neurosis*. New York: Norton.

Ferenczi, S. (1924). *Thalassa: A Theory of Genitality*. Albany: Psychoanalytic Quarterly, 1936.

———(1949). Confusion of tongues between the adult and the child (the language of tenderness and passion). *International Journal of Psycho-Analysis* 30:225–330.

Ferm, V. (1950). *A History of Philosophical Systems*. New York: The Philosophical Library, pp. 207, 464.

Flew, A. (1951). Locke and the problem of personal identity. *Philosophy* 26:53–68.

Fliess, R. (1948). An ontogenetic table. In *Psychoanalytic Reader* Vol. 1. New York: International Universities Press.

Flugel, J. C. (1953). The death instinct, homeostasis and allied concepts. *International Journal of Psycho-Analysis,* supplement, pp. 43–73.

Ford, C. S., and Beach, C. A. (1951). *Patterns of Sexual Behavior*. New York: Harper.

Frenkel-Brunswik, E. (1954). Psychoanalysis and the unity of science. *Proceedings of the American Academy of Arts and Sciences* 80:271–350.

Freud, A. (1936). *The Ego and the Mechanisms of Defense.* Writings of Anna Freud, vol. 2. New York: International Universities Press, 1966.

————(1949). Aggression in relation to emotional development: normal and pathological. *Psychoanalytic Study of the Child* 3-4:37–42.

————(1952). A connection between the states of negativism and of emotional surrender (Abstract). *International Journal of Psycho-Analysis* 33:265.

Freud, S. (1900). The interpretation of dreams. *Standard Edition* 4/5. London: Hogarth, 1953.

————(1905). Three essays on the theory of sexuality. *Standard Edition* 7:125–243. London: Hogarth, 1953.

————(1907). *Delusion and Dream in Jensen's* Gradiva. New York: Moffat Yard, 1917.

————(1908), "Civilized" sexual morality and modern nervous illness. *Standard Edition* 9:177–204. London: Hogarth, 1959.

————(1910). Leonardo da Vinci: a psychosexual study of an infantile reminiscence. *Standard Edition* 11:63–137. London: Hogarth, 1957.

————(1911). Formulations on the two principles of mental functioning. *Standard Edition* 12:218–226. London: Hogarth, 1958.

————(1913). The claims of psychoanalysis to scientific interest. *Standard Edition* 13:165–192. London: Hogarth, 1955.

————(1914). On narcissism: an introduction. *Standard Edition* 14:73–102. London: Hogarth, 1957.

————(1915a). Instincts and their vicissitudes. *Standard Edition* 14:117–140. London: Hogarth, 1957.

————(1915b). The unconscious. *Standard Edition* 14:161–204. London: Hogarth, 1957.

————(1917a). A difficulty in the path of psychoanalysis. *Standard Edition* 17:135–144. London: Hogarth, 1955.

————(1917b). Introductory lectures on psychoanalysis. *Standard Edition* 15/16. London: Hogarth, 1963.

————(1919). The uncanny. *Standard Edition* 17:217–256. London: Hogarth, 1949.

————(1920). Beyond the pleasure principle. *Standard Edition* 18:3–64. London: Hogarth, 1955.

————(1921). Group psychology and the analysis of the ego. *Standard Edition* 18:64–143. London: Hogarth.

——(1923a). The ego and the id. *Standard Edition* 19:3–68. London: Hogarth Press, 1961.

——(1923b). The infantile genital organization. *Standard Edition* 19:139–145. London: Hogarth, 1961.

——(1924a). The dissolution of the oedipus complex. *Standard Edition* 19: London: Hogarth, 1961.

——(1924b). The economic problem in masochism. *Standard Edition* 19:159–170. London: Hogarth, 1961.

——(1925a). An autobiographical study. *Standard Edition* 20:7–74. London: Hogarth, 1959.

——(1925b). Negation. *Standard Edition* 19:234–239. London: Hogarth, 1961.

——(1926). Inhibitions, symptoms, and anxiety. *Standard Edition* 20:77–178. London: Hogarth, 1959.

——(1930). Civilization and its discontents. *Standard Edition* 21:64–145. London: Hogarth, 1961.

——(1931). Female sexuality. *Standard Edition* 21:225-243. London: Hogarth, 1961.

——(1932). New introductory lectures on psychoanalysis. *Standard Edition* 22:5–122. London: Hogarth, 1964.

——(1938). Splitting of the ego in the defensive process. *Standard Edition* 23:275–278. London: Hogarth, 1964.

——(1940). An outline of psychoanalysis. *Standard Edition* Vol. 23. London: Hogarth, 1964.

Fromm, E. (1947). *Man for Himself: An Enquiry into the Psychology of Ethics.* New York: Rinehart.

——(1949). Psychoanalytic characterology and its application to the understanding of culture. In: *Culture and Personality,* ed. S. St. Sargent and M. W. Smith. New York: Viking Fund, p. 5.

——(1955). *The Sane Society.* New York: Rinehart.

Frondizi, R. (1953). *The Nature of the Self: A Functional Interpretation.* New Haven: Yale University Press.

Fürstenau, P. (1964). Ich-Psychologie und Anpassungsprobleme: eine Auseinandersetzung mit Heinz Hartmann. *Jahrbuch der Psychoanalyse,* 3:30–55.

Gedo, J. E. and Goldberg, A. (1973). *Models of the Mind.* Chicago: University of Chicago Press.

Geleerd, E. R., Hacker, F.J., and Rapaport, D. (1945). Contribution to the study of amnesia and allied conditions. *Psychoanalytic Quarterly* 14:199–220.

Gill, M. M. (1963). *Topography and Systems in Psychoanalytic Theory.* New York: International Universities Press.

Glover, E. (1943). The concept of dissociation. In: *The Early Development of the Mind.* New York: International Universities Press, 1956.

————(1945a). Examination of the Klein system of child psychology. *Psychoanalytic Study of the Child* 1:75–118.

————(1945b). *The Psycho-Pathology of Prostitution.* London: L.S.T.D. Publications.

————(1956). *The Early Development of the Mind.* New York: International Universities Press.

————(1961). Some recent trends in psychoanalytic theory. *Psychoanalytic Quarterly* 30:86–107.

Godard, J. L. (1969). *Le Gai Savoir.* Film review by Vincent Canby, *New York Times,* September 29, 1969.

Goethe, J. W. (1809–1829). Die Maximen und Reflexionen. In: *Gedenkausgabe der Werke, Briefe und Gespräche,* ed. P. Stöcklein 9:499–676. Zurich: Artemis, 1949.

————(1830). Fragmente zur vergleichenden Anatomie. IVN: *Gedenkausgabe der Werke, Briefe, und Gespräche,* 17:435, ed. E. Beutler. Zurich: Artemis, 1952.

————(1832). *Faust.* Trans. Louis MacNeice. New York: Oxford University Press, 1960, p. 287.

Gonseth, L. (1948). Remarque sur l'idée de complementarité. *Dialectica* 2.

Goodman, S. (1965). Current status of the theory of the superego. *Journal of the American Psychoanalytic Association* 13:172–180.

Greenacre, P. (1953). Certain relationships between fetishism and the faulty development of the body image. *Psychoanalytic Study of the Child* 8:79–98.

————(1955). Further considerations regarding fetishism. *Psychoanalytic Study of the Child* 10:187–194.

————(1957). The childhood of the artist. *Psychoanalytic Study of the Child* 12:47–72.

————(1958a). Early physical determinants in the development of the sense of identity. (Abstract). *Journal of the American Psychoanalytic Association* 6:131–142, 6:612–627.

————(1958b). The family romance of the artist. *Psychoanalytic Study of the Child* 13:9–36.

————(1958c). The imposter. *Psychoanalytic Quarterly* 27:359–382.

————(1958d). The relation of the imposter to the artist. *Psychoanalytic Study of the Child* 13:521–540.

Greenson, R. R. (1953). On boredom. *Journal of the American Psychoanalytic Association* 1:7–21.

————(1954). The struggle against identification. *Journal of the American Psychoanalytic Association* 2:200–217.

Greenwalt, N. (1958). *The Call Girl*. New York: Ballantine.

Grinker, R. R. (1955). Growth inertia and shame: their therapeutic implications and dangers. *International Journal of Psycho-Analysis* 36:242–253.

————(1957). On identification. *International Journal of Psycho-Analysis* 38:379–390.

Hartmann, H. (1939). *Ego Psychology and the Problem of Adaptation*. New York: International Universities Press, 1958.

————(1948). Comments on the psychoanalytic theory of instinctual drives. *Psychoanalytic Quarterly* 17:368–388.

————(1950). Comments on the psychoanalytic theory of the ego. In: *Essays on Ego Psychology: Selected Problems in Psychoanalytic Theory*. New York: International Universities Press, 1964.

————(1951). Technical implications of ego psychology. *Psychoanalytic Quarterly* 20:31–43.

————(1952). Mutual influences in the development of the ego and the id. In: *Essays on Ego Psychology*. New York: International Universities Press, 1964.

————(1956a). The development of the ego concept in Freud's work. *International Journal of Psycho-Analysis* 37:425–438.

————(1956b). Notes on the reality principle. *Psychoanalytic Study of the Child* 11:31–53.

————(1960). *Psychoanalysis and Moral Values*. New York: International Universities Press.

Hartmann, H., and Kris, E. (1945). The genetic approach in psychoanalysis. *Psychoanalytic Study of the Child* 1:11–30.

Hartmann, H., Kris, E., and Loewenstein, R. M. (1947). Comments on the formation of psychic structure. *Psychoanalytic Study of the Child* 2:11–38.

———(1949). Notes on the theory of aggression. *Psychoanalytic Study of the Child,* 3-4:9–36.

Heidegger, M. (1927). *Sein und Zeit.* Tübingen: Max Niemeyer, 1953.

———(1957). *Identität und Differenz.* Pfullingen: G. Neske, 1957.

Hendrick, I. (1939). *Facts and Theories of Psychoanalysis.* New York: Knopf.

———(1951). Early development of the ego: identification in infancy. *Psychoanalytic Quarterly,* 20:44–61.

Hermann, I. (1929). Das Ich und das Denken. *Imago* 15:325–348.

———(1936). Sich-Anklammern, Auf-Suche-Gehen. *Internazionale Zeitschrift für Psychoanalyze* 22:349–370.

———(1943). *As Emberiseg Osi Ostonei.* [The Primordial Instincts of Man]. Budapest: Pantheon.

Hoffmann, E. P. (1935). Projektion und Ich-Entwicklung. *Internationale Zietschrift für Psychoanalyze* 21:342–373.

Jacobson, E. (1953a). The affects and their pleasure-unpleasure qualities in relation to the psychic discharge processes. In: *Drives, Affects, Behavior,* ed. R. M. Loewenstein. New York: International Universities Press.

———(1953b). Contributions to the metapsychology of cyclothymic depression. In: *Affective Disorders,* ed. P. Greenacre. New York: International Universities Press.

———(1954). Contribution to the metapsychology of psychotic identification. *Journal of the American Psychoanalytic Association,* 2:239–262.

———(1964). *The Self and The Object World.* New York: International Universities Press.

James, M. (1960). Premature ego development: some observations upon disturbances in the first three months of life. *International Journal of Psycho-Analysis,* 41:288–294.

James. W. (1902). *Varieties of Religious Experience.* New York: Longmans, Green, 1935, p. 191.

Jonas, H. (1966). *The Phenomenon of Life: Toward a Philosophical Biology.* New York: Harper and Row.

Jones, E. (1927). The early development of female sexuality. *International Journal of Psycho-Analysis,* 8:459–472.

——(1947). The genesis of the superego. In: *Papers on Psycho-Analysis,* 5th ed. London: Baillière, Tindall and Cox.

——(1955). *The Life and Work of Sigmund Freud.* New York: Basic Books, Vol. 2.

——(1957). Ibid., Vol. 3.

Kant, I. (1788). *Kritik der praktiscen Vernunft,* ed. K. Vorlander. Leipzig: Felix Meiner, 1920.

——(1871). *Kritik der reinen Vernunft,* ed. T. Valentiner. Leipzig: Felix Meiner, 1922.

Kantner, P. (1969). "We Can Be Together." Words and music by P. Kantner. Icebag Corporation. (A Jefferson Airplane record.)

Kanzer, M. (1961). Ego interest, egoism, narcissism. Presented at the Panel on Narcissism, American Psychoanalytic Association, Fall meeting.

Katan, A. (1951). The role of "displacement" in agoraphobia. *International Journal of Pshcho-Analysis* 32:41–50.

Kaywin, L. (1957). The concept of self-representation. *Journal of the American Psychoanalytic Association* 5:293–301.

Keats, John (1814–1821). *The Letters of John Keats,* ed. H.E. Rollins. Cambridge: Harvard University Press, 1958.

Keiser, S. (1947). On the psychopathology of orgasm. *Psychoanalytic Quarterly* 16:378–390.

Keniston, K. (1965). *The Uncommitted: Alienated Youth in American Society.* New York: Harcourt, Brace & World.

Keyser, C. J. (1922). The group concept. In *The World of Mathematics,* vol. 3, ed. J. R. Newman. New York: Simon and Schuster, 1956.

Khan, M. M. R. (1963). Ego ideal, excitement and the threat of annihilation. *Journal of the Hillside Hospital* 12:195–217.

——(1964). Ego distortion, cumulative trauma, and the role of reconstruction in the analytic situation. *International Journal of Psycho-Analysis* 45.

Kierkegaard, S. (1843). *Repetition: An Essay in Experimental Psychology.* Princeton: Princeton University Press, 1946.

Kilian, H. (1971). *Das enteignete Bewusstsein: Zur dialektischen Sozialpsychologie.* Neuwied und Berlin: Luchterhand.

Klein, M. (1948). *Contributions to Psycho-Analysis.* London: Hogarth.

————(1955). On identification. In: *New Directions in Psycho-Analysis,* ed. M. Klein et al. New York: Basic Books.

Koffka, K. (1935). *Principles of Gestalt Psychology.* New York: Harcourt Brace.

Kramer, P. (1955). On discovering one's identity: a case report. *Psychoanalytic Study of the Child* 10:47–74.

Kris, E. (1935). The psychology of caricature. In *Psychoanalytic Explorations in Art.* New York: International Universities Press, 1952. pp. 173–188.

————(1950a). Introduction to *Aus der Anfängen der Psychoanalyse,* by S. Freud. London: Imago.

————(1950b). Notes on the development and on some current problems of child psychology. *Psychoanalytic Study of the Child* 5:24–46.

————(1952). *Psychoanalytic Explorations in Art.* New York: International Universities Press.

————(1955). Neutralization and sublimation: observations on young children. *Psychoanalytic Study of the Child* 10:330–346.

Kubie, L. S. (1939). A critical analysis of the concept of a repetition compulsion. *International Journal of Psycho-Analysis* 20:390–402.

————(1941). The repetitive core of neurosis. *Psychoanalytic Quarterly* 10:23–43.

————(1948). Instincts and homeostasis. *Psychosomatic Medicine* 10:15–29.

————(1956). Influence of symbolic processes on the role of instincts in human behavior. *Psychosomatic Medicine* 18:189–208.

————(1963). The central affective potential and its trigger mechanisms. In *Counterpo:nt: Libidinal Object and Subject,* ed. H. S. Gaskill. New York: International Universities Press.

Lacan, J. (1953). Some reflections on the ego. *International Journal of Psycho-Analysis* 34:11–17.

Laing, R. D. (1967). *The Politics of Experience.* New York: Ballantine.

Lawrence, D. H. (1928). *Lady Chatterley's Lover.* New York: Grove, 1957.

Leibnitz, G. (1949). *Die Hauptwerke,* ed. G. Kruger. Stuttgart: Alfred Kroner.

Lenzen, V. F. (1954). *Causality in Natural Science.* Springfield: Thomas.

Levi-Strauss, C. (1966). *The Savage Mind.* Chicago: University of Chicago Press.

Lifton, R. J. (1970). *History and Human Survival.* New York: Random House.

————(1971). Protean man. *Archives of General Psychiatry* 24:298–304.

Lipset. S. M. (1961). A changing American character? In Lipset and Lowenthal (1961), pp. 136–174.

Lipset, S. M., and Lowenthal, L., eds. (1961). *Culture and Social Character: The Work of David Riesman Reviewed.* New York: Free Press of Glencoe.

Locke, J. (1690). *An Essay Concerning Human Understanding,* ed. A. C. Fraser. Oxford: Clarendon, 1894.

Loewald, H. W. (1951). Ego and reality. *International Journal of Psycho-Analysis* 32:10–18.

Loewenstein, R. M. (1957). Psychoanalytic theory of masochism. *Journal of the American Psychoanalytic Association* 5:197–234.

Lorenz, K. (1935). Companionship in bird life. In *Instinctive Behavior,* ed. and tr. C. H. Schiller. New York: International Universities Press, 1957.

————(1937). The nature of instinct. Ibid.

Lorenz, K., and Tinbergen, N. (1938). Taxis and instinct. Ibid.

Lynd, H.M. (1958). *On Shame and the Search for Identity.* New York: Harcourt Brace.

Mahler, M. (1952). On child psychosis and schizophrenia: autistic and symbiotic infantile psychoses. *Psychoanalytic Study of the Child* 7:286–305.

————(1958). Problems of identity. (Abstract). *Journal of the American Psychoanalytic Association* 6:131–142.

Mahler, M. and Elkisch, P. (1953). Some observations on disturbances of the ego in a case of infantile psychosis. *Psychoanalytic Study of the Child* 8:252–270.

Mahler, M., and Gosliner, B.J. (1955). On symbiotic child psychosis: genetic, dynamic, and restitutive aspects. *Psychoanalytic Study of the Child* 10:195–212.

Mahler, M., Pine, F., Bergman, A. (1975). *The Psychological Birth of the Human Infant: Symbiosis and Individuation.* New York: Basic Books.

Mandell, A. J., and Schuckit, M. (1971). Western humanism, modern liberal politics and psychiatric training: relatives, friends and enemies. Presented at the Annual Meeting of the American Psychiatric Association in Dallas, Tex., May 1972.

Mann, T. (1954). *Confessions of Felix Krull, Confidence Man,* tr. D. Lindley pp. 113–114. New York: Knopf, 1955.

Masserman, J. H. (1952). Psycho-analysis and biodynamics. *International Journal of Psycho-Analysis,* supplement, 13–42.

Mead, G. H. (1936). *Movements of Thought in the Nineteenth Century.* Chicago: University of Chicago Press.

———(1954). Mind, Self and Society. Chicago: University of Chicago Press.

———(1956). *The Social Psychology of George Herbert Mead,* ed. A. Strauss. Chicago: University of Chicago Press.

Mead, M. (1969). *Culture and Commitment: A Study of the Generation Gap.* New York: Doubleday/Natural History Press.

Messinger, S. L., and Clark, B. K. (1961). Individual character and social constraint: a critique of David Riesman's theory of social conduct. In: Lipset and Lowenthal (1961), pp. 72–88.

Meyer, A. G. (1954). *Marxism: The Unity of Theory and Practice.* Cambridge: Harvard University Press.

Meyer, B. C. (1964). Psychoanalytic studies on Joseph Conrad. *Journal of the American Psychoanalytic Association* 12:32–58, 357–391, 562–586, 802–824.

Meyer, R. W. (1948). *Leibnitz and the Seventeenth Century Revolution,* tr. J. P. Stern. Chicago: Henry Regnery, 1952.

Meyerson, E. (1908). *Identity and Reality,* tr. K. L. Loewenberg. London: Allen and Unwin, 1930.

Miller, M. L. (1948). Ego functioning in two types of dreams. *Psychoanalytic Quarterly* 17:346–355.

Milner, M. (1952). Aspects of symbolism in comprehension of the not-self. *International Journal of Psycho-Analysis* 33:181–195.

———(1957). *On Not Being Able to Paint.* New York: International Universities Press.

Mitscherlich, A. (1965). *Auf dem Wege zur Vaterlosen Gesselschaft: Ideen zur Sozialpsychologie.* Munich: Piper.

Monod, J. (1970). *Le Hasard et la Nécessité.* Paris: Ed. du Seuil.

Moustakas, C. E., ed. (1956). *The Self: Explorations in Personal Growth.* New York: Harper.

Murphy, G. (1958). *Human Potentialities.* New York: Basic Books.

Murtagh, J. M., and Harris, S. (1957). *Cast the First Stone.* New York: McGraw Hill.

Needham, J. (1931). *Chemical Embryology.* London: Macmillan.

Nelson, M. C. (1967). On the therapeutic redirection of energy and effect. *International Journal of Psycho-Analysis* 48:1–15.

Nietzsche, F. (1883). *Thus Spoke Zarathustra.* ed. and tr. W. Kaufman. p. 389. New York: Viking Press, 1959.

Novey, S. (1955). Some philosophical speculations about the concept of genital character. *International Journal of Psycho-Analysis* 36:88–94.

———(1966). The sense of reality and values of the analyst as a necessary factor in psycho-analysis. *International Journal of Psycho-Analysis* 47:492–501.

Nunberg, H. (1932). *Principles of Psychoanalysis.* New York: International Universities Press 1955.

Olinick, S. (1957). Questioning and pain, truth and negation. *Journal of the American Psychoanalytic Association* 5:302–324.

Orr, D. W. (1942). Is there a homeostatic instinct? *Psychoanalytic Quarterly* 11:322–335.

Ortega y Gasset, J. (1939). The self and the other. In *The Dehumanization of Art and Other Writings on Art and Culture. pp. 163–187.* New York: Doubleday, 1956.

———(1949). In search of Goethe from within. *Partisan Review* 16:1167–1168.

———(1973). *An Interpretation of Universal History.* New York: W. W. Norton.

Parr, A. E. (1926). *Adaptiogenese und Phylogenese.* Berlin: Springer.

Perry, J. W. (1953). *The Self in Psychotic Process: Its Symbolization in Schizophrenia.* Berkeley: University of California Press.

Parsons, T. (1970). The impact of technology on culture and emerging new modes of behavior. *International Social Science Journal* 22:607–627.

Parsons, T., and White W. (1961). The link between character and society, pp. 89–135. In Lipset and Lowenthal (1961).

Peller, L. E. (1965). Comments on libidinal organizations and child development. *Journal of the American Psychoanalytic Association* 13:732–747.

Piaget, J. (1932). *The Moral Judgement of the Child.* Glencoe, Ill.: The Free Press, 1960.

———(1936). *The Origins of Intelligence in Children.* New York: International Universities Press, 1952.

———(1937). *The Construction of Reality in the Child,* tr. T. M. Cook. New York: Basic Books, 1954.

———(1953). *Logic and Psychology.* New York: Basic Books, 1957.

Piers, G., and Singer, M.B. (1953). *Shame and Guilt: A Psychoanalytic and Cultural Study.* Springfield: Thomas.

Rapaport, D. (1951a). The autonomy of the ego. In *Psychoanalytic Psychiatry and Psychology,* ed. R. P. Knight and C. Friedman pp. 248–258. New York: International Universities Press.

———(1951b). *Organization and Pathology of Thought.* New York: Col.. .a University Press.

———(1952). The conceptual model of psychoanalysis. In *Psychoanalytic Psychiatry and Psychology,* ed. R. P. Knight and C. Friedman pp. 221–247. New York: International Universities Press.

———(1959). An historical survey of psychoanalytic ego psychology. In Erikson (1959).

Rapaport, D., and Gill, M. (1959). The points of view and assumptions of metapsychology. *International Journal of Psycho-Analysis* 40:153–162.

Reich, A. (1953). Narcissistic object choice in women. *Journal of the American Psychoanalytic Association* 1:22–44.

Reich, C. A. (1970). *The Greening of America.* New York: Random House.

Reich, W. (1970). *The Function of the Orgasm.* New York: Orgone Institute Press, 1942.

Rhinehart, L. (1971). *The Dice Man.* New York: William Morrow.

Ricoeur, P. (1970). *Freud and Philosophy: An Essay on Interpretation.* New Haven: Yale University Press.

Riesman, D. (1949). The saving remnant: an examination of character structure. In *Individualism Reconsidered and Other Essays,* pp. 99–120. Glencoe, Ill.: Free Press, 1954.

Riesman, D., Denney, R., and Glazer, N. (1950), *The Lonely Crowd: A Study of the Changing American Character.* New Haven: Yale University Press.

Riesman, D. and Glazer, N. (1961). The lonely crowd: a reconsideration in 1960. In Lipset and Lowenthal (1961), pp. 419–458.

Riezler, K. (1950). *Man: Mutable and Immutable.* Chicago: Regnery.

Riviere, J. (1936). On the genesis of psychical conflict in earliest infancy. *International Journal of Psycho-Analysis* 17:395–422.

Róheim, Géza (1919). *Spiegelzauber.* Leipzig and Vienna. Int. Psych. Verlag.

———(1948). Metamorphosis. *American Imago* 5:167–172.

Rollman-Branch, H. S. (1960). On the question of primary object need. *Journal of the American Psychoanalytic Association* 8:686–702.

Roszak, T. (1969). *The Making of a Counter-Culture.* New York: Doubleday.

———(1972). *Where the Wasteland Ends: Politics and Transcendence in Postindustrial Society.* New York: Doubleday.

Rueckert, F. (1822). *Rueckert's Werke, Auswahl in acht Teilen,* ed. E. Gross and E. Hertzer p. 214. Berlin-Leipzig: Bong, n.d.

Runciman, S. (1955). *The Medieval Manichee: A Study of the Christian Dualistc Heresy.* Cambridge: University Press.

Russell, B. (1967). *The Autobiography of Bertrand Russell, 1872–1914.* Boston: Little, Brown.

Ryder, N. B. (1965). The cohort in the study of social change. *American Sociological Review* 30:843–861.

Sachs, H. (1933). The delay of the machine age. In *The Creative Unconscious: Studies in the Psychoanalysis of Art.* Cambridge: Sci-Art Publ., 1942.

Sandler, J. (1960). On the concept of the superego. *Psychoanalytic Study of the Child* 15:128–162.

Sandler, J., and Rosenblatt, B. (1962). The concept of the representational world. *Psychoanalytic Study of the Child* 17:128–148.

Sartre, J. P. (1943). *Being and Nothingness.* New York: Philosophical Library, 1956.

Schachtel, E. G. (1959). *Metamorphosis: On the Development of Affect, Perception, Attention and Memory.* New York: Basic Books.

Schafer, R. (1969). The loving and beloved superego in Freud's structural theory. *Psychoanalytic Study of the Child* 15:163–190.

Schilder, P. (1935). *The Image and Appearance of the Human Body.* New York: International Universities Press, 1950.

Schiller, F. (1795). Der Spaziergang. In *Schillers Sämtliche Werke, Säcularausgabe.* Stuttgart and Berlin: Cotta'sche Buchhandlung, 1904.

Schmideberg, M. (1946). On querulance. *Psychoanalytic Quarterly* 15:472–501.

———(1953). Some aspects of jealousy and of feeling hurt. *Psychoanalytic Review* 50:1–16.

Schroedinger, E. (1944). The statistical law of nature. *Nature* 153:704.

———(1945). *What is Life?* New York: Macmillan.

———(1958). *Mind and Matter.* Cambridge: University Press.

Schumpeter, J. A. (1954). *History of Economic Analysis.* New York: Oxford University Press, pp. 436–437.

Schur, M. (1958). The ego and the id in anxiety. *Psychoanalytic Study of the Child* 13:190–220.

———(1966). *The Id and the Regulatory Principles of Mental Functioning.* New York: International Universities Press.

Searles, H. F. (1960). *The Nonhuman Environment in Normal Development and Schizophrenia.* New York: International Universities Press.

Seeman, M. (1959). On the meaning of alienation. *American Sociological Review* 24:783–791.

Silesius, A. (1657). *Aus des Angelus Silesius Cherubinischem Wandersmann.* Leipzig: Insel Verlag, n.d.

Sofer, E. G. (1961). Inner-direction, other-direction, and autonomy. In Lipset and Lowenthal (1961), pp. 316–348.

Sontag, S. (1966). *Against Interpretation.* New York: Farrar, Straus and Giroux.

Spemann, H. (938). *Embryonic Development and Induction.* New Haven: Yale University Press.

Spiegel, L. A. (1959). The self, the sense of self, and perception. *Psychoanalytic Study of the Child* 14:81–112.

Spitz, R. A. (1945). Hospitalism: an inquiry into the genesis of psychiatric conditions in early childhood. *Psychoanalytic Study of the Child* 1:53–57.

———(1946). Hospitalism: a follow-up report. *Psychoanalytic Study of the Child,* 2:113–117.

———(1957). *No and Yes: On the Genesis of Human Communication.* New York: International Universities Press.

———(1959). *A Genetic Field Theory of Ego Formation.* New York: International Universities Press.

———(1963). Life and the dialogue. In *Counterpoint: Libidinal Object and Subject,* ed. H. S. Gaskill. New York: International Universities Press.

———(1964). The derailment of dialogue: stimulus overload, action cycles and the completion gradient. *Journal of the American Psychoanalytic Association* 12:752–775.

———(1965). The evolution of dialogue. In *Drives, Affects, Behavior,* ed. H. Schur. New York: International Universities Press.

Spitz, R.A., and Wolf, K. M. (1949). Autoerotism. *Psychoanalytic Study of the Child* 3-4:85–120.

Steiner, G. (1965). Nightwords. In *Language and Silence: Essays on Language, Literature and the Inhuman.* pp. 68–77. New York: Athenaeum, 1967.

Stern, W. (1919). *Die menschliche Persönlichkeit.* Leipzig: Barth.

———(1921). *Die differentielle Psychologie in ihren methodischen Grundlagen.* Leipzig: Barth.

———(1938). *General Psychology from the Personalistic Standpoint.* New York: Macmillan.

Stoller, R. J. (1973). *Splitting: A Case of Female Masculinity.* New York: Quadrangle/NYT Book Co.

Strachey, J. (1957). Editor's note to S. Freud, On Narcissism. *Standard Edition* 14:69–71. London: Hogarth.

Strauss, A. L. (1959). *Mirrors and Masks: The Search for Identity.* New York: Free Press of Glencoe.

Sullivan, H. S. (1953). *The Interpersonal Theory of Psychiatry.* New York: W. W. Norton.

Szasz, T. S. (1952). On the psychoanalytic theory of instincts. *Psychoanalytic Quarterly* 21:25–48.

————(1961). *The Myth of Mental Illness: Foundations of a Theory of Personal Conduct.* New York: Hoeber.

Tielhard de Chardin, P. (1955). *The Phenomenon of Man.* New York: Harper, 1959.

Thigpen, C. H., and Cleckley, H. M. (1957). *Three Faces of Eve.* New York: McGraw-Hill.

Thom, R. (1975). *Structural Stability and Morphogenesis.* New York: W. A. Benjamin.

Thompson, H. S. (1966). *Hell's Angels: A Strange and Terrible Saga.* New York: Random House.

Tinbergen, N. (1951). *The Study of Instinct.* Oxford: University Press.

Titchmarsh, E. C. (1959). *Mathematics for the General Reader.* New York: Doubleday.

Toomey, J. H. (1959). Analytic orientation in psychiatry. *New York State Journal of Medicine.*

Venable, V. (1945). *Human Nature: The Marxian View.* New York: Knopf.

von Uexküll, J. (1921). *Umwelt und Innenwelt der Tiere.* Berlin: Springer.

————(1934). A stroll through the world of animals and men. In *Instinctive Behavior,* ed. C. H. Schiller. New York: International Universities Press, 1957.

Waelder, R. (1937). The problem of the genesis of psychical conflict in earliest infancy. *International Journal of Psycho-Analysis* 18:309–473.

Waelder, R, et al. (1958). Neurotic ego distortion: panel discussion. *International Journal of Psycho-Analysis* 39:243–275.

————(1967). Inhibitions, symptoms and anxiety: forty years later. *Psychoanalytic Quarterly* 36:1–36.

Weil, A. (1972). *The Natural Mind: A New Way of Looking at Drugs and the Higher Consciousness.* Boston: Houghton Mifflin.

Werner, H. (1957). The concept of development from a comparative and organismic point of view. In *The Concept of Development,* ed. D. B. Harris. Minneapolis: University of Minnesota Press.

West, R. (1940). *Black Lamb and Gray Falcon.* New York: Viking.

Westerman-Holstijn, A. J. (1930). Tendenzen des Toten, Todestriebe und Triebe zum Tode. *Imago* 16:207–231.

Williams, B. O. (1964). Personal identity and individuation. In *Essays in Philosophical Psychology,* ed. Donald F. Gustafson. New York: Doubleday.

Williams, R. H. (1942). Scheler's contribution to the sociology of affective action, with special attention to the problem of shame. *Philosophy and Phenomenological Research,* 11:348–358.

Winnicott, D. W. (1948). Pediatrics and psychiatry. In Collected Papers. New York: Basic Books, 1958. pp. 157–173.

———(1952). Psychoses and child care. In *Collected Papers.* New York: Basic Books (1958).

———(1953). Transitional objects and transitional phenomena. *International Journal of Psycho-Analysis* 34:1–9.

———(1954). Metapsychological and clinical aspects of regression within the psycho-analytical set-up. In *Collected Papers.* New York: Basic Books, 1958.

———(1962). The theory of the parent-infant relationship. *International Journal of Psycho-Analysis* 43:238–239.

Wittels, F. (1935). A type of woman with a threefold love life. *International Journal of Psycho-Analysis* 16:462–473.

Wolff, P. H. (1960). *The Developmental Psychologies of Jean Piaget and Psychoanalysis.* New York: International Universities Press.

Zeeman, E. C. (1976). Catastrophe theory. *Scientific American,* April.

Zetzel, E. R. (1955). Recent British approaches to problems of early mental development. *Journal of the American Psychoanalytic Association* 3:534–543.

Zola, E. (1880). *Nana.* Pocket Books, 1941.

INDEX

Abraham, K., 270
adaptation
  concept of, in context of evolutionary
    theory and metapsychology of self,
    223–226
  problems of, Hartmann's approach to, as
    anticipation of psychology of whole
    person, 234–238
Agel, J., 345
aggression, use of, and use of sexuality as
  defense against "feeling negated" in de
  Sade, 314–317
Agoston, T., 86, 87, 92
Albee, Edward, 314, 317
Alexander, F., 34
alienated man, de Sade on new morality and
  new freedom for, 317–321
Allport, G. W., 149
Andersen, Hans Christian, 360
Anthony, E. J., 7
Apfelbaum, B., 226
Arlow, J. A., 234
Aristotle, 30
Artaud, Antonin, 340
Augustine, St., 166, 321

Bak, R., 75, 97
Balint, A., 64, 65
Balint, M., 64, 65, 66, 171, 207, 209, 265
Barag, G., 92

Beach, C.A., 53
being and nothingness, archetypical ideas of,
  36–42
"being negated"
  genetic reconstruction of experience of,
    309–312
  manifestation of experience of, 300–309
    in clinical observation, 300–305
    effect of, on psychoanalytic situation,
     305–309
  See also malignant no
Bellak, L., 99
Benedek, T., 64
Bennis, W. G., 325-326, 327, 331, 335, 337
Bergler, E., 89, 122n
Bergman, P. 249, 250, 255
Bergson, Henri, 28
Berkeley, George, 127
Bernfeld, S., 34, 50
Beyond the Pleasure Principle, and problem of
  identity, 101–111
Bibring, E., 64, 65, 104, 105
Bing, J. F., 207, 209
Bohr, Nils, 70, 117, 167–168, 244n
Boltzmann, L., 34, 36, 46n
Bonaparte, M., 117
Bowlby, J., 7, 121n
Boyer, L. B., 75, 90
Brenner, C., 234
Brodbeck, A., 147–148
Brodey, W. M., 309